The Encyclopedia of Animals
The Care of Exotic and Domestic Pets

Designed and produced by Aventinum
English language edition first published in 1994 by Sunburst Books, Deacon House, 65 Old Church Street, London SW3 5BS

© Aventinum, Prague 1994

Text by Jiří Čihař, Jan Dobrovský, Pavel Harcuba and Helena Kholová
Translated by Ivy Kovandová and Václav Sochor
Illustrations by Zdeněk Berger, Alena Čepická, Inka Delevová, Lubomír Drožď, Ladislav Junger, Vítězslava Klimtová, Jaromír Knotek, Libuše Knotková, Jan Maget, Vlasta Matoušová, Jiří Polák, Marie Preclíková, Miroslav Rada, Hana Zpěváková-Sokoltová
Graphic design by Pavel Helísek

ISBN   1 85778 029 9
Printed in Slovakia by Neografia, Martin
1/19/07/51-01

The Encyclopedia of Animals
The Care of Exotic and Domestic Pets

Contents

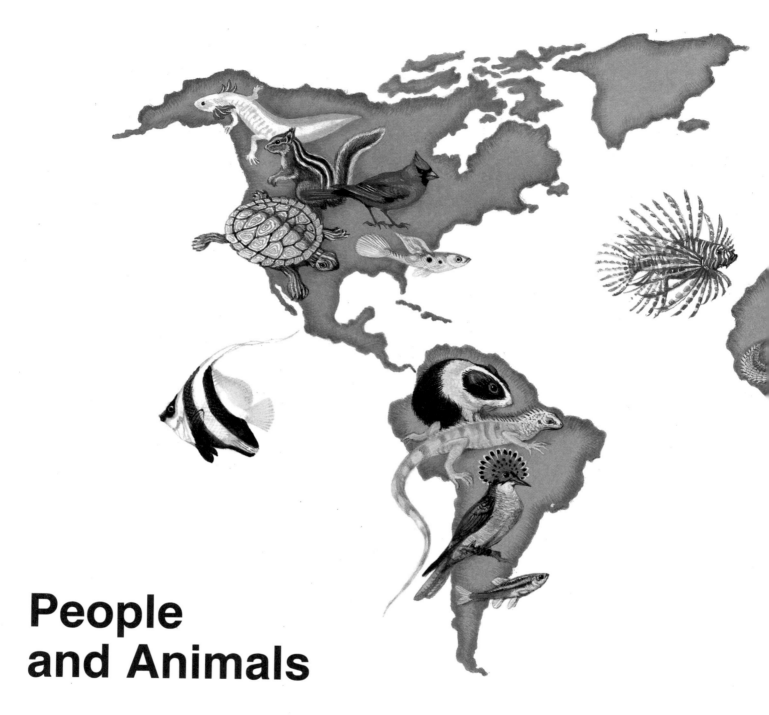

People and Animals

Around the huts and villages of primitive tribes one will often find some kind of animal or bird that has been tamed. This is often done for practical purposes. Toads, for example, bred in the homes of South American Indians, are used to catch troublesome insects, while elsewhere animals are simply kept for pleasure and company. Such relationships between people and animals have been found among tribal dwellers all over the world, and so it may be assumed that, even in ancient times, people sought companions among the wildlife of their environment.

Archaeologists have proved that as long ago as the mid-Stone Age, fishermen and gatherers of wild fruits were often accompanied by a domesticated dog. In the Middle East, about 12,000 years ago, people were already breeding the first herd animals – goats and sheep. It was about that time, too, that the taming of cats began; their statues and remains can still be found in the towns of Anato-

lia and the region that was once Palestine, dating from about 8000 BC. From these modest fragments and primitive statues we cannot tell whether this animal was semi-wild, or whether people kept it in temples or in their own homes.

Many works of art, dating from the third millennium BC, have been discovered from which we can learn something about people's attitudes to their four-legged friends. The drawings and carvings of different breeds of hunting and fighting dogs are precise and elab-

orate in detail, while their ornamental collars and protective armour indicate that their owners valued them highly. Reliefs from Mesopotamian palaces show large numbers of animals in action, as well as in tranquil scenes. On the walls of tombs and temples of ancient Egypt, remarkably well-preserved coloured frescoes show that a place of honour was set aside for sacred cats and different breeds of dogs as well as other exotic animals, such as monkeys, antelopes and birds. Drawings of the palace gardens show us that the Egyp-

tians kept ornamental fish and waterfowl.

The people of ancient Greece and their contemporaries in Minoan Crete also had a profound liking for animals, but by far the greatest success in breeding a variety of animals was found in eastern Asia, China and later Japan. From these countries we have the oldest proof of pure breeds of animals being kept as pets, such as goldfish, miniature quail and other birds. Even insects, such as crickets and cicadas, were bred in tiny bamboo cages. Many Chinese breeds of dogs have survived almost unchanged for several thousand years, a familiar example being the Chow Chow.

The abilities of Chinese breeders have been recognised in Europe for a long time, whereas discoveries still being made in the New World are a source of constant surprise. The ancient Indian peoples of Mexico and of the advanced civilizations in the Andes bred not only domestic animals such as llamas, guinea pigs and turkeys, but also very distinct breeds of dogs. We still have one of these – the Chihuahua – and although the others have vanished as proper breeds, their likenesses can be seen in modern European breeds.

Besides breeding animals whose existence had always been linked with humans, collectors would also go in search of particularly beautiful, interesting or sacred species in their

natural surroundings. Once found, such animals would be kept in gardens or special buildings. Here and there, reports on the breeding of such animals have been preserved. They reveal that people of ancient times were inclined to interweave this knowledge with belief in magic and superstition.

In time, however, these special animals lost their magic status and were kept only as pets. They were very expensive even then, and some much admired creatures are still with us today. These include peacocks brought from India by the Egyptians, and parrots that enjoyed such popularity in Rome in early medieval times, and were known as *papa gallus* (Pope's jungle-fowl).

From this we can see that the breeding of different animals for our own pleasure has roots reaching far into the depths of human history. We have inherited many breeds and improved species from our ancient ancestors, although of even greater value is the breeding skill and knowledge that has been passed down to us.

Creating a Natural Environment

Although for centuries people are known to have kept many different kinds of animals, in modern times new requirements have come

to the fore. No longer are we satisfied with watching a tiny, lone fish swimming around in a large glass bowl, or a bird perched sadly in its small cage. People have begun to notice the special relationships that are found in nature and now animal keepers try, in the limited space of their homes, to create tiny areas that provide a suitable habitat for these creatures to live in. All sorts of combinations of plants and objects (unusual stones, pieces of wood, shells) can be constructed to provide a setting that resembles part of nature itself. To be able to do this successfully requires knowledge about the life cycle of the flora and fauna and about their natural habitats.

So let us take a look at the exotic landscapes from where we have brought a few specimens to live in conditions that are quite alien to them. A comparison of their natural habitats with those that we have prepared for them will help us to make our pets comfortable and happy, and also ensure that their new artificial habitat — aquarium, terrarium or aviary — is not just a jumble of randomly placed, unsuitable pieces of stone and wood, but a comfortable and well-balanced unit.

South American Fresh-water Pools

Among the hundreds of ornamental fish kept in aquariums, the common favourites and those most frequently bred are fish from the tranquil fresh-water pools of South America. Just a glance at such a pool will reveal the basic conditions required for these little fish to thrive, and from this we can learn how to make our own fresh-water aquariums. The water of the pools and rivers of South America is usually soft, sometimes slightly acid, always warm (about 25 °C/11 °F) and richly overgrown with vegetation. The little fish live mostly on tiny plankton which flourish in the warm water, but here, too, live numerous pre-

dators and several herbivorous species. Each creature has different habits. Some like to chase about in the clear waters, others prefer to hide in the thick vegetation, some live on the bottom of the pool and yet others keep to the surface. Some of these fish live quite alone, others in pairs and still others in large or small shoals.

Now that you are aware of all this information, you can decide which varieties to have and in what combination you would like to keep them. The exquisite angelfish are sociable little fish that live in shoals and are quite timid. For these you must prepare a deep aquarium – for they live in deeper waters, and it must be thickly overgrown with narrow-

leaved water plants among which they like to hide. You must take care not to choose aggressive or predatory species as their companions. They like peaceful neighbours.

In nature losses are the rule; the offspring of most fish are eaten by the predator species or even by their own parents or relatives. The breeder is interested in breeding as many fish as possible and losses by such 'natural selection' are not tolerated in the aquarium. At spawning times the breeding pairs separate themselves from the other fish and in an aquarium special conditions are often prepared for them. In nature, spawning is often dependent upon weather changes, a rainy period, for instance. For this reason the aquarist must prepare a tank with soft water for the breeding pair.

In the wild fish take no care of their surroundings. Many species search for food at the bottom of pools where they rummage about, turning up the mud. Such fish, the cichlids, for example, cannot be kept in aquariums with water vegetation, because they would uproot and destroy it.

Pools that contain many species and are rich in plankton conceal much danger for the tiny fish, many of which have learned ways of escape such as jumping up above the surface. They jump so far out of the water that the aquarium must be covered for safety; in the wild they would land back in the water, but

in a living room such a jump could be fatal for them.

The Tropical Jungles of Indo-China

In the depths of the tropical jungle a very special microclimate prevails: high temperatures of 25–30 °C (77–86 °F) remain stable not only throughout the day, but throughout the whole year. Even more constant is the high humidity that usually never drops below 90 per cent. The air here is dead calm, without the slightest breeze. These conditions affect the growth of both flora and fauna. The insufficient light forces plants to climb up the trunks and branches of higher trees to better positions, especially the lianas and epiphytes. The leaves of plants are very large and smooth, allowing rain water to run down them easily. Frequently they have open cells (hydathodes) from which surplus water can be released and then drops of water will be seen suspended from the leaf tips. The hanging gardens on the tree trunks and branches are the habitats of many tiny creatures, such as spiders, insects, centipedes and grubs. These, in turn, provide a luscious hunting ground for little vertebrates, especially amphibians, such as frogs and reptiles. The geckos are the best climbers, although many snakes can move with great agility through

the tree branches. Naturally this is the haunt of many predators, from whom the little creatures protect themselves in ingenious ways. Many of them rely on the invisibility and mimicry practised by different insects, such as leaf insects, stick insects, some butterflies and beetles, while some of the geckos lose themselves entirely by blending in with the tree bark. Other creatures prefer to escape in the most acrobatic ways. Many of them launch themselves into a gliding flight (the flying lizard, the *Chrysopelea* snakes and the *kuhli* gecko).

The jungle community is immensely abundant and diverse and it is obviously impossible in captivity to provide the required conditions for many jungle species, particularly the flying creatures. Even the most modest of the rainforest fauna need a high and stable temperature. You can obtain a high humidity either by continual misting or by using an aquaterrarium. There is also the difficulty of supplying such little creatures with their varied jungle diet; in captivity they have to become accustomed to substitutes – domestic crickets, vinegarflies for the insectivorous, fruit for the frugivorous, and pieces of meat or fish for the predators.

On the Banks of African Rivers

The banks of African rivers, thickly overgrown with tall vegetation, are ideal nesting places for little songbirds. There they find cover, nesting materials and adequate food among the tall plants, bushes and forest growth. The tiny African singing birds, such as Green Avadavats and weaverbirds, often nest together, or in small colonies. They have many enemies who often rob them of their eggs or take the young from the nests.

For this reason these birds nest in places that are inaccessible to snakes and other predators. They build their nests in the thin branches of bushes, in reeds or in tall grasses such as elephant grass. The nests are round or bottle-shaped, often with a long 'chimney-like' entrance. Both parent birds work on the nest-building, and they also take care of the young fledgelings together.

These are modest little birds both in the wild and in captivity. In their natural habitats they have to cope with considerable fluctuations of temperature during both day and night as well as alternating periods of rain and drought. Most of them, however, need a lot of light and sunshine. For this reason it is advisable to give them extra lighting during the shortest days of the year. They must also have sufficient clean water for drinking and in which to bathe, otherwise they will die. Generally speaking, these are compatible species so it is possible to keep a few pairs together.

In the aviary, try to make a replica of their natural surroundings by planting bushes or shrubs in pots, and do not forget a large bowl of water for bathing in. Nesting is encouraged by hanging nesting baskets or boxes in the aviary, as well as providing the birds with nesting material such as hay, sisal and coconut fibre. African grass seed can be substituted with millet, niger and other cultivated strains. Live food, such as vinegar flies and pupae, is essential for feeding the fledgelings, and egg mixtures also provide protein. These exotic creatures must be protected from frosts and especially from freezing winds.

The Mutual Relationships of Animals

Every responsible person who keeps animals simply for pleasure is aware that suitable conditions must be provided for them. The condition for successful breeding, however, is quite different. Every species has different requirements and the caring breeder has to pay special attention to this. In the wild animals have a free choice as to where they live, or at least the possibility of escape from an uncomfortable situation. In a restricted breeding area this is out of the question and here bad conditions will lead to stress, to a decline in the production of offspring or even to animals of the same species killing each other.

Even the least observant nature lover must realize that in the wild there are some animals that are loners and others that live in groups, that certain species pair only at the time of mating, while some remain faithful to each other throughout their whole lives. We also know that some species need constant contact; they press close to each other, demonstrating their feeling in many different ways, but other animals live in shoals, flocks or herds and behave as though indifferent to one another. These peculiarities must be borne in

mind and respected during captive breeding.

It is quite obvious that predatory species must be bred separately or at most in pairs. Invertebrates in particular are so savage that they do not hesitate to hunt and eat their own kind. Spiders, for example, must be bred separately; the same applies to scorpions, mantises and similar creatures.

Numerous aquarium fish also need 'privacy'. These are either predators or species that have exclusive territorial demands. The Siamese Fighting Fish (*Betta splendens*), for example, lives on minute organisms. The female of this species is extremely intolerant of other females and a fight could lead to the death of her opponent. For this reason, the male fighters are kept separately in small tanks. However, these fishy 'warriors' do not attack females of their own kind or fish of another species and so a pair of 'fighters' can be kept in a mixed aquarium. Other, normally peace-loving little fish cannot tolerate the presence of any other species at spawning time. Voracious predators, such as pike, simply cannot stand being together in a tank. It is not unusual if from a large spawn only one fish remains, having consumed all the other fry. On the other hand, there are some fish that cannot be bred alone; they need some sort of company, if only of another species, so they can join a shoal and have a feeling of security.

Among the higher vertebrates the situation is still more complex. In this case, the character of an individual may be decisive. Even among normally peaceful little guinea pigs, hamsters or brown rats, aggressive individuals can be found that have to be reared in isolation. The young females are frequently aggressive, although not at mating time or when caring for their young. These small animals should be carefully observed especially when changes in their communities can be expected, such as when the young are reaching adulthood, or when the animals are being moved to another home. Another important point to note is the density of numbers of animals kept in a limited space, for this is when stress and fighting will develop, fertility will be curtailed and the animals will begin to behave quite unnaturally and may even kill each other. In such cases they must be separated at once, thus reducing their numbers to an acceptable degree.

It often happens that a person wants to tame and train an animal by special methods. In this case the animal has to be kept away from its own kind. If, for instance, one wishes to teach a parrot to speak, then the young bird, preferably a female, should be kept alone and if possible out of sight of other parrots. The keeper must maintain close contact with such a bird at all times and talk to it often to prevent it from getting depressed or lonely.

A similar situation applies to domesticated animals such as dogs and cats. For them, a human family replaces the company of their own kind and they must be given lots of attention and time. The other requirements of such species are also of importance. For example, some members of the cat family are solitary animals that, when in the wild, live a solitary life in their quite extensive territory — apart from when mating and when caring for their kittens. Such cats would find it difficult to live peacefully in larger groups. Tom cats, in particular, are very quarrelsome. On the other hand, dogs, as animals used to living in packs, are much more tolerant of other dogs, although they too will fight for their place in the hierarchy of the pack. The more the dog becomes used to a certain handler, the more likely it is to show strong signs of possessiveness or jealousy. Thus the successful breeder and trainer of domestic animals also needs to be a psychologist who understands the characters and temperaments of the animals. Through observing animals' behaviour much invaluable, thought-provoking information can be obtained.

Breeding Invertebrates

Invertebrates make up the majority of living creatures on our planet. If we roughly calculate mammals, birds, reptiles and amphibians in thousands of species, and fish in tens of thousands of species, then there are *millions* of species of inverte-

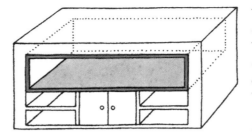

It is more difficult but also more practical to build the aquarium as a part of the furniture, such as within a niche inside a wall fitment.

The simplest way of breeding phytophageous insects – a container with a live plant under a protective net.

brates. They comprise a colourful spectrum of pet keepers' interests, from the insignificant almost microscopic organisms to little creatures several millimetres long. However, not every invertebrate makes an ideal pet. Beginners are not advised to

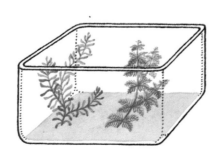

A simple all-glass aquarium will not only serve for keeping fish or other animals, but may also be an impressive decorative element in your home.

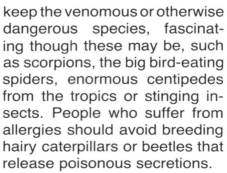

A 5-litre (8³/₄-pint) jar (or a bigger container) will serve as a general-purpose breeding vessel. Filled with corrugated cardboard or crushed paper, it will make a good environment for keeping crickets.

keep the venomous or otherwise dangerous species, fascinating though these may be, such as scorpions, the big bird-eating spiders, enormous centipedes from the tropics or stinging insects. People who suffer from allergies should avoid breeding hairy caterpillars or beetles that release poisonous secretions.

There are, of course, many invertebrate species that are too demanding and difficult to keep and breed. These include most of the sea animals, for which expensive sea aquariums, requiring special maintenance, have

to be provided. Also unsuitable as pets are those species that take several years to mature and that require an exceptionally specialized habitat, or food that is rarely available in captivity. Some, such as the magnificent caterpillars from the Antherae family, live solely on leaves that are seldom grown in Europe. However, there is still an inexhaustible variety of invertebrates that require modest breeding conditions and whose appearance and way of life are always intriguing.

The advantage of making pets of invertebrates is that numerous groups can be kept in a fairly small place. Besides breeding them for an exclusive

Phytophageous insects can also be kept in closed containers (with a live plant in a bottle with water). The neck of the bottle must always be well sealed to prevent the insects from drowning. For species that pupate underground, the container should be equipped with a bowl of soil, peat or sand.

purpose, such as crickets intended as food for another species, you can use aquariums, terrariums or special breeding facilities, such as ants' nests (formicariums) as interesting interior decoration.

A variety of fresh-water animal life can be kept in a medium-sized, all-glass aquarium that does not require aeration, filtering or, in many cases, even heating. An aquarium planted with fine-leaved, small vegetation, enhanced by colourful stones and unusually shaped entangled roots makes a pretty scene, and it is sufficient to add to this swimming beetles, water bugs, dragonfly larvae or water snails to create a tiny living piece of nature indoors. More exotic insects can be kept in terrariums planted with decorative vegetation. Such creatures require heated terrariums set with tropical plants, the most suitable being brome grass, which grows well on branches or pieces of bark.

Butterfly breeders do not have to limit themselves only to caterpillars, for nourishing plants cultivated in flower pots and protected by a mosquito net can be very attractive. Invertebrates can also be kept and bred on balconies and patios or in the garden. Butterflies can be bred, providing they are protected from their natural enemies, such as birds.

One advantage of choosing invertebrates is that they rarely live to an advanced age. The life span of many species is but a few weeks, at most months, allowing the breeder who has achieved the desired results to replace the species with a different one for the next season.

The breeding of invertebrates is not only a matter of decorative or biological interest, it has a practical significance too. Species of economic import-

Slugs are undemanding and interesting invertebrates to keep, especially the different dry land species.

ance include bees and silkworms. Others, undemanding because of their high reproduction ability, are an ideal source of food for pet vertebrates, from aquarium fish to exotic amphibians, reptiles, birds and mammals. The breeding of invertebrates as food enables the expert to obtain remarkable results with these exotic species.

Fresh-water Invertebrates

Fresh waters are home to many species such as strapworms and ecinoderms, so the selection for keepers is really vast. The most popular choices are some of the molluscs and arthropods, which can often be found in their natural habitats. Tropical snails will have to be purchased at aquarist shops, where the eggs of the fairy shrimp or other crustaceans are also on sale.

The species itself should be chosen according to what you wish to achieve. Short-term keeping, when animals caught in their natural surroundings are observed for only a few days or weeks, does not require special facilities; a glass tank of 1–5 litres (1.75–8.85 pints) volume is adequate. For longer-term captivity, however, a 10–15 litres (2–3.5 gallons) or even in special cases a 20-litre (4.5 gallons)

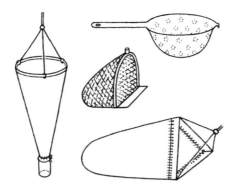

Food organisms for the invertebrates can be picked directly from their natural environment. A plankton net will help catch plankton, a strainer will serve for catching aquatic insects, a dredge is useful for catching the organisms living close to the bottom, such as worms, and a scraper will help to separate algae and other sources of food attached to stones, etc.

aquarium is desirable. Cover the bottom of the tank with well-washed or heat-sterilized sand and gravel (either boiled, or thoroughly heated through when dry in an oven). Then easily grown aquarium vegetation such as water milfoil (*Myriophyllum*), different kinds of grass (*Vallisneria*), waterweed (*Elodea*) and similar floating vegetation can be planted.

Careful observation of the natural habitats of species captured in the wild will reveal their requirements. For breeding purposes species from still or, exceptionally, slightly flowing water can be used. The easiest species to breed are the inhabitants of small pools, found submerged in sand or puddles. You must not put these little creatures into chlorinated tap water. Either rainwater or previously boiled, cooled tap water should be used. Vegetation brought in from the wild must be thoroughly washed and any wood used should preferably have been

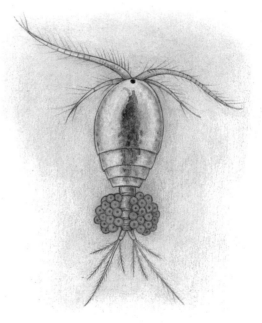

Cyclops, an important plankton organism and valuable food for both fish and invertebrates.

specially purchased for this use; only scrap wood that has been lying outside in water for a long time, and has been boiled or heat-sterilized, may be put into the aquarium.

The smallest animal organisms, plankton, can be caught by using a cone-shaped net made of fine silk, attached to

A well-planted aquarium makes a good home not only for fish but also for a number of water invertebrates.

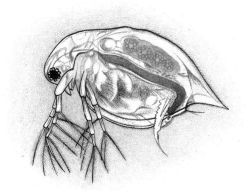

Water fleas are another important component of stagnant water plankton – also a valuable food for the aquarium.

a long rod, with glass or tap-like closures. For the larger animal organisms a coarse kitchen sieve is used, or else a net of loosely woven material or a strainer purchased at an aquarium supply shop. Entomological pincers are used to take the insects and snails from the sieve. Animal organisms and gill-breathing animals, such as tiny crustaceans, can be transported in jars of water, while most water insects can be carried in closed boxes lined with damp moss. Water beetles and heteropterans can easily be removed from even the tiniest crevice or cranny, but be careful, many of them are excellent fliers and they will escape if given a chance.

They should all be transported in the shortest time possible. The main thing is to ensure that the water temperature does not change too quickly. The containers must also be protected from direct sunlight and in high temperatures it is advisable to wrap them in something damp, such as moss or a damp piece of cloth, or else they can be transported in a vacuum flask. You must also protect domestic species from unsuitable or fluctuating temperatures, so the location of the aquarium must be carefully chosen.

Most invertebrates need natural food that can be found in the wild. Predatory animals, such as diving beetles and their larvae and the large water heteropterans, can be fed with surplus fish spawn or crustaceans such as *Artemia* that you have bred yourself. A magnifying glass or microscope of low magnification can be used for observation of the tiny animal organisms.

Water Snails

Of the European water snails the following thrive best in aquariums, the genera *Radix* and *Lymnaea* and the ramshorn snail *Planorbarius,* which live off all sorts of organic remains, only *Lymnaea* nibble the aquarium vegetation. If the snails are found to be gnawing at their shells, this indicates a lack of calcium in the water and a piece of limestone should be put in to rectify the situation. Of the tropical molluscs, Ampullaria is available, but it needs water of over 20 °C (68 °F) in temperature. The brine shrimp (*Artemia salina*) is suitable food for predatory water organisms. Put the purchased eggs into water to which you have added five per cent pure kitchen salt (fluoride-free) and keep them at a temperature of around 20 °C (68 °F). To 1 litre ($1^3/_4$ pints) of liquid add a teaspoonful of *Artemia salina* eggs. The larvae hatch within one to two days and they usually need to be fed at once. To breed *Artemia salina* to adulthood, they must be kept in a shallow bowl of salty liquid and fed with algae, preferably *Dunaliella salina.*

Aquatic slugs are all good inhabitants of aquariums, including the phytophageous ramshorns, predatory great pond snails or undemanding species of the *Viviparus* genus.

Water Insects

You will probably have to catch water insects yourself out in the countryside, because they are not on sale at most aquarist shops. Choose species from still water because they require water with a low oxygen content. The aquarium should be planted with sufficient water vegetation. If you are keeping fast swimmers, then plant more vegetation at the sides or in one part of the tank. The tank must always be covered with a dense net or a solid covering with holes in it, to prevent the insects from escaping. The most suitable species for keeping and breeding at home are dragonflies (Odonata), water heteropterans (Heteroptera), dytiscidae beetles, the water scavenger beetles (Hydrophilidae) and trichoptera beetles.

Ischnura elegans is one of the dragonfly and damselfly species that live in swarms in still water. Its larval stage (nymph)

Predatory water bugs – water scorpions and water stick insects – will stay in the aquarium for a long time.

can be recognised by the transparent pointed leaf-like suspension from its tail. It requires a thickly overgrown large tank with a sandy bottom. Enough room must be left above the

Of the great variety of sedge flies, those of stagnant waters can be kept with success. These include those of the genus *Limnophilus* whose larvae build cases from small shells.

water for protruding twigs or reeds to allow the developed nymphs to climb out of the water. The larvae are very rapacious and live on water fleas,

water beetles, mosquito larvae and, if desperate, on pieces of earthworms or meat, which you can hold in pincers and move around in front of the damselfly larvae. The adult insect will not survive in captivity.

The **Water Scorpion** (*Nepa cinerea*) is a water bug up to 22 mm (0.75 in) long, from muddy waters. It breathes in air through a long respiratory tube at its tail, which it raises to the surface. It can deliver a painful sting from its front legs, which operate like a jack-knife, or from a bite from its mouth. Water scorpions should be bred separately in small, shallow tanks thickly planted with vegetation, from where they pounce on tiny insects, crustaceans and fish fry. The water scorpion flies well, and as the top of its body is flattened it can slide through the narrowest crevices.

The **Long-bodied Water Scorpion** (*Ranatra linearis*) is up to 40 mm (1.5 in) long, and is the more mobile relative of the water scorpion, which can be kept in similar conditions. Both of these insects live for a long time and when fully grown they will winter in mud. In captivity, they remain quite healthy through the winter at a temperature of 10 °C (50 °F).

The **Water Boatman** (*Notonecta glauca*) is a 15 mm (0.6 in) long heteropteran that is unusual in that it swims on its back with its belly upwards. It catches small insects on the surface and crustaceans in the water. Several kinds of boatmen can be kept together in a large tank but not with fish or amphibians which they like to attack. They fly well in temperatures above 15 °C (59 °F).

Sigara falleni is about 7 mm (0.25 in) long and resembles the water boatman. It swims belly-down and when in danger flies straight up from the water surface. It lives on the remains of plant life and animal organisms and can be kept together with other animals. However, these should be peaceful species living on plankton because *Sigara falleni* often takes predator insects and even fish.

Agabus bipustulatus is a bug about 10 mm (0.4 in) long that lives in shallow water such as pools and rainwater barrels. It consumes minute animal organisms. It is an excellent swimmer and flier. Its voracious larvae live near the bottom of the pool or barrel and can be up to 20 mm (0.75 in) long.

The **Great Diving Beetle** (*Dytiscus marginalis*). This is a very agile beetle up to 30 mm (1.2 in) long that needs a large tank with sufficient animal feed (larvae and the like). The larva, which is up to 50 mm (2 in) long, is predatory and easily overcomes fish of the same size. For this reason these beetles cannot be kept with other aquarium life. When fully grown they fly well.

The **Great Silver Water Beetle** (*Hydrous piceus*) Europe's largest water beetle, measuring up to 50 mm (2 in). It lives on water vegetation and algae and its larvae are voracious. This is a rare little beetle, so it should be re-

Water beetles, especially the large species of diving beetles and the water scavenger beetle, are good subjects to observe. The scavenger beetle is not very fastidious because it feeds on plants.

turned safely to its natural habitat when no longer needed for observation.

Caddis Flies (*Trichoptera*) are found in stagnant or gently flowing water. They are herbivorous, so if kept in an overgrown tank there is no need to worry about their food. They must, however, be provided with enough suitable building material for their caddises, as their small dwellings are known, such as small stones, sand, wood and tiny shells. The larvae pupate in water inside the caddis. The adult fly has a wing span of up to 6 cm (2.3 in) and is inconspicuous in colour.

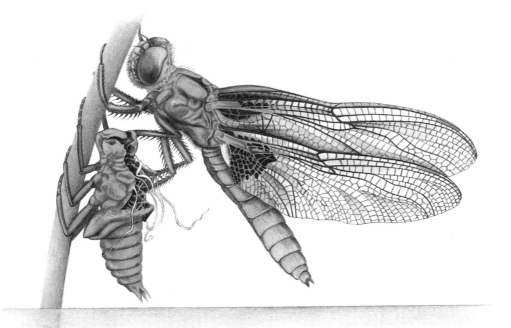

The larvae of the elegant dragonfly are very predatory and their development is prolonged. It is, therefore, better to catch them when they are large enough and raise them until they change into the insects.

Cockroaches, Mantises and Stick Insects

The best insects to breed in an insectarium are the large tropical species that are masters at disguising themselves. By changing the shapes of their bodies and their colour they are able to blend perfectly with their surroundings. With few excep-

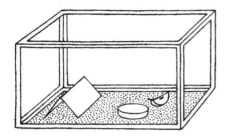

The terrarium for cockroaches can be very simple: it should include only a simple hiding place, a bowl with wet cotton wool and food. It should be well secured.

tions, these are peaceful little creatures that can be kept in large numbers in one terrarium. They can be bought in specialist shops supplying exotic animals or from breeders. They require a high and spacious terrarium,

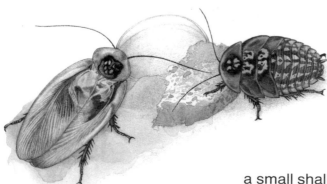

Exotic cockroaches grow to imposing sizes but their requirements do not differ much from those of the smaller species. The enormous South American Blabery requires a somewhat higher temperature.

planted with suitable vegetation, or at least containing lots of little twigs along which they can climb. To feed these herbivorous little creatures you must place a very large glass or vase containing nutritious plants in the tank. Make sure the glass has a well-sealed neck to prevent the tiny insects from falling in and drowning. The terrarium should be heated with a weak 15 W light bulb, and it should be covered with a dense net or a lid with tiny air holes to prevent the animals from escaping.

Cockroaches (Blattaria) live on refuse and breed very fast, so you must make sure, when breeding them, that the terrarium is always kept firmly closed, otherwise the youngest, very nimble nymphs could escape and infest your home. The larger species from the tropics are the most suitable for keeping, such as *Leucophaes surinamensis* or the green cockroaches of the Panchloridaea family or the enormous Blabery. All of them need moisture, a temperature of around 28 °C (82 °F), adequate hiding places and pieces of fruit, meat, dried blood and similar food. They should be supplied with water in

a small shallow glass container, plugged with cotton wool which should be changed twice a week.

The **Praying Mantis** (*Mantis religiosa*) is a robust, voracious in-

sect. In Europe the most easily obtainable mantis is the Praying Mantis (*Mantis religiosa*), which is 8 cm (3 in) long. It lives on twigs or on plants near a window. It flies well, so you must ensure that the window is always kept closed. They must be kept singly as they are cannibals. They should be well supplied with live insects, grasshoppers, maggots, moths and so on. In an emergency, you can kill insects for them, using pincers. Once a day the terrarium needs a gentle spraying with water. The Praying Mantis needs a temperature of over 20 °C (68 °F) and the adults live for about six months.

The order Phasmida, which are dispersed all over the world in more than 2,500 species, make very special pets. They are among the larger insects — some of the tropical species grow to over 20 cm (8 in) in length — but most are suitable for the inexperienced breeder. They are kept at temperatures over 20 °C (68 °F) but not more than 35 °C (95 °F), in which they could not survive. They are generally herbivorous and many are not at all selective. They live for a few months only. The females often lay unfertilized eggs — they multiply parthenogenetically. In some species one male will mate with several thousand females. Their eggs are barrel-shaped and are laid freely on the ground, covered with soil, or fixed to plants. They like a shady spot, fairly high humidity and always require fresh food. If the food is insufficient they are likely to bite each others' tails.

The **Common Stick Insect** (*Carausius morosus*) is the best known and most widespread stick insect. It has to be kept at temperatures around 20 °C (68 °F) and is fed on leaves from roses, plum trees and privet,

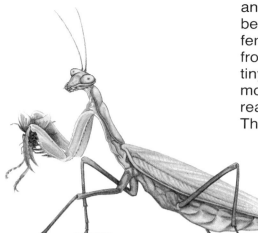

The predatory Praying Mantis and its exotic relatives are among the most voracious insects.

and in the winter on ivy, blackberry or spiderwort leaves. The females lay some 400 eggs from which, after three months, tiny nymphs emerge. Three months later they will have reached adulthood.

The **Mediterranean Stick In-**

The Indian locust (in the picture) and the South European *Bacillus rossii* are most frequently kept in captivity.

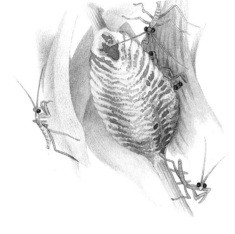

The Mantis lays its eggs in a special foamy cocoon. Outdoors, the young hatch in spring, but in captivity they emerge sooner.

The Australian *Extatosoma tiaratum* has a bizarre appearance. Like many of its relatives, it is noted for its marked sexual dimorphism.

sect (*Bacillus rossii*) is smaller than the Common Stick Insect and lives in southern Europe. It is fed on birdseed. The Australian stick insect, *Extatosoma tiaratum,* is noted for its strange body shape, conspicuous hermaphroditism and bizarre movements. It needs a temperature of around 25 °C (77 °F), and feeds on leaves from rosaceous plants and especially blackberry bushes.

The **Leaf Insect** (*Phyllium bioculatum*) is more demanding than the previous species. It originates in tropical Asia and consequently needs temperatures

above 26 °C (79 °F), a higher humidity and a thickly grown terrarium with an abundance of branches. These insects are difficult to breed because they often reject substitute food. The male differs considerably from the female. It closely resembles leaves, but even so it flies very well.

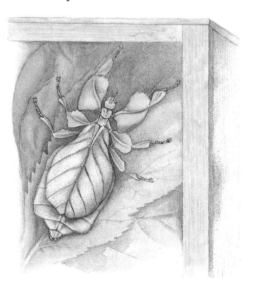

The large tropical species of the genus *Phyllium,* which are close relatives of Locusts, are among the most striking insects kept by fanciers.

Butterflies

Butterflies are quite easy to breed, so even a beginner can keep the most beautiful tropical species in an insectarium. It is no problem to obtain local butterflies, careful observation in the countryside will reveal clusters of butterfly eggs on the leaves of plants, or little caterpillars, and these can be carried away on the leaves. You can breed exotic species from eggs ordered from specialist firms or

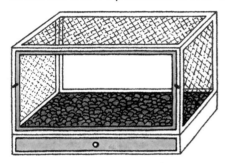

A caterpillar house is the best breeding facility for butterflies. Its front wall is made of glass, the other walls are of fine netting and the bottom is removable.

by mail order. The caterpillars of most butterflies are herbivorous, some living off specific plants and others off the leaves of a variety of plants. Literature on butterflies is vast and readily available so that all the essential information on how to feed and keep the different species is easy to come by.

The caterpillar of the *Cerula vinula* is very popular because of its pretty colours and unusual behaviour.

The 'domestic' caterpillar – the Silkworm – has been bred for more than 1,000 years and bears marked traces of man's purposeful breeding effort.

Keep the caterpillars in a large, airy caterpillar house with walls made of densely woven netting or a similar textile, although one wall may be of glass to make observation possible. Put the plants on which they feed in a very large container and change them frequently. Spread absorbent paper or newspaper on the floor. It is advisable to have a removable floor to facilitate the removal of excrement and debris. Put the eggs in flat glass bowls, where a certain level of moisture is maintained, until they hatch. The little caterpillars are then put into a large jar and later into a caterpillar house. Most caterpillars change their coats twice. As they develop, they cease to

take food and search for a place to pupate. Those that pupate on the ground should be placed in a bowl with some soil.

The **Puss Moth** (*Cerura vinula*)

has a wing span of up to 7 cm (2.75 in). It is widespread throughout Europe and the temperate zones of Asia and North America. The caterpillars live on poplar and willow trees from April to July. They pupate in a hard cocoon and winter on branches. Keep them in small caterpillar houses on a balcony or windowsill.

The **Buff-tip Moth** (*Phalera bucephala*) has a wing-span of up to 5.5 cm (2.5 in). When seen with its wings closed, it strongly

The Tiger Moth, an abundantly occurring European insect, is easily bred from a long-haired caterpillar.

resembles a broken twig. It lives in deciduous woodland, and its caterpillars are most voracious. They eat the leaves of linden, oak, willow, hazel, beech and even fruit trees. The pupae winter below ground.

The **Tiger Moth** (*Arctia caja*) hatches from eggs in the late summer months. After wintering, the caterpillars complete their development in the spring. These are long-haired, brown caterpillars that will eat anything, they pupate in a cocoon in the ground and can often be found while seeking a place to pupate. Take them home and place them in a bowl of earth, from where you can expect a moth to emerge after a few weeks.

The **True Silkworm Moth** (*Bombyx mori*) is of economic importance for it is the source of natural silk. It is so domesticated that it could hardly breed without the help of people. Neither the moth nor the caterpillar is particularly pretty, so few people are interested in keeping them. Breeders keep the caterpillars in open trays lined with fresh mulberry leaves for food. The caterpillars pupate in silken cocoons on mulberry twigs in the trays.

The **Chinese Oak Silkworm** (*Antherea pernyi*) is the producer of what is known as shantung silk. The related Japanese species, *Antherea yamamai,* also produces very fine fibres. Both insects live on the oak tree. Both their food and the temperature during breeding influence the colours of these moths. When fully grown, they are good fliers and must therefore be kept in large caterpillar houses, or, if kept outside, under a net to protect them from birds. The moth has a wingspan of up to 12 cm (4.75 in).

The **Atlas Moth** (*Attacus atlas*) from southeast Asia is one of the biggest moths, with a wing span of more than 20 cm (8 in). Before pupating, its caterpillars are over 10 cm (4 in) long. It lives on the leaves of citrus fruit trees and tea plants, as well as on bird food. The caterpillars should be kept at temperatures above 23 °C (73 °F) and in a high humidity.

The **Small Tortoiseshell** (*Aglais urticae*), **Peacock** (*Inachis io*) and the **Red Admiral** (*Vanessa atalanta*), European day butterflies, make very rewarding pets. Their caterpillars can be found in great numbers on nettles. The Red Admiral produces several generations a year, so its caterpillars can be found from spring until autumn. They pupate freely, suspended from plants, so their whole development can be carefully studied. The butterflies winter in places where temperatures are low, such as cellars or corridors.

The Peacock is among the butterflies that live on nettles. Breeding is easy and results are good.

Beetles

Beetles, which comprise the most numerous of all insect orders, live in a variety of environments. Some are predators and others herbivorous. Do not use the venomous species for breeding, especially the oil beetles of the *Meloe, Lytta* and *Mylabris* genera. It is also inadvisable to keep any of the rare and protected species. It is best to breed carnivorous beetles and those that live on a variety of organic remains. These can be kept in small terrariums arranged like parts of the beetles' natural habitats. For example, a piece of the woodland floor with stones and vegetation such as clivina and the moisture-loving notiophilus, can make a damp mossy background for the genus *Feronia.* The plant eaters,

Almost all Ladybirds are predators and can easily be bred in captivity. The Eyed Ladybird feeds on aphids on pine twigs.

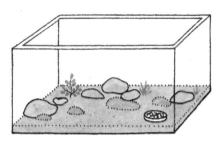

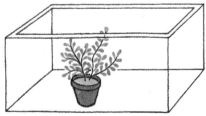

Various breeding facilities can be used for keeping beetles. Ground Beetles can be kept in a terrarium with a landscape-like arrangement inside, offering hiding places under stones. The phytophageous species, such as Chrysomels, are best kept on a plant grown in a pot. Wood-decaying species can be kept in a block of wood.

ladybirds and aphid hunters can be kept in nutritious growth in a caterpillar house. Many different beetles place their larvae in wood or under tree bark: examples are the longicorn beetle and the deathwatch beetle. Cultivate the food plants they need in little blocks of wood. Other species live in mould, such as the Stag Beetle or Rhinoceros Beetle; for them you must prepare a suitable container filled with mould. The disadvantage of these insects is the long time they take to develop – the larvae of the cock-chafer or may-bug and of some of the longicorn beetles live for as long as four years, and the larvae of the stag beetles for as long as five.

Feronia vulgaris and *F. burmeisteri* are beetles about 15mm (0.5in) long, usually found in fields, gardens and forests. They live on tiny invertebrates and are easy to breed. Their terrarium must always be slightly damp, although the sand and peat bed must not become sticky. The slender, fast-moving larvae, which are about 1cm (0.4in) long, catch soft insects and pupate in the ground.

The **Two-spot Ladybird** (*Adalia bipunctata*), the **Seven-spot Ladybird** (*Coccinella septempunctata*) and the **Eyes Ladybird** (*Anatis ocellata*) live on a variety of aphids in their larval and adult stages. You can breed

them in a caterpillar house, where they must be supplied daily with leaf-grown twigs full of aphids, such as the rose aphid. The adult beetle needs as many as 40 aphids a day. The larvae usually pupate on the leaves of plants.

Rose Chafers (*Cetonia aurata*) are beautiful beetles that are fed on sugar water or nectar and flower pollen. Their larvae live in the ground, in compost or mould. They take about a year to develop and pupate in a firm cocoon. The tropical Rose Chafers of the Pachnoda family are great favourites. They come in beautiful and striking colours and are easy to care for in a heated terrarium, thickly grown with tropical plants. Feed them on soft fruits and various sugary liquids.

The **Colorado Beetle** (*Leptinotarsa decemlineata*), whose larvae live on different plants, is also one of the most frequently kept beetles. Note that it is illegal to release these creatures in the wild as they are a serious crop pest. Beetles noted for

The Seven-Spot Ladybird and many of its relatives feed on the rose aphid and many other smaller aphid species. They do not like the bean aphid.

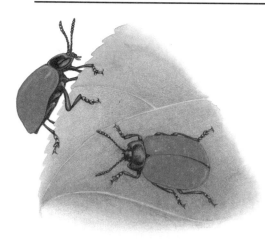

The various species of the Chrysomels are comparatively easy to breed. It is an advantage that both the larvae and caterpillars often live on the same plant. The picture shows the Red Poplar Leaf Beetle.

their lovely colours are the **European Leaf Beetle** (*Cryptocephalus sericeus*), the **Red Poplar Leaf Beetle** (*Melasoma populi*) and the **Alder Beetle** (*Agelastica alni*). The larvae of *Cryptocephalus* live on poplar, birch, oak and other trees. When fully grown, the beetles seek the flowers of the Asteracaea. The poplar beetle lives on poplar and willow trees while the alder is home to *Agelastica alni.* All of these beetles should be kept on food plants in a caterpillar house. The **Longhorn Beetle** (*Cerambycidae*) is quite demanding to breed be-

cause it takes so long to mature. For this reason you should look for its half-grown larvae among food plants and then care for them at home until they develop fully. The easiest to come by are the **Lesser Aspen Longhorn** (*Saperda populnea*) and the **Greater Poplar Longhorn** (*S. carcharias*) whose larvae live on the thin saplings and twigs of poplar and aspen and sometimes even on willow. The affected tree can be recognised by

swellings on small branches in places where the larvae have settled. Cut off these little branches or twigs and then keep the larvae in a closed jar. The wood must not be allowed to dry out or become mildewed.

The beautiful and rare **Musk Beetle** (*Aromia moschata*) can be found on the living wood of willows, where its larvae develop. If you are lucky enough to find a partly developed larva on a willow tree, take it home to ob-

A very fine insectarium with the tropical Rose-Chafers of the genus *Pachnoda* – the velvety beetles contrast nicely with the lush plants.

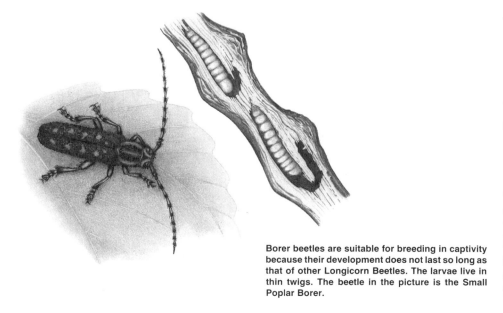

Borer beetles are suitable for breeding in captivity because their development does not last so long as that of other Longicorn Beetles. The larvae live in thin twigs. The beetle in the picture is the Small Poplar Borer.

serve it there. It pupates in the wood or mould of a hollow tree. When fully grown this beetle needs feeding on sweet juice and sap, and the pollen or nectar of flowers.

The **Longicorn Beech Beetle** (*Cerambyx scopolii*) lives in hornbeam, beech, willow and poplar as well as in fruit trees, so its larvae are easy to find. The adult beetles are fed on a sugary liquid and twigs from fruit trees. The terrarium must be kept closed and be made of glass because these beetles can easily bore their way through wood and even plastic.

Ants

The breeding of ants differs considerably from that of other invertebrates to the extent that you cannot breed individuals or even randomly collected groups; only parts of colonies taken with the female – the queen – can be kept successfully. The nests of some ant species are very large and crowded, so if ants are to be kept in a formicarium then the species must be chosen very carefully. For beginners, it is best to start with the small species that form small colonies and are peaceful, non-belligerent and, what is more, herbivorous. These would include the south European ants of the *Messor* genus, which live mostly on various seeds.

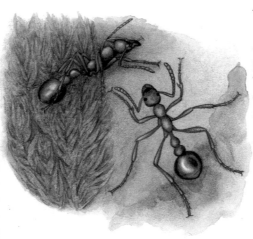

The ant *Manica rubida* is easy to rear. It is predatory and likes to nest in small stumps. Although it has a sting, it is very placid.

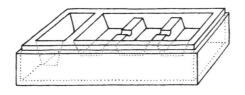

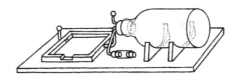

Small plaster formicariums or simple containers with a nest of a natural material, with an easily accessible range and a separate compartment for feeding.

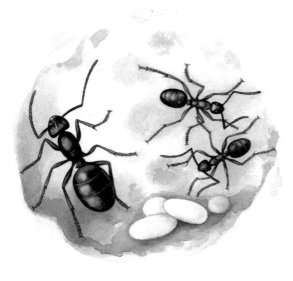

The alate female is the key element in the nest, but in captivity it is seldom able to rear the workers. It is much easier to bring a female together with several workers and the brood (preferably the pupae) to the formicarium. The ants in the picture are the Wood Ant and *Formica rufa*.

The formicarium should be constructed according to the ant species you intend to breed. Most literature describes small plaster types with two small chambers and hollows where wet cottonwool can be placed to maintain the desired humidity. Such little formicariums are suitable for small ants of the *Leptothorax* genus, whose colonies hold no more than a few hundred workers. Larger and more agile species can be kept in a glass container with compartments connected by glass or metal tubing. Cork stoppers or rubber elements should not be used because ants can easily penetrate them. Put in material for the ants to use when building

their nests. The small *Leptothorax* ants will be happy with a piece of bark or worm-eaten pieces from an old tree stump, whereas the *Formica* ants require pine needles, and a little sand and soft soil meet the needs of the *Lasius* genus.

The **Moss Ant** (*Leptothorax muscorum*) is a tiny omnivorous species that can be kept in a small formicarium and fed on drops of honey, pieces of fruit and dead, soft insects. The ants can quench their thirst on water-soaked cottonwool. If eggs or larvae are found in the formicarium, add more albumin to the diet. Any unconsumed food should be removed after about three hours.

The **Wood Ant** (*Camponotus ligniperda*) forms large colonies. In the countryside you may often see a young just-fertilized female looking for a place to build her nest. Place her in a large glass jar with a layer of sand on the bottom and a piece of old wood. Give her a piece of water-soaked cotton wool, and feed her on a little honey and sugar and pieces of dead insects or fruit, although, as a rule, the little female will reject food. It is most interesting to watch how she cares for her eggs and larvae, and then, later, to observe the first workers, for whom a larger formicarium of several chambers will have to be provided.

Manica rubida is a large rusty-coloured species that is excellent for breeding. It lives in fairly small colonies in the ground, under stones or in small tree stumps. This ant is not very agile nor is it belligerent, although it has a sting. It is certainly voracious and feeds on other insects. Put part of the nest, with the eggs or larvae and the female, in a large glass container with a layer of sand on the bottom.

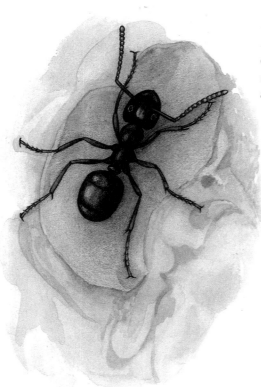

Ant breeding provides an excellent opportunity to study the social relationships among the different worker ants, the common care of the young and other aspects of ant society. If you make a larger run in the formicarium you should be able to observe the tracing activity of the ants in which they are guided by smell and mark their routes with pheromones.

The ant *Dendrolasius fuliginosus* lives inside trees where it forms large colonies. It is not difficult to breed this species in captivity.

Dendrolasius   fuliginosus nests inside trees where it builds a complex box-like construction of corridors and chambers in decayed crevices or hollows. It is possible to take away part of the nest with some ants and to keep them for a time in a 5-litre (8.5-pint) glass jar. They are herbivorous and should be fed on sweet foods.

The sizes of the different ants have not been given because they are a highly organized insect society that has several castes. These are primarily workers, males whose size varies even in the same colony. For instance, in the Moss Ant genus the largest worker is twice as long as the smallest. The female is big and robust, the males are smaller and comparably thinner. The soldiers, equipped with enormous stings, are considerably bigger than the workers.

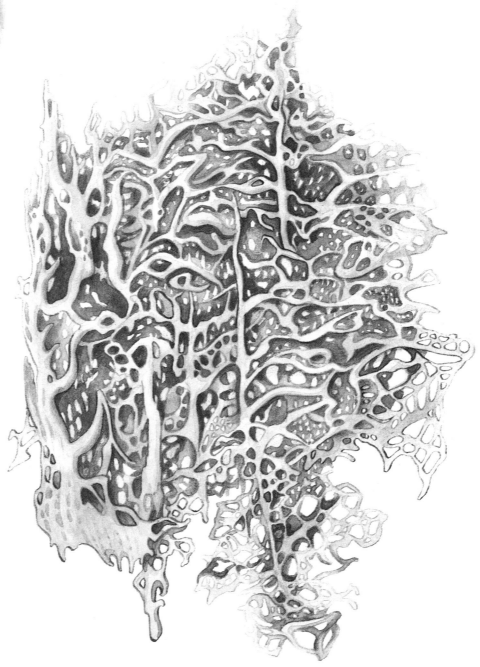

This ant builds complex nests of black 'carton' inside the hollow trunks. If the keeper is able to find such a nest and take it away to put it in a large formicarium, the nest structure looks like a fine work of art.

Gastropods

Although slugs and snails are not the most popular creatures, snails often have beautifully coloured and shaped shells. As pets, they are both interesting and neither is difficult to keep. They are of considerable negative and also positive economic importance to horticulture, and one species, the Edible Snail, is

The Garden Snail is an animal of economic importance.

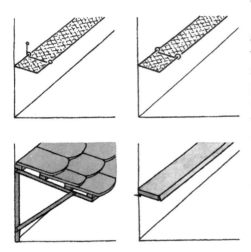

How to prevent the snails from escaping from the pen: roof-like structures of netting, metallic sheet, roof tiles or wood.

bred on a large scale for culinary purposes.

Local snails can be kept successfully in a terrarium, in the open in a part of the garden surrounded with a fence, made preferably of metal turned inwards

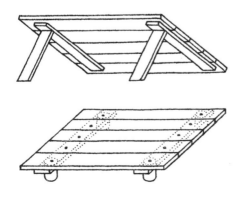

Screens made of planks provide shade.

at the top to prevent the snails from escaping. As snails are bisexual, any two are capable of producing young. Most gastropods are herbivorous, so feed them on lettuce leaves, dandelions, vegetables and fruit. Slugs are especially fond of mushrooms. Cover the bottom of the terrarium with a layer of sand for drainage, then turf, stones and a few pieces of wood. Tropical gastropods must be kept in a heated terrarium.

The **Edible Snail** (*Helix pomatia*) is one of Europe's biggest gastropods. These can be kept in the shade, in a garden pen or a terrarium covered with netting and glass to ensure a regular humidity inside. Place lettuce leaves and other food on a stone for them to eat. If the weather is hot and dry, they must be lightly sprayed quite often. Besides food, gastropods require lime and crushed eggshells or crushed calcium tablets must be added to their diet or, in an emergency, weathered plaster. Snails lay their eggs in the ground. For this reason you should place a large, deep bowl of earth in the terrarium. Later, if possible, transfer the young ones to a smaller bowl.

The **Grove Snail** (*Cepaea nemoralis*), whose striped shell

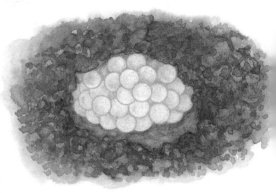

The Garden Snail buries its eggs in the ground after laying them.

measures about 2 cm (5 in), is one of the prettiest and most changeable snails. It lives in the lower levels of gardens and parks.

The **Garden Snail** (*Cepaea hortensis*) lives in similar, although somewhat damper, spots. Both of these snails can easily be bred in a terrarium, but they have to be provided with small branches along which to climb. They eat the same food as the Edible Snail.

The genus *Helicella* are white or yellowish snails with brown- or black-striped, flat shells. They live in dry grassy places and are not at all difficult to breed, not requiring any special care. They are happy with a rather dry terrarium containing tufts of grass and dry sticks along which to climb. The most prolific species is ***Helicella candicans***, whose

The shells of large snails are often nicely coloured; for example those of the Helicellae and Cepaeae (in the picture).

shell measures about 16 mm (0.6 in) in diameter. *H. ericetorium* is the same size, while *H. unifasciata* and *H. striata* are only half as big, at 8 mm (0.3 in). The **Giant Slug** (*Limax maximus*) is up to 16 cm (6.25 in) long and requires a large terrarium. The smaller, nicely coloured slugs include *Milax marginatus*, *Arion circumscriptus* and *A. hortensia*. Slugs require a terrarium of high humidity. They are vegetable eaters and enjoy field plants, fruit and mushrooms. The terrariums in

which gastropods are kept must be frequently and thoroughly cleaned of all food remains, excrement and slime left on the walls and other parts of the terrarium.

Achatina fulica is the most frequently bred of all giant tropical gastropods. Its shell is more

During adverse conditions *Helicella obvia* spends the time firmly attached to a stone or twig.

than 20 cm (8 in) in diameter; a fully grown *A. fulica* can weigh as much as 500 g (17.5 oz). They are native to the damp vegetation along the banks of West African rivers and lakes and were at one time taken by people to tropical Asia where they now do immense harm in the fields and plantations. Keep them in heated terrariums at temperatures above 26 °C (79 °F) and with high, airy humidity. This species feeds on various vegetables and fruit. They are fast growing gastropods and require large doses of lime. They dig holes in the damp soil, in which they lay a cluster of about eight eggs. The disadvantage for the keeper is that this is a nocturnal gastropod, which also takes its food mostly at night.

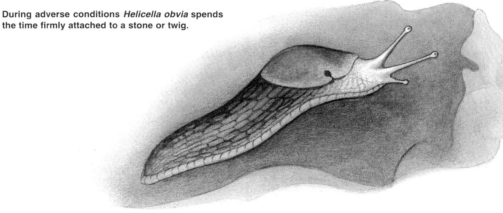

The Garden Slug is the most commonly available species: it is a common pest which can most easily be collected at night or after rain.

The Giant Slug can hardly be overlooked.

Tips on Breeding Invertebrates

Invertebrates are an important part of the diet of a variety of domestically bred animals. For this reason we shall give a few tips on how to breed invertebrates for food. Such species do not, of course, need elaborate living accommodation and can be kept in places such as cellars or sheds. A large strong plastic box, a 5-litre (1 gal.) jar, an old wooden drawer or any other large container is all one needs for breeding invertebrates for food. Feeding and caring for them is very simple.

The favourite food of many aquarium fish, terrarium dwellers, birds and mammals are maggots – smaller common white worms, thread worms and larger species. Earthworms live in the soil and feed on bits of vegetation. They require a box measuring about $50 \times 50 \times 25$ cm ($20 \times 20 \times 10$ in) lined with peat, leaf-mould and garden soil. Common white worms need a little box measuring about $30 \times 25 \times 15$ cm ($12 \times 10 \times 6$ in). It is quite difficult to breed common white worms and maggots rarely flourish in captivity. To try to keep them alive longer, feed them on the larvae of midges and mosquitoes. These can be bred in

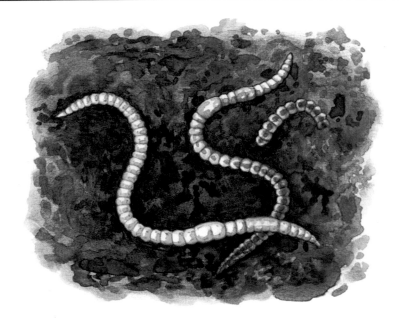

The whitish pinworm makes fine food for fish, terrarium animals, birds and some mammals.

small garden containers – it is not advisable to breed them indoors.

The **Common White Worm** (*Enchytraeus albidus*) is about 35 mm (1.3 in) long and lives in the moist, decaying remnants of organic substances. Fill the breeding box with peat, leaf-mould and cooked oats, or soaked bread rolls with added vitamins A and D. This can be topped up with scalded lettuce leaves or cooked vegetables, which should be placed in a little hole that is covered over with a piece of glass. Place a few maggots on the peat substrate.

Any food left over should be removed and replaced. The breeding boxes should stand on a raised shelf or table in a cool dark place, preferably in a cellar.

The smaller **Grindal Worm** (*Enchytraeus buchholtzi*) is bred in the same way and is more suitable as food for fish fry.

The **Common Earth Worm** (*Lumbricus terrestris*) and the **Dung Worm** (*Eisenia foetida*) are only two of the 30 or more species of hairless worms and maggots living here, most of which can be reliably distinguished only by experts. Most worms multiply in captivity, especially those living in compost, hotbeds or dung. They can stand higher temperatures and so propagate and develop quickly. Keep the worms in covered boxes filled with a deep layer of leaf-mould upon which you have placed straw, lettuce leaves, vegetables and so on. The layers of leaf-mould can be alternated with layers of fallen leaves or stable manure, or with a mixture of clover and straw.

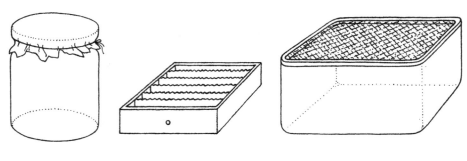

Common containers for support culture. A jar with dense netting on top, a drawer with corrugated cardboards for the crickets and a simple aquarium covered with a netting.

Different earthworm species can be bred successfully in boxes filled with earth. Good quality humus is obtained as a by-product.

Adequate moisture is essential for breeding worms. Unlike the White Worms, which surface on their own, you will have to dig out the worms.

Worms of the genus *Tubifex* are about 4 cm (1.5 in) long, red maggots that live in little tunnels in the muddy beds of standing water. They can be bought in

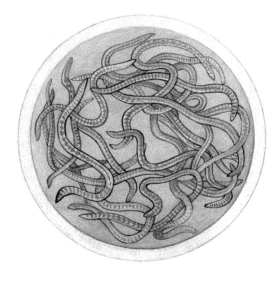

Tubificid worms are among the easiest aquatic organisms to keep.

aquarist shops or fished out of their natural habitat. You can take them from the mud by spreading it on the base of a flat tin, when the little worms will begin to cluster together, making them easy to collect. If you put the mud and worms in a net or sieve above water in a container, they will slide into the water themselves. Placed in a container under slowly dripping water they will remain alive for several days.

The larvae of the midge *Chi-*

ronomus plumosis are 20–28 mm (0.75–1.0 in) long, thick and bright red. They, too, live in tunnels in the mud of large tanks and in slowly flowing rivers. They can be purchased in aquarist shops and kept in containers under tap water.

Water fleas of the genera *Cladocera* and *Copepoda* are tiny plankton crustaceans, especial-

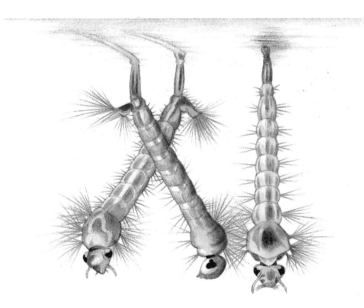

The larvae of the northern house mosquito and other larvae make perfect food for fish and other aquatic animals taking food near the water surface.

ly important as food for aquarium fish. They can be caught with a plankton net attached to a fishing rod. Some of the Copepoda or the larger crustaceans can be kept alive in an aquarium for several days, especially if the water is oxygenized with an aeration device.

Hints on Insect Breeding

Insects are an essential food for many animal species kept in captivity, so it is worthwhile for every breeder of the more demanding species to raise small breeds of abundantly multiplying insects. As these are often species that could become pests or unpleasant companions, they must be kept under very secure conditions.

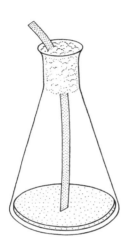

An Erlenmeyer flask adapted for the breeding of pomace flies.

The **Cricket** (*Gryllus domesticus*) is an almost ideal species to keep because it needs only a shallow box or drawer lined with a piece of corrugated paper, folded several times. This makes a welcome hiding place for the crickets, which are night creatures that avoid daylight. The box in which they are kept must have a tightly fitting lid, or be covered with densely woven netting, and should be placed in a warm room and heated to a temperature of about 30 °C (86 °F) using an electrical bulb or an infra-red heater. Feed the crickets with fruit, vegetables, dried blood, a variety of plants and the like. There must be a bowl of earth in the box, in which the female crickets can

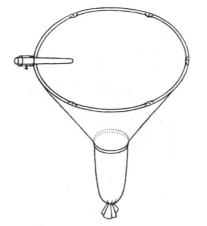

Though seldom used, the shake-down net is useful for catching insects falling from trees.

lay their eggs. The bowl must be changed regularly and put into smaller elements where the young insects can hatch out undisturbed. Fully grown, healthy crickets must be chosen if you intend to start breeding; the female is recognised by her ovipo-

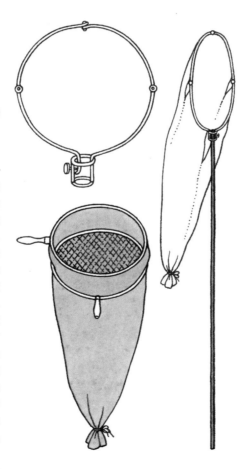

Aids for collecting small invertebrates in their natural habitat. Top: the folding frame of a dragging net and a complete dragging device. Bottom: a separating sleeve.

sitor. Allow the cricket time to lay her eggs and then the nymphs can be collected regularly according to size. The females lay 200–300 eggs, the hatching period of which lasts from three to six weeks according to the temperature.

The **Darkling Beetle** (*Tenebrio molitor*) is a beetle about 18 mm (0.7 in) long, whose larvae make a welcome food for most animals. You can breed them in either a plastic box or a wooden one with well-sealed edges, about 25 cm (10 in) high. Strips of glass about 3 cm (1.2 in) wide should be stuck to the inside of the upper edges of the boxes to prevent insects from escaping. Otherwise it is not necessary to cover them. A 15 cm (6 in) layer of chaff or oats must be put on the bottom of the box before releasing a few beetles into it. Their diet is fruit, vegetables and bread rolls with added vitamins. Give them water in a small, shallow bowl stuffed with cotton wool. The eggs must be placed in a warm, preferably dark place. The most suitable temperature is 25–28 °C (77–82 °F). After two weeks the tiny larvae are ready for collecting.

The **Mediterranean Flour Moth** (*Ephestia kuehniella*) is a tiny moth whose caterpillars are a favourite food of terrarium dwellers. Breed them in a large, 3 litre (5.25 pint) bottle one-third filled with a mixture of wheat chaff, coarse flour and dried yeast. On top of the mixture place a piece of corrugated cardboard where the caterpillars will pupate. After putting about twenty fully grown moths into the bottle, it must be well sealed with a piece of rag and a rubber band. To get a lot of caterpillars quickly, the bottle should be gently warmed from below, otherwise it should be kept in the dark at a temperature of 22–24 °C (71–75 °F).

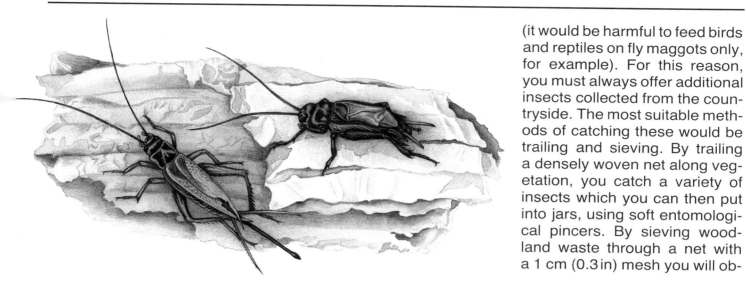

The House Cricket, an undemanding species, provides different kinds of food during its development – from small nymphs to large adults.

(it would be harmful to feed birds and reptiles on fly maggots only, for example). For this reason, you must always offer additional insects collected from the countryside. The most suitable methods of catching these would be trailing and sieving. By trailing a densely woven net along vegetation, you catch a variety of insects which you can then put into jars, using soft entomological pincers. By sieving woodland waste through a net with a 1 cm (0.3 in) mesh you will ob-

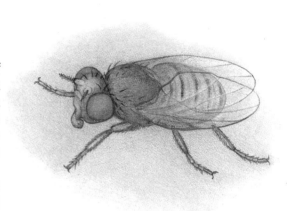

The pomace fly, one of the most popular experimental organisms among invertebrates, is noted for a rapid alternation of generations.

replaced with a whole piece of rag and the jar brought into a warm room. Within two weeks a new generation of vinegar flies will have developed, and these can then be divided between two jars.

Such domestic breeding is not the only way of obtaining food for insectivorous species

Meal worms – larvae of the meal beetle – are indispensable in the insect culture.

tain woodland insects, which you can carry home in a linen bag and then carefully pick out with pincers. Insects can also be shaken out of bushes and trees into an upturned umbrella or a thick net.

The **Vinegar Fly** (*Drosophila melanogaster*) is an excellent food for the smallest species and the young of terrarium animals. The female fly can be caught flying around decaying fruit and fruit juice left in a glass. You can breed vinegar flies in jars in which you have put pieces of crushed, decaying fruit, bits of white bread and a little yeast. Cover the jars with paper through which a hole has been pierced that is big enough for the flies to get out but too small for bigger flies to get in. When there are enough vinegar flies in the jar, the paper must be

Cultures of the store pests, such as the Mediterranean flour moth, require careful handling.

Aquarium Keeping

For thousands of years little fish have been bred in the Far East. In Thailand the **Siamese Fighting Fish** (*Betta splendens*), a well-known species of labyrinth fish, has always been purposely bred and the fights between the males are still a popular entertainment in that part of the world. There is evidence that in Japan, China and Korea many varieties of veil tails were bred in the eighth century BC; solitary fish were usually kept in decorative china bowls.

This 'goldfish' was introduced into Europe by the Portuguese and British in the seventeenth century. It soon became fashionable among European nobility to keep such fish in round bowls without plants in elegant drawing rooms. A long time elapsed before people learned how important it is for aquarium fish to have plants in their tank and that a close and well-balanced relationship must be maintained between the fish and the water plants. The growing of plants in fish tanks brought about a revolution in aquarium fish culture late in the nineteenth century. Tropical fish were imported into Europe on a large scale. The first aquarium fish to reproduce successfully in Europe was the **Paradise Fish** (*Macropodus opercularis*), in France in 1870.

Many aquarium fish come from tropical and subtropical countries where they live in various environments, such as periodically drying shallow waters, both stagnant and flowing, and tropical forest creeks that are rich in nutrients, as well as in large rivers and lakes. Most are native to South and Central America, the adjacent islands and Australia. Only a small pro-

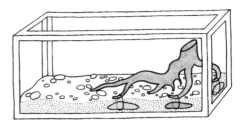

A recommended way of fixing a root among stones on the bottom of the tank.

portion come from countries in the temperate zones: the tanks where these species are kept are called cold-water aquariums.

It is, of course, impossible to provide in a tank all the factors to which the fish are exposed when living in their natural habitats. However, the aquarist must at least provide those conditions that are essential for the fish to live and reproduce in captivity.

Before deciding what type of tank to choose, you must have a clear idea what purpose the tank is to serve; whether you want to have just a decorative aquarium, a tank for brood fish, a spawning tank, or a tank in which to rear young fish. An all-

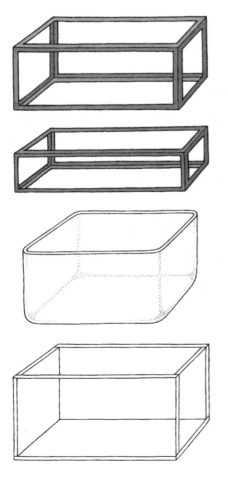

Tanks made from sheets of glass within a metal frame are almost completely out of use today. All-glass cast tanks are used mainly for rearing fish and for quarantine purposes. Tanks stuck by means of silicone cements have begun to predominate in recent years.

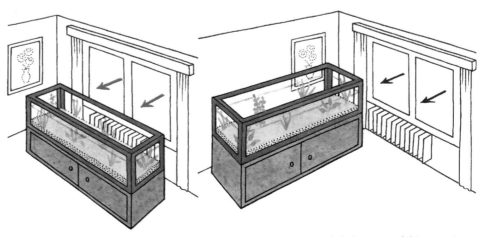

Locating the tank. Left: incorrect; right: correct.

Side view through the bottom and the rear wall of the tank.

Potted plants can be placed on the bottom in special-purpose tanks.

glass tank will normally suffice for spawning and rearing the fry. A large glass tank is the best tank in which to keep brood fish or to rear a large fish stock; it is also the best type of decorative aquarium. Aquariums are available in a variety of sizes in specialist aquarist shops.

The size of a decorative aquarium must be in balance with the furniture in the room. For example, one or more large aquariums look nice when they are built into a wall unit. A decorative aquarium should be as large as possible, 60 litres (13 gallons) minimum. The best location for a decorative aquarium is on the southeastern or southwestern wall of the room where there is plenty of daylight but no prolonged exposure to direct sunshine. It is essential to leave some free space at the sides of the tank and above it: there must be room for electrical wiring and other essential requisites, including an aeration device (compressor), filter and so on. There must be a fixed lamp above the tank. You will have to feed the fish and catch them from above, and some other operations will also require the same direction of access, so there must be enough room above the aquarium.

Tanks for brood fish, the spawning aquariums and tanks for the fry are usually placed in a separate room where they are supported on firm stands, welded from shaped iron. The tank requisites are the same as mentioned above.

The water in which these fish

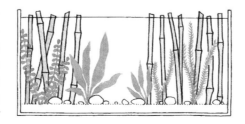

Alternative ways of furnishing a tank.

normally live has a chemical composition that is entirely different from the chemistry of the water normally available from domestic taps. Tropical pools and water courses receive large amounts of rainwater, so this water is usually very soft and contains only a very small quantity of minerals. On the other hand, such water usually contains much humus and clay, which give it a characteristic colour and cloudiness.

As the correct water chemistry is vital for the aquarium fish to prosper and reproduce successfully, tap water must be conditioned to reduce its hardness and offset the effects of any chemicals (such as chlorine) added to it in the waterworks. The so-called temporary hardness, caused by acid carbonates, can easily be removed by boiling. The carbonates will then change into an insoluble incrustation, and the chlorine will evaporate and escape. Permanent hardness, however, is caused mainly by calcium sulphate (gypsum). To remove it, the water must be boiled and then diluted with soft (distilled) water.

Water hardness is directly associated with water reaction, which may be alkaline, neutral or acid. The reaction is defined

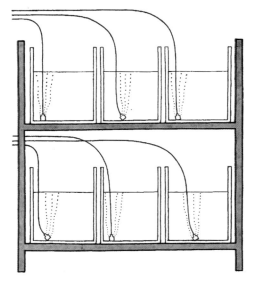

A stand with containers to rear fry.

as the hydrogen-ion concentration in the water and is denoted as pH. The pH of neutral water is 7.0. At a higher pH the reaction is alkaline and at a lower pH it is acid. Various general-purpose colour-scale indicators are available from aquarist shops to determine water pH: the indicator is dropped into a white or glass bowl containing the water being tested and its colour is then compared with the colour on the pH value scale. Transistor-type pH meters are also available and their measurements are very accurate.

If the water in the tank is required to be more acid, it is recommended that you filter it through peat. Filtering through crushed marble or the addition of a small amount of sodium hydroxide will increase the pH value.

Fresh water must be prepared outside the tank. Once the water has the required pH characteristics and the bottom of the tank has been prepared, the aquarium can be filled. A few days later the filled tank, planted with aquatic plants, can be safely stocked with fish. Good lighting, the correct temperature and plenty of oxygen must be provided.

Light is required mainly by the aquarium plants and the tanks must be therefore kept in places that are exposed to direct sunshine for two to three hours daily (preferably in the morning), or else additional light should be provided. Bulbs or fluorescent lamps may serve as the light source; they can be turned on and off automatically to keep a regular light regime in the aquarium. Daylight lasts for 12—14 hours in the native countries of the majority of aquarium fish, so artificial light that prolongs the day in winter is very beneficial to the fish.

Various types of heating elements, connected to a thermostat, are used to keep the water in the tank at the required temperature. The aquarium should

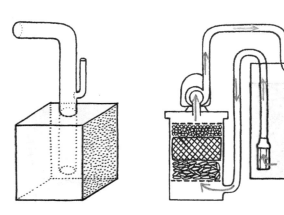

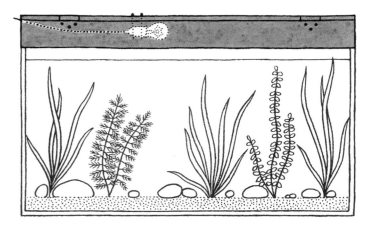

The source of light must be well shielded at the front to prevent dazzle.

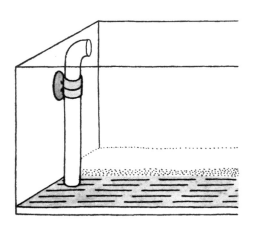

Filters: internal rubber-foam filter, outer filter with pump, soil filter.

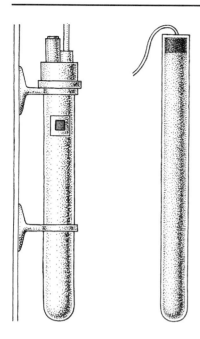

The heating elements either allow you to adjust the temperature as required or provide a constant temperature.

have a floating thermometer and the water temperature should be checked regularly.

The higher the temperature, the lower the content of oxygen that is dissolved in water. An artificial supply of oxygen is necessary therefore, using small compressors and a microbubble generator. It is advantageous to oxidize the water by using filters to remove pollutants and maintain the flow in the tank.

Glass fishing 'bells' and nets are among the essential requisites of every aquarist. The fish may be caught in nets and removed from the tank together with water by means of the 'bell'. It is also important to have a mud separator, which helps to remove organic residue from the bottom, a razor blade on a handle to scrape algae off the inner sides of the glass of the tank, and various floating feeders to prevent the feed from dispersing over the water surface.

First consider what type of aquarium you need. For reasons of sanitation, young, growing fish are usually reared in tanks free of any decoration, either without plants or with plants in pots. On the other hand, a decorative aquarium has to be tastefully planted, the taller plants being placed close to the rear wall so as not to mask

the shorter ones. The bottom of the tank should slope slightly from the back to the front and must be well layered. The bed should consist of washed, coarse river sand, pebbles of different sizes, coarse river gravel, or a combination of these materials. The inside of the tank must look natural. Small caves may be built on the bottom with stones, and roots that have formed interesting shapes may be spread in the tank. (Any wood used must have been thoroughly cleaned.) Suitable pieces of wood can be found in peat water and in peat bogs; such wood is already partly mineralized and does not decay. Some water plants may be tied to the roots using a nylon thread.

Limestone is not a suitable material to form the bed because it dissolves in water and increases its hardness.

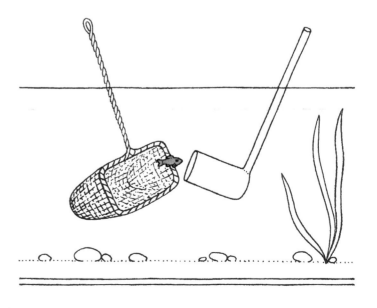

Using the fishing net and bell to catch the fish.

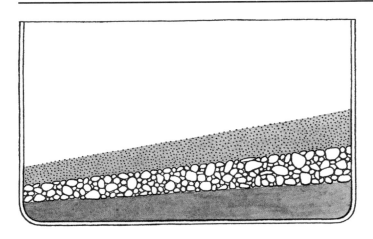

Some plants require the nutrient substrate to be covered with a layer of coarse gravel and a layer of sand.

The number and species of fish to be kept in the tank depend on the size of the tank, the sizes of the fish, and the requirements of the fish in terms of technical equipment. The most natural-looking tanks are the Dutch-type aquariums in which only a few fish swim through thickets of water plants. If such a tank is equipped with efficient aeration or filtration, the number of fish in it can be higher. Usually we allow 2 litres (3.5 pints) of water per fish of 3–5 cm (1–2 in) long.

Adequate feeding is an important factor in aquarium fish culture. Live food is best. This includes plankton, cyclops, water fleas (Cladocera), rotifers (Rotatoria), benthos, the well-known tubifex worms, Chironomidae larvae (*Chironomus plumosos*) and other insect larvae living in water. Some aquatic fish live on algae and aquatic plants, which can be replaced by chopped and scalded lettuce. Predatory aquarium fish may also be given the fry of other fish, usually young guppies (*Poecilia reticulata*).

Specialized aquarist shops sell various food replacements for various fish groups or species. The composition of such artificial feeds fulfils the require-ments of the fish; the fish eat them readily and grow well.

The food consumed by different fish varies in both quality and quantity. Some, such as the Live-bearing Tooth-carps (Poeciliidae), consume large amounts of food which they digest imperfectly, so their excrement soon spoils the water. The stock density of such fish in the tank should therefore be lower than that of fish that make better use of their food, such as the Tetras (Characidae). Overfeeding the fish in the tank must be avoided; unconsumed food will decay and spoil the water.

Some aquarium fish only feed on one specific kind of food. The Wrestling Halfbeak (*Dermogenys pusillus*), which picks flying insects from the water surface, is a typical example. The well-known Archerfish (*Toxotes jaculatrix*) possesses the remarkable ability to shoot down an insect from a leaf above the water's surface by spitting a jet of water at it.

Like any breeder or keeper, the aquarist must take care of the health of his or her stock. Fish that are sick can often be recognised by sight: they become pale in colour, look slow and their skin and gills are covered with tumours, ulcers or white tubercles. Sometimes a whitish or greyish film occurs on the surface of their bodies, sometimes their scales are raised or their spine is bent.

Sick fish are hard to cure and a specialist's help is usually necessary, so it is better to look after the fish with the utmost care and keep them safe from infection to prevent disease from occurring.

The following key principles must be observed:

1 Provide the best possible environment for the fish.
2 Avoid keeping too many fish together or too many fish in the tank.
3 Add a new fish or plant to the aquarium only after

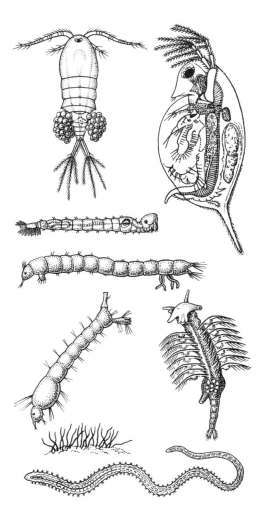

Plankton and benthic organisms at a high magnification.

Aquarium Plants

Aquarium plants are an important decorative feature and also an important part of the biological balance in the tank. Through photosynthesis, or its processes, plants convert organic waste (mainly the compounds of nitrogen) into the substances they need for their nutrition and growth. While doing this, they also release much oxygen into the water.

Every aquatic plant species has its own specific requirements of light, temperature and food. These requirements must be met if the plants are to thrive in the tank. Plants from tropical forest creeks, shaded by rank vegetation, need less light in the tank than plants from sunlit tropical pools and rivers. Artificial light must be provided to prolong the daylight for the plants in the tank in autumn, winter and spring.

If the plants are to grow well, they must root in a suitable substrate. In their original habitats, most of these plants are submerged for only part of the year, but in the tank they have to remain underwater permanently. In order to survive, they need plenty of light, adequate temperature and good nutrition.

Marsh plants, whose nutrient demand is comparatively high, could not prosper in washed sand on the bottom of a tank. Instead, they must be planted in small pots filled with clay or turf soil and the pots immersed in the sand on the bottom of the tank, or else a small amount of clay or turf soil can be put into the lower layers of the bed. Approximately every three or four weeks, it is necessary to remove the fish and plants, drain the tank, clean it and fill it again. This will provide the plants with a fresh supply of nutrients.

Fish of the *Synodontis* genus often take food in an upside-down position.

a two- to three-week stay in a quarantine tank.

4 Avoid catching live food (plankton and the like) in reservoirs stocked with fish, otherwise infection might be introduced to your tank with the food.

5 Feed the fish adequately (avoid overfeeding) and give them varied food.
6 Maintain and clean the tank regularly and check the equipment often.
7 Remove sick fish from the tank without delay.

The mouth of halfbeaks is adjusted to taking insects from the water surface.

Common Java Moss (*Vesicularia dubyana*) is a moss from the jungles of southeast Asia where it grows both in and out of water. In the tank it forms large decorative sessile or freely floating clusters. It often reduces the pH of the water. Many aquarium fish seek this moss to spawn in.

Floating Moss (*Salvinia minima*), native to southern Brazil, is a small moss that floats on the water's surface. It needs plenty of light and the air above the surface must be warm and humid. The fish of the Anabantidae family build their foamy nest on this moss, whose rootlets provide a perfect spawning substrate for fish that spawn under water, such as the fish of genus *Aphyosemion.*

Java Fern (*Microsorium pteropus*) is a fern of the tropics and subtropics of southeast Asia. It has no special demands as to water quality. The optimum temperature for this plant is 20–25 °C (68–77 °F). It takes in nutrients through its whole body surface and via the root system. The roots must not be planted into the bottom, but tied with nylon thread to a stone or a piece

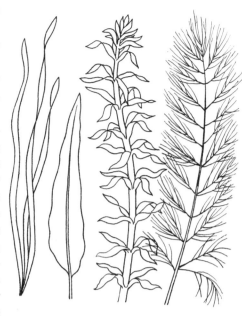

The leaves of some aquatic plants.

of wood and left to attach themselves to the substrate.

Floating Water Sprite (*Ceratopteris pteroides*) from tropical Asia and America is a free-floating fern that prospers in medium-hard to soft water and at a high humidity on sites exposed to light. It has very frail leaves on which suckers grow.

Fanwort (*Cabomba australis*), native to southern Brazil, Uruguay and Argentina, is a photophilous (light-loving) plant, that has floating or submerged leaves. The plant must be protected from water slugs, which will nibble at its fine leaves.

Hygrophila (*Hygrophila polysperma*) is a marsh plant from Indonesia where it grows in shallow shore-side waters. If provided with plenty of light, it

Ludvigia palustris

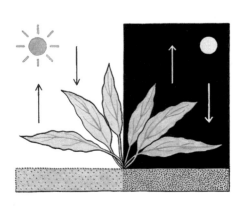

The principles of photosynthesis.

50

Salvinia minima

grows vigorously at temperatures between 18 and 25°C (64–77°F). To propagate it, its parts are clipped and left to root. **Giant Vallisneria** (*Vallisneria gigantea*) is an aquatic plant with a large root system and a short stem. It needs deep, large tanks that allow enough room for its long leaves, up to 2.5 cm (1 in) wide, to float freely on the water surface. Clay sand, rich in nutrients, is needed for good growth of its huge root system. If the plant is exposed to sunshine for several hours, it will produce a wealth of flowers. The male flowers are set in leaf axils and the female flowers, held on long coiled stems, stick out above the water surface. The pollination is a remarkable process: the male flowers detach themselves from the plant to float freely on the water surface where they open fully. The water current or the wind drives them to the female flowers which are thus pollinated. Then the spiral-like stem of the female flower shrinks to draw the pollinated flower down onto the bottom where it ripens into a pod. Seeds seldom develop in the aquarium. Like other species of the same genus, the plants will

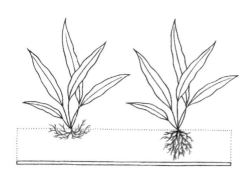

A plant on the bottom. Left: incorrectly planted; right: correctly planted.

also reproduce vegetatively. Young plants grow from the runner-like stolons; they can be cut off and planted separately. **Tape Grass** or **Eel Grass** (*Vallisneria spiralis*) is less demanding with regard to nutrients and will grow well even in washed sand. It occurs in masses in the tropical and subtropical regions of the Old World. Like *Vallisneria gigantea,* it requires plenty of light. Even in the aquarium it is

Microsorium pteropus

Vesicularia dubyana

able, in a sunny place, to produce seeds that will germinate. All plants of this genus have frail leaves that break easily. The damaged tissue soon dies away. Such damage is often caused by aquatic snails or careless handling.

Water Trumpet (genus *Cryptocoryne*) is found in the swamps that develop along the water courses in tropical forests in Asia. The water there is soft, slightly acid and low in organic matter. Plants of this genus will prosper in aquariums if a peat extract is added to the water. They take up most of the nutrients through their root system. The water in the tank should be 25–27 °C (77–80 °F) and no deeper than 30–35 cm (12–14 in). The plants readily propagate by rhizomes or root suckers.

Cryptocoryne affinis, from the Malay Peninsula, is one of the most popular aquarium plants. It is very hardy and able to grow

Vallisneria gigantea

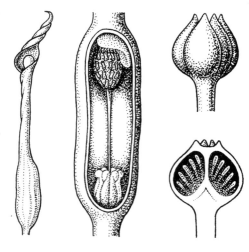

Cryptocorynes flowers

Cryptocoryne affinis

Cryptocoryne wendtii

cultivation is easy, so it is especially good for large tanks. It propagates by suckers and seeds.

Echinodorus latifolius forms rosettes of low-set leaves. If there is plenty of light, it propagates readily by suckers growing from creeping runners.

The family *Aponogetonaceae* are plants from Africa and the tropical belt of Asia. Most of the species are permanently submerged and require alternating seasons of growth and rest. To create this alternation, the temperature should be maintained at 18–20 °C (64–68 °F) in winter and at a level of up to 24 °C (75 °F) in summer. Plants of this family need light locations that are sunlit for several hours even in darker places. It has no special demands for water quality; even hard, limy water will dolt propagates by suckers or trailing runners.

Cryptocoryne wendtii, native to Sri Lanka, requires a sunlit site. It is hardy and has no special demands for water quality or temperature. It readily produces suckers, so its vegetative propagation is easy.

There are many other popular aquarium plants in the *Cryptocoryne* genus, including *Cryptocoryne becketi* with olive-brown-green leaves, purplish-red on the underside and slightly wavy at the edges; *Cryptocoryne exelrodii* from Sri Lanka, with dark, diagonally striped leaves; and *Cryptocoryne cordata,* native to Java, Borneo and the Malay Peninsula, with green, heart-shaped leaves, usually red-brown on the underside.

Amazon Sword Plants (plants of the genus *Echinodorus*) come from the tropical and sub-tropical regions of South and Central America where they exist as partly aquatic and partly terrestrial plants in marshes and in shore-side areas. In the rainy season they are flooded and produce submerged leaves; in the dry season they grow as marsh plants and produce flowers. All species need light and sunny sites. Their periods of growth alternate regularly with periods of rest during the year. The plants grow well in both soft and hard water. Optimum temperatures for their growth range between 17 and 28 °C (63–82 °F). The majority of the species requires additional light during winter. The genus *Echinodorus* has a number of species of different sizes and their leaves and inflorescences have different shapes.

Echinodorus cordifolius is native to Mexico and the southern states of the USA. Its leaves float on the water surface or stick out above the water. Its

Vallisneria spiralis

Echinodorus magdalensis

muddy banks of stagnant waters. The bottom of the tank must contain plenty of nutrients and the water temperature should range between 20 and 22 °C (68–71 °F). If plenty of light is provided, they set flowers and produce germinable seeds. Suckers can be used daily. Propagated by seeds, they are planted in coarse river sand. The plants stick out above the water surface and after pollination the seeds usually ripen in water. Small insects carry pollen from one flower to another. It is not easy to produce seeds that will develop.

Aponogeton fenestralis has leaves that look like a fine net, with no tissue between the nerves. It is rare and delicate and usually does not survive long when grown in a tank with other plant species. It cannot live in stale aquarium water. There must be enough light to allow the plant to prosper but not enough to let algae grow through its net-like leaves. In summer the water must be about 22 °C (71 °F) and in winter 15–18 °C (59–64 °F).

Aponogeton undulatus is a modest plant inhabiting stagnant and slowly flowing waters. It is a good plant for small aquariums. There are many hybrids between this species and related plants, whose seeds usually have a poor chance of growing or do not germinate at all.

Arrowhead plants (genus *Sagittaria*) are marsh plants, most of which are native to North America. They grow wild in sunlit places where they root in the

Aponogeton fenestralis

for vegetative propagation. No special water quality is required. **Sagittaria eatonii** is a very short plant. If enough light is provided, it forms dense and decorative growth. The flower-bearing axil sticks out above the water surface.

Hygrophila polysperma

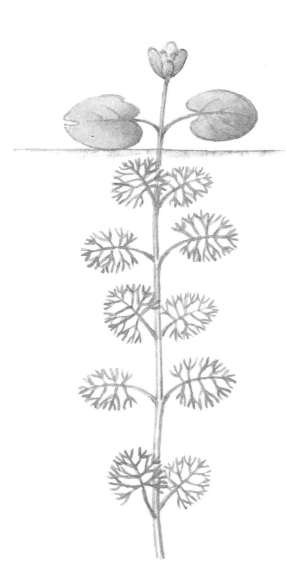

Cabomba australis

Keeping Characins (Characidae)

Characins, members of the family Characidae, live in the fresh water of the jungles of Central and South America, especially in the basin of the River Amazon and its tributaries. Our knowledge of the geographical distribution of many species of this family is poor. The quality of the water in which the Characins live depends on various geological conditions, and on the climate and local vegetation. Some waters are crystal-clear, some are brownish to black, others opaque, depending on the clay they carry.

In the aquarium, characins prefer water with neutral to slightly acid pH (pH 6–7). They are kept in large aquariums where most of them gather in large shoals. They will show all their graceful beauty and striking colouring as they glide through tufts of plants from shade to sunlit places, quickly changing speed and direction. Almost all characins love shade, or must at least have a shaded place in which to hide, so the tank in which these fish are to be kept should resemble a shoreline habitat with a darker bottom, and contain plants that do not demand much light (*Microsorium, Cryptocoryne*) and large pieces of branch. Dark paper or cloth is used to cover the back wall of the tank. The water in the tank must be filtered and checked regularly for nitrates. If the nitrate level is too high the fish become ill and often die.

Most of the characins grow to a length of up to 10 cm (4 in). The requirements of the different fish are suggested by their colour: species with bright shining markings come from the dark waters, coloured by plant pigments. These bright colours help the fish to see one another and to orient themselves in the shoal.

Many characins feed on plankton, some eat the bottom fauna (benthos), others are predatory, several species are plant-eaters (phytophagous). In aquariums they readily take dry food specially prepared for the different species or groups of species. The food must have a high nutritive value and must be varied.

It is not always easy to breed characins, although group spawning of healthy and well-fed fish takes place fairly frequently. They spawn over a tangle of fine-leaved plants. Their eggs are very tiny, hardly noticeable when they fall to the bottom or onto plants, from where the fish like to pick and eat them during and after spawning. The eggs will develop successfully only in very soft water, so it is necessary to have a separate small tank in which to keep the spawning fish and to rear the young. Such a spawning tank should contain soft water to which some peat extract is add-

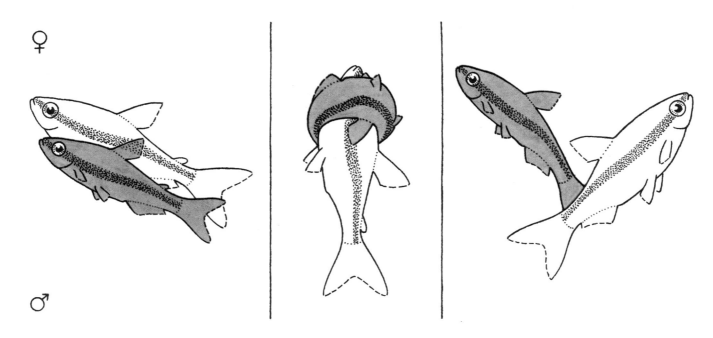

The spawning pattern of Tetras.

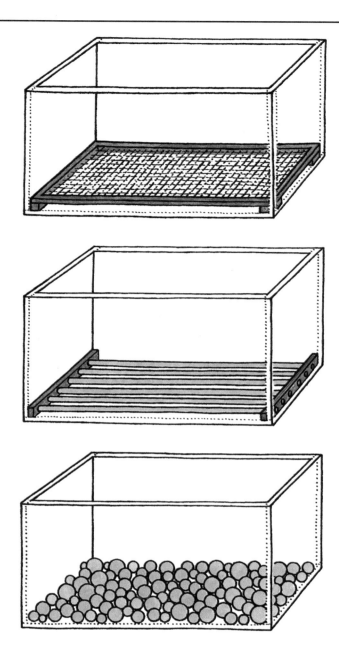

Types of spawning grates.

a change in pH caused by the decomposition of remnants of undigested food might kill the fry. It is not easy with many characin species to provide and maintain the optimum water quality required for the development of the eggs and fry, so the breeder must be very experienced.

The **Cardinal Tetra** (*Cheirodon axelrodi*) is among the best known and most popular of aquarium fish. It grows to a length of less than 5 cm (2 in). It is a native of the western tributaries of the Rio Negro and the Orinoco basin. The female differs from the male by having a rounder belly. In open waters the fish spawn in the evening or at night. For optimum development of the eggs, the water must be soft, such as rainwater or snow water that has been left to stand for some time, or distilled water with a very small addition of tapwater (pH 5.2–5.8). At a temperature of 27–28 °C (80–82 °F), the fry emerge after about 20 hours and begin to swim after five days. They prefer fine food, including rotifers and the nauplii of cyclops or brine shrimp. As small amounts of common aquarium water are added, the fry are gradually transferred from soft to harder water. The young are fastidious about water purity and new fresh water must be frequently added to replace the old (50 per cent replacement every two weeks).

The **Neon Tetra** (*Paracheirodon innesi*) originates from the upper Amazon and its tributary, the Rio Purus. Adults are about 4 cm (1.5 in) long and the males are more slender than the females. Outside the breeding season they are kept at a temperature of 16–22 °C (61–71 °F) but for spawning the water must be warmer, 23–24 °C (73–75 °F). There must

ed. There should be a spawning grate and a fine-leaved plant. The pair of parent fish kept there must be removed promptly as soon as the eggs are laid.

At an optimum temperature, the fry hatch after 18–36 hours. They have sticky glandules on the back of their heads by which they attach themselves to plants, the walls of the tank and

the grate. After about five days they discard the consumed yolk sac, their air bladder fills and the small fish begin to swim. This is the moment when they start taking food such as the finest plankton, infusorians and the like. Small amounts of normal tapwater are added to the fry tank every day for gradual adaptation. This also helps to reduce the possible variation of the pH:

be very soft water (pH 6.2–6.8) in the spawning tank. A small addition of peat extract is essential for good development of the eggs and fry. The fish spawn in fine-leaved plants. The fry will emerge after 24 hours and begin to swim after about five days. Further rearing is the same as for the Cardinal Tetra.

The **Black Widow** or **Black Tetra** (*Gymnocorymbus ternetzi*), native to Brazil, is an undemanding tetra that even the beginner can keep with little difficulty. The female grows to 5.5 cm (2.1 in) long; the males are shorter. They can withstand temperatures as low as 16 °C (61 °F) in winter. Older fish (especially the females) have a duller colouring than the young. Tapwater will suffice for their spawning and for the development of the fry. At a temperature of about 25 °C (77 °F) the fry hatch after 24–26 hours. They will feed on rotifers and other kinds of fine live food.

The **Glow-light Tetra** (*Hemigrammus erythrozonus*) is a quiet, tolerant fish from Guyana, growing to a length of 4.5 cm (1.75 in) at the most. It does well in mixed stocks. It is reared in a small tank containing about 10 litres (2 gallons) of comparatively hard water with an addition of

Cardinal Tetra (*Cheirodon axelrodi*)

peat extract. The parents spawn in dense tangles of water plants at a temperature of 26–28 °C (79–82 °F). The fry need very clean water, so whenever sludge is removed, new water at an optimum temperature must be added, after having been left to stand for a while. The Glow-light Tetra feeds on fine food.

The **Red Tetra** (*Hemigrammus rhodostomus/becheri*), which comes from the lower course of the Amazon, is a gregarious fish about 4 cm (1.5 in) long. The male is somewhat more slender than the female. In the aquarium this species is resilient and easy to breed. It prefers larger tanks for spawning, which always takes place in the dark, shortly before daybreak. The parents must be removed promptly after spawning, otherwise they would consume the eggs. The fry are very fastidious about food quality: first they take the finest particles of food – infusorians and rotifers – and not until they have reached an age of eight days can they take the smallest nauplii of brine shrimps. The fry of the Red Tetra are very sensitive to the content of waste products in water and to shocks, abrupt changes of light and any inconsiderate handling of the tank. Fish of this species are sexually

mature at an age of five to seven months.

The **False Rummy-nose Tetra** (*Petitella georgiae*) is native to the upper waters of the Amazon and the River Huallaga (near the city of Iquitos) where it lives in large shoals. It grows to a length of 6 cm (2.3 in) and bears a very close resemblance to the Red Tetra from which it is distinguished by the pattern on the root of the tail and on the caudal fin. It needs very soft

Neon Tetra (*Paracheirodon innesi*)

water, in which it spawns at a temperature of 25–26 °C (77–79 °F). The fry, having similar requirements to those of the Neon Tetra, hatch after 30–36 hours.

A female and male Black Tetra

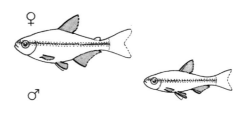

A female and male Glow-light Tetra

Glow-light Tetra (*Hemigrammus erythrozonus*)

Congo Tetra (*Phenacogrammus interruptus*)

The **Flame Tetra** or **Red Tetra from Rio** (*Hyphessobrycon flammeus*), living in waters in the neighbourhood of Rio de Janeiro, only grows up to 4.5 cm (1.5 in) long. It is undemanding and even a beginner can culti- vate it with success. In winter it has no difficulty in living in waters as cold as 16 °C (61 °F).

Red or Gloomy-nosed Tetra (*Hemigrammus rhodostomus*)

In mixed aquariums it is kept in shoals. The male has a more striking colouring than the female and is also somewhat larger. Flame Tetras spawn in pairs or in shoals at a temperature of 20–24 °C (68–75 °F) near fine-leaved plants. The fry hatch after 24–26 hours and when they start swimming they keep close to the bottom where they consume both live food and purchased mixtures.

The **Ornate Tetra** (*Hyphessobrycon bentosi*) is found in the lower course of the Amazon and its tributaries, and in Guyana, where it lives in shoals. It is 4–6 cm (1.5–2.3 in) long and is recommended for combined stocks in larger tanks. For spawning it prefers harder water at a pH of about 6.5–7. It is very fertile and able to produce 500–600 young at one spawning. The fry are able to consume comparatively large particles of food, such as the nauplii of the Brine Shrimp. During the first weeks of rearing the water temperature must remain as constant as possible. The optimum range is 24–26 °C (75–79 °F).

Female and male False Rummy-nose Tetra (*Petitella georgiae*)

Black-line Tetra or Scholze's Tetra (*Hyphessobrycon scholzei*)

Flame Tetra or Red Tetra from Rio (*Hyphessobrycon flammeus*)

The **Black-line Tetra** or **Scholze's Tetra** (*Hyphessobrycon scholzei*) is a modest fish about 5 cm (2 in) long, originating from the neighbourhood of the city of Pará in Brazil. It is popular among aquarists because it is peaceful and very prolific; up to 1,600 fry can be reared from one pair. It spawns readily at a temperature above 23 °C (73 °F) even in the presence of

The young are sensitive to an increase of nitrates in the water. The spawning takes place in tufts of plants. The eggs are not very clingy and usually fall to the bottom. Many of them remain unfertilized, sometimes because they have overripened inside the female's body, sometimes because of the poor fertility of the male.

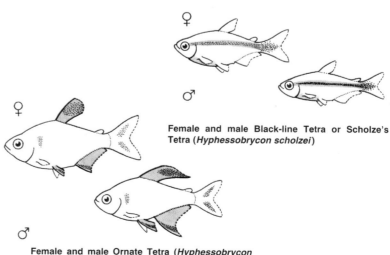

Female and male Black-line Tetra or Scholze's Tetra (*Hyphessobrycon scholzei*)

Female and male Ornate Tetra (*Hyphessobrycon bentosi*)

their eggs on finely leaved plants in larger tanks (about 20 litres/4.3 gallons) at a temperature of 26 °C (79 °F). The young can be reared successfully even in tapwater that has been left to stand for some time. The fry emerge some 36 hours after fertilization of the eggs and begin to swim three days later. They can be given crushed hard-boiled egg yolk or fine live food. The fish grow quickly but irregularly, so they must be graded by size because the larger young may eat the smaller if there is a lack of other food.

Serpae Tetra (*Hyphessobrycon serpae*)

other fish. It prefers larger tanks. Both the young and adult fish readily take any kind of food, including remnants of plants which they pick from the bottom of the tank.

The **Serpae Tetra** (*Hyphessobrycon serpae*), living in the Amazon and in the Rio Guaporé on the border between Bolivia and Brazil, is about 5 cm (2 in) long and requires about the same conditions for breeding and rearing as *Hyphessobrycon bentosi*. The dark spot behind the head may be absent in some aquarium populations, or may be very small. A shoal of these tetras is very impressive in a densely overgrown tank with numerous hiding places. The Serpae Tetra does not live much longer than two years. It spawns readily, but needs very clean water, free from nitrates, and is susceptible to diseases such as infectious dropsy.

The **Red-eyed Tetra** (*Moenkhausia sanctaefilomenae*), a native of the Paraná in Paraguay and the Paranaiba (Paraná's upper course) in Brazil, grows to a length of 7 cm (2.75 in). A large tank is necessary for its successful cultivation. The optimum water temperature for this fish is 20–25 °C (68–77 °F). Separate pairs lay

Moenkhausia sanctaefilomenae

61

The **Emperor Tetra** (*Nemato-brycon palmeri*) is a popular aquarium fish, from Colombia. The males and females can be distinguished easily: the male is up to 7 cm (2.75 in) long and has pointed caudal and dorsal fins,

Emperor Tetra (*Nematobrycon palmeri*)

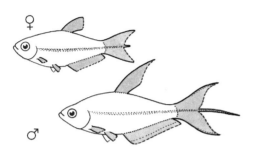

Male and female Emperor Tetra

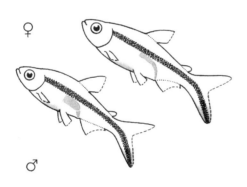

Male and female *Impaichthys kerri*

duce a small number of eggs which they stick onto plants. The fry emerge after 30 hours and begin to swim at an age of five days.
Impaichthys kerri lives in the

whereas the females are smaller and their fins are rounded. Emperor Tetras are very active in the tank and the males often fight to protect their territories. They prefer large tanks where they are kept at a temperature of about 26 °C (79 °F); at lower temperatures the older fish are usually reluctant to take food. A small tank with 5–10 litres (1–2 gallons) of very soft water (pH about 6) and a tuft of fine-leaved plants will suffice for spawning. Emperor Tetras pro-

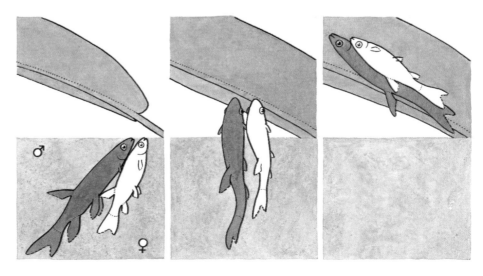

Spawning of the Spraying Characin

river Aripuaná in the northern areas of the Matto Grosso plateau in Brazil. It grows up to 5 cm (2 in) long. The male is larger than the female and has a glossy blue adipose fin whereas the adipose fin of the female is orange to deep red. Although its native waters in Brazil are comparatively soft, it can be kept with success in medium-hard water. However, the fry need very soft water with an addition of a plant extract. The spawning is short and very lively. At a temperature of about 26 °C (79 °F) the fry hatch after 16 hours, begin to swim after four to five days, and are able to consume the nauplii of the Brine Shrimp (*Artemia salina*) immediately. The fry grow very quickly and are easy to rear, but are very sensitive to the nitrate content of water: a high content of nitrates encourages the development of bacteria in the fish's digestive tract and this leads to the formation of dangerous exudates in the body cavity (an enlarged abdominal cavity), to inflammations of the intestines and flatulence.

The **Penguin Fish** (*Thayeria boehlkei*), 6 cm (2.3 in) long, is native to the upper waters of the river Marañon. It does well in mixed stocks in aquariums. The tank must always be well covered by glass because the fish could leap above the water surface if they were disturbed. In the spawning season, the female is distinguished from the male by having a larger belly. The Penguin Fish spawns in a large tank, 30–40 litres (6.5–8.5 gallons) in size, filled with neutral water at 26 °C (79 °F) with an addition of some peat extract. There should be several plants in the tank, and one to two males with three to five females. First, the fry feed on fine food (rotifers), later they are given the nauplii of the brine

shrimp or cyclops. Penguin fish are prolific breeders, producing up to a thousand young at one spawning.

The **Congo Tetra** (*Phenacogrammus interruptus*) is a native of the River Congo (Zaire) and like the majority of African characins, it is comparatively large. The males are about 12 cm (4.75 in) long; the females are smaller. As with most characins, it is more impressive to view a large shoal of Congo Tetras, so ideally they are kept in big tanks of 100 litres (22 gallons) of water or more. The optimum water pH is about 7. During spawning and fry-rearing, the temperature should be kept at 26–27 °C (79–80 °F). The fry emerge from the brownish eggs after six to seven days and can swim immediately. They feed on fine live food (rotifers and nauplii

Penguin Fish (*Thayeria boehlkei*)

of cyclops or brine shrimp). The development of the eggs is encouraged by the addition of a very small amount of peat extract and by the aeration or filtration of the water.

The **Spraying Characin** (*Copella arnoldi*) lives near the surface in the lower course of the Amazon and in the River Pará in Brazil. The male grows to a length of 8 cm (3 in), the female is smaller. It requires a large tank, well covered by glass

Impaichthys kerri

to prevent the fish, which like to leap above the surface, from getting outside the aquarium. The Spraying Characin prefers slightly acid water. There should be large-leaved plants in the tank. During spawning, the fish leap out of the water and lay their eggs on the glass cover or on the underside of leaves over-

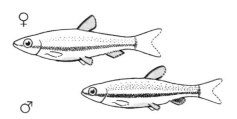

Female and male Red Pencilfish

hanging the water. In order to prevent the eggs from drying out, the male sprays them by lashing his tail fin from time to time. The water temperature in the tank should be between 21 and 24 °C (70—75 °F). The fry emerge from the eggs after 36 hours and fall off the glass or leaf into the water where they are fed with rotifers or other fine food of animal origin.

The **Red Pencilfish** (*Nannostomus beckfordi*) inhabits the waters of a very large part of South America: the rivers of Guyana,

Female and male Dwarf Pencilfish

the lower and middle course of the Amazon, the basin of the Rio Negro and the River Paraná. It grows 6.5 cm (2.5 in) long. The male is more slender than the female, has a round dorsal fin and his colouring is richer. The species exists in a number of forms, distinguished by their colouring. They are kept in small tanks with oxidised clean, soft water at a temperature of 25—28 °C (77—82 °F). The fish prefer live plankton to dry food or substitute mixes. For the rearing of the fry, the water must be soft (pH 6.6—6.8). A tuft of fine-leaved plants is the best spawning bed, where most of the eggs have a chance of escaping the parents' notice. If the brood fish have a clear view of the territory where they spawn, they often

eat all the eggs they have laid. About 100—200 young are usually reared from one spawning. The fry are fed rotifers and other very fine food.

The **Dwarf Pencilfish** (*Nannostomus marginatus*) lives in the waters of Surinam and western Guyana. It grows to 4 cm (1.5 in) long. The female is larger and more robust than the male. It spawns well in an all-glass aquarium of 3—4 litre (5—7 pint) with fine-leaved plants and the same water as used for the spawning of the Golden Pencilfish. The brood fish produce few eggs and the female eats them greedily. To prevent this, it is recommended to partition the spawning tank with a glass plate: when the fish have spawned in one part of the aquarium they are separated from the plants carrying eggs, and then the plants on which the eggs are stuck are transferred to another tank. The same is then done in the other half of the spawning aquarium. The fry hatch about 30 hours after spawning and are

Dwarf Pencilfish (*Nannostomus marginatus*)

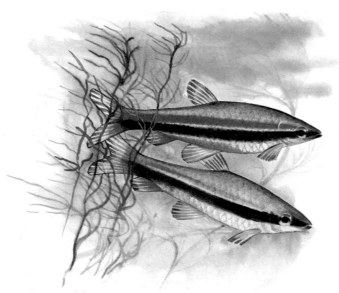

Red Pencilfish (*Nannostomus beckfordi*)

Three-banded Pencilfish (*Nannostomus trifasciatus*)

able to take large particles of food (nauplii of cyclops and others).

The **Three-banded Pencilfish** (*Nannostomus trifasciatus*)

Espe's or Barred Pencilfish (*Nannostomus espei*)

from the middle course of the Amazon, Guyana and the Rio Negro, is one of the delicate fish, fastidious about water composition and purity. Its size is about 6 cm (2.3 in). The brood fish stick their eggs onto plants and the fry hatch at a temperature of 27–28 °C (80–82 °F) within 24 hours.

The **Espe's** or **Barred Pencilfish** (*Nannostomus espei*) was first described as recently as 1956. It lives in the River Mazaruni in western Guyana and is one of the smallest pencilfishes: the adult specimens are as short as 3.5 cm (1.4 in). The male has a longer anal fin than the female. The fry are hard to rear because they grow very slowly and are very sensitive to changes in water quality.

The **Tube-mouthed Pencilfish** (*Nannostomus eques*) from the middle course of the Amazon and from the Rio Negro, is up to 6 cm (2.3 in) long. The male is smaller than the female and his pelvic fins have a white border. This fish swims permanently in a slanted position with its head upwards. It mostly stays in

shoals near the water surface. It has different colouring in the daytime and at night: during the day it has dark stripes along its body, whereas at night it shows two irregular wide bands going across. It is very timid, so it is not a good fish to keep together with other species. When the brood fish spawn they stick 60–200 eggs on to the underside of the leaves of the broad-leaved water plants such as *Cryptocoryne*. The fry emerge after 24–36 hours and start swimming immediately. At first they take fine live food (rotifers) but later they can be given substitutes.

The **Striped Anostomus** (*Anostomus anostomus*), from the basin of the Amazon and Orinoco, is a fish up to 18 cm (7 in) long, that swims obliquely with its head downwards. It is kept at temperatures between 24 and 27 °C (75–80 °F) in large aquariums, densely overgrown with plants and strewn with pieces of wood providing numerous shelters. The Striped Anostomus is an omnivorous fish and will also nibble at algae on submerged objects and on the walls of the tank. It needs plenty of room: the stronger

Tube-mouthed Pencilfish (*Nannostomus eques*)

specimens often guard their territory very closely and drive others away. Accurate data on the reproduction of this fish are not yet available.

Striped Anostomus (*Anostomus anostomus*)

Keeping Cyprinids (Cyprinidae)

The cyprinids are distributed over an enormous area; they live almost everywhere except in South America, Australia and Madagascar. They can be encountered in the most varied environments of the tropics, subtropics and the temperate zones. The family Cyprinidae comprises both large species, which are commercially cultivated, and small fish in bright colours, suitable for aquariums. All cyprinids are freshwater species and they are seldom choosy about food. The adults, as well as the young, largely prefer

Striped Barb (*Barbus fasciatus*)

Spawning of the Cyprinids

Female and male Striped Barb or Zebra Barb

medium-hard water (pH about 7). They do not require such pure conditions as the characins.

Cyprinids spawn readily on to various substrates, on both broad-leaved and fine-leaved plants, and above both sandy and stony bottoms. As the brood fish usually consume their eggs, they must be removed from the tank immediately after spawning. The fry keep close to the bottom where they take fine live food as well as food substitutes. After hatching, the fry remain suspended on the walls of the tank, on plants and other submerged objects: they stick to these surfaces by means of a gummy secretion on the back of the head. During this stage they are very sensitive to any disturbance; therefore it is recommended that you shade the spawning tank when they first lay their eggs and expose the tank again when the fry begin to swim.

The **Striped Barb** or **Zebra Barb** (*Barbus fasciatus*) comes from India, Sumatra and Borneo. It grows to 10–12cm (4–4.75 in) long. The male is distinguished from the female by an oval white spot in the middle of the upper jaw. It is not easy to rear and keep the Striped Barb.

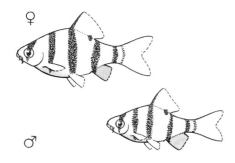

Female and male Five-banded Barb

The males are very aggressive, and are even liable to kill the female during spawning, especially if the tank is small. The eggs are very sticky and the brood fish like to consume them, so both male and female must be removed from the tank promptly after spawning. The water in which they are to spawn must be very soft. The fry are very vulnerable to an increased carbon content. The adult fish are kept in large tanks overgrown with water plants.

The **Five-banded Barb** (*Barbus pentazona pentazona*) is a native of Indonesia and the Malay Peninsula. In the aqua-rium it is an undemanding fish. In the spawning season the females have a much larger belly than the males. In captivity they grow to a length of 5 cm (2 in). Tap water, left to stand for a while, can be used to keep the Five-banded Barb. The water must be replaced from time to time because the fish do not digest their food completely and the waste quickly increases the nitrate content of the water. Five-banded Barb spawns at a temperature of about 26 °C (79 °F). One female will produce 300–400 eggs from which the young emerge after 26–30 hours. The fry begin to swim after six weeks and feed on small particles of food of animal origin (rotifers, nauplii). The fish reach sexual maturity at the age of ten to twelve months.

The **Sumatra Barb** or **Tiger Barb** (*Barbus tetrazona tetrazona*) has its native waters in Sumatra and Borneo. It is a very energetic and fairly robust fish, 7 cm (2.75 in) long. Some of the Sumatra barbs will bite off the fins of the slower fishes in the aquarium community, so it is better to remove such aggressive specimens from the tank. The water must be soft, clear and well filtered and the tank should be large as this fish needs space. The temperature in the tank should be 21–23 °C (70–73 °F). One female ejects up to 700 eggs and the fry hatch at 24 °C (75 °F) within 36 hours and begin to swim at the age of five days.

The **Stoliczka's Barb** (*Barbus stoliczkanus*) is a barb from Burma, 6 cm (2.3 in) long, with no special demands as to water quality. Adults can withstand temperatures fluctuating between 18 and 25 °C (64–77 °F). The fry hatch at 25 °C (77 °F) within 24 hours and readily take live food.

The **Ornamental Barbs** (*Pun-*

Sumatra or Tiger Barb (*Barbus tetrazona*)

tius sp.) first appeared in an aquarium fish market in 1971 in Odessa in the former USSR. Its native waters are not known but the barb has been found to be a close relative of the preceding species. The males take on their typical red colouring at the age of about one year. The Odessa

Five-banded Barb (*Barbus pentazona pentazona*)

Barb reproduces easily in captivity. The eggs and fry require a temperature of 25–26°C (77–79 °F) and comparatively soft water.

The **Zebra Danio** (*Brachydanio rerio*) from eastern India is a comparatively undemanding fish, 4.5 cm (1.75 in) long, that can easily withstand temperatures as low as 16 °C (61 °F). When larger shoals are kept,

Stoliczka's Barb (*Barbus stoliczkanus*)

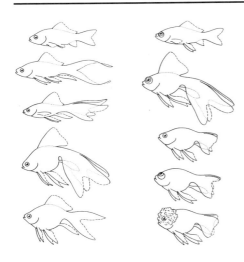

Fins, head and egg shapes of Goldfish

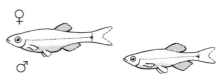

Female and male White Cloud Mountain Minnow

the fish will form pairs themselves and usually it is the female who chooses her partner to spawn with. They will spawn in warm tapwater left to stand for a while, at about 24 °C (75 °F). The parents must be removed promptly after spawning to prevent them from eating their eggs. The fry emerge after three days and begin to swim after another five days. They feed on rotifers, infusorians and a special powdered diet. The young fish grow irregularly and should be graded by size.

The **Leopard Danio** (*Brachydanio frankei*) is often listed as a colour mutation of the Zebra Danio; its actual place of origin is unknown. It crossbreeds easily with the preceding species and the progeny are fertile. The Leopard Danio is more warmth-loving than the Zebra Danio, and is very prolific and easily reproduced. The conditions of

rearing are practically the same as for the Zebra Danio.

The **Goldfish** (*Carassius auratus* var. *bicaudatus*) has been cultivated in China for more than a thousand years. An enormous number of races have been developed, in which grey, white, black, red and other colours combine with various shapes of the body, head and eyes (e.g. the Telescope Veiltail, the Comet, the Lionheads and others). These fish are assessed very strictly and carefully to meet the strict breeder standards. The proportion of first-class specimens is comparatively small, because a large percentage of the offspring revert to the original form of *Carassius auratus auratus.* The greatest care is still taken in breeding these fishes in China and Japan where they are kept in outdoor breeding facilities. The enormous number of offspring (several thousand from one spawning) make it impractical to keep the goldfish in aquariums.

The **White Cloud Mountain Minnow** (*Tanichthys albonubes*) is a popular fish that even

the novice aquarist can keep with success. It comes from the regions of Canton in China and Hong Kong. The 4 cm (1.5 in) long White Cloud Mountain Minnow has variable colouring in both aquariums and in its native waters. The female has a much larger belly than the male and the male has smaller dorsal and anal fins. The water in the tank can be left unheated in winter because the White Cloud Mountain Minnow can survive temperatures as low as 5 °C (41 °F). In the warm season it prospers at temperatures around 20 °C (68 °F). The brood fish spawn in tangles of fine-leaved water plants and usually leave eggs untouched, so they need not be removed from the tank after spawning. At a temperature of about 23 °C (73 °F) the fry hatch after two to three days and need another three to four days to

Zebra Danio (*Brachydanio rerio*)

Goldfish (*Carassius auratus* var. *bicaudatus*)

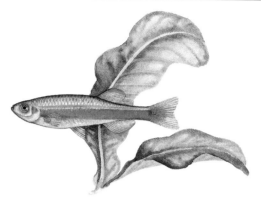

White Cloud Mountain Minnow (*Tanichthys albonubes*)

start swimming. The fish stay near the water surface where they pick up fine live or dry food. The **Harlequin Fish** or **Red Rasbora** (*Rasbora heteromorpha*), the most popular and best known of all rasboras, comes from the rivers of the Malay Peninsula, Thailand and eastern Sumatra. The male is more slender than the female and has a dark V-shaped spot tapering to the base of the pelvic fins. The fish look most impressive when they are in a shoal, which, in fact, is their preferred mode of life. They are kept in medium-sized tanks densely overgrown with broad-leaved plants (e.g. those of the genus *Cryptocoryne*). On sunny days they will often spawn in tanks stocked with other fish, but the eggs can develop only in soft water with addition of peat extract. At a temperature of 28 °C (82 °F) the fry hatch after 24–28 hours, begin to swim after five hours, and take small food such as

Red-tailed Black Shark (*Labeo bicolor*) – top; Green-fringed Lip Labeo (*Labeo frenatus*) – bottom

rotifers and nauplii of the Brine Shrimp. After spawning and removal of the brood pair, the tank should be kept in the dark until the fry begin to swim.

The **Red-tailed Black Shark** (*Labeo bicolor*) and the **Green-fringed Lip Labeo** (*Labeo frenatus*) from Thailand are about 10 cm (4 in) long, and only rarely reproduce in captivity. However, they can live a long time in large aquariums densely overgrown with plants. They feed on live food but will also take algae or scalded lettuce.

Leopard Danio (*Brachydanio frankei*)

Harlequin Fish or Red Rasbora (*Rasbora heteromorpha*)

The Spiny Loaches (Cobitidae)

The small fishes of the family Cobitidae are distributed all over Europe and Asia up to the Pacific coast. Some European species of the genera *Cobitis* and *Sabanajewia* can be kept with success in unheated aquariums. Only species native to the tropical and subtropical areas of Asia and the adjacent islands require aquariums with heated water.

The spiny loaches have long, slender bodies, adapted to life on the bottom. They are shy creatures and many of them belong to species that are active at night. The water in a tank where spiny loaches are kept must be well oxidized and medium hard. The bottom should be soft and preferably covered with fibrous peat. The fish will bury themselves in the bottom where they

Two genera, *Acanthophthalmus* and *Botia,* are the most common spiny loaches kept in aquariums.

The **Coolie Loach**, **Leopard Eel**, **Prickly Eye** or **Striped Loach** (*Acanthophthalmus kuhli*) is among the most frequently imported species. There are a number of subspecies of this fish: the subspecies *A. kuhli sumatranus* lives in Sumatra, another subspecies lives in Borneo and several others are found in other places in southeast Asia and the adjacent islands. They grow to a length of 5–10 cm (2–4 in). There are minor differences between the sexes: the females have round bellies when they are full of eggs; males have an extended dark spot on their pectoral fins. All species of spiny loaches are

The Coolie Loach seldom reproduces in captivity. Carp pituitary hormones, injected under the skin, must be used to stimulate the female to spawn. This treatment can be given only by experienced aquarists. During spawning the pair of brood fish ascend in a spiral-like movement to the water surface, the male embracing the female. They then eject a cloud of eggs and sperm and fall to the bottom afterwards, one after the other. The yield of eggs amounts to several thousand but many remain unfertilized. They must be transferred immediately to warm, clean, oxidized water that is aerated or filtered. At a temperature of 26 °C (79 °F) the fry hatch within 24 hours. During the first fourteen days the greenish-coloured fry have well-

Myer's Loach (*Acanthophthalmus myersi*)

Coolie Loach, Leopard Eel, Prickly Eye or Striped Loach (*Acanthophthalmus kuhli*)

seek their food (benthos). Coarse sand on the bottom is not good for spiny loaches because it may damage their skin, leading to chronic inflammation or a fungal disease.

very vulnerable to abrupt changes in water chemistry, especially to the presence of heavy metals (mainly copper). They are kept in soft water (pH about 7), which must have been pre-treated with a solution that fixes heavy metals. These solutions can be purchased in aquarist shops.

developed, forked external gills that are later replaced by true gills hidden under gill covers. The fry take their first food as early as 72 hours after the eggs were laid. They are fed with food of animal origin, which must fall to the bottom.

Myer's Loach (*Acanthophthalmus myersi*), native to Thailand,

Female and male Clown Loach or Tiger Botia

Clown Loach or Tiger Botia (*Botia macracantha*)

The **Orange-finned Loach** (*Botia modesta*), a native of Indo-China, the Malay Peninsula and Indonesia, grows to a length of 10 cm (4 in) in the aquarium. It is aggressive and so must be kept separately from other fish. As with other East Asian loaches, such as *Botia hymenophysa,* all attempts to breed it in captivity have failed so far.

Singapore, Sumatra and Java, is another species that reproduces in captivity in the same way as the Coolie Loach. As with other loaches, the tank must always be well covered, because the fish are able to jump out of the tank or pass through the smallest hole between the edge of the tank wall and the cover glass.

The **Clown Loach** or **Tiger Botia** (*Botia macracantha*), a fish up to 30 cm (12 in) long, comes from the waters of Sumatra, Borneo and the Sunda Islands. In captivity it grows to a length of 15 cm (6 in) at the most. It is kept at a temperature of about 24 °C (75 °F) in large and densely planted tanks with many shelters. The Clown Loach is very shy and seeks dimly lit places. The water must be clean and well oxidized and the bottom must be soft.

Orange-finned Loach (*Botia modesta*)

71

The Armoured Catfish (Loricariidae)

A catfish of the family Loricarii-
dae, called the Armoured Catfish, lives in the fresh waters of
the northern and central parts of
South America. Its body is covered by a bony armoured coat
and its mouth has broad lips that
serve as a sucking organ. The
fish often moves by attaching its
lips to stones or plant roots and
drawing its body forwards. Most
of the species can be kept easily
in soft to medium-hard water at
temperatures of 21–25 °C (71–
77 °F).

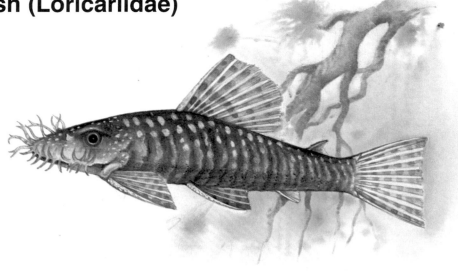

Blue Chin Xenocara (*Ancistrus dolichopterus*)

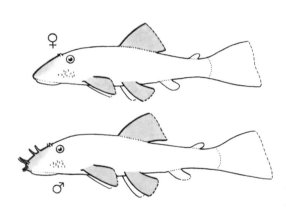

Female and male Blue Chin Xenocara

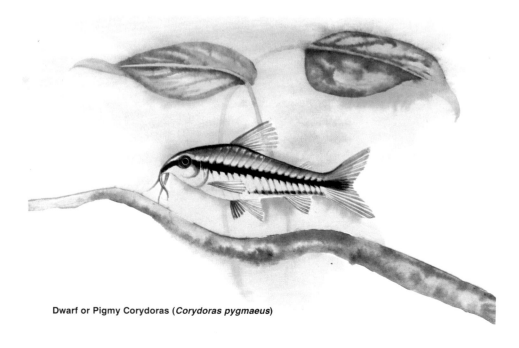

Dwarf or Pigmy Corydoras (*Corydoras pygmaeus*)

Dasyloricaria filamentosa is
an armoured catfish living in
Colombia in the watershed of
the River Magdalena. Its normal
length of up to 25 cm (10 in) is
never achieved by specimens
kept in aquariums. The upper
part of the male's pectoral fin is
covered by dark bristles and his
head is round. The pectoral fins
of the female are smooth and
her head is pointed. They are
kept in large tanks with dense
tangles of water plants and will
take food of both animal and
plant origin and also scrape algae off the tank walls. The
breeding pairs spawn in various
hollows and recesses and between stones at a temperature
of 24 °C (75 °F). The male takes
great care of the orange eggs
and will refuse food until the fry
hatch, which happens after nine
days.

The **Blue Chin Xenocara** (*Ancistrus dolichopterus*) is a native
of the rivers of Guyana and the
basin of the Amazon. Its length
is about 13 cm (5 in). The front of
the head of the male carries upright forked tentacles which do
not develop in the female. The
Blue Chin Xenocara spawns at
a temperature of about 28 °C
(82 °F) in recesses that the fish
itself builds under stones or
pieces of wood. The fry emerge
from the eggs on the fifth day after spawning and begin to swim
after another four days. The
adult fish are thorough in re-
moving algae from the leaves of
plants and walls of the tank.
Having no special demands,
they will take food of both animal and plant origin, such as
leaves of spinach, lettuce and
the like.

The **Upside-down Catfish** (*Synodontis nigriventris*) of the family Mochocidae is native to the African River Congo. The female grows to 8 cm (3 in) long, the male is shorter (6 cm/2.3 in). This fish is of interest because of its habit of swimming near the surface of the water, upside-down, showing its dark belly. It picks food from the water surface and from the undersides of leaves. The aquarium should be densely planted and there should be free-floating plants on the surface. The Upside-down Catfish is very shy and is most active at night. It has no special reproduction of the Upside-down Catfish in captivity.

Keeping the Mailed Catfish (Callichthyidae)

Catfish of the family Callichthyidae are very popular among aquarists. They live near the bottom in the fresh waters of South America. The body of each of these fish is covered by bony plates on the flanks. There are two to four fleshy barbels on each side of the small mouth, which is set low on the head. and in stagnant water. They are able to breathe atmospheric oxygen: they swallow air at the water surface and absorb oxygen via their intestinal mucous membrane which has a dense network of blood vessels. They are kept in a shallow aquarium containing medium-hard water with neutral reaction (pH 7). The bottom should consist of fine sand or small pebbles in which the fish, always seeking food, cannot get injured. The catfish of the genus *Corydoras* feed on everything they can find on the bottom, including the dead parts of plants and the organic resi-

Leopard Corydoras (*Corydoras julii*)

requirements for water chemistry. Food of plant origin is essential for this omnivorous fish. The adult fish are placid. Nothing is known as yet about the

Species of genus *Corydoras* are among the most popular Mailed Catfish. These small catfish are found in large shoals in the slow-flowing water courses

due of food. The optimum temperature for these fish is between 15 and 27 °C (59–80 °F). They usually have no problem in reproducing in captivity. Spawning can be induced by repeatedly decreasing the temperature by 2–3 °C. During spawning itself, the male holds the female's barbels with his pectoral fins, presses himself to her and ejects his milt. At that moment the female lays three to five eggs in the cradle formed by her pelvic fins. Then the female finds and cleans a place in the aquarium where she will stick the eggs. The fry usually hatch at a temperature of 20–23 °C (65–73 °F) after five to eight days. When they begin to swim, they can take quite large particles of food from the bottom.

The **Peppered Corydoras** (*Corydoras paleatus*) is native to eastern Brazil and the basin of the River Plate. It grows to a length of about 7 cm (2.75 in). The male is smaller and more slender than the female and has a pointed dorsal fin, whereas the dorsal fins of the females are round. The Peppered Corydoras is kept at a temperature of 18–26 °C (64–79 °F) in tanks with a soft bottom where the fish

Peppered Corydoras (*Corydoras paleatus*)

like to dig. It feeds on animal and plant food but does not damage developed and healthy plants in the aquarium. It can be kept together with smaller peaceable fish.

The **Bronze Corydoras** (*Corydoras aeneus*), about 7 cm (2.75 in) long, lives in the waters of Venezuela, Brazil and Trinidad. Like the Peppered Corydoras, it belongs to the very hardy group of aquarium fish, which even the complete beginner can keep without difficulties.

The **Gold-striped Corydoras** (*Corydoras schultzei*) is regarded by some experts as a separate species and by others as a variety of the Bronze Corydoras. It lives in the small tributaries of the Amazon and grows to a length of about 6.6 cm (2.6 in).

The **Leopard Corydoras** (*Corydoras julii*), from the smallest tributaries of the Amazon, is 6 cm (2.3 in) in length at the

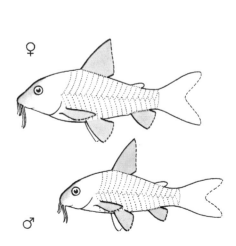

Female and male Peppered Corydoras (*Corydoras paleatus*)

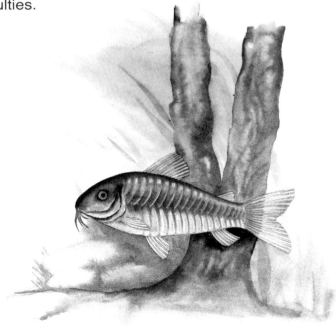

Bronze Corydoras (*Corydoras aeneus*)

Gold-striped Corydoras (*Corydoras schultzei*)

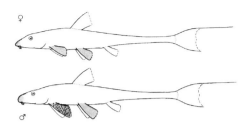

Female and male *Dasyloricaria filamentosa*

ras, it reacts to abrupt changes in water chemistry by swimming nervously and by gasping frequently at the surface.

The **Cascadura** (*Hoplosternum thoracatum*) is distributed over

most. It is shy and sensitive to water temperature, which has to be about 24 °C (75 °F). It is the male, not the female, that cleans the surfaces onto which the eggs are to be stuck (usually the underside of aquatic plants). **Dwarf** or **Pygmy Corydoras** (*Corydoras pygmaeus*) is the smallest of all corydoras species, as short as 3 cm (1.2 in). It inhabits the basin of the Rio Madeira in Brazil where it lives in large shoals. Aquarists may keep it in a small tank. Like other species of the genus *Corydo-*

Cascadura (*Hoplosternum thoracatum*)

a very large territory of the northern part of South America and in the islands of Trinidad and Martinique. As it grows up to a length of 18 cm (7 in), it is suitable only for large aquariums. The male is distinguished from the female by having larger pectoral fins with much thickened fin rays. The Cascadura is noted for its care of its progeny. The male builds a bubble nest on the water surface under large floating leaves or another solid surface and the eggs are closely guarded.

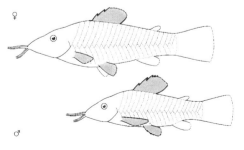

Female and male Cascadura

Glassfish and their Relatives

The popular aquarium fish of the very numerous order Perciformes include the small Glassfish (Centropomidae), some species of the family Centrarchidae (Sunfish and Black Bass, Toxotidae, Nandidae and Scatophagidae (Scats and Argus fish). Most of them are undemanding as to water quality and are not difficult to keep.

The **Indian Glassfish** (*Chanda ranga*) is a fish about 5 cm (2 in) long, living in the waters of India, Burma and Thailand. The male is a golden colour and the female is silvery. The air bladder of this transparent fish is easily discernible when viewed against light, and takes different shapes in the male and female (see illustration). In the tank this

Spawning of the Indian Glassfish

glassfish needs crystal-clear water and plenty of live food (water fleas, Cyclops and the like) and refuses dried food and food substitutes. They are kept

Black-banded Sunfish (*Enneacanthus chaetodon*)

in shoals at a temperature of 22–25 °C (71–77 °F) in medium-large, well-lit tanks. Three to six teaspoonfuls of salt are added to each 10 litres (2 gallons) of water. The fish spawn at a temperature of about 26 °C (79 °F), onto fine-leaved plants, and the fry hatch after 24 hours. When they begin to swim they take very fine live food (rotifers, nauplii of cyclops and brine shrimp). The fry do not actively hunt their prey, they only take the food that passes by their mouth.

The **Black-banded Sunfish** (*Enneacanthus chaetodon*) lives in stagnant waters and slow water courses in North America from New Jersey to Maryland. In its native waters it

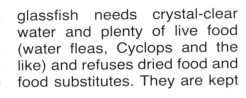

Indian Glassfish (*Chanda ranga*)

grows to a length of 10 cm (4 in) but in the aquarium it is no longer than 5 cm (2 in). There is a dark crescent-shaped spot on each gill cover of the female. The Black-banded Sunfish is very hardy and can survive drops in water temperature down to freezing point in winter. It only eats live plankton. Spawning takes place at a water temperature of about 22 °C (71 °F). The male first digs a hollow in sand and the female lays her eggs there. The male takes care of the eggs and the fry: he cleans the eggs of any organic residue and will not take food for the first five days after the hatching of the fry.

Schomburgk's Leaf Fish (*Polycentrus schomburgki*), which grows to a length of 7–10 cm (2.75–4 in), is native to the northern areas of South America and the island of Trinidad. The females are brownish, the males are velvety-black with blue or green spots and flecks. They are kept either in a separ-

76

Schomburgk's Leaf Fish (*Polycentrus schomburgki*)

Female and male Badis

ate tank or in a community with other fish of the same size to which Schomburgk's Leaf Fish, which is not very tolerant, can do no harm. They hide among plants during the daytime and leave their shelter in the evening. They take coarse food and like to catch young guppies. At a temperature of 26 °C (79 °F), the fish spawn on the underside of the leaves of water plants. The male takes care of the offspring. The fry are fed with fine live food.

The **Badis** (*Badis badis*) is a fish up to 8 cm (3 in) long that is native to India where it inhabits stagnant waters, well warmed by the sun. It is kept in large, densely overgrown tanks, affording numerous hiding places among stones. The optimum temperature for this fish is between 26 and 28 °C (79–82 °F). The eggs are laid in hollows or in a pot prepared for this purpose by the breeder. The male takes over the care of the eggs and fry.

The **Scat** or **Argusfish** (*Scatophagus argus*) lives near the sea coast, in the estuaries of rivers that empty into the Indian and Pacific oceans along the coast of southern Asia, Indonesia and Australia. Under natural conditions it grows to 30 cm (12 in) long but in aquariums its usual length is 10 cm (4 in). The Scat needs plenty of food of plant and animal origin. It is kept in a large tank without plants and with gravel on the bottom. A powerful filter must be available to remove the large amount of excrement these fish produce. The aquarium requires regular maintenance. The adult fish do well in water to which a small amount of salt has been added. No conclusive data on the reproduction of the Scat in captivity are as yet available.

The **Archerfish** (*Toxotes jaculatrix*), native to the fresh and and brackish (mixed fresh and salt) waters of southern and southeast Asia, the Philippines, Australia and Indonesia, grows

to a length of 15 cm (6 in). It is one of the warmth-loving fish, and should be kept at a temperature of 26–28 °C (79–82 °F) in large tanks overgrown with aquatic vegetation. Three to four teaspoonfuls of salt should be added for each 10 litres (2 gallons) of water. The fish possesses the remarkable ability to shoot down with a jet of water any insect that sits on plants above the water surface. It then feeds on its prey. In the aquarium it will take small crickets, flies and other insects that it picks from the surface. No information is available on its reproduction in captivity.

Badis (*Badis badis*)

The Egg-laying Tooth Carps (Cyprinodontidae)

The family of Egg-laying Tooth Carps (Cyprinodontidae) embraces 450 species of small brightly coloured fish living in all tropical regions of the world with the exception of Australia. Many of them are popular among aquarists. They inhabit pools and small lakes that may dry up either partly or completely in the dry season. The species has had to adapt to these adverse conditions to survive. The fish living in waters that dry out completely are short-lived and will die before the pool dries. Their eggs, which have a very thick, hard envelope, can survive on the bottom. The development of

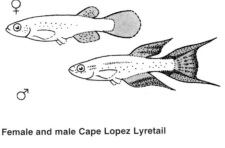

Female and male Cape Lopez Lyretail

Cape Lopez Lyretail (*Aphyosemion australe*)

Spawning of the Egg-laying Tooth Carps

the embryo in the egg stops completely during the dry season and is resumed when the pool is filled with water again in the rainy season. A number of other factors also influence the development of the eggs, such as the amount of oxygen and the concentration of carbonates in the water. Depending on their origin in waters that dry out completely or partially, some species of Egg-laying Tooth Carp bury their eggs in the bottom while others stick them onto the leaves of plants.

In captivity, pairs or groups of Egg-laying Tooth Carps are kept in small or very small tanks.

To rear the fry successfully, the breeder must respect the requirements of the different species and provide conditions in which the eggs may develop. The common practice is to suck the eggs from the spawning tank and put them into peat with a neutral pH. The peat is then moistened and placed in plastic bags. Water is poured onto the peat after some time to allow the interrupted development to continue. The time of interruption varies with the species of the fish. The fry are fed with small particles of food. Few species of Egg-laying Tooth Carps live longer than a few months.

The **Cape Lopez Lyretail** (*Aphyosemion australe*) lives in the muddy shore-side waters of the River Congo basin as far up as Gabon. Unlike the brightly

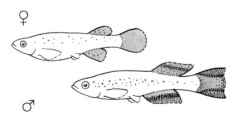

Female and male Steel-blue Aphyosemion

coloured male, the female is light brown and has no extended fins. The Cape Lopez Lyretail, 5.5 cm (2.2 in) long, is a peaceable fish that has to be kept in a small tank with very soft and slightly salted water. There should be fine-leaved and floating plants in the tank. The fish can be reared successfully in small shaded tanks where the brood fish spawn on to fine-leaved plants at a temperature of about 24 °C (75 °F) for a fairly long period. The eggs are sucked off with a glass tube and are placed in a shaded dish with a thin layer of water. The fry will hatch after ten days. They begin to swim immediately, catching fine live food.

The **Steel-blue Aphyosemion** (*Aphyosemion gardneri*), living in Nigeria and western Cameroon, grows to a length of 6 cm (2.3 in). It requires the same conditions of rearing as the preceding species, but the fish lay their spawn in peat on the bottom of the tank. After spawning, the parent fish are removed and the water depth above the peat is reduced to about 2 cm

Christy's Lyretail (*Aphyosemion christyi*)

(0.75 in) and left to evaporate; the peat must remain wet, however, so the tank must then be covered with glass. The tank must be thoroughly shaded, as the eggs are sensitive to light. Soft water is poured on to the peat after six weeks and the fry will hatch within several hours.

The **Christy's Lyretail** (*Aphyosemion christyi*) is a 5 cm (2 in) long fish native to the middle course of the Congo. The best time for spawning is from the early spring to the end of June. The female lays a large number of quite small eggs on plants; the eggs then develop in water. The fry will hatch after about 14 days and must be graded by size some time later to prevent the stronger species from attacking the weaker ones.

The **Golden Pheasant** (*Aphyosemion sjoestedti*) lives in drying pools in southern Nigeria and western Cameroon. It is a comparatively large fish, up to 12 cm (4.75 in) long. Pairs of this species have to be kept in isolation in large tanks with dense tangles of plants. They are given coarse live food, including small fish (young guppies). The Golden Pheasant spawns in fine sand at a temperature of about 22 °C (71 °F). As soon as the eggs are laid they must be sucked off and placed in a shallow dish, covered with a lid and kept in a dark place (for example, a drawer or box) at room temperature for six to eight weeks. The eggs must be regularly checked and those affected by mould must be eliminated. The fry hatch after three to nine weeks and three days later they begin to swim and take food. They grow fast and reach sexual maturity within two to

Steel-blue Aphyosemion (*Aphyosemion gardneri*)

three months. During rearing the stronger specimens must be selected and put into another tank to prevent them from attacking their weaker siblings.

Aphyosemion geryi lives in the tropical forest waters of the lowland parts of Guinea and Sierra Leone. The male grows to 4.5 cm (1.75 in) long, is larger

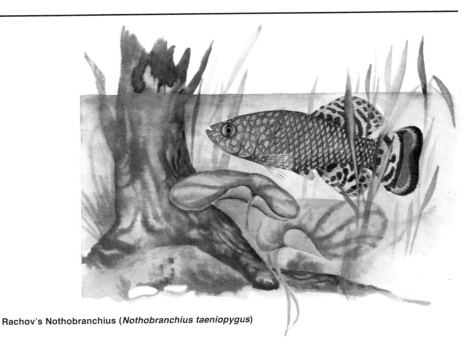

Rachov's Nothobranchius (*Nothobranchius taeniopygus*)

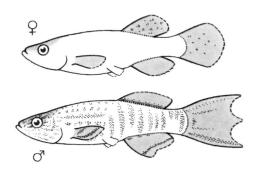

Female and male Golden Pheasant

than the female, and has a red throat. The eggs develop rapidly in 10–12 days at a temperature of 25–27°C (77–80°F). The eggs are very small, so they may easily escape the breeder's notice. The fry begin to swim about 24 hours after hatching and are able to take small live food immediately.

Rachov's Nothobranchius (*Nothobranchius taeniopygus*) is distributed in eastern Africa from Uganda to Mozambique. Its length is 5 cm (2 in). The male

is somewhat larger than the female. The fertilised eggs develop in five to six weeks. (Water must be poured on to the peat to keep it moist.) Rachov's Nothobranchius is a short-lived fish. It is kept in warm water at about 20°C (68°F) in a medium-sized tank. The fish are able to reproduce as early as their third to fourth week. The males are aggressive, so pairs should be kept separately. They are fed live food (plankton, crustaceans and the like).

The **Striped Aplocheilus** (*Aplocheilus lineatus*) comes from western India and Sri Lanka and grows up to 12 cm (4.75 in) long. The female has characteristic vertical stripes

Male and female Rachov's Nothobranchius

which are less conspicuous in the male, and her anal fin is round, whereas that of the male is pointed. This predatory fish is kept in large tanks with medium-hard water and floating plants. It is quite easy to breed this species. The brood pair spawn onto fine-leaved plants and the fry emerge from the eggs 14–17 days later. The adults must be removed from the tank after

Golden Pheasant (*Aphiosemion sjoestedti*)

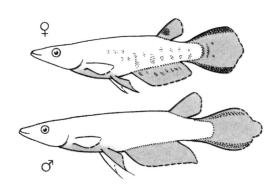

Female and male Blue Panchax

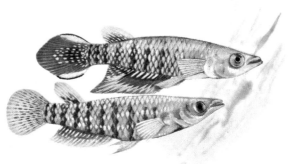

Female and male *Epiplatys dageti*

Striped Aplocheilus (*Aplocheilus lineatus*)

spawning. Given fine live food, the fry reach sexual maturity at six months.

The **Blue Panchax** (*Aplocheilus panchax*) up to 8 cm (3 in) long is native to India, Sri Lanka and the Indonesian region. In the aquarium it is unsociable and rapacious, and individual pairs must be kept in isolation in

Epiplatys dageti

Blue Panchax (*Aplocheilus panchax*)

small or medium-sized tanks. The parent fish eject their eggs and sperm onto water plants and the fry hatch after about 14 days. At first the young are given fine animal food, later they are able to consume larger food particles.

Epiplatys dageti, which lives in the swamps of southwestern Ghana and the Ivory Coast, is a peaceable fish, 5 cm (2 in) long, that stays near the water surface. The tank must be of medium size with medium-hard water and floating plants. The fish feeds on live food. The females lay their eggs among the rootlets of floating plants. Spawning sometimes extends over several weeks. The plants with eggs on them must be suc-cessively transferred to another tank. The fry of *Epiplatys dageti* are light-shy, so the tank should be protected against intensive light. At 25 °C (77 °F) the fry emerge from the eggs after ten days. They feed on live food and grow fast: the sex of the fish can be distinguished after eight weeks. At nine months they are able to reproduce.

The Live-bearing Tooth Carps (Poeciliidae)

The **Live-bearing Tooth Carps** (fish of the family Poeciliidae) are native to the fresh waters of the northern parts of South America, Central America, Mexico, the south of the USA, and the Caribbean islands. They are noted for a marked sexual dimorphism: the anal fin of the male has been transformed into a mating organ, called a gonopodium, with which he fertilises the eggs inside the female's body. The fertilized eggs continue to grow in the mother's body and when the fry are born they are fully developed and able to live independently. Some species of this family bear only a few young per spawning, others up to several hundred. One fertilization will usually suffice for several successive litters.

The Live-bearing Tooth Carps are easy to keep in aquariums because they have fairly

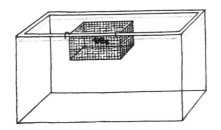

Birth cell for the viviparous female fish hanging inside the tank

broad requirements for water quality. They are omnivorous and can be fed with both live and dry food as well as artificial substitute diets, which should contain ingredients of plant origin. The females of many species consume their own fry, so there must be a spawning grate in the tank or else the females must be removed before the eggs are laid and placed in a special plastic container known as the birth cell. This has two small holes in the bottom through which the female cannot pass, while the young can easily escape from their mother's reach to the water in the free part of the tank in which the cell is suspended. The fact that the female is about to bear her young is usually indicated by a dark spot on each side of her belly in front of the pelvic fin ('pregnancy spots').

The fry of the Live-bearing Tooth Carp are comparatively large. They greedily eat both dry feed and substitutes, and grow fast. Most of the species have very variable colouring; a crossing of various colour mutations

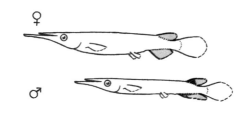

Female and male Wrestling Halfbeak

may lead to very interesting results. Of course, in such a breeding programme the fish must first be divided by sex and the males and females must be kept apart. The specially selected pairs are then placed in special tanks.

The **Platy** (*Xiphophorus macu-*

Platy (*Xiphophorus maculatus*)

Copulation in viviparous fishes

Swordtail (*Xiphophorus helleri*)

latus) comes from Guatemala and Mexico. It is highly variable in colouring and genetically unstable. The female, up to 6 cm (2.3 in) long, is larger than the male. The platys are kept in medium-sized tanks at a temperature of 22–24 °C (71–75 °F). The fish consume a large quantity of food but digest it poorly, so the water in the tank

larger than the male, grows to a length of 12 cm (4.75 in). The lower part of the male's caudal fin is elongated to form a typical 'sword'. Aquarists have bred a number of colour and shape mutations of this fish, such as the golden form, or the 'lyretail' form in which both lobes of the caudal fin are equally extended. The **Variegated Platy** (*Xiphophorus variatus*) is a native of Mexico. Its length is about 7 cm (2.75 in). The female is larger than the male. The Variegated

Platy should be kept is about 20 °C (68 °F) and the water should be medium hard. Rearing with a thorough selection and systematic breeding programme may lead to progeny of interesting colour combinations and fin shapes.

The **Guppy** (*Poecilia reticulata*) is among the most common and undemanding of aquarium fish. The Guppy comes from the northern parts of South America. It is noted for a high variability of form and colour, allowing a great range of mutations to be produced. Aquarists who specialize in breeding this fish exhibit the products of their breeding work and compete with one another at various national and international guppy shows where the fish are assessed according to strict rules. The females are 5–6 cm long (2–2.3 in). The males are shorter and their veil-like tails and dorsal fins hold all colours of the rainbow. Females of a similar appearance to the males have been artificially bred recently. The female can

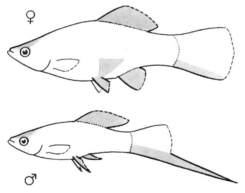

Female and male Swordtail

Variegated Platy (*Xiphophorus variatus*)

must be thoroughly filtered and frequently replaced. There are usually 40–120 young in one litter – in exceptional cases up to 150. As soon as the young leave their mother's body, they break the egg envelope and start swimming.

The **Swordtail** (*Xiphophorus helleri*) lives in Guatemala and southern Mexico. The female,

Platy will cross readily with all aquarium forms of the swordtails and the crossbred fish are often very interesting and highly valued. The optimum temperature at which the Variegated

be distinguished easily from the male by the black pregnancy spot in front of her anal fin. Birth lasts for about two hours. One larger female may bear 200 young or even more. Both young and adult guppies will take artificial and dried food.

The **Black-bellied** or **Blue Limia** (*Poecilia melanogaster*), from Jamaica and Haiti, requires a tank with water at about 22 °C (71 °F), but can withstand higher temperatures without damage. It likes sunshine, so the tank should be located in a sunny place. About 50–80 young are born in one breeding season. Besides live food, they will eat dried and artificial food.

The **Sailfin Molly** (*Poecilia velifera*) belongs to the larger robust live-bearing tooth-carps. In its native waters in Yucatan it grows to about 15 cm (6 in) long, though in the aquarium it is shorter, at 10–12 cm (4–4.75 in). The male has a conspicuously large dorsal fin. As with the Veil-tail Guppy, there are a large number of colour mutations and varieties of this species. The Sailfin Mollies need varied food of both plant and animal origin.

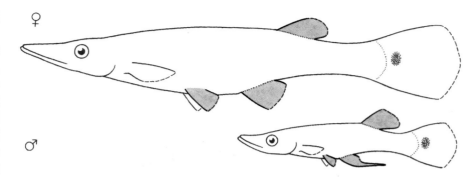

Female and male Pike Top Minnow

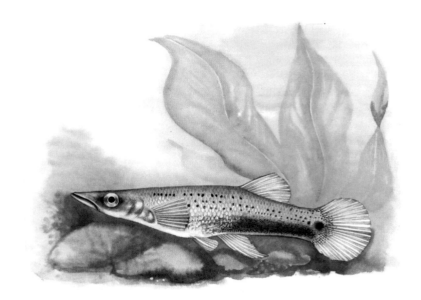

Pike Top Minnow (*Belonesox belizanus*)

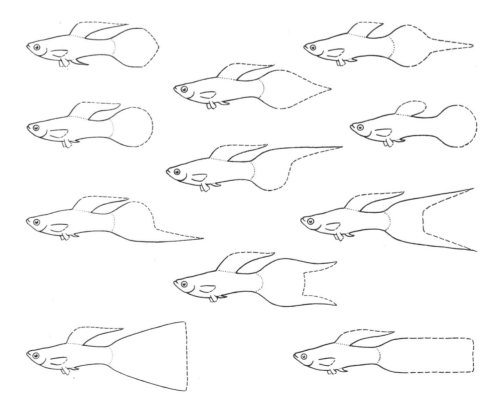

The caudal fin shapes in the male guppy

Green algae are important for the development of the male's enlarged dorsal fin. The tank must be large, well covered with glass, and with thick plant growth. The water in the tank should be about 24 °C (75 °F) or just over.

The **Pike Top Minnow** (*Belonesox belizanus*) is the largest fish of the Poeciliidae. The female is up to 20 cm (8 in) long; the males are much shorter. Fish of this species inhabit the eastern part of Central America. In captivity they need large tanks with dense aquatic vegetation where they will mostly hide near the water surface. The water temperature should be kept at 25–30 °C (77–86 °F). This species is a predator and is unsuitable for mixed aquariums.

Male and female Guppy (*Poecilia reticulata*)

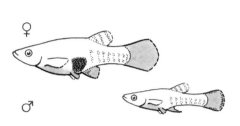

Female and male Black-bellied or Blue Limia

often hunts them relentlessly. The fry feed straightaway on water-fleas and other such food. The **Wrestling Halfbeak** (*Dermogenys pussilus*) of the halfbeak family (Hemirhamphidae) has some traits similar to those of the Pike Top Minnow. It is a live-bearing species and its

Sailfin Molly (*Poecilia velifera*)

It requires varied food: small fish, tadpoles, larvae of insects and worms. Like a pike, it catches its prey by attacking it suddenly from a hiding place. The Pike Top Minnow has an extremely flexible upper jaw, enabling it to swallow very large chunks of food. The males and females are kept apart and can be left together only when the female has been given enough food. Before mating, the male usually takes up a threatening posture in which his body is bent

and the gonopodium stretched forwards. The act of the mating itself is very quick. Five to six weeks after mating the female bears up to 100 comparatively large young (2.5–3cm/1–1.2in). It is advisable to use a birth cell to protect the newborn young, because the female

upper jaw, as with the preceding species, is extremely flexible. The halfbeak comes from Thailand, the Malay Peninsula and the large islands of the East Indies. Its length is about 7cm (2.75in). It feeds on insects that have fallen on to the water surface, by catching them in their short upper jaw. Its native waters are both fresh and brackish, so it is advisable to add some salt to the water in the tank (two teaspoonfuls of cooking salt per 10 litres/2 gallons water). The fish will take dryland insects (*Drosophila,* young crickets and the like). About eight weeks after mating the female bears eighteen to twenty young.

Black-bellied or Blue Limia (*Poecilia melanogaster*)

Keeping Cichlids (Cichlidae)

The family Cichlidae are freshwater fish, native to South and Central America and Africa, and there are also three Asiatic species. All have roughly the same body form, but they differ in size, colouring and behaviour. They

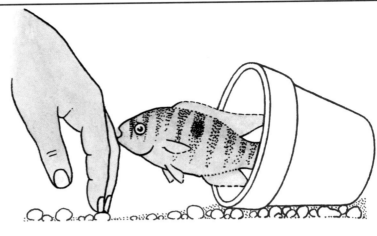

Some fishes will even defend their eggs against a man's hand.

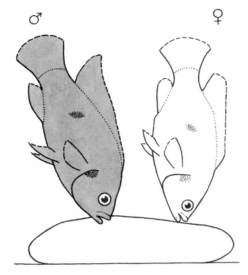

♂   ♀

also differ in their requirements for breeding and rearing. The males are usually larger and more colourful than the females. Many of them defend their territory, both in their native waters and in a tank. Some cichlid species feed on plant food, others on plankton, others again are predators. Many species are notable for their particular care of their eggs and young, which they defend bravely against any enemy. They are mostly kept in large tanks without plants be-cause they like to dig into the bottom as they seek food or prepare for spawning. If, in spite of this, the aquarist still wants to put plants in the tank, it is better to plant them in pots and place the pots among larger stones. Although most of the cichlids inhabit stagnant and slow-moving waters, the water in the tank must be well filtered to remove the large amount of sludge that the fish stir up. There should be coarse sand and both smaller and larger pebbles on the bot-

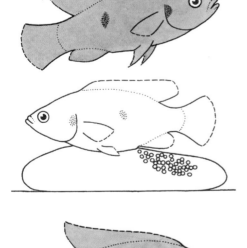

Spawning in some Cichlids, laying their eggs on stones.

Fire-mouth Cichlid (*Cichlasoma meeki*)

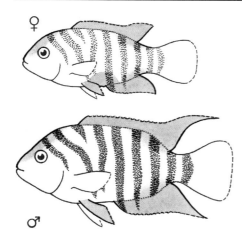

Female and male Zebra or Convict Cichlid

tom, as well as large stones and decorative logs and roots in order to provide shelter and caves for the fish. A pot, a piece of tile, a flat stone or a piece of coconut shell may be put on the bottom of the tank for the spawning of the different species.

Most of the cichlids are aggressive, so individual pairs must be kept in isolation. They often defend their territory with great tenacity against fish of the same or other species and it may easily happen that a strong male will kill an intruder. However, the cichlid family is large and also comprises some peaceable species that can be kept in mixed aquariums together with other fish.

The **Fire-mouth Cichlid** (*Cichlasoma meeki*), from the waters of Guatemala and the Yucatan Peninsula, grows to a length of 15 cm (6 in). The male is larger than the female and has long, tapering fins. It is kept in larger tanks at a temperature of 22 °C (71 °F). As the fish are comparatively quiet outside the breeding season, they can be kept together with certain other aquarium fish. They feed on larger animal food and pieces of fish flesh, such as fillet. They spawn at a temperature of about 26 °C (79 °F). With her belly turned up,

the female lays her eggs on solid surfaces inside caves or pots put on the bottom of the tank. The fry hatch 48–60 hours later. Both parents protect the eggs and fry; they fan them by waving their fins and remove any white, infertile eggs that have been infected by a fungus. When the young emerge, the parents dig a small hollow in the sand and put their offspring there. They crush large chunks of food in their mouths and spit them in among the young.

The **Zebra Cichlid** or **Convict Cichlid** (*Cichlasoma nigrofasciatum*) grows 8–10 cm (3–4 in) long. It comes from the lakes of Atitlán and Amatitlán in Guatemala. It is very active in the aquarium, constantly stirring up and digging about in the bottom. Outside the breeding season it is not particularly aggressive and can be kept in the tank together with larger fish. It prefers recesses in stones or flowerpots for spawning, and both parents take care of their eggs and fry, defending them with great courage against any intruder, including the hand of

the aquarist. Besides coarser chunks of animal food, they also eat food of plant origin, such as scalded lettuce or soaked oat flakes. A red (xanthoric) form of the Zebra Cichlid has been bred artificially. It has a milky-white colouring and red eyes. The female has a reddish belly.

The **Festive** or **Flag Cichlid** (*Cichlasoma festivum*), a fish up to 15 cm (6 in) long, is native to western Guyana and the Amazon basin. It is peaceable and quiet except in the spawning season when, during a short period, it is able to wreak havoc in the tank so that usually very little is left of the plant growth. The female does not hesitate to move quite large stones or logs if they lie in the way of her chosen spawning bed. The Festive Cichlid is kept in large tanks at a temperature of 24 °C (75 °F). The parent fish spawn on leaves of plants or on large stones at a temperature of 26 °C (79 °F). Both parents take care of their offspring. The fry feed on fine live food such as rotifers.

The **Blue Acara** (*Aequidens pulcher*) is a comparatively

Zebra or Convict Cichlid (*Cichlasoma nigrofasciatum*)

large fish, up to 20 cm (8 in) long, sometimes longer, from Colombia and Panama. Unlike the female, the male has tapering dorsal and anal fins. Fish of this species do not destroy the plants or the bottom. They require well-filtered, clean water, which must be replaced frequently because they do not do

Barred Cichlid (*Cichlasoma festivum*)

well in stale water. They spawn several times a year at a temperature of about 26°C (79°F). The female lays her eggs on a cleaned, flat stone and fans them with her fins. The fry hatch after 60–70 hours and feed on fine live food. The parents take

Keyhole Cichlid (*Aequidens maronii*)

care of their young for a very long time.

The **Keyhole Cichlid** (*Aequidens maronii*) is a native of the waters of Guyana and grows to be about 10 cm (4 in) long. The male is larger than the female. It is a quiet fish that can be kept in densely overgrown aquariums in the company of other fish. It is not very fussy about food and does not destroy the plants, or dig into the bottom. It spawns at a temperature of 26°C (79°F) on stones, logs and roots and the parents take intensive care of their young for a long time. The fry feed on rotifers and other fine animal food.

The **Flag Cichlid** (*Aequidens curviceps*) is a small cichlid,

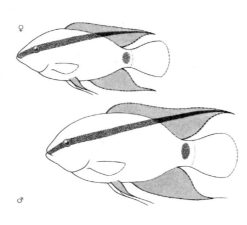

Female and male Barred Cichlid

8 cm (3 in) long at the most, from the Amazon river system. It is quiet and peaceable, suitable for mixed aquariums, and does not destroy the bottom or the plants. It is kept at about 23°C (73°F) and spawns at 26°C (79°F) on flat stones. While the female lays her eggs the male guards the spawning bed against intruders and then he fertilizes the eggs while the female is on guard. The offspring are guarded by both parents.

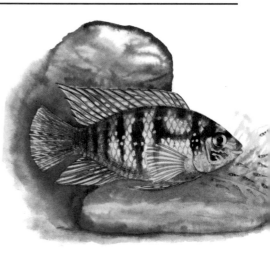

Blue Acara (*Aequidens pulcher*)

When the fry begin to swim, they will feed on small animal food.

The **Oscar's Cichlid** or **Velvet Cichlid** (*Astronotus ocellatus*) is up to 35 cm (13.5 in) long and is native to the Amazon, Paraná, Rio Negro and Rio Paraguay. The young fish are chocolate-brown with dark-rimmed, light spots and patterns; older specimens are grey-brown. The males often have three round flecks on their dorsal fin. These big cichlids are kept in large tanks with stony bottoms free of plants or with plants anchored in pots. Velvet Cichlids are very quarrelsome and rapacious and consume large quantities of food (various larvae, worms, slugs, live fish, pieces of beef, crickets and the like). They spawn at a water temperature of 26°C (79°F) and lay their eggs on stones. During the first few days the young hang from the sides of their parents' bodies.

The **Devil Fish** (*Geophages jurupari*), from the basin of the Amazon and rivers in Guyana, grows to a length of 15 cm (6 in). It is kept at temperatures above 22°C (71°F) in large tanks in which plants grow. Although the fish dig into the bottom they do not damage the plants. They feed on small animal foodstuff:

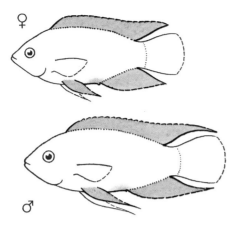

Female and male Flag Cichlid

instinct for caring for her young. She keeps a characteristic reticulated pattern on her back and

Oscar's or Velvet Cichlid (*Astronotus ocellatus*) – an adult and a young fish

fish up to 12 cm (4.75 in) long, from the middle course of the Amazon and its tributaries. It

plankton crustaceans, tubificids and the larvae of chironomids. The fish spawn on stones. Two to three days later the parents take eggs into their mouths and keep them there until the fry hatch, i.e. about ten days. The best food are rotifers and small plankton crustaceans.

The **Golden-eyed Dwarf Cichlid** (*Nannacara anomala*), from the waters of western Guyana, Venezuela, Colombia and Bolivia, is a small fish growing to a length of only about 7 cm (2.75 in). It is kept in tanks of medium size, densely overgrown with plants and filled with soft water. The female has a remarkable

flanks during the spawning season and then for as long as she is protecting her young; she never leaves her eggs or fry and guards them against any intruder and often also against the male whom she may even kill. It is therefore advisable to remove the male from the tank immediately after spawning.

The **Scalare** or **Angelfish** (*Pterophyllum scalare*) is a popular

has a very tall body and flattened flanks. The sexes are hard to distinguish outside the breeding season, except that the male has a more prominent cushion of fat above the eyes. Scalares are kept in small shoals in large, deep tanks at a water temperature of 22–24 °C (71–75 °F). Scalares are shy, seeking shelter among plants. The presence of other, more

Devil Fish (*Geophagus jurupari*)

Flag Cichlid (*Aequidens curviceps*)

active fish in the tank disturbs them. At a temperature of about 26 °C (79 °F) they lay up to one thousand eggs on the cleaned, broad leaves of plants. The breeder should transfer the eggs with the plants into a separ-

89

ate tank with intensive aeration, because the adult fish do not take particular care of the offspring. The fry emerge after 36–60 hours and need several days to begin swimming; they take fine animal food such as rotifers and nauplii of chironomids and the brine shrimp.

The **Discus** (*Symphysodon discus*) comes from the middle

course of the Amazon and Rio Negro and Rio Xingu. Like its relatives, the **Green Discus** (*S. aequifasciatus*), **Blue Discus** (*S. aequifasciatus haraldi*) and **Brown Discus** (*S. aequifasciatus axelrodi*), it belongs to an interesting group of aquarium fish which are also very difficult

Female and male Scalare or Angelfish

to keep. All grow to a length of 15–20cm (6–8in) and require a large, shaded tank with thick

plant growth, filled with soft, slightly acid water that has to be replaced frequently. The food should be as varied as possible. The fish of the Discus group are peaceable and comparatively sociable; they are disturbed only by extremely nimble companions in the tank. They spawn at a temperature of about 28 °C (82 °F) in large tanks with a dense growth of plants and with very soft water at a pH of 6.2–6.5. When the fry begin to swim, they feed on a secretion from their parents and when they are shaken off by a quick movement they will attach themselves again to the body of either parent. To keep these fish and rear their young is a test of the breeder's skill, as they are very particular about the composition and temperature of the water and the nature of their food.

Agassiz's Dwarf Cichlid (*Apistogramma agassizi*) is a cichlid of about 7cm (2.75in) long from the Amazon river system. The

Golden-eyed Dwarf Cichlid (*Nannacara annomala*)

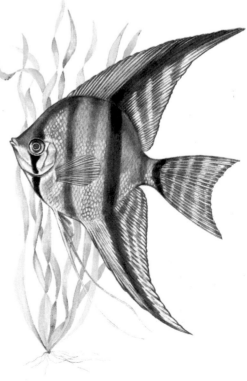

Scalare or Angelfish (*Pterophyllum scalare*)

90

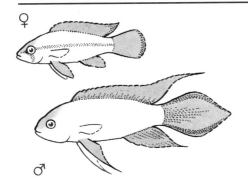

Female and male Agassiz's Dwarf Cichlid

perature of 26°C (79°F) onto solid surfaces, preferably in hollows and caves. The fry hatch three days after spawning and the female carries them off into hollows in sand where she guards them. Fourteen days

Ramirez's Dwarf Cichlid (*Apistogramma ramirezi*)

male has a brighter colouring than the female and his dorsal and anal fins taper off. This small cichlid does well in densely overgrown tanks of medium size, with shelters for the fish.

Agassiz's Dwarf Cichlid (*Apistogramma agassizi*)

Borelli's Dwarf Cichlid (*Apistogramma borellii*)

The water should be soft, slightly acid, thoroughly aerated and frequently replaced. Agassiz's Dwarf Cichlid spawns at a tem-

after they begin to swim freely, the cichlid fry are able to live independently.

Ramirez's Dwarf Cichlid (*Apistogramma ramirezi*) and **Borelli's Dwarf Cichlid** (*A. borellii*), relatives of Agassiz's Dwarf Cichlid, have similar requirements for breeding and rearing. The fry of all these small cichlids require fine live food, such as rotifers or the early, developmental stages of the brine shrimp.

Astatatilapia burtoni is a splendid cichlid from the tropics of eastern and central Africa. It grows to a length of about 10 cm (4 in). The male is larger than the female and has brighter colouring. Fish of this species need a large tank and must be kept separately because they attack smaller species – sometimes fatal to the weaker specimens. Plant growth in the tank should afford many hiding places for weaker fish that have not yet reached sexual maturity. *A. bur-*

toni is kept at a temperature of about 24°C (75°F) but its spawning takes place at higher temperatures – about 28°C (82°F). During the act of spawning, the male lies down on his side on a stone cleaned in advance, spreads his anal fin to show a striking pattern (spots with the form and colour of eggs) and ejects his milt. The female tries to pick the egg-like spots from the male's anal fin

Back to front: Discus (*Symphysodon discus*), Green Discus (*Symphysodon aequifasciatus*), Blue Discus (*Symphysodon aequifasciatus haraldi*)

Female and male Ramirez's Dwarf Cichlid

and in doing this she sucks the milt into her mouth. She then lays her eggs on the stone and afterwards picks them up in her mouth where they mix with the sperm. The fertilized eggs will develop in the sac in her throat.

Thomas's Dwarf Cichlid (*Pelmatochromis thomasi*)

Astatatilapia burtoni

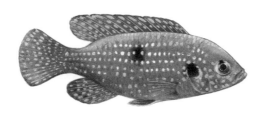

Jewelfish or Red Cichlid (*Hemichromis bimaculatus*)

Red Dwarf Cichlid or Kribensis (*Pelvicachromis pulcher*)

The fry hatch after 16 to 20 days and soon begin to swim, although they will seek refuge in their mother's mouth for another week, if danger threatens.

The **Jewelfish** or **Red Cichlid** (*Hemichromis bimaculatus*), another African cichlid from the basins of the Niger, Nile and Congo, is up to 12 cm (4.75 in) long. The red colouring is more striking in the female than in the male. These predatory cichlids

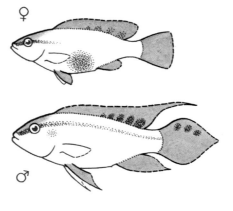

Female and male *Pelvicachromis pulcher*

need a large tank and it is advisable to separate the older specimens from young. They often dig into the bottom, so it is better to leave the tank without plants. The Jewelfish is kept at a temperature of about 20 °C (68 °F) and spawns at about 26 °C (79 °F). The parents take great care of their eggs and fry and the young fish are very sturdy and voracious.

Thomas's Dwarf Cichlid (*Pel-*

Melanochromis auratus

long, leave their mother after 22–26 days. The number of young is small, usually no more than 40 from one spawning.

The **Cobalt-blue Cichlid** (*Pseudotropheus zebra*), about 14 cm (5.5 in) long, is also native to Lake Malawi. It is a quarrelsome cichlid: sometimes even the male and female, kept in a separate pair, will attack each

Cobalt-blue Cichlid (*Pseudotropheus zebra*)

matochromis thomasi) lives in the Kenema region of Sierra Leone. It grows to a length of 10 cm (4 in). Fish of this species are undemanding and peaceable and are kept in medium-hard water at a temperature of 23–25 °C (73–77 °F). They spawn on stones at 28 °C (82 °F) and treat their young with great care. The fry feed on fine food of animal origin (rotifers, nauplii).

The **Red Dwarf Cichlid** (*Pelvicachromis pulcher*) is native to the southern part of Nigeria. The male is 10 cm (4 in) long, the female 7 cm (2.75 in). They are kept in tanks of medium size at a temperature of about 24 °C (75 °F). There may be plants in the tank. At a temperature of 28 °C (82 °F) the female, lying belly-upwards, lays eggs inside a cave or a pot and the male then fertilises the eggs. Some keepers recommend the female to be removed from the tank after spawning in order to prevent her from disturbing the male in his care of the offspring. The fry are easy to rear; they take fine food (rotifers, nauplii and the like). The adult fish should be kept in separate pairs. **Melanochromis auratus** lives near the rocky coast of the Lake

Malawi. It grows to 6–7 cm (2.3–2.75 in) long and is one of the peaceable cichlids that do not hurt smaller fishes, although they do attack larger ones sometimes. Algae are important in their food but they do not damage the plants in the tank. The female keeps fertilized eggs in a sac in her throat and the young, about 1 cm (0.3 in)

other. The tank should be large, affording numerous shelters among large stones. After spawning, the female keeps her young in her mouth; for this period she should be kept in isolation in a separate tank where there is no danger to the fry. This is an omnivorous species that will even take algae voraciously.

The Labyrinth Fish (Anabantidae)

The family Anabantidae, also known as the Labyrinth Fish, is distributed across the tropical regions of Asia and Africa, where these fish inhabit various shallow muddy waters, larger pools, paddies and similar places. Their environment — water that is poor in oxygen, varying depths, etc. — led to a special adaptation among the fish of this family: all labyrinth fishes have an auxiliary breathing organ that enables them to take in oxygen from the air. This

Siamese Fighting Fish (*Betta splendens*)

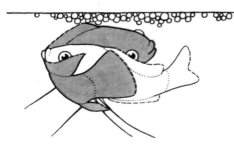

Spawning of Labyrinth Fishes

organ, called labyrinth, developed as an enlargement of the first gill arch and is lined with a mucous membrane copiously supplied with blood. The fish picks air bubbles from the water surface into its mouth and the labyrinth absorbs the oxygen from these bubbles.

Some species of Labyrinth Fish build bubble nests under the water surface, others under the leaves of plants. The surface membrane of the bubbles is hardened with a special secretion that the male produces in his mouth. The eggs of some species contain numerous oil droplets that keep them floating on the water surface. The male takes care of the eggs in the bubble nest. (The males of some species do not build a nest in this way or carry the eggs in their mouths.) The young enjoy parental care until they are able to swim freely. The female should be removed from the tank immediately after spawning to prevent her from disturbing the male in his duty. The fry of the Labyrinth Fish take the finest (powder) food, including rotifers, small developmental stages of cyclops and the brine shrimp. Their growth is

often very irregular, so they must be graded by size and put into separate tanks.

Fish of the family Anabantidae are mostly peaceable and sociable and can be kept in mixed aquariums.

The **Siamese Fighting Fish** (*Betta splendens*) is one of the most popular Labyrinth Fish. It is native to Indo-China and Thailand and grows to a length of about 6 cm (2.3 in). The males, unlike the female, have lobe-like fins. The males often fight with one another and strong specimens may sometimes kill weaker ones; in some cases they may even attack weaker females. Siamese Fighting Fish do not need large tanks. Plants should float on the water and the water temperature should be above 25 °C (77 °F). The male builds a bubble nest at a temperature of 27–28 °C (80–82 °F) and lures the female underneath this nest by displaying his brilliant fins. Then the male firmly embraces the whole body of the female and at that moment both of them eject their reproductive secretions. The eggs are heavier than water and fall to the bottom where the male picks them up carefully

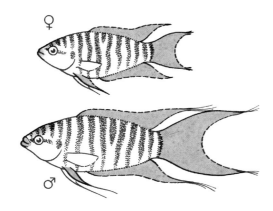

Female and male Paradise-fish

and spits them into the bubble nest. Sometimes the female helps him to do this. However, as soon as the spawning is over, the female must be removed from the tank, otherwise the male might kill her. The fry emerge 24–35 hours after fertilization and are protected by the male until they are able to swim independently. The young feed on fine food and are easy to rear.

The **Paradise-fish** (*Macropodus opercularis*) lives in the waters of Korea, China, Vietnam and Taiwan and grows to about 9 cm (3.5 in) long. The male is larger than the female and has tapering fins. Paradise-fish are kept in small or medium-sized tanks at a temperature of 15–20 °C (59–68 °F). They are quarrelsome and so are unsuitable for mixed aquariums. There should be free-floating plants in the tanks intended for spawning to make it easier for the male to build his nest, and a thicket of submerged plants where the female can hide from the aggressive male. Spawning takes place at a temperature of 20–24 °C (68–75 °F) and the female must be removed from the tank after the act. The male protects the nest and eggs with the utmost care. The fry of the Paradise-fish take rotifers and the nauplii of aquatic crustaceans.

The **Pearl** or **Mosaic Gourami**

(*Trichogaster leeri*) is a fish up to 11 cm (4.3 in) long from the Malay Peninsula, Thailand, Sumatra and Borneo. The male is more slender than the female and his dorsal fin tapers to a point. The Pearl Gourami is a very friendly, though rather shy fish suitable for a mixed aquarium. The adequate water temperature for this fish is about 23 °C (73 °F); the tank should be partly overgrown with aquatic vegetation and there should be free-floating plants on the water surface. Pairs of these fish spawn at a temperature of 26 °C (79 °F) underneath a bubble nest. The male takes care of the eggs and fry until they can swim independently.

The **Three-spot Gourami** (*Trichogaster trichopterus*), native to the same regions as the preceding species, grows to a length of 15 cm (6 in) and its colouring varies greatly in the aquarium. It has the same requirements as the pearl gourami and takes the same food, which must be live and varied.

The Three-spot Gourami is a very prolific breeder, producing 500–1,000 eggs, or even more at one spawning. The male protects the offspring until they begin to swim on their own. The development of the eggs from fertilization to hatching lasts three days at a temperature of 28 °C (82 °F). The auxiliary breathing organ develops in the fry at an age of three or four months, which is a critical time for them. During this period the temperature throughout the water must remain constant, including the layer near the surface. If the water is just slightly colder near the surface, the fish may become cold and die.

The **Thick-lipped Gourami** (*Colisa labiosa*) is a fish about 8 cm (3 in) long from southern Burma. The colouring of the male is brighter than that of the female. The Thick-lipped Gourami can be kept in a mixed aquarium together with other fish at a water temperature of 27–30 °C (80–86 °F). The eggs have a large oil content and so

Paradise-fish (*Macropodus opercularis*)

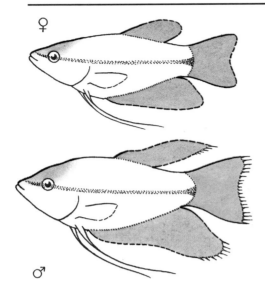

♀

♂

Female and male Pearl or Mosaic Gourami

at a temperature of 30 °C (86 °F) in a tall bubble nest into which parts of plants are interwoven. During the spawning the male produces short, sharp audible sounds and is also able to spit water a short distance above the water surface. It is not easy to feed the early fry because they refuse feeding stuffs other than very fine live food (rotifers). The **Honey Gourami** (*Colisa chuna*), native to northeastern India, is the smallest of the gouramis, growing no longer than 4–4.5 cm (1.5–1.75 in). Various colour forms are known to exist in their native waters and aquarists have developed another

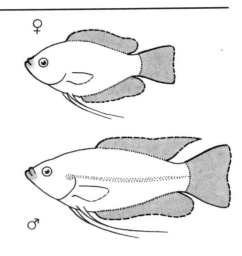

♀

♂

Female and male Thick-lipped Gourami

do not fall to the bottom. The male takes great care of the young in a bubble nest.

The **Dwarf Gourami** (*Colisa lalia*) is only about 25 cm (2 in) long and comes from India. The male's colouring is much brighter than that of the female. It is a peaceable and somewhat shy fish, suitable for mixed aquariums. It thrives in well-lit, not too deep tanks with plant growth. The parent fish spawn

variant, the golden form. The fish is easy to keep in the aquarium. The young are reared at a temperature of about 24 °C (75 °F). The fry take very fine

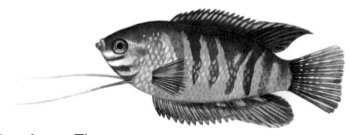

Thick-lipped Gourami (*Colisa labiosa*)

food such as certain infusorians (*Parametium*) or small rotifers. Like other fish of the genus *Colisa,* the Honey Gourami is susceptible to various diseases, the treatment of which is difficult and often unsuccessful.

The **Dwarf Croaking Gourami** (*Trichopsis pumilus*), from Vietnam, Thailand, the Malay Peninsula and Sumatra, is no longer

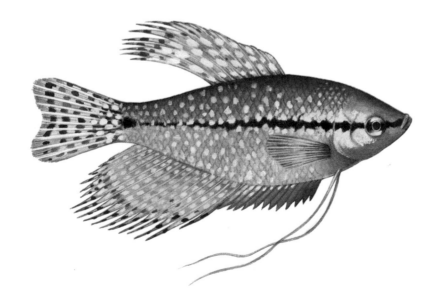

Pearl or Mosaic Gourami (*Trichogaster leeri*)

♀

♂

Female and male Dwarf Gourami

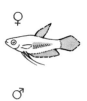

Female and male Dwarf Croaking Gourami

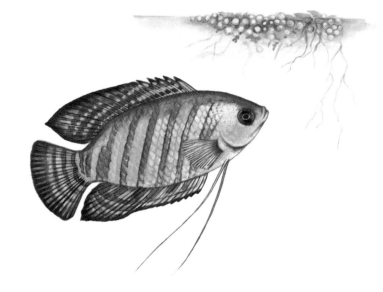

Dwarf Gourami (*Colisa lalia*)

Dwarf Croaking Gourami (*Trichopsis pumilus*)

than about 3.5cm (1.4in). It is kept in small tanks with both submerged and free-floating plants, in soft, slightly acid water. The Dwarf Croaking Gourami takes animal and artificial foodstuffs voraciously. The

Three-spot Gourami (*Trichogaster trichopterus*)

Honey Gourami (*Colisa chuna*), the male above

spawning nest, built by the male, is a foamy ball on the underside of the leaf of a water plant, in a pot laid on the bottom, or in other such places not too far above the bottom. At a temperature of 28°C (82°F) the fry will hatch in 36 hours. As soon as they begin to swim independently, they are able to

though most of them are difficult to keep. The majority inhabit the brackish waters (i.e. mixed fresh and sea water) in the estuaries of rivers. In the aquarium,

on which they jump and crawl in mud or climb up the roots of shore-side vegetation. In captivity the Mudskipper is kept in a shallow tank with stones and

Kissing Gourami (*Helostoma temmincki*)

Mudskipper (*Periophthalmus barbarus*)

consume comparatively large chunks of food, including the nauplii of the brine shrimp. During the courtship, the males emit croaking sounds, audible at a distance of several metres from the tank.

The **Kissing Gourami** (*Helostoma temmincki*), from the Malay Peninsula, Thailand and the Sunda Islands, grows to a length of 30 cm (12 in), but in the aquarium it is much shorter. It is kept in a large tank and fed with both animal and vegetable food (algae). The optimum temperature for spawning is 28–30°C (82–86°F). The male does not build a spawning nest, but leaves the eggs to float on the surface. The parent fish should be removed after spawning, otherwise they might consume their eggs. These fish have a habit of pressing their thick-lipped mouths together as if they were kissing. In fact, they do this to defend their territory.

Keeping other Fish

Certain other fish are also kept in warm-water aquariums, al-

slightly salted water must be provided for these fish.

The **Mudskipper** (*Periophthalmus barbarus*) lives near the sea coast in the neighbourhood of river estuaries of the Red Sea and eastern Africa through southeast Asia and the Sunda Islands to Australia. In its natural habitat it grows to a length of 15 cm (6 in). This fish has eyes on the top of its head and very long first rays to its dorsal fin and it can live outside water for a comparatively long time. They have strong pectoral fins

roots protruding above the water surface. The water should be slightly salted and the tank must be well covered with glass. Both water and air temperature should be between 26 and 30°C (77–86°F). These shy creatures catch live food and should be fed with insects (crickets, flies and others) and worms. They have not yet been bred successfully in captivity.

The **Spotted Spiny Eel** (*Mastacembelus pancalus*) is a 20 cm (8 in) long fish from India. It is kept in large tanks with dense

Spotted Spiny Eel (*Mastacembelus pancalus*)

plant growth and fine sand on the bottom in which the fish often buries itself. It leaves its shelter at dawn. The water in the tank must be slightly salted. The adult fish spawn near the water surface in fine-leaved plants. The fry begin to swim independently after three days and feed on the nauplii of the brine shrimp. Fish of this species can be kept in mixed aquariums with other fish.

The **Green Pufferfish** (*Tetraodon fluviatilis*) lives in sea water, fresh water and brackish water near the coast in Indonesia. It grows to a length of 17 cm (6.8 in). Swimming by waving its pectoral fins, it uses its caudal fin as a rudder. The intestine of this fish contains a number of sacs. If it is disturbed or if it feels threatened, the fish can fill itself with water or air and puff itself up to a much larger body size. Its sharp, strong teeth can crush even the thick shells of snails which form the main part of its diet. The fish produces croaking sounds that can be heard several metres from the tank. It is kept in a large tank with a clean sandy bottom and hiding places for the fish among stones. The water should be salted by adding one tablespoonful of sea or cooking salt to 10 litres (2 gallons) of water. The eggs are laid on stones and the male protects the eggs until the fry hatch. Then he carries them to a hollow in the sand where he takes care of them until they begin to swim independently.

The **African Snakehead** (*Ophiocephalus africanus*) is a predatory fish 30—35 cm (12—13.75 in) long, living in muddy pools and drying water courses where the water temperature may be as high as 40 °C (104 °F). This fish, like all snakeheads, has an auxiliary respiratory organ in its gill chamber through which it breathes oxy-

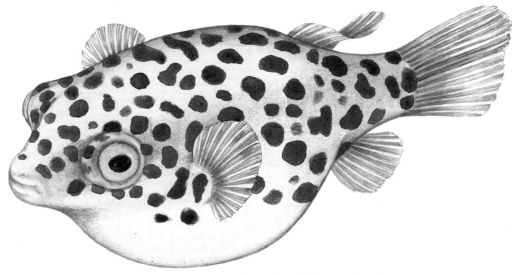

Green Pufferfish (*Tetraodon fluviatilis*)

gen from the air on the water surface. It is easily frightened and will often spring above the surface, so it is necessary to cover the tank with solid glass. The African Snakehead feeds on live fish. It spawns in nests of plants built just below the water surface. The eggs contain air droplets which allow them to float on the surface. The male takes care of the nest and eggs.

The **Elephant-nosed Fish** (*Gnathonemus petersi*), from the muddy waters of West Africa, is a fish that is active at night when it seeks food on the bottom. Like all species of the order

Mormyridormes, it has a weak electric organ which it uses for orientation in the muddy waters in the dark and in seeking food. It is kept at temperatures above 24 °C (75 °F) in large tanks with frequent partial replacement of water. All attempts to reproduce the fish in captivity so far have failed.

Many small European fish can be kept in aquariums, garden pools and small ponds. The conditions in which they are kept must be consistent with those of their natural habitat in the temperate climatic zone where most of the water cour-

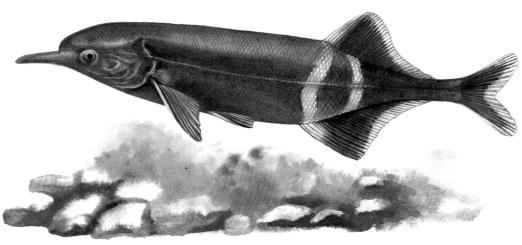

Elephant-nosed Fish (*Gnathonemus petersi*)

ses freeze in winter and even in summer often remain colder than 10–15°C (50–59°F). Before deciding what species to keep you must always consider what type of waters the fish come from and what requirements they have as to temperature, the amount of oxygen dissolved in the water and food.

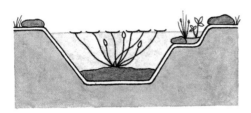

Diagram of a simple garden pool.

Fish from mountain and submontane torrents need large tanks with clear soft water and coarse sand and pebbles on the bottom. The tank should be put in a shaded place, preferably by a northern window. Fresh, cold water must be added often to replace stale water in the tank: it is advisable to provide a continuous water flow through the aquarium.

Fish that live in rivers, pools, lakes and ponds should be kept

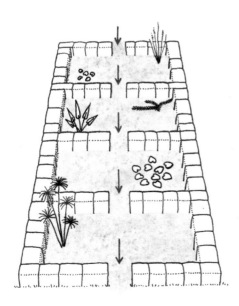

System of separate flow-through pools.

in tanks with somewhat harder, warmer water but, again, the water must be thoroughly filtered and frequently replaced. Plants for cold-water aquariums, garden pools and small ponds can be transplanted from rivers, pools and ponds, but bear in mind that many aquatic and marsh plant species are protected by law from collection in the wild.

Rather than in a tank, fish that are native to your own geographical region can be kept in a pool or a small pond in a garden, or in a small creek with a constant inflow of fresh water, for example in a rock garden. During winter the fish should be caught and put in indoor tanks with intensively filtered water, the temperature of which must be kept at or below 15°C (59°F). In such conditions the fish may be given live or artificial food of the same kind that is given to tropical fish. If the fish grow too large for an indoor tank, they can simply be released in suitable water outdoors and replaced by younger specimens.

The **Goldfish** (*Carassius auratus auratus*) is the most widely known and most strikingly coloured of the fish kept in ornamental ponds, pools and fountains. It has its home in the Far East where the Koi, or Gold Carp, was also bred. Goldfish can also be kept in large tanks with water at a pH slightly above 7. Goldfish spawn in fine plants.

The **Bitterling** (*Rhodeus sericeus amarus*), a fish about 8 cm (3 in) long, is usually found in stagnant or slow-flowing waters. It has an interesting reproductive system. During the breeding season the female develops a long egg-laying organ which she inserts between the valves of Swan Mussels (*Anodonta* and *Unio*) in order to lay her eggs where they will be pro-

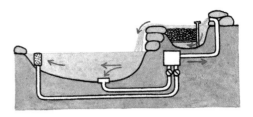

A more sophisticated garden pool with forced water circulation.

tected. Afterwards, the male ejects his milt just above the mussel, which sucks the sperm in through its respiratory opening, thus fertilising the Bitterling eggs. The eggs then develop safely until the young hatch and leave the mussel. The Bitterlings are kept in small shoals in large tanks with thick plant growth and with several mussels on the soft bottom. The optimum temperature for the fish is between 10 and 20°C (50–65°F).

The **Moderlieschen** (*Leucaspius delineatus*) lives in stagnant and slow-flowing waters over a clean bottom. It often forms large shoals. This fish grows to a length of 6–9 cm

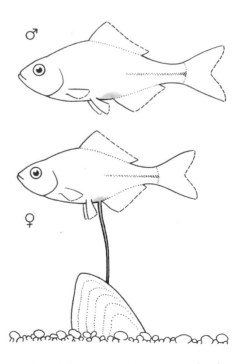

Female and male Bitterling and the way they lay their eggs.

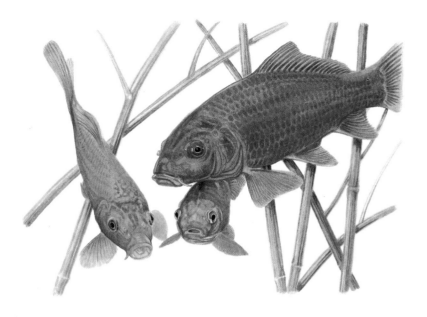

Goldfish (*Carassius auratus auratus*)

quires water with a high oxygen content. At spawning time the male takes on striking colouring. The **Stone Loach** (*Noemacheilus barbatulus*) is a fish 10—12 cm (4—4.75 in) long, living near the bottom of both stagnant and flowing waters. In an aquarium or reservoir it requires a sandy bottom with numerous roots and stones where it seeks shelter. It feeds on small invertebrates. The water in which the Stone Loach is kept must be of medium hardness, 6—18 °C (43—64 °F), with a high oxygen content.

The **Weather Fish** (*Misgurnus fossilis*), a larger relative of the Stone Loach, from the family of Spiny Loaches (Cobitidae), grows to a length of 25 cm (10 in). It inhabits slow-flowing and stagnant, muddy waters and often buries itself in the mud. In water with a low oxygen content it gulps in air from which

(2.3—3.5 in). In captivity it is kept in small reservoirs or large aquariums densely overgrown with plants, where it may breed successfully.

The **Minnow** (*Phoxinus phoxinus*) usually grows to about 8 cm (3 in) long (exceptionally up to 12 cm/4.75 in). It lives in the clean upper reaches of rivers and in stony- or sandy-bottomed streams. It can be kept in garden streamlets or small resorvoirs with a constant flow of water. The Minnow re-

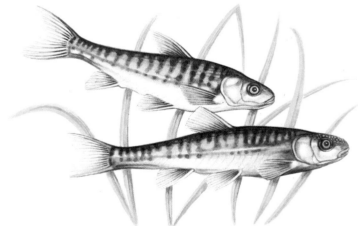

Minnow (*Phoxinus phoxinus*)

it extracts oxygen through an auxiliary breathing organ in its intestinal mucous membrane, which has a complex lung-like system of blood vessels. Young weather fish are kept in large aquariums where the temperature may rise as high as 25 °C (77 °F) in summer. They can

Bitterling (*Rhodeus sericeus amarus*)

also be kept in small ponds in a garden, but in such situations it is not easy to control the stock when the fish bury themselves in the mud.

be hard, stony or covered with coarse sand to which larger stones are added to provide shelters for the fish. In the tank the fish soon become tame and

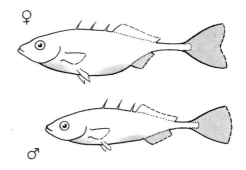

Female and male Three-spined Stickleback

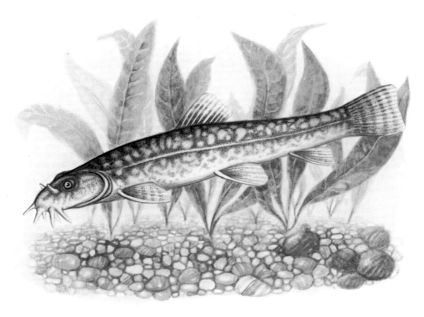

Stone Loach (*Noemacheilus barbatulus*)

The **Miller's Thumb** or **Bull-head** (*Cottus gobio*) is a typical small fish living in the clean and fast-moving waters of the upper reaches of rivers and brooks. Its length is about 10 cm (4 in). Miller's Thumb is easy to keep in an aquarium. The bottom must

may take food (tubificids, chironomid larvae and the like) from the keeper's hand. The female lays her eggs on the underside of a hollow stone. The male protects the eggs and chases other fish away. The Miller's Thumb requires clean, well-aerated

water, preferably in a flow-through tank. It feeds on live food but will also take artificial foodstuffs.

The **Three-spined Stickleback** (*Gasterosteus aculeatus*), a fish growing to a length of 10 cm (4 in) at the most, is distributed along the sea coast of Europe. It was probably originally stocked in inland waters by aquarists. The Three-spined Stickleback is a very adaptable fish, suitable for aquariums as well as for garden ponds. In summer it can withstand water temperatures above 20 °C (68 °F) but in winter the water must be much colder. In the breeding season the male uses parts of plants and various fine roots to build a messy nest on the bottom of the tank. He then drives several females into the nest, where he fertilizes their

Weather Fish (*Misgurnus fossilis*)

Three-spined Stickleback, the male above

Pumpkinseed Sunfish (*Lepomis gibbosus*)

males dig dish-like hollows in the bottom where the females lay their eggs. The male then guards the nests and drives all other fish away. The Pumpkinseed Sunfish is suitable for garden ponds and small reservoirs in parks. It feeds exclusively on animal food.

The **Golden Orfe** (*Leuciscus idus orfus*), 30—40 cm (12—16 in) long, sometimes longer, is a popular ornamental fish of lar-

eggs. The male protects the eggs and the hatched young against all intruders, including even the keeper's hand. In the breeding season the male's belly acquires an orange crimson colouring. The Three-spined Stickleback feeds on any fine live food.

The **Pumpkinseed Sunfish** (*Lepomis gibbosus*) comes from the waters of North America and has also become acclimatized to European waters. It grows to 15—20 cm (6—8 in) long but in an aquarium it will not reach this length. It is best kept

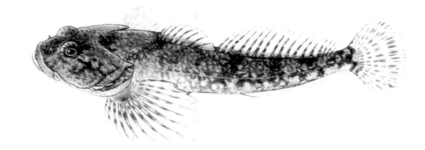

Miller's Thumb or Bullhead (*Cottus gobio*)

in a small shoal, without other fish, in a large tank with thick plant growth and a sandy bottom. In the breeding season the

ger garden reservoirs and park ponds where it often breeds successfully. It has no special requirements as to water quality and temperature. The small specimens take fine animal food, the larger ones also catch small fish. The Golden Orfe spawns on aquatic plants and tree rootlets exposed by water.

Golden Orfe (*Leuciscus idus orfus*)

The Sea Aquarium

Keeping sea fish in aquariums, until recently the exclusive hobby of a small number of specialists, has now spread throughout a broad range of aquarists as a result of the availability of various technical aids. Never-

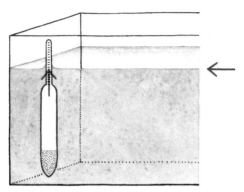

Salt water density should be read on the densimeter at the height of the water level.

theless, the keeping of sea creatures in aquariums is still far from free of problems. One of the major problems is the accumulation of the waste products of the sea animals. In a fresh-water tank much of the waste materials is removed by plants, but plants will not thrive in sea water, so the keeper must find other ways of disposing of the

waste. It is an advantage that sea water, which contains a large quantity of dissolved salts, is very stable, maintaining its pH at 7—8.5.

It is no problem to prepare sea water from a mixture of salts that are available in shops, which the keeper dissolves in water. The main point here is to control the density of the solution with a hydrometer. The water density required by almost all sea fish and other marine creatures is 1.011 to 1.028. The prepared solution must be

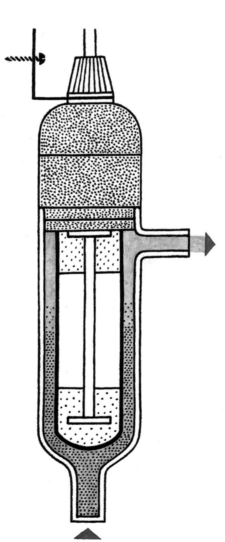

left to stand for several days before it can be stocked with fish. The bottom of the sea aquarium need not consist of several layers because it will not hold any plants; it will suffice to cover the bottom with a thin layer of pebbles of different sizes, or with coarse sand that will not be stirred up. The tank can be decorated with pieces of coral, empty shells of sea slugs and stones and rocks. If plenty of light is provided, algae will soon grow on the bottom and the stones. Algae are the only plants in the sea aquarium that can process organic waste and enrich the water with oxygen. Constant filtration is necessary to maintain the quality of the water.

High-performance pump-type filters are best: they thoroughly mix all the water in the tank, remove larger particles of contaminants, and whirl the water to enrich it with oxygen. The filters are filled with activated charcoal and nylon fibre which can be combined with ceramic material or crushed coral, basalt or granite. No extra aeration is needed in a tank with such a filter. This is advantageous because the aerators produce air bub-

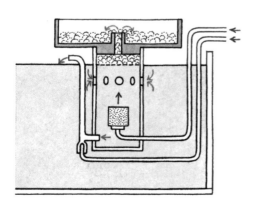

Diagram of the defoamer (protein separator).

A design for installing a UV radiator: water driven by a pump runs around a discharge lamp.

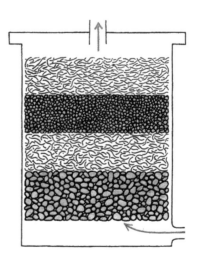

The sequence of substrate layers in a sea-water filter: there is a coarse gravel or crushed ceramic material on the bottom; coarse nylon fibre is spread over it; this is covered by a layer of activated charcoal, and fine nylon fabric is spread over the top.

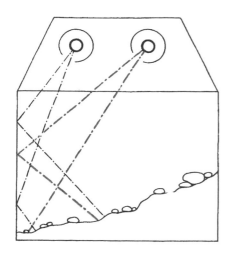

Because of the high refraction in sea water it is advisable to focus light on to the front wall of the tank.

some crabs and shrimps, starfish and sea urchins. Their striking colours and bizarre body forms are fascinating, especially on the bottom of the aquarium.

The **Beadlet Anemone** (*Actinia equina*), widely distributed in the Adriatic and Black Seas and along parts of the coast of Europe, grows to a size of 4–12 cm

very long arms which it cannot fold like the preceding species. Its colour variations comprise various shades of brown, red and blue. It is kept in small tanks at a temperature up to 18 °C (64 °F). Water filtration and clarification are necessary. Any food not swallowed by the anemone must be removed immediately to prevent deterioration of

Beadlet Anemone (*Actinia equina*)

bles that may drift outside the tank and these droplets of water contain salt that may damage the surface of the furniture.

As it is necessary to remove protein from the water, the sea aquarist will need a defoamer. Condensed protein forms slimy foam in the defoamer, which is then easy to remove. The defoamer should be in operation 12–18 hours every day. Ozone (O_3) can be used as a disinfectant in the water and to provide better oxygenation. Ozonisers are available in special aquarist shops, and carry detailed instructions for their use. The normal dose is about 0.5 mg per hour. Ozone overdosage may kill the inhabitants of the aquarium, so it is probably better to use ultra-violet radiators to irradiate the water that flows through the filter.

If treated with due care, the sea creatures may live in the tank for several years.

A list of organisms that can be kept in a sea aquarium would include various sea invertebrates, particularly sea anemones,

(1.5–4.8 in). It usually attaches itself firmly to a surface by the underside of its body, although it is also able to move at a slow speed of about 8 cm (3 in) per hour. Its mouth disc with tentacles is closed during the day and opens in the evening. This species of sea anemone has no particular requirements as to water temperature, but probably does best at a temperature of about 20 °C (68 °F). In the aquarium it will feed on small fish, pieces of beef or large plankton organisms; each chunk, gripped in a pair of forceps, is laid on the anemone's tentacles, which then propel it to the mouth.

The **Snakelock Anemone** (*Anemonia sulcata*) is an inhabitant of the Mediterranean Sea and the European Atlantic coast up to the English Channel. It has

the water. Like all anemones, the Snakelock Anemone is sensitive to changes in water chemistry and temperature.

The **Hermit Crab** (*Diogenes pugilator*) hides the soft, unprotected parts of its body in the empty shell of a sea slug which it carries along with it. It lives in the Mediterranean, Black and Adriatic seas and grows to a size of 10–20 cm (4–8 in). When the shell becomes too small for its body, it finds another one. Hence, lack of suitable shells is often the cause of failure in keeping this creature in the aquarium. The optimum temperature is about 18 °C (64 °F). The Hermit Crab is kept in large tanks with sand or gravel on the bottom. It eats pieces of meat and remnants of food left by other animals on the bottom and thus does an important job in keeping the aquarium clean.

The **Shrimp** (*Crangon crangon*), living in all European seas, is a crustacean 4–10 cm (1.5–4 in) long. It thrives in water at a temperature of about 20 °C (68 °F). Small specimens often become the prey of sea anemones, lobsters and fish. Shrimp are sensitive to the oxygen content of water, so intensive clarification and aeration are necessary. They feed on

Snakelock Anemone (*Anemonia sulcata*)

ped meat is the best food for the starfish.

Sea Urchins (*Echinoidea*) live in colonies anchored on coastal cliffs near the sea surface. The optimum temperature for sea urchins is about 20 °C (68 °F). Only the smaller species, 5–7 cm (2–2.75 in) in size, are kept in aquariums. Their main food in the sea is molluscs;

Hermit Crab (*Diogenes pugilator*)

small pieces of fish flesh, small worms or plankton.

The Starfish, the **Small Gibbous Starlet** or **Cushion Star** (*Asterina gibbosa*), living in all European seas, grows to a size of 3–4 cm (1.2–1.5 in) and is very suitable for marine aquariums. It requires a temperature of 22–24 °C (71–75 °F) and is predatory, like all starfishes, so it must not be kept in the same tank as defenceless organisms that live on the bottom. There should be coarse sand and flat rocks on the bottom and the water must be thoroughly filtered and oxygenated. Chop-

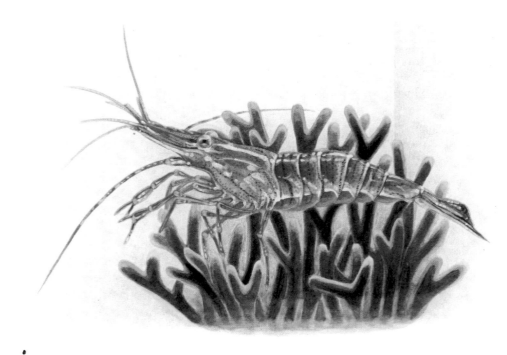

Shrimp (*Crangon crangon*)

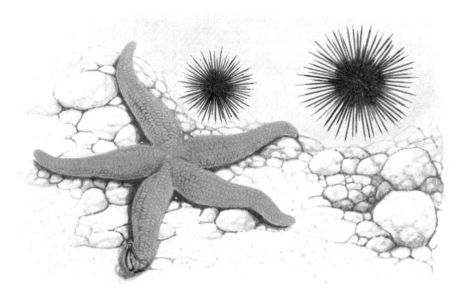

Small Gibbous Starlet (*Asterina gibbosa*) and Sea Urchins (*Echinoidea*)

in the aquarium they will take pieces of fish flesh, beef heart and lettuce. Using forceps, the chunks of food are laid on the creature's prickles and the urchin then propels these towards its mouth situated in the middle of the ventral part of its body.

The **Seahorse** (*Hippocampus hippocampus*), native to the shallow, densely overgrown, sandy shores of European seas, swims in a vertical position and moves by waving its dorsal and pectoral fins. It at- taches itself to algae and other submerged objects by its tail. Like all seahorses, it is fastidious about water purity and oxygen in the water. It requires a temperature between 18 and 20 °C (64—68 °F). In the aquarium it is given small crustaceans (brine shrimp and the like), small fry of freshwater fish and other fine live food. Any unconsumed remnants of food must be removed from the tank immediately. Seahorses move slowly and awkwardly, so they become easy prey of crabs and larger fish. The male keeps the fertilized eggs in a special sac on his belly. The young swim out of the sac after four weeks, attach themselves to aquatic plants and begin to take food immediately.

The **Great Pipefish** (*Syngnathus acus*), a relative of the seahorses, grows to 30—50 cm (12— 20 in) long. It should be kept under roughly the same conditions as seahorses but is not so particular about water purity and temperature. The male keeps the fertilized eggs in his abdominal sac. If such a male is captu- red, an attempt can be made to rear the young pipefish. They are fed on the nauplii of the brine shrimp, which the Great Pipefish fry consume in large quantities. If the young are to be reared, the water must be absolutely clean and thoroughly aerated.

The **Sphinx Blenny** (*Aidablennius sphynx*) is a fish up to 7 cm (2.75 in) long, living in European coastal waters with sandy and stony bottoms. In the aquarium it is kept at a temperature of about 20 °C (68 °F). There should be coarse sand, rocks and caves built from stones on the bottom of the tank. The fish will spawn in the caves and the nest containing the eggs will be protected by the male. The water must be thoroughly oxygenated. The Sphinx Blenny will take chopped mussels, pieces of fish flesh and chunks of other food of animal origin.

Another Blenny, **Salaria tentacularis**, distributed along the

Seahorse (*Hippocampus hippocampus*)

Sea Urchin (*Strongylocentrotus droebachiensis*): detail of mouth part

107

European sea coast, lives in sandy places and often hides in empty shells. Like other blennies, *Salaria tentacularis* is

prises about 20 species, is a close relative of the freshwater pufferfish of the genus *Tetraodon* (Green Pufferfish), but grows to a larger size (over 30 cm/12 in). It is recommended that you keep only one fish in the tank. If the Porcupine Fish is disturbed or frightened it fills its auxiliary bladder with an enormous amount of water so that it looks like a large spiny ball. Its spines stick out in all directions, deterring any intruder from coming close. If the fish swims near the water surface at such a moment, it fills itself with air and swims on the surface with its belly upwards. Sometimes,

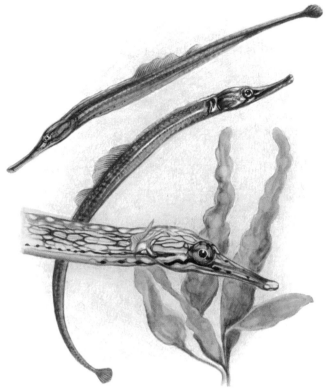

Great Pipefish (*Syngnathus acus*)

a predator and is quarrelsome. In the breeding season the female lays eggs in various hiding places in the tank and the male takes over the care of the offspring. The eggs develop for five to six weeks. The young fry are fed with brine shrimp nauplii. The male, who guards the eggs, is very aggressive and will often even attack the female.

The **Common Shrimpfish** or **Razorfish** (*Aeoliscus strigatus*), a distant relative of the seahorse and pipefish, almost always swims with its head pointing directly at the bottom. It is very active and requires much live food. Its length is up to 18 cm (7 in). In the aquarium it is kept in small shoals in clean, well-aerated water and is fed with brine shrimp.

Blennies: back, *Aidablennius sphynx*; front, *Salaria pavo*

The **Common Porcupine Fish** (*Diodon hystrix*), a representative of the family of porcupine fish (Diodontidae) which com-

however, it fails to let the air out and dies. It feeds on molluscs which it bites out of their shells. In the aquarium it can be given

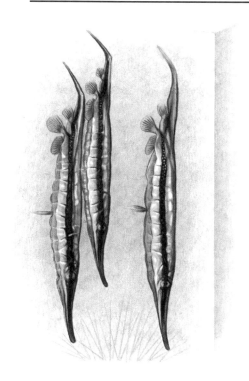

Common Shrimpfish or Razorfish (*Aeoliscus strigatus*)

to the fact that the fish needs foods that the keeper is unable to offer.

The **Arabian Snapper** (*Lutjanus kashmiri*) is an undemanding coral fish, having no special requirements provided it is kept in clear, well-aerated sea water. Young specimens, up to 4–6 cm (1.5–2.3 in) are particularly suitable for aquariums: if properly

ficial foodstuffs. As soon as they smell food they begin to swim quickly and greedily through the tank. They consume a large quantity of food, so the water in the tank must be intensively filtered and any mud or sludge must be separated regularly.

The **Yellow Longnose Butterfly Fish** (*Forcipiger longirostris*) is a typical coral fish and a strict

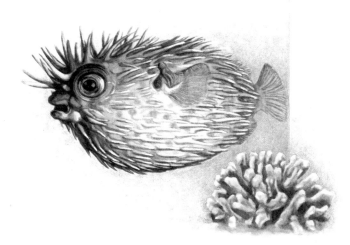

Common Porcupine Fish (*Diodon hystrix*)

pieces of fish or large forms of live food.

The **Six-line Grouper** (*Grammistes sexlineatus*), from the tropical Indopacific region and the Red Sea, is a predatory fish, up to 25 cm (10 in) long, living around coral reefs. If it is frightened or if it is taken out of the aquarium it exudes a poison that soon kills all the other fish, so it is better to keep it in isolation in a large tank with numerous hiding places. Even the young fish 4–6 cm (1.5–2.3 in) long are able to swallow large pieces of food. It feeds on small fish and larger sea invertebrates, pieces of fish flesh and the like.

The **Harlequin Sweetlip** (*Plectorhynchus chaetodontoides*), native to the coral seas from the Malay Peninsula up to the eastern Pacific region, is a very fastidious fish whose breeding in captivity is seldom successful. These failures are probably due

fed they grow quickly. They take larger animal food and pieces of meat, and will not refuse arti-

food specialist. Using its long jaws it takes small worms and invertebrates hidden in the coral

Harlequin Sweetlip (*Plectorhynchus chaetodontoides*)

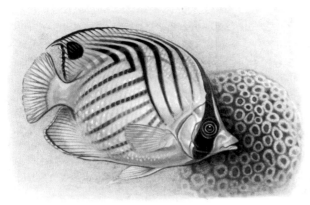

Golden Butterfly Fish (*Chaetodon auriga*)

means of a powerful pump filter. The Golden Butterfly Fish is a good fish with which to begin keeping coral fishes.

The **Powder-blue Surgeonfish**

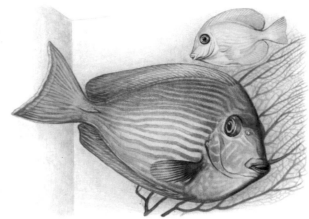

Blue Tang (*Acanthurus coeruleus*)

reefs. In captivity it soon becomes accustomed to substitute food (worms, pieces of meat) which it picks from the bottom or from the coral. It is kept in a large tank where it can move freely. Aeration, filtration and regular removal of mud are essential.

The **Golden Butterfly Fish** (*Chaetodon auriga*), a close relative of the Yellow Longnose Butterfly Fish, occurs in large shoals in warm coral seas. It is probably the most common species of coral fish kept in aquariums. It is undemanding and takes substitute food without much hesitation. Smaller shoals of this fish are kept in large tanks in which the water must be filtered and aerated by

(*Acanthurus leucosternon*) has, like all other surgeonfish (family Acanthuridae), a sharp spine that can be depressed into a socket; this weapon may cause an injury to the keeper's hand if he or she touches the fish carelessly. This common coral fish of the Indopacific region feeds mainly on vegetable food; in captivity it will take frozen or fresh spinach and lettuce and it is soon able to consume live food.

The **Blue Tang** (*Acanthurus coeruleus*), from the tropical seas, is an adaptable and undemanding fish in a marine aquarium. It is herbivorous and takes food greedily (such as frozen or fresh spinach) in captivity.

The **Moorish Idol** (*Zanclus cornutus*) is a beautiful coral fish from the Indian Ocean. It is difficult to keep in the marine aquarium because it often refuses food. It grows to a length of up to 25 cm (10 in). Although it is

Powder-blue Surgeonfish (*Acanthurus leucosteron*)

Moorish Idol (*Zanclus cornutus*)

The **Blue Streak** (*Labroides dimidiatus*), native to the coral reefs of the Indopacific, Persian Gulf and Red Sea, is 10 cm (4 in) long and belongs to the species known as the 'cleaner fish'. In its natural habitat it gathers and eats parasites from the bodies of all other fish living around the coral reefs. Even the large predators allow these small fish to clean their fins and flanks and also the gills and the inside of the mouth without doing any harm to them. In captivity, these fish soon take to a substitute meaty diet. They are very fastidious about the purity and quality of water, so they should be put in water that has been left to stand for at least a month and in which other fish are also kept. *Balistoides niger* is distributed in the Indian and Pacific oceans where it grows to a length of 50 cm (20 in). Its jaws are able to crush the hard shells of marine invertebrates, including sea-urchins. This fish is hardy and requires a large tank. In the aquarium it feeds on larger live food, e.g. insect larvae, larger worms and pieces of fish flesh. The **Red-lined Triggerfish**

one of the most attractive fish in the marine aquarium, it cannot be recommended either to beginners or even to more experienced aquarists.

The **Common Clownfish** (*Amphiprion ocellaris*), a fish about 9 cm (3.5 in) long, comes from the coral seas of the Indopacific region and the Red Sea. The male is smaller than the female. Fish of this species are sociable and can be kept in groups of several specimens. In their natural environment they live in symbiosis with the sea anemones of the genus *Stoichactis,* among whose tentacles they hide, as they are immune to the they should also be kept together with these anemones. They are kept in large tanks at a water temperature of 26–27 °C (79–81 °F) and are given pieces of meat or liver. The anemone fish are usually undemanding aquarium fish. However, *Amphiprion sebae*, a species related to *A. ocellaris,* grows to a length of 12 cm (5 in) and is quarrelsome and aggressive, so individual pairs must be kept in isolation.

Top: Common Clownfish (*Amphiprion ocellaris*); bottom: *Amphiprion sebae*

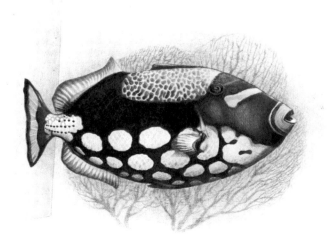

Balistoides niger

Red-lined Triggerfish (*Balistapus undulatus*)

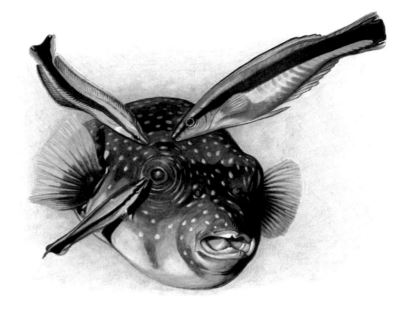

Blue Streak (*Labroides dimidiatus*) picking parasites from the body surface of a fish of the species *Arothron hispidus*.

Emperor Angelfish (*Pomacanthus imperator*); back: a young fish

The **Emperor Angelfish** (*Pomacanthus imperator*) is a coral fish up to 40 cm (16 in) long, living in the Indopacific region and in the Red Sea. Like other species of the family Pomacanthidae it has different colouring when it is young and when it is adult. It does well in captivity if it is kept in a large aquarium with clean sea water. However, if the keeper fails to pay due attention to water quality, the angelfish becomes frail and susceptible to various diseases. Fed once every two or three days, it takes

(*Balistapus undulatus*), inhabiting the same region as the preceding species, is up to 30 cm (12 in) long. It is somewhat aggressive, so it must be kept in isolation. If treated with care, both *Balistapus undulatus* and *Balistoides niger* can live in aquariums for a number of years.

Blue Angelfish (*Pomacanthus semicircularis*); top: a young fish

Red Firefish (*Pterois volitans*)

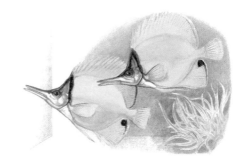

Yellow Longnose Butterfly Fish (*Forcipiger longirostris*)

Six-line Grouper (*Grammistes sexlineatus*)

through the Indian Ocean up to the Pacific, is among the most commonly kept fish of the family Pomacanthidae. It is not choosy about food and will soon acclimatize to aquarium conditions. However, it is often invaded by singlecell parasites and also suffers from bacterial skin diseases. It can be kept in the company of other, larger sea fish, with which it gets along well.

The **Red Firefish** (*Pterois volitans*) is one of the most common firefish kept in captivity. Its natural habitat is the Indian Ocean and the Red Sea, where it reaches a length of about 35 cm (13.5 in). It is easy to keep in an aquarium but must be handled with care as its fin rays

larger live food and soon adapts to a diet of pieces of meat or liver.

The **Blue Angelfish** (*Pomacanthus semicircularis*), distributed from the eastern African coast

have poison on their tips. In the aquarium the Red Firefish can grow to a length of 25–30 cm (10–12 in). It feeds on small fish, larger crustaceans and pieces of meat.

Rascasse volante

Terrariums

The hobby of keeping amphibians and reptiles enjoys increasing popularity among both adults and youngsters, although the price to be paid for such animals is often high and the keeper is not always sure that the animal will survive long or that he or she will be able to rear the young. Great practical skill and sound theoretical knowledge are necessary as a rule for success.

Many amphibians and reptiles are now seriously endangered in the wild. If their biology is learned in detail and if optimum rearing methods are developed, a valuable contribution could be made to their conservation. Unfortunately, animals captured in natural habitats still outnumber those reared in captivity. For this reason amphibians and reptiles should not be kept merely as pets; the keeper should always try to reproduce them and to rear the young. The

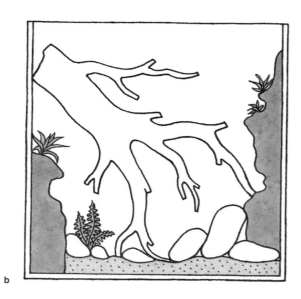

Types of terraria: a) desert; b) semi-arid;
c) tropical; d) an aquaterrarium

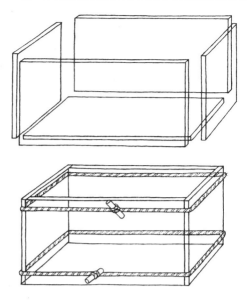

Making an all-glass tank

complete biology of many of these animals is still unknown, so any observations of their behaviour, plus photographic documentation and published notes, will be useful to other keepers and in many cases even to scientists.

Amphibians and reptiles are kept in special enclosures or tanks, called terrariums. Before buying a terrarium you must be sure what animals you want to keep and how many. Some amphibians and reptiles have many specific requirements.

Most terrariums have a rectangular or square ground plan; some (those standing in corners) are triangular when viewed from above. Various materials can be used to build a terrarium, such as glass, wood, plastic or metal. All-glass tanks are best for aquatic animals. Other creatures are kept in terrariums with a metal frame or in glued containers. The frame is made from iron sections and the remaining parts are glass, plastic or metal sheet. There must be large air holes in the side walls, covered with wire netting painted with an anti-corrosive coat-ing and held in a wooden frame. To provide access to the animals in the terrarium, there should be either a glazed door or sliding glass sheets that move in grooves in the front wall. Any gap in these movable parts must always be as small as possible because reptiles, especially snakes, are able to pass through unbelievably small openings. If you wish to keep a pair, or a group, of animals for breeding you will need several tanks. They may all be held on one metal stand or distributed among other furniture in the room.

Amphibians and reptiles are poikilothermic animals – having a body temperature that matches the temperature of their surroundings. For the keeper this means that in the terrarium the temperature must be the same as in the animals' natural habitats. Reptiles from the temperate climatic zone require an average temperature of about 14–18 °C (57–64 °F) in the daytime and 19–20 °C (55–68 °F) at night; the subtropical species need 20–30 °C (68–86 °F) in the daytime and 18–22 °C (64–71 °F) at night; the tropical reptiles need 20–30 °C (68–86 °F) in the daytime and 22–24 °C (71–75 °F) at night. The commonly used heat sources are bulbs, resistance heaters, heat plates and the like. If several species are kept, all having about the same demand for heat, the required temperature can be maintained throughout the whole room and the separate terrarium can be equipped with only one weak electric heat source.

Daylight does not usually suffice, so additional light must be provided. Bulbs may be used, serving simultaneously as sources of heat in the terrarium, but fluorescent lamps are more economical.

Daily sprinkling is essential to maintain the optimum humidity in the aquarium. In addition, many tree species of tropical forest amphibians and reptiles will drink by licking drops of water from leaves and other surfaces. The water (preferably rain water) used for the spraying must be 20–30 °C (68–86 °F).

Plants are used in the terrarium mainly for decoration, but they are also important for the reproduction of some tree frogs. The plants are cultivated, according to well-tried gardeners' instructions, either directly in the substrate on the bottom of the terrarium or in pots or boxes. No plants are grown in what we call hygienic terrariums as the bottoms of such terrariums are covered or strewn with paper, coarse sawdust, plastic foam, polystyrene and other easily removable or washable materials. Hardened vinyl products can be used to provide various shelters or to imitate tree branches.

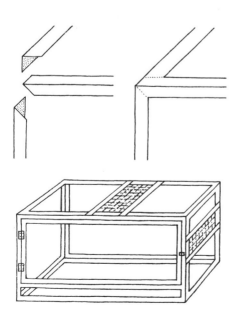

Cutting and assembling steel sections to build a steel-frame tank

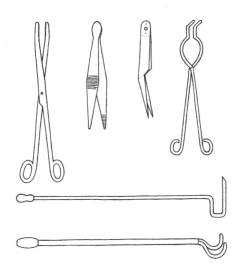

Tools used in keeping a terrarium

Terrarium animals need plenty of fresh air. To provide adequate ventilation, the air holes must be so located in relation to the heat source as to make the air flow. It is recommended to make the air holes in part of one of the side walls and also in part of the ceiling.

The terrarium must be cleaned regularly if the animals kept in it are to do well. Immedia-te removal (as far as possible) of excrement is important. The material that is to be used to replace the old bedding must have been thoroughly sterilised by heat. Natural materials such as sand, gravel and peat should be replaced at least once every three months. The whole terrarium and everything inside it should be thoroughly washed and disinfected once a year at least.

It is very difficult to create the best possible conditions for animals in the limited space of a terrarium. Nevertheless, the basic factors, including day length, temperature, humidity and overwintering, should be controlled to be as similar to those in their natural habitats as possible. To avoid disappointment, you must learn as much as possible about the animals' natural surroundings and their climatic conditions *before* the chosen animal or animals are bought.

Garden terrariums, although not so frequently used as indoor ones, are very suitable for reptiles and amphibians of the temperate and subtropical zones. These are, as a rule, enclosures set in terrain where many features of the animals' natural surroundings can be imitated. A garden aquarium is built as a solid-bottom pool furnished with a drain outlet for excess water. A terrarium should have a run with walls reaching some 30–50 cm (12–20 in) underground to prevent the animal from undermining them. The walls must be high, at least three times as high as the animals' length. There should be a roof over part of the run and a heated place may be provided to help the animals survive unfavourable weather without harm. A net

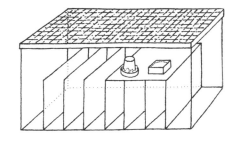

A tank for cricket breeding

must be spread above the terrarium to protect the animals from intruders (cats, birds).

Conditions for overwintering must be provided for animals native to the temperate geographical zones. Such animals should spend their winter rest in suitable cool places (cellars, larders, refrigerators and the like) where they are kept in small tanks with a thick layer of suitable substrate, such as peat, peat moss, sand and leaf mould, at a temperature of 3–8 °C (31–46 °F). These tanks

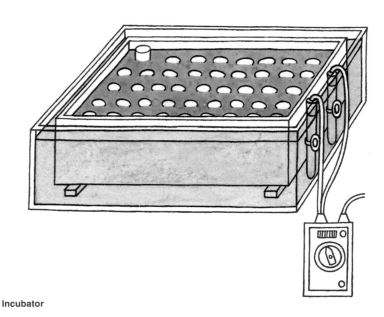

Incubator

must be inspected from time to time and slight moisture maintained in the substrate. Before hibernation, the animals should have fasted for about three weeks and evacuated their gut. The temperature should be reduced step by step. Animals in poor health should not be hibernated.

If the animals in the terrarium take food without reluctance they can be fed as frequently as they are able to consume the food. The best composition of diets for amphibians and reptiles has not yet been determined, so the keeper must often resort to experimentation. There is a wide variety of food of animal origin, including water fleas, tubificids, earthworms, mosquito larvae, slugs, spiders, vinegar flies, house flies, crickets, cockroaches, meal beetles, and frozen fish, chickens and mice. The keeper can either buy most of these feeding stuffs or may instead breed the animals that will serve as the food. The keeping of such species is described in the preceding chapters on the management of auxiliary stocks of invertebrates (pages 38—41), on keeping aquarium fish (pages 44—113) and in the later chapter on keeping small mammals (pages 210—229).

Insects captured by dragging are an important ingredient of the diets of insectivorous terrarium species. Foodstuffs normally available in shop (eggs, lean beef, fish fillet, curd cheese, biscuits and so on) are also of great importance. Various fresh and stewed fruits, fresh and frozen vegetables, sprouted grains leaves and flowers of nonpoisonous herbs are the major vegetable sources of nutrients. Minerals and trace elements are essential. To provide them, crushed eggshells and preparations containing calcium, phosphorus, potassium, sodium,

iron, trace elements, amino acids, sugars and carotene are added to the diet. Half-rotten, decayed or otherwise defective food should never be used.

If often happens that terrarium animals refuse food. This may be caused by exhaustion of the animal, transport shock, invasion by parasites, disease, in-

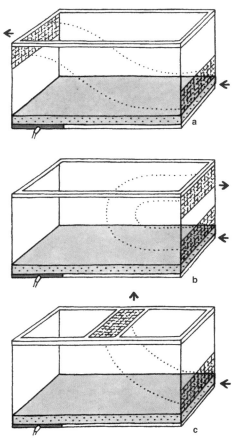

Ventilation in a terrarium: a) wrong; b) suitable; c) possible

jury, adverse conditions or the wrong food. If the vet's help and a change of conditions fail, you may have to resort to force feeding. A pair of long forceps or a syringe is used to introduce the food into the animal's gullet. The forceps must have rounded

ends. To feed the animal, grip the moistened food between the forceps, press the animal's jaws gently and carefully part them from the front and push the food carefully into the gullet. Then wait to see if the animal starts to swallow the food itself. If it tries to vomit, massage its throat to propel the food further down. If using a syringe, mash the food and make it a little runny (for example with raw eggs) if necessary. Use a large syringe with a thin rubber tube instead of a needle. Moisten the tube, introduce it gently into the animal's gullet and empty the syringe slowly.

Success in rearing the young of amphibians and reptiles in a terrarium depends on a number of factors, particularly nutrition, temperature, light and humidity. In some species the male and female may be left together all the time and allowed to rear their young. In other species the male and female must be kept apart outside the mating season. During egg laying or birth, the parents must often be watched to ensure that they do not harm their offspring.

The eggs and larvae of amphibians are kept in tanks under roughly the same conditions as aquarium fish. As the larvae grow, they must be distributed by size into larger tanks. Incubators with the correct conditions for the hatching of the eggs must be available for the reproduction of egg-laying reptiles. The simplest unit of this kind is a plastic container with several air holes and a suitable substrate into which the eggs are set. The incubator is either left in the terrarium or kept in another suitable place at the correct temperature, and the humidity inside it is maintained by spraying the substrate. Sophisticated separate tanks with automatically controlled temperature

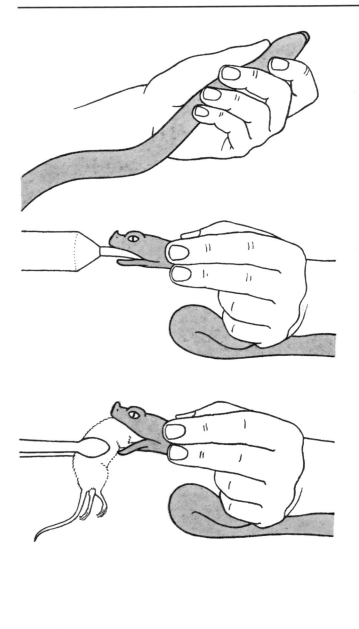

Artificial feeding

possible. Easily replaceable materials such as paper, plastic foam and sawdust should be used as the substrate. Every new animal should be inspected thoroughly for possible surface injuries or parasites. It is

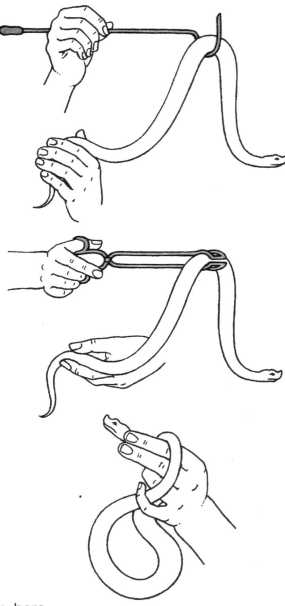

and humidity can also be used. Small tanks are used for rearing the young, who are kept in small groups in which their condition can be easily observed; the weaker and stronger young must be kept apart.

A special quarantine terrarium should be available for new arrivals. Animals obtained from another keeper, as well as those captured in their habitat, should

spend four to six weeks here. These terrariums must be easy to clean and disinfect and their equipment must be as simple as

Handling a venomous snake

120

also recommended to examine their faeces microscopically for the presence of intestinal parasites and micro-organisms that are transmissible to people. Food consumption should be checked every day. Reptiles must be observed to see whether they shed their skins without problems. If any animal falls ill, a veterinary surgeon should be consulted as to the best treatment.

The Tailed Amphibians (order Caudata)

Newts and salamanders, included in the order of tailed amphibians, are native to the northern hemisphere, especially North America and Europe, although some species also live in South America and Africa. No such creatures are found in the Indomalayan region or in Australia.

The order Caudata consists of about 250 species, most of which live outside water when they are adult, but need moisture throughout their whole life. They cannot withstand high

How the newt lays eggs on aquatic plants

temperatures, so rarely occur in tropical regions.

The salamanders and the dry-land stages of the newts are most active in the dusk and at night. During the day and when the weather is hot and dry, they hide under stones, in hollows in the rocks or in holes dug by other animals.

The size of the tailed amphibians varies from tiny 2 cm (0.75 in) creatures up to giants about 1.5 m (5 ft) long.

The tailed amphibians have neither an eardrum nor a middle ear, so they cannot hear sounds carried on sound waves in the air; however, they do feel very keenly the vibrations that travel through both earth and water. Their sense of smell is also well developed and they use it in seeking food. All salamanders are carnivorous and their prey includes various insects and other invertebrates; the large species feed on fish and other small vertebrates.

Like many aquarium fish, some tailed amphibians are known to practise courtship play. The purpose of this play is to make the female pick up the spermatophores, i.e. clusters of spermatozoa stuck together with jelly. The male lays them on the bottom and the female picks them up with her cloaca and then lays separate fertilized eggs on plants. Larvae with external gills hatch from the eggs

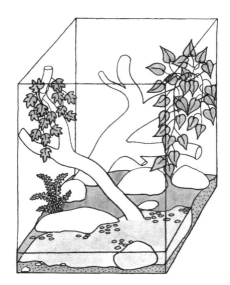

Garden terrarium

Aquaterrarium

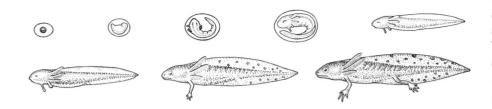

The development of the newt

and later undergo a metamorphosis. During the course of their development their gills are gradually replaced by lungs so that after the metamorphosis the animals are able to live on dry land. Nevertheless, there are a number of species that remain in water all their life.

Many amphibians lay a large number of eggs, but both the eggs and the larvae often fall prey to other animals, so that only a small number of offspring

A pouch with eggs (*Hynobius keyserlingi*)

survive to adulthood under natural conditions. If the right conditions are provided, a much higher number of young can be reared in captivity. The hatched larvae are reared in the same way as fish fry. The first food they take are rotifers, nauplii of cyclops and the brine shrimp, or artificial food. Overfeeding must be avoided. As the larvae grow,

they are distributed by size in larger tanks.

Hynobius keyserlingi, distributed over the vast territory from the Ural mountains to Sakhalin Island, grows to a length of 14 cm (5.5 in). It lives in forest pools and swamps. Salamanders of this species are kept in an aquaterrarium at a water temperature of up to 20 °C (68 °F) in summer and 3–5 °C (37–41 °F) in winter. The dry part of the terrarium is bedded with moss and bark in which the salamander will hide and the tank is decorated with cold-loving ferns. The salamander feeds on small insects, spiders, earth worms and the like. It mates early in spring at a temperature of up to 5 °C (41 °F). The female lays sacs containing eggs on aquatic plants and the male attaches his spermatophores to them. Larvae hatch

from the eggs after 15–36 days and undergo their metamorphosis after 30–60 days.

The **Japanese Giant Salamander** (*Andrias japonicus*) is native to the Japanese islands and is the largest of all the tailed amphibians, growing to a length of up to 1.5 m (5 ft). It inhabits the clear waters of mountain torrents and brooks. In captivity it is kept in a large tank with flowing water of over 10–15 °C (50–59 °F); during the warm season it can be kept in a garden pool. The Japanese Giant Salamander feeds on small vertebrates: fish, amphibians and mammals. The female lays 300–500 eggs stuck together with a jelly-like matter. The male fertilizes the eggs and protects them until the young hatch (after 60–80 days).

The **Olm** (*Proteus anguineus*) is only found in the wild in the cold underground waters of Dalmatia and in Italy and is very strictly protected. It is kept in shaded aquariums in water at about 10 °C (50 °F). It feeds on worms, slugs and small fish. Adult specimens are up to 25 cm (10 in) long. The Olm gives birth to live young (viviparous) in the cold cave waters of its natural habitat, but in the waters of the aquarium it lays eggs from

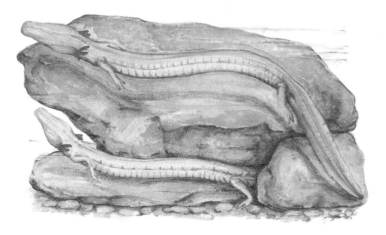

Olm (*Proteus anguineus*)

seldom leaves the water. It is kept in an aquarium with about a 20 cm (8 in) layer of water and for the summer season it can be left in an outdoor pool. In autumn the male and female are kept separately in larger aquariums at a temperature of about 8 °C (48 °F). In spring, an increase of temperature to 17–20 °C (63–68 °F) will induce the

Japanese Giant Salamander (*Andrias japonicus*)

which the young, looking like smaller copies of the adults, hatch after three months.

The **Red-bellied Newt** (*Cynops pyrrhogaster*) is a 10–12 cm (4–4.75 in) long inhabitant of stagnant and densely overgrown waters in Japan and eastern China. It is kept in an aquaterrarium with water plants at a temperature of about 20 °C (68 °F) in summer and 3–6 °C (37–43 °F) in winter. Plankton, mosquito and chironomid larvae, insects and worms are the main ingredients of its diet. Mating takes place in April and May. The female lays 50–100 eggs on aquatic plants.

Ribbed Salamander (*Pleurodeles waltli*) mating

Ribbed Salamander (*Pleurodeles waltli*)

Red-bellied Newt (*Cynops pyrrhogaster*)

The **Ribbed Salamander** (*Pleurodeles waltli*) lives in the larger bodies of stagnant waters in Spain and Morocco and only

Hynobius keyserlingi

123

newts to mate. They feed on earthworms, insects, small fish and pieces of lean beef. Adult Ribbed Salamanders are up to 30 cm (12 in) long. During mating the male carries the female on his back and holds her with his forefeet. The female lays up to 800 eggs on water plants. The development of the larvae up to their metamorphosis lasts about three months.

The **Marbled Newt** (*Triturus marmoratus*), distributed over southwest Europe (the south of France and Spain and Portugal) is up to 14 cm (5.5. in) long. It inhabits shaded and wet places in moss, under stones, roots and the like. It is kept in an aquaterrarium with cushions of moss and with shelters under stones and roots. The Marbled Newt feeds on small insects and other invertebrates. Spawning takes place late in February at a water temperature of about 10 °C (50 °F). The female lays her eggs from the end of March until mid-May.

The **Fire Salamander** (*Salamandra salamandra*), a strictly protected amphibian up to 25 cm (10 in) long, is distributed throughout a vast territory from northwest Africa through southern and central Europe to southwest Asia. Its habitat is wet and shady forests, mostly of broadleaved trees, where the salamander lives in the proximity of clear forest brooks. In captivity it needs an aquaterrarium with a large dry area and suitable hiding places. The optimum temperature is 15–18 °C (59–64 °F) in summer and 2–5 °C (36–41 °F) in winter. The Fire Salamander can be kept with success in an outdoor terrarium. It feeds on earthworms, molluscs and insects. Its breeding season extends from April to August. About ten months after mating, the female finds water where she gives birth to fully

developed young. The average litter size is 10–30 young. Two to three months after birth the young undergo metamorphosis. After metamorphosis the salamanders spend the rest of their lives on dry land near water.

The **Spotted Salamander** (*Ambystoma maculatum*) inhabits the eastern areas of the USA where it lives in wet places near water. It is kept at a temperature of 18–21 °C (64–70 °F) in a large aquaterrarium where the water tank occupies about two-thirds of the total area. The

Marbled Newt (*Triturus marmoratus*)

Fire Salamander (*Salamandra salamandra*)

Spotted Salamander, up to 20 cm (8 in) long, feeds on worms, molluscs and small insects (crickets and the like). At breeding time the female lays clusters of up to 200 eggs.

The **Red Salamander** (*Pseudotriton ruber*) is native to the northwestern and central regions of the USA where it lives on the banks of clear brooks in mountains and highlands. In captivity this salamander, up to about 12 cm (4.75 in) long, does well in an aquaterrarium with a large body of water at a temperature of 18–20 °C (64–68 °F). After metamorphosis the young salamanders are bright red in colour, with small dark spots; older specimens are dark red with a brownish tint. In captivity they will feed on worms, molluscs and smaller insects.

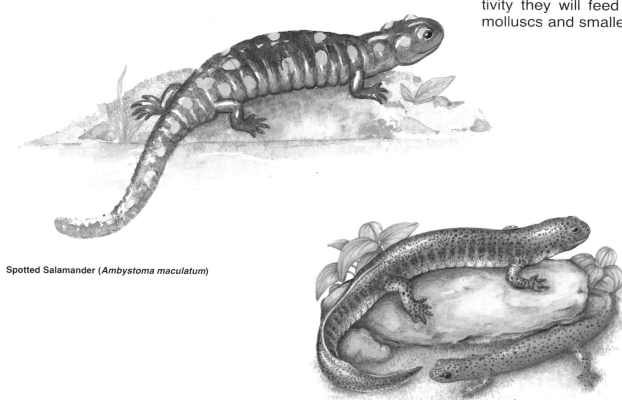

Spotted Salamander (*Ambystoma maculatum*)

Red Salamander (*Pseudotriton ruber*)

Triturus alpestris

Frogs and Toads (order Anura)

The order Anura comprises over 3,500 species. They are distributed in the tropical and subtropical regions of the whole world. In the north, several species reach to the Arctic Circle and in South America they are found as far south as Patagonia. However, anurans will not be encountered on the tops of mountain ranges, in deserts or on some islands in the Pacific Ocean.

Although some species always stay in water, the majority leave water after metamorphosis and spend most of their life on dry land.

Most of the small species feed on insects, worms, spiders and similar prey. Larger species may occasionally capture small animals, birds and other vertebrates.

In their natural habitats, the males find the nearest waters of sufficient depth, fill their throat sacs or resonant drums with air and produce various sounds to lure females by forcing the air out of the sacs through the glottis.

Like the majority of fish, the eggs of frogs and toads are fertilised outside the body. The male's forefeet firmly embrace the female who ejects several sets of eggs which the male fertilises. Some species lay eggs in clusters, other in strings.

A larva hatches from the egg and clings to objects under the water using its suction organ. Only the smallest tadpoles have external gills; in older tadpoles the gills disappear into the branchial cavity behind the head. Anuran tadpoles feed on algae but in captivity they will take suitable artificial food. Vegetable matter is generally the preferred food of tadpoles and frogs, although there are some exceptions. When the tadpole begins to metamorphose into a frog, its oral disc loses its horny rim. First the tadpole acquires rear legs, then forelegs, while the tail shortens, although it is still visible when the young adult leaves the water.

The **Surinam Toad** (*Pipa pipa*)

Midwife Toad (*Alytes obstetricans*)

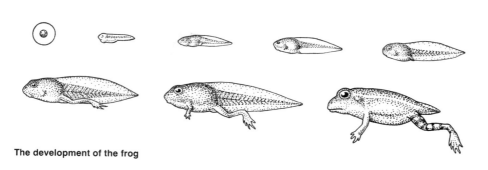

The development of the frog

is a large toad up to 25 cm (10 in) long, from Peru, Guyana, Surinam and Brazil, where it usually inhabits stagnant waters. In captivity it needs a large aquaterrarium with floating plants, where the toad is kept at a temperature of 22–26 °C (71–79 °F). It is fed with tubificids, earthworms, chironomid larvae and other aquatic invertebrates.

During mating, the male grips the female's flanks between his forefeet and the pair swims from the bottom to the water surface where both will turn their bellies up and then return to the bottom afterwards. At the moment when the cloacae of both male and female are turned upwards, the male slightly loosens his grip to let the female eject several eggs into the narrow space between her back and the male's belly. The male then fertilises the eggs. Then follows a short rest before another act of fertilisation. This continues until the female's back carries 30–120 eggs. Later, the skin on the female's back swells and encases every egg. The eggs develop into tadpoles, which do not leave the 'hatchery' on their mother's back until metamorphosis. About 20 days elapse from the mating to when the small toads emerge.

The **Fire-bellied Toad** (*Bombina bombina*) is a small toad 36–60 mm (1.4–2.3 in) long, inhabiting small bodies of stagnant water from southern Scandinavia and central Europe to the Urals. It can be kept in an aquaterrarium with water at about 20 °C (68 °F). The Fire-bellied Toad is given insects (crickets) and other small invertebrates. For hibernation the temperature should be reduced to 3–7 °C (37–45 °F). Soon after the winter season the females lay either separate eggs or clusters of eggs on water plants. The tadpoles emerge from the eggs after a week and undergo metamorphosis after two to three months.

The **Midwife Toad** (*Alytes obstetricans*) lives in western Europe, except Great Britain; the area of its distribution reaches to the Alps and Pyrenees in the south and to the eastern regions of Germany in the east. It is a 4–5 cm (1.5–2 in) long nocturnal

Fire-bellied Toad (*Bombina bombina*)

toad that hides under stones, among roots or in holes in the ground during the day. It feeds on slugs, earthworms, small insects and similar food. In captivity it does well in an aquaterrarium with a large dry area and suitable hiding places. The Midwife Toad mates on dry land. The female lays a string of about 60 eggs and the male winds the string round the thighs of his hindlegs. He keeps the eggs wet until the tadpoles emerge: shortly before hatching he finds a pool where the tadpoles hatch from the eggs.

The cusp on the heel of the Common Spadefoot Toad

The **Common Spadefoot Toad** (*Pelobates fuscus*), a 6–8 cm (2.3–3 in) long nocturnal toad with vertical, slit-like pupils, is found in Europe from France to the Urals. It inhabits sandy places near rivers and ponds in

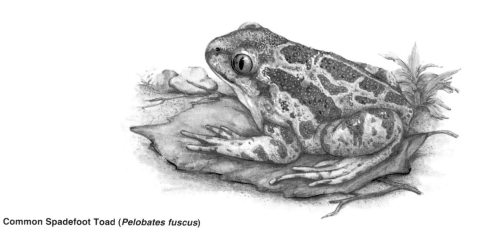

Common Spadefoot Toad (*Pelobates fuscus*)

Flaming Poison-arrow Frog (*Dendrobates pumilio*)

flies and similar small animal food. The adult males are quarrelsome, so individual pairs must be kept in isolation. During mating the male ejects his

Granular Poison-arrow Frog (*Dendrobates granuliferus*)

lowlands. In an aquaterrarium with a large 'dry' area of wet, loose substrate it requires a temperature of 20–25 °C (68–77 °F). It is most active in the evening and at night and spends the day buried in sand. It has huge cusps on its heels with which it can quickly bury itself underground. The Common Spadefoot Toad feeds on insects, slugs, worms and other small animal food. Mating takes place during March to May. The female lays strings of 1,200–2,500 eggs, which she weaves around water plants. Metamorphosis follows after two to three months, but sometimes the tadpoles may overwinter in water and many have grown to a length of 15 cm (6 in) before metamorphosis.

The **Nose-horned Frog** (*Megophrys monticola nasuta*) lives in the tropical forests of the Malay Peninsula, Borneo and Thailand. It is a large toad up to 16 cm (6.5 in) long, requiring a large aquaterrarium with a water column of 8–10 cm (3–4 in). The best temperature for this toad is between 22 and 26 °C (71–79 °F). It feeds on various large insects, earthworms and slugs and can easily swallow even a small mouse. It is recommended that you put pieces of corky bark on the

water surface in the breeding tank. The eggs laid by the female will float loose on the water until they touch and cling to the bark. Then the bark and the eggs can be transferred to a separate tank with intensive aeration and filtration of the water to prevent fungi from affecting the eggs. The tadpoles, with typical horn-like projections on their heads, will hatch after about ten days and metamorphose after another three months.

The **Flaming Poison-arrow Frog** (*Dendrobates pumilio*), only 17–24 cm (6.5–8.5 in) long, inhabits the tropical forests of Nicaragua, Costa Rica and Panama. In captivity it requires a wet tropical terrarium with plenty of branches and plants with funnel-like leaves (*Bromelia*). The temperature in the terrarium should be 23–27 °C (73–80 °F). It feeds on small crickets, insects larvae, vinegar

sperm on a *Bromelia* leaf and the female lays six to sixteen eggs onto it. As the tadpoles hatch, they slip down to the water contained in the funnel--like leaves. In the terrarium the *Bromelia* plants can be replaced by small plastic pots filled with water. After 60 days the small frogs leave the water. One female Flaming Poison-arrow Frog can lay eggs eight to ten times a year.

The **Granular Poison-arrow Frog** (*Dendrobates granuliferus*) lives in the tropical forests of Nicaragua, Panama and Costa Rica. In captivity it requires a large tropical terrarium with *Bromelia* plants and a temperature between 23 and 27 °C (73–80 °F). It can be given vinegar flies and other small insects.

The **Blue Poison-arrow Frog** (*Dendrobates azureus*) from Surinam is about 4 cm (1.5 in) long. It needs a wet, tropical terrarium with suitable shelters built from pieces of bark, stones and other materials. Unlike the two preceding species, this little frog lives mainly on the ground and does not spend much time climbing in shrubs and trees. The temperature in the tank should be about 25 °C (77 °F). The Blue Poison-arrow Frog will take small insects (vinegar flies, small crickets). In the breeding season the female lays two eggs on a solid surface (a Petri dish can be used in the terrarium) which she has moistened in advance. The male fertilises the eggs and 20 days later tadpoles will emerge. The female and sometimes also the male carry the tadpoles to water where they finish their development.

Asian Painted Frog (*Kaloula pulchra*)

ing them. The frogs produce poison in their dermal glands and release it when they are touched. The keeper should wear rubber gloves whenever he or she wishes to touch them. A painful inflammation will occur on the skin if the poison penetrates through a scratch.

The **Asian Painted Frog** (*Kaloula pulchra*) is up to 8 cm (3 in) long, distributed from Sri Lanka through India up to southern China and Vietnam and the Indomalayan islands. It is kept in an aquaterrarium with a large dry area and suitable plants. The optimum temperature for the bull-frog is between 25 and 28 °C (77–82 °F). It feeds on

Nose-horned Frog (*Megophrys monticola nasuta*)

There are about 90 species of poison-arrow frogs and all are venomous and unsuitable for children or inexperienced keepers. Their striking colouring warns enemies against attack-

Blue Poison-arrow Frog (*Dendrobates azureus*)

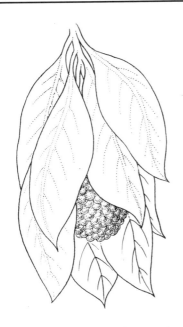

The foam nest of *Rhacophorus leucomystax*

insects, earthworms, slugs and other small invertebrates.

The **European Marsh Frog** (*Rana ridibunda*) is 15 cm (6 in) long. It lives near stagnant or slow-flowing waters in northern Africa, southern and central Europe, in the Crimea, in the Caucasus, in Asia Minor and central Asia. In captivity it requires a temperature of 15–22 °C (59–71 °F) and can be kept in a large aquaterrarium or in a garden terrarium. Insects and crickets (collected by dragging, etc.)

European Marsh Frog (*Rana ridibunda*)

should predominate in its food. Marsh Frogs are active both during the daytime and at night. To hibernate, they bury themselves in the mud under water. The females lay 3,000–10,000 eggs in irregular clusters and the tadpoles metamorphose three to four months after hatching. At breeding time the males have conspicuous dark calluses on their forefeet.

The **American Bullfrog** (*Rana catesbeiana*), from the Atlantic coast of the USA to eastern Colorado, the eastern part of New Mexico and the southern regions of Canada, grows to be 20 cm (8 in) long. Its habitat is on the edges of stagnant and slow-flowing waters. The American Bullfrog requires a temperature of 18–24 °C (64–75 °F) and is kept in a large aquaterrarium with a water column of 10–15 cm (4–6 in). It feeds on insects, worms, small fish, small amphibians and other smaller vertebrates. The mating season is from March to June. The female lays 10,000–20,000 eggs from which the tadpoles emerge after five to 20 days. They metamorphose towards the end of summer.

The **Burrowing Bullfrog** (*Pyxicephalus adspersus*) is native to central and southern Africa. It is the largest of the African bullfrogs, growing as long as 25 cm (10 in). Its homeland is in the savanna regions. In captivity it needs an aquaterrarium with a large dry area (leaf mould and sand). The temperature should be maintained at between 22 and 28 °C (71–82 °F). The frogs will take large insects and small vertebrates (mice). The female lays 3,000–4,000 eggs and the tadpoles develop very quickly: they take only eighteen days to change into small frogs.

Rhacophorus leucomystax, a frog up to 8 cm (3 in) long, inhabits a vast area from the east-

American Bullfrog (*Rana catesbeiana*)

ern Himalayas to southern China and is found as far south as Java and Kalimantan and as far east as the Philippines. It lives in tropical forests in the vicinity of water. All four feet of this flying frog have a web between the long fingers and serve as 'parachutes', allowing the frog to jump and glide over a long distance. *Rhacophorus leucomystax* can be kept in a tropical terrarium with a small water tank, with twigs and creeping plants, and with peat as a substrate and moss as bedding. The temperature in the terrarium should range between 22 and 28 °C (71–82 °F). The flying frogs are

Burrowing Bullfrog (*Pyxicephalus adspersus*)

most active in the dark. They feed on insects. In the breeding season the female whips up a special secretion using her

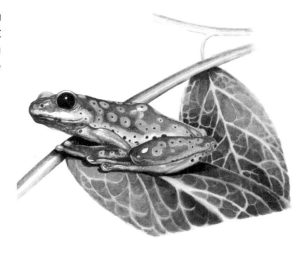

Painted Red Frog (*Hyperolius marmoratus*)

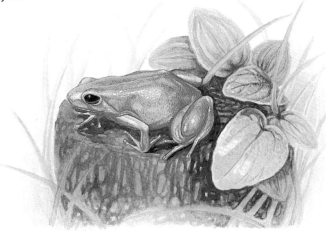

Rhacophorus leucomystax

Golden Mantella (*Mantella aurantiaca*)

the back wall and some of them should be placed aslant. At breeding time the terrarium should be shaded because the eggs of the mantella are vulnerable to exposure to direct sunshine. Daily spraying in the terrarium is essential during the development of the eggs. The frogs stick semicircular clusters of eggs on the underside of the peat plates. The plates and eggs are then transferred to a separate shaded tank containing shallow water. The tadpoles metamorphose after about two months.

The **Painted Red Frog** (*Hyperolius marmoratus*) is a marbled African frog living near the water on shore-side vegetation. Moisture-loving plants with long narrow leaves should be grown in the aquaterrarium because the frogs like to sit on such leaves. The temperature should be maintained between 22 and 28 °C (71−82 °F). The tank must be ventilated because these frogs require a comparatively low air humidity (up to 70 per cent). If the humidity is higher they soon fall ill and may even die.

The **South American Bullfrog** (*Leptodactylus pentadactylus*)

hindfeet, to make a foamy nest which she fixes in branches overhanging the water surface. About 50−100 eggs are laid in this nest. The hatched tadpoles fall into the water where they finish their development.

The **Golden Mantella** (*Mantella aurantiaca*) is a small frog about 2 cm (0.75 in) long that lives in the screw pine stands in Madagascar. In captivity it does well in a small tropical terrarium with plants and a small water tank. Pressed peat plates should be laid on the bottom and against

South American Bullfrog (*Leptodactylus pentadactylus*)

131

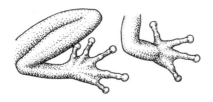

is a frog up to 20 cm (8 in) long from the Lesser Antilles, Costa Rica and the tropical regions of South America. It inhabits tropical forests and often lives near water. In captivity it thrives in a large aquaterrarium with good hiding places under bark or among rocks etc. The optimum temperature is between 22 and 26 °C (71−79 °F). The South American Bullfrog can be given larger insects, worms, molluscs and small vertebrates. At breeding time the females build a foamy nest at the water's edge; the tadpoles undergo part of their development in the nest and the rest of their development in water.

Common Tree Frog (*Hyla arborea*)

Bell's Ceratophrys (*Ceratophrys ornata*)

The **Robber Frogs** (*Eleutherodactylus* sp.) are a genus consisting of about 200 species distributed in the Antilles, in the south of the USA and in Central America. All these small frogs live in tropical and subtropical forests. In captivity they can be kept in a small tropical terrarium with plants and a small water tank at a temperature of 24−28 °C (75−82 °F). Small insects (vinegar flies, small crickets and others) are the main ingredients of their diet. The Robber Frogs grow to a length of 14−80 mm (0.5−3 in). Mating takes place on dry land. The females lay their eggs among wet leaves, in moss, under pieces of wood or under stones. The development of these frogs does not include a tadpole stage, so the small frogs hatch straight from the eggs.

Bell's Ceratophrys (*Ceratophrys ornata*) is a frog 10−12 cm (4.−4.75 in) long that inhabits the swamps and shore-side vegetation around pools and along slow-flowing waters in Brazil and Argentina. The tropical terrarium where Bell's Ceratophrys is to be kept should have a small water tank and the floor should be covered with a mixture of peat and sand. The temperature should be between 22 and 28 °C (71−82 °F). There must be no sharp objects in the terrarium because the frogs are very vulnerable to skin injuries. Their diet consists of large insects and small vertebrates. Bell's Ceratophryses are often aggressive and may bite the keeper.

The **Common Tree Frog** (*Hyla arborea*) is distributed over an extensive area from western Europe through North Africa and Asia Minor to Siberia. The natural habitat of this well-known frog, 4−5 cm (1.5−2 in) long, is in shrubs and tree tops. The most suitable terrarium for keeping this frog is cube-shaped and should be decorated with twigs and plants and furnished with a small water

The **Green Tree Frog** (*Hyla cinerea*) lives on trees and shrubs near water, from North Carolina to Texas. It is one of the smaller species of tree frogs and grows to a maximum length of 6 cm (2.3 in). In a terrarium with twigs and plants and a small water tank it does well at a tempera-

Green Tree Frog (*Hyla cinerea*)

Robber Frog (*Eleutherodactylus* sp.)

tank. The temperature should be maintained at between 18–24°C (64–75°F). In the terrarium the Common Tree Frog will take various insects as its food. Mating takes place in spring. The females lay 800–1,000 eggs on the bottom of the tank. The tadpoles metamorphose after two to three months.

Hyla caerulea is a large frog up to 10 cm (4 in) long, from Australia and Papua New Guinea, where it is usually found in for-

est regions. It is kept in a tropical terrarium with tree branches and twigs and a small water tank. The temperature should be between 23 and 28°C (73–82°F). The diet of the frog consists of large insects. The females lay eggs on the bottom of the tank.

ture of 22–26°C (71–79°F). It feeds on small insects. Mating takes place in spring and, like other tree frogs, the female lays clusters of eggs on the bottom of the water tank.

Hyla caerulea

Marsupial Frog (*Gastrotheca marsupiata*)

The **Marsupial Frog** (*Gastrotheca marsupiata*), native to the wet tropical forests of Ecuador, needs a terrarium of medium size with plants and twigs and a water tank. The optimum temperature is between 22 and 27 °C (71–80 °F). The Marsu-

Rohde's Tree Frog (*Phyllomedusa rohdei*)

pial Frog grows up to 6 cm (2.3 in) long, and is given insects, worms, molluscs and other small animal food. After mating, the female carries the fertilised eggs in a subcutaneous sac on her back, where they develop for two or three weeks. When the tadpoles reach a certain stage of development, the female opens the hole of the sac and releases the offspring into water where they finish their development and metamorphose.

The **Red-eyed Tree Frog** (*Agalychnis callidryas*), up to 7 cm (2.75 in) long, is native to the wet tropical forests of Central America, and does well in a large tropical aquaterrarium with plenty of plants, including large-leaved species. The temperature in the terrarium should range between 24 and 28 °C (75–82 °F), and humidity should be between 80 and 90 per cent. In captivity the Red-eyed Tree Frog will feed on large insects. In the breeding season the female lays eggs between the leaves of plants above the water surface. The tadpoles emerge after six to eight weeks and fall of the trees to finish their development in water.

Rohde's Tree Frog (*Phyllomedusa rohdei*) is a small species whose length does not exceed 4 cm (1.5 in). It is distributed in the tropical forests of Brazil and Paraguay. In captivity it will be content with a small tropical aquaterrarium with plants and a small water tank where the temperature is main-

tained between 22 and 28 °C (71–82 °F). Rohde's Tree Frog feeds on small insects and other invertebrates. The female lays her eggs between two or three leaves stuck together above the water surface. When the tadpoles hatch they fall off into the water where they later undergo their metamorphosis.

European Green Tree Frog (*Bufo viridis*)

The **European Green Toad** (*Bufo viridis*) is well-known everywhere in Europe except the Iberian Peninsula, Great Britain and northern Scandinavia. It also lives in North Africa and in Asia as far north as Mongolia. Its habitat spreads from lowlands to high altitudes, for example up to 4,500 m (14,500 ft) above sea level in the Himalayas. This toad, up to 10 cm (4 in) long, can be kept in both indoor and outdoor terrariums. It requires numerous hiding places. The substrate may comprise a mixture of sand and peat. There should be a smaller tank of water in the terrarium

Red-eyed Tree Frog (*Agalychnis callidryas*)

and the temperature should be maintained between 18 and 24 °C (64–75 °F). In captivity the Green Toad readily feeds on insects, worms, molluscs and other food of animal origin. Mating takes place in spring and the female lays a string of eggs 2–5 m (6.5–16 ft) long. The tadpoles usually hatch within a week and finish their metamorphosis in one to three months.

The **Giant Toad** (*Bufo marinus*), growing to a length of 24 cm (9.5 in), is distributed from the southern states of the USA to tropical South America. It has also been introduced in Florida and in some Caribbean and Pacific islands. Its habitat is tropical forests, so in captivity it should be kept at a temperature of 22–28 °C (71–82 °F) in a large tropical terrarium with numerous hiding places, vegetation and a small tank of water.

Its diet should consist of large insects (crickets, cockroaches), earthworms and small vertebrates. The Giant Toad mates in April and May. The female lays 3,000–10,000 eggs. The tadpoles that hatch from the eggs will metamorphose in 50–60 days. The secretions produced by the large parotid glands of these toads are poisonous so the keeper must wash his hands with soap and water every time they are touched.

The **Cuban Toad** (*Peltaphryne peltocephala*), from the damp regions of Cuba, grows up to 20 cm (8 in) long. It can be kept in a terrarium with shelters and a small water tank. The bottom should be covered with a mixture of peat and sand. The temperature in the terrarium should be 22–28 °C (71–82 °F). The toads are fed with large insects, worms and molluscs. In spring the female lays strings of

Giant Toad (*Bufo marinus*)

several thousand eggs. The hatched tadpoles will change into small toads in about two months.

When large toads are handled it is advisable to wear rubber gloves. These toads have large glands called parotisa on both sides of their heads. When the toads are touched these glands release a secretion that irritates the mucous membranes.

Cuban Toad (*Peltaphryne peltocephala*)

Turtles and Tortoises (order Chelonia)

The characteristic feature of the order Chelonia is their armour, consisting of two parts. The dorsal (top) part is called the carapace and the ventral (bottom) part is called the plastron. The carapace and plastron are either fused at the sides or are connected by fibrous tissue. There is an opening for the head and the pectoral (front) limbs in the front and another opening for the pelvic (hind) limbs and

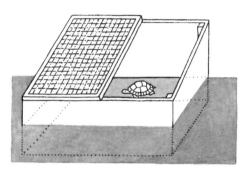

Outdoor terrarium for dry land turtles

tail at the back. The jaws of turtles and tortoises are toothless and horny, like the beak of birds. Most of them have feet with five toes used either for digging (in dry-land species) or for swimming (the water species). The feet of the water species have a web between the toes

and the feet of the marine species look like oars.

Most of the Chelonia are peace-loving. In a world full of predators they practise passive defence; most turtles and tortoises can hide their head, feet and tail between their carapace and plastron and then close the openings with their feet, armoured with hard scales. Some species can even move the fore and hind parts of the plastron, thus firmly closing up their armour.

The Chelonia require both vegetable and animal food sources in their diet. The dry-land species feed largely on vegetable food, whereas those living in water prefer food of animal origin. All reproduce by laying eggs, which the female always lay in sand, humus or other such material on dry land. Turtles and tortoises live for a long time. It is very probable that the Aldabra Tortoise (*Geochleone gigantea*), native to the Seychelles, can reach an age of 200 years.

Today there are about 220 species of Chelonia in existence. The **Common Snapping Turtle** (*Chelydra serpentina*) lives in stagnant and flowing waters from the southern regions of Canada through the eastern parts of the USA and Central America to the northern part of South America. It grows

Common Snapping Turtle (*Chelydra serpentina*) catching its prey

to a length of about 40 cm (16 in) and reaches a weight of about 20 kg (44 lb), sometimes more. It is kept in a large aquarium or aquaterrarium with a small dry area. The optimum temperature for this turtle is between 20 and 28 °C (68–82 °F). The Snapping Turtle deserves its name because in both its natural habitat and in captivity it snaps at any intruder and the keeper must be very careful when handling it. The Snapping Turtles often attack one another, so it is recommended that you keep them in isolation. Their mating season is from May to November. The female lays 10–50 eggs on dry land and the embryos develop inside the eggs for 60–130 days. Like the females of many other turtles, the female Snapping Turtle carries the male's sperm in her spermatothecae, so she does not need a male for the repeated laying of fertilized eggs.

The **Alligator Snapping Turtle**

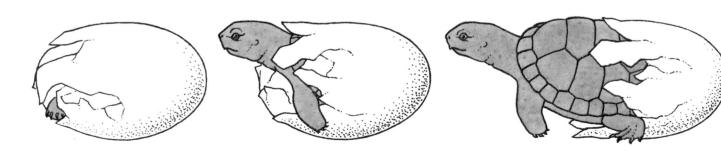

Hatching turtle

(*Macroclemys temmincki*), inhabiting the stagnant and slow-flowing waters of the southeastern regions of the USA, grows up to 60 cm (24 in) long (the carapace) and can be kept in a large aquarium or aquaterrarium with a small dry area. The temperature should be maintained at between 22 and 28 °C (71–82 °F). The Alligator Snapping Turtle feeds on various water animals, mainly fish. It has a worm-like projection on its tongue which it uses to lure fish. It moves this special bait around in its open mouth while lying still on the bottom and when an unwary fish gets too close to its mouth, it sucks it in with the flow of water and the beak-like jaws catch the prey. This may also happen in captivity if the turtle is given live food. Besides fish, the turtle may occasionally take pieces of lean beef, fillets of fish and other similar foodstuff. The Alligator Snapping Turtle mates from February to April. The fe-

Red-eared Turtle (*Chrysemys scripta elegans*)

35 cm (10–14 in) long, with striking colouring. It is distributed from the USA down to the northern areas of South America where it inhabits stagnant and slow-flowing waters. The colouring of the young is particu-

waters from southern Canada to Florida and southeast Texas. In the aquaterrarium it requires a temperature of 20–26 °C (68–79 °F). It feeds on large insects,

larly striking. The Red-eared Turtle needs a temperature of 20–28 °C (68–82 °F) and is kept in a large aquaterrarium; it can also be kept in a pool inside

male lays 10–55 eggs in June. The young hatch 80–120 days later.
The **Common Musk Turtle** (*Sternotherus odoratus*) inhabits stagnant and slow-moving

Alligator Snapping Turtle (*Macroclemys temmincki*)

Common Musk Turtle (*Sternotherus odoratus*)

worms and small fish. The Common Musk Turtle is small, growing no longer than 14 cm (5.5 in). The female lays two eggs several times a year and the young hatch within 110–115 days.
The **Red-eared Turtle** (*Chrysemys scripta elegans*) is 25–

a greenhouse in winter and in a garden pool or garden aquaterrarium in summer. The young need higher temperatures than the adult turtles. They are fed on various aquatic invertebrates, fish, pieces of beef and the like and the diet must be enriched

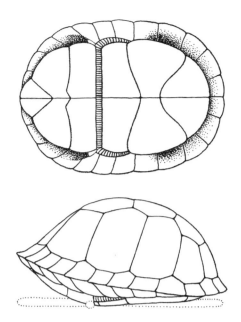

When it feels danger, the turtle *Terrapene carolina* can close its carapace with part of its movable plastron.

Common Box Turtle (*Tarrapene carolina*)

on dry land near expanses of water. It is kept at a temperature of 20–28 °C (68–82 °F) in a terrarium with a small water tank. The Common Box Turtle feeds on both animal and vegetable food and will even enjoy eating mushrooms and forest fruits. There are credible reports that this turtle, up to 20 cm (8 in) long, may reach an age of 100 years. In June, the female lays four to six eggs and buries them underground. The young hatch in September and October. Some eggs may overwinter underground, however, and the young will emerge the following spring.

The **Black-breasted Leaf Turtle** (*Geomyda spengleri*), from southeast Asia, lives near forest brooks, although it spends most of its time on dry land. It is kept in an aquaterrarium at a temperature of 20–28 °C (68–82 °F). Water should occupy about one-third of the area of the aquaterrarium. The Black-breasted Leaf Turtle, growing to a length of 14 cm (5.5 in), feeds

with minerals and vitamins. The mating season of the Red-eared Turtle is April and May. The females lay 2–30 eggs and bury them in the substrate. The young hatch after about two and a half months. The Red-eared Turtle can live up to 25 years in captivity.

The **Common Box Turtle** (*Terrapene carolina*). Popular among keepers, this turtle is found from southern Canada to the southwestern USA. It lives

Black-breasted Leaf Turtle (*Geomyda spengleri*)

on worms, molluscs, fish and pieces of beef. Vitamins and minerals should be added to the diet.

The **Indian Roofed Turtle** (*Kachuga tecta*), from India and Pakistan, has a carapace up to 20 cm (8 in) long and lives near stagnant and slow-flowing waters. The aquaterrarium where it is kept must have clear

Malayan Box Turtle (*Cuora amboinensis*)

Indian Roofed Turtle (*Kachuga tecta*)

hibernation it is kept in a small box, filled with a 25 cm (10 in) layer of peat, leaves and sand in which the tortoise will bury itself. The ideal temperature for its

Stripe-necked Terrapin (*Clemmys caspica rivulata*)

water at 24–28 °C (75–82 °F). Bacterial diseases often affect the carapace of this turtle, so clean water and a clean aquaterrarium are essential. The turtle will take food of both vegetable and animal origin, including lettuce, clover, cabbage, slices of apple, tomatoes, crickets, larvae of meal beetles, earthworms, slugs and pieces of beef.

The **Malayan Box Turtle** (*Cuora amboinensis*) is native to Indo-China, the Sunda Islands and the Philippines. It is kept in a large aquaterrarium at a temperature of 22–30 °C (71–86 °F) and takes both animal and vegetable food. The maximum length of these turtles is 20 cm (8 in). The mating season is from March to May. After about two months the females lay eggs on dry land and the young turtles hatch from the eggs in 70–90 days.

The **European Swamp Turtle** (*Emys orbicularis*), up to 25 cm (10 in) long, is distributed in southern and central Europe, southeast Asia and northwest Africa. Stagnant and slow-flowing waters are its typical home; the turtles often creep out of the water to bask in the sun. In captivity it requires a large aquaterrarium where the temperature should be maintained between 20 and 27 °C (68–80 °F). In

summer these creatures do well in a garden run with a pool. They should be fed on various invertebrates, such as worms and slugs, but will also eat fish and pieces of beef. The mating season is between April and June. The female buries 3–15 eggs in dry land. The young hatch from the eggs in eight to ten weeks. Another European water species, the **Stripe-necked Terrapin** (*Clemmys caspica rivulata*), which is native to southeast Europe, is kept in a similar way. Both hibernate in clean water at a temperature of 4–7 °C (39–45 °F).

The **Mediterranean Spurthighed Tortoise** (*Testudo graeca*) is a dry-land species, native to southern Europe, southwest Asia and north Africa where it lives in the forest steppes and semidesert areas. It grows to a length of about 30 cm (12 in). It is omnivorous and takes the leaves of various herbs, fruits and vegetables, as well as minced meat, cottage cheese, slugs and worms. Vitamins and minerals must be administered regularly to both young and adults. The Spurthighed Tortoise is kept in a terrarium at a temperature of 22–30 °C (71–86 °F) and in summer it can be left in a garden run. If the tortoise is to reproduce, it must hibernate adequately. In

winter rest is 2–5 °C (35–41 °F). Mating takes place early in spring soon after hibernation. The female then lays 8–15 eggs with a calcareous shell and buries them underground. The young will hatch after 60–110 days.

Hermann's Tortoise (*Testudo hermanii*) is native to the Balkan Peninsula, Italy, Sicily, Sardinia and Corsica, southern France, the Balearic Islands and southeastern Spain. It lives in forests and in steppe and semidesert regions. In captivity it requires the same conditions as the Mediterranean Spurthighed Tortoise: a large terrarium with a dish of water for drinking and a temperature of 22–30 °C (71–86 °F). In summer it can be left outdoors in the garden. It feeds on the leaves of herbs, fruits, vegetables, cottage cheese, minced meat and other foodstuffs. Mating takes place in spring after hibernation and the female lays two to ten eggs from which the young hatch after 60–100 days.

The **Marginated Tortoise** (*Testudo marginata*) from Greece, Sardinia and Sicily (where it was introduced and domesticated) has the same requirements as the two preceding species and its biology is also the same.

The **Spiny Soft-shelled Turtle** (*Trionyx spiniferus*) inhabits stagnant and slow-flowing waters over a vast area from the south of Canada down to north Mexico. It is kept in an aquaterrarium in water at 22–28 °C (71–82 °F). It grows up to 35 cm (14 in). It spends its life in water and goes on to dry land mainly in the breeding season. In the aquaterrarium it will take insects, crustaceans, slugs, fish, pieces of meat and pieces of fish fillet. Larger specimens may bite the keeper, so they must be handled with care. In the dry part of the aquaterrarium, the female lays one to three sets of eggs (5–30 eggs in each set) in spring to August. The young emerge from the eggs after two to three months.

The **Mata-mata** (*Chelus fimbriata*) has its habitat in the stagnant and slow-flowing waters of South America from Peru through Venezuela and Surinam to central Brazil. It grows up to 40 cm (16 in) long, so it must have a large aquarium or aquaterrarium with a small dry area. The water should be heated to 24–30 °C (75–86 °F) and there must be enough water to allow the Mata-mata to sit on the bottom and reach the water surface easily with its mouth. The food

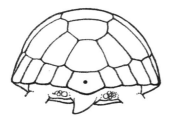

Comparison of Hermann's Tortoise with the Mediterranean Spur-thighed Tortoise

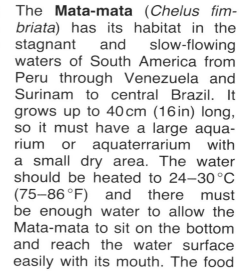

Mediterranean Spur-thighed Tortoise
(*Testudo graeca*)

Hermann's Tortoise (*Testudo hermanni*)

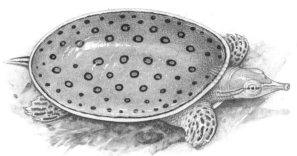

The Spiny Soft-shelled Turtle (*Trionyx spiniferus*)

given to the adult Mata-mata
should include insects, worms,
molluscs and the like. The
Mata-mata must be handled
with care because it is liable to
bite the keeper. Its head is carried on a long neck, allowing
Mata-mata to reach as far as
the rear end of its carapace.
The incubation time of the eggs
is about seven months.
The **Snake-necked Turtle**
(*Chelodina longicollis*), native to
the eastern regions of Australia,
grows to 15–25 cm (6–10 in)
long. It is kept in an aquater-

Snake-necked Turtle (*Chelodina longicollis*)

rarium at a temperature of 24–
30 °C (75–86 °F), with a small
dry area. This turtle feeds on
fish, worms, molluscs, pieces of
fish fillet or beef and other food
of animal origin. The young
hatch from the eggs in 85–114
days.

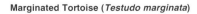

Marginated Tortoise (*Testudo marginata*)

141

Crocodiles (order Crocodilia)

Twenty-one species of crocodile live in the warm areas of Africa, Asia, America and Australia. Their habitat is water. They have a huge tail with flat sides, which propels them along when they swim. Their legs are held close to the body. They only crawl out of the water when

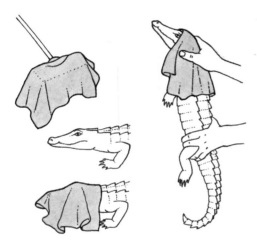

Handling a crocodile

they need to bask in the sun or lay their eggs, but they never go far and will quickly return to the water if they are frightened.

The bulging eyes and protruding nostrils are the most noticeable features on the head of any of the crocodiles. This allows them to breathe easily in the water and watch out for prey.

All crocodiles reproduce by means of eggs. The eggs have hard calcareous shells and the females lay them on dry land. In some species the parents take care of their young: first the female builds a large heap of leaves, grass, twigs and earth and lays the eggs in it; then she protects the eggs during the development of the embryos. Two to three months later the young begin to emerge, while the parents help them to claw through the upper part of the nest. In some cases the parents even carry their newborn young in their mouth from the nest to water.

Crocodiles are meat eaters. The adults feed on fish, birds and smaller mammals; the young eat insects, molluscs, amphibians and small fish.

At the end of the last century and early in the twentieth century, tens of thousands of crocodiles were hunted and killed, so today almost all types are on the list of endangered species.

There are highly exaggerated reports concerning the age and size of crocodiles. The greatest age so far documented is for one American alligator that reached the age of 85 years in captivity. The longest crocodile ever shot was 7.5 m (24.5 ft) long, but older records suggest that the Nile crocodile grew to be as long as 10 m (33 ft).

Naturally, these large reptiles can only be kept by an experienced keeper who can provide the correct conditions for them.

The **American Alligator** (*Alligator mississippiensis*) inhabits the fresh and brackish waters of the southeastern regions of the USA from Texas to South Carolina and Florida. This large reptile, and, in fact, any other crocodile, can only be kept by those who have a greenhouse with a run and a water reservoir of adequate size. The optimum temperature required by this alligator is 22–30 °C (71–86 °F). Adult alligators are fed on fish, birds and small mammals, the young will take insects, molluscs, small fish and pieces of fish fillet or meat enriched with minerals and vitamins. Adult specimens grow up to 6 m (19.5 ft) long. Their mating season is in April. The female builds a heap of leaves, twigs, grass and earth up to 1 m (3 ft) high in which she lays 20–60 eggs. The young alligators hatch after about three months.

The **Spectacled Caiman** (*Caiman crocodylus*), from the wetlands and slow-flowing waters in the basins of the Orinoco and the Amazon in South America, and from some areas of Central America, grows to a length of about 2 m (6.5 ft). It can be kept in a large aquaterrarium at a temperature of 24–30 °C (75–86 °F). It feeds mainly on fish but will also chase small mammals and birds. Young Caimans should be given insects, molluscs, small fish and pieces of meat. Minerals and vitamins must be added to their food.

Spectacled Caiman (*Caiman crocodylus*)

Nile Crocodile (*Crocodylus niloticus*)

The female lays 14–30 eggs in a heap of plant debris and the young emerge after 75–105 days.

The **Nile Crocodile** (*Crocodylus niloticus*), an African species also found in Madagascar, the Seychelles and the Comoro Islands, is an inhabitant of rivers, lakes and marshes. Its length is up to 7 m (23 ft). Like the alligator, it can do well in captivity if it has enough room and a large pool in the greenhouse where it is kept at a temperature of 22–30 °C (71–86 °F). The food it takes is the same as that given to the alligator. The female buries her eggs in sand near water in places well heated by the sun. There may be 15–100 eggs in each set buried. The young emerge after about two months. Incubators are used for hatching all crocodiles in captivity.

American Alligator (*Alligator mississippiensis*)

Lizards (sub-order Lacertilia)

Lizards, the largest group of reptiles, comprise 3,000 species of small and large animals. Most of them live in tropical and subtropical areas; few inhabit the temperate zones, although there are several species whose

Common Gecko – view from below

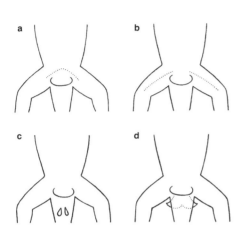

Types of sexual dimorphism: a) preanal pores; b) femoral pores; c) pair of group of larger scales in front of the cloaca; d) swellings under the cloaca. These traits are absent or suppressed in the females.

distribution reaches to the Arctic Circle. They can be found in various surroundings: on the ground, underground, in water, in tree tops, in deserts and semideserts, in savannas and in wet tropical forests.

Many lizards have a cartilaginous plate in the caudal vertebrae at the end of the body, at which point their tail easily breaks off. This is an important feature of passive defence: the predator chasing the lizards often captures the tail but the rest of the prey escapes. The lost tail will grow again, but the caudal part of the spine is now replaced by a tough tissue.

Most lizards reproduce by laying soft, leathery eggs; only the eggs of the geckos have a hard shell. Some species are ovoviviparous, which means that the embryo develops in an egg that remains in the female's body. True viviparity is rare among lizards (it does occur among some Australian skinks).

Lizard species range in size from some centimetres long to animals growing to a length of about 3 m (10 ft). Their diet includes food of both vegetable and animal origin. Some species are vegetarians, others are carnivores, while yet others eat everything. The lizards that live in the temperate climatic zones fall into a state of lethargy in the winter season; the length of this winter sleep depends on the actual conditions in which the animals live.

With three exceptions, lizards are not venomous. These are two species of the family of venomous lizards (Helodermatidae) and one species of the family of earless lizards (Lanthanotidae). The bite of these lizards produces a toxic reaction similar to that caused by venomous snakes.

The **Leopard Gecko** (*Eublepharis macularius*) is a popular terrarium animal. It is up to 25 cm (10 in) long and lives in India, Afghanistan, Iran and Iraq

Common Gecko (*Tarentola mauretanica*)

where it inhabits stony, semi-desert areas with sparse vegetation. It is kept in a half-dry terrarium, with plenty of hiding places, at a temperature of 22—30 °C (71—86 °F). Insects are the main ingredient of its diet, although it will also take a piece of fruit from time to time. The female lays two eggs with a leathery skin and buries them in the substrata. Laying takes place several times a year. The incubation time of the eggs is 60—80

calcium which should be given to them in their food. Two eggs are laid several times a year, and the female hides them in various holes or buries them

Ashy Gecko (*Sphaerodactylus cinereus*) — adult and young one

Leopard Gecko (*Eublepharis macularius*) — adult and young one

days. The size of the newly hatched young is about 7 cm (2.75 in).

The **Common Gecko** (*Tarentola mauretanica*) is distributed in the Mediterranean countries where it lives in dry semidesert areas. Its length is up to 15 cm (6 in). In captivity the Common Gecko requires a half-dry terrarium with a back wall built from stones or bark. The optimum temperature for this species is between 22 and 30 °C (71—86 °F). The main ingredient of its diet is insects; in the terrarium it can be given crickets, as well as insects collected by dragging. When the females lay their eggs they need additional

Flying Gecko (*Ptychozoon kuhli*) — ventral view

people's houses. In captivity it requires a small terrarium with tree branches and creeping plants. The temperature should

underground. Then the young emerge from the eggs after 100 days, sometimes later.

The **Ashy Gecko** (*Sphaerodactylus cinereus*) is a native of the Antilles and was also introduced in Florida where it has acclimatised. It is small — no longer than 5 cm (2 in). It lives on the trunks of trees, on rocks and in

Flying Gecko (*Ptychozoon kuhli*)

be maintained at between 22 and 28 °C (71–82 °F). The Ashy Gecko feeds on small insects. The female lays one egg five times a year. The incubation time of the egg is about 90 days. The **Flying Gecko** (*Ptychozoon kuhli*) inhabits the tropical forests of the Malay Peninsula, Sumatra, Kalimantan and Java. It grows up to 20 cm (8 in) long. It has lobes of skin on the sides of its head and on its flanks, and wide webs on its tail. It uses these like a parachute to glide long distances from one tree to another. It is kept at a temperature of 24–30 °C (75–86 °F) in a wet terrarium of medium size with many tree branches and plants. Its diet consists of large insects (crickets and the like). The female lays eggs on the bark of the tree. A net must be spread over the eggs on the bark and the newly hatched young must be removed immediately, to prevent the parents from consuming their own eggs or young. The embryos develop in the eggs for ten weeks before they emerge as young geckos.

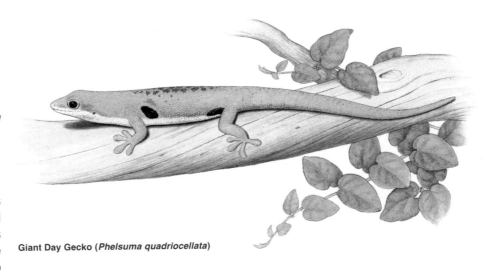

Giant Day Gecko (*Phelsuma quadriocellata*)

be kept must be large and its back wall must be lined with bark. The temperature should range between 22 and 30 °C (71–86 °F). The Tokay feeds on large insects and small vertebrates. It is recommended that they are kept in pairs. The female lays two eggs with a calcareous shell every 20–30 days during the warm season, and sticks them onto the walls of the terrarium. The young emerge after 120 days.

and trees. In captivity it requires a large terrarium with branches of small trees and other plants, and the temperature should be maintained at 24–30 °C (75–86 °F). The Madagascar Gecko feeds on insects and soft sweet fruit. Only one pair can be kept in a terrarium, because geckos of this species are quarrelsome and will attack one another. The female sticks two eggs on to the tree bark and the young hatch from these eggs after 60–80 days.

The **Giant Day Gecko** (*Phelsuma quadriocellata*), which inhabits shrubs and trees in Madagascar, grows to a length of 10–12 cm (4–4.8 in). It is kept in a large terrarium decorated with branches and plants on which the creature can climb. The optimum temperature in the terrarium is between 24 and 30 °C (75–86 °F) and ideal humidity is between 60 and 80 per cent. Like the other *Phelsuma* species, it feeds on insects and soft sweet fruits; once or twice a week it should be given a mash of cottage cheese, eggs and sugar with added mashed banana or pineapple. This gecko must also be kept in separate pairs. Mating takes place several times a year and will produce two to three fertilized sets of

Madagascar Gecko (*Phelsuma madagascariensis*)

The **Tokay** (*Gekko gecko*), from southwest Asia, is one of the largest Geckos: it may be up to 35 cm (14 in) long. It lives on trees, on rocks and in the vicinity of human dwellings. The terrarium in which the Tokay is to

The **Madagascar Gecko** (*Phelsuma madagascariensis*) grows to a length of 25 cm (10 in) and is among the most popular terrarium lizards. Its homeland is in Madagascar and the Seychelles where it lives in shrubs

eggs. The female sticks the eggs in twos on tree bark or onto plants and the young emerge from the eggs after 50–70 days. **Phelsuma lineata** is another native of Madagascar, where it

Tokay (*Gekko gecko*)

Turkestan Plate-tailed Gecko (*Teratoscincus scincus*)

Asia and western China. Its size is up to 20 cm (8 in). It requires a dry terrarium with a 10–20 cm (4–8 in) layer of fine sand in which it likes to bury itself. The

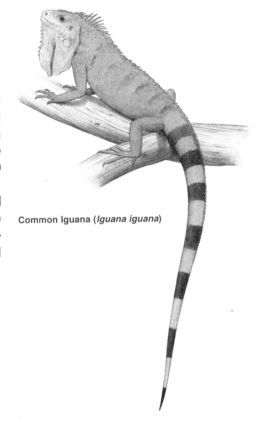

Common Iguana (*Iguana iguana*)

lives in trees and shrubs. It is kept in pairs in a tropical terrarium with tree branches and plants, at a temperature of 24–30 °C (75–86 °F). Its diet consists of crickets and other insects and soft, juicy fruits. The adults, up to 12 cm long, mate several times a year. The female lays one to two eggs and sticks them on various objects in the terrarium. In spring and summer the interval between layings is 20–30 days. The young emerge after 50–80 days.

The **Turkestan Plate-tailed Gecko** (*Teratoscincus scincus*) is found in the desert and semi-desert regions of Iran, central

Phelsuma lineata

temperature should be maintained at between 25 and 33 °C (77–91 °F). This popular gecko

147

is fed on insects, spiders and other small invertebrates. Mating takes place in April and May. The female produces two to

Male Anoles send optical signals from their necks to defend their territories.

three eggs in several layings and buries them in sand. The young geckos hatch after 40–60 days.

The **Common Iguana** (*Iguana iguana*), up to 2 m (6.5 ft) long, is a species of the Iguanidae family and is distributed in Central and South America. Its homeland is in tropical forests where it often lives close to water. It is kept in a large terrarium with thick branches and plants, and a shallow pool. The optimum temperature ranges between 24 and 32 °C (75–90 °F). The adults are more or less herbivorous and are given fruits, vegetables and leaves of herbs, but also curd cheese, eggs and some beef. The young prefer insects and eat very little vegetable food. Minerals and vitamins must be added to their diet and the terrarium should be sprayed every day. The female lays and buries 25–70 eggs, the incubation time of which is 70–90 days.

The **Cayman Islands Ground Iguana** (*Cyclura nubila*) inhabits rocky sites overgrown with trees and shrubs in Cuba and other islands in the Caribbean. It grows to about 1.5 m (5 ft) long and requires a large terrarium with hiding places (caves and the like), heated to 25–30 °C (77–86 °F). It is fed on vegetables, fruit, curd cheese, boiled eggs, insects, small vertebrates and similar food. The Cayman Islands Ground Iguana is very choosy about food and will not accept the same food for long. Mating takes place in spring and the females lay 6–30 eggs, usually in May. The young emerge in August and September.

The **Green Anole** (*Anolis carolinensis*), native to the southeastern regions of the USA and the Bahamas, is up to 22 cm (8.5 in) long and lives in trees, rocks and even inside people's homes. It can be kept in a large terrarium decorated with plants and branches at a temperature of 24–30 °C (75–86 °F). One terrarium may be stocked either with a pair of Green Anoles or with a male and several females. They feed on various insects. The female lays one egg with a leathery shell at fortnightly intervals from spring to autumn and the young hatch from the eggs after 50–70 days.

The **Knight Anole** (*Anolis equestris*) comes from Cuba where it mostly lives in trees. It grows to a length of about 55 cm (22 in) and requires a large terrarium with plants and tree branches, heated to 24–30 °C (75–86 °F). It feeds on insects but will also take small vertebrates. The males guard their territory by puffing out their strikingly coloured throats and nodding their heads. The Knight Anole should be kept in pairs. The female usu-

Plumed Basilisk (*Basiliscus plumifrons*)

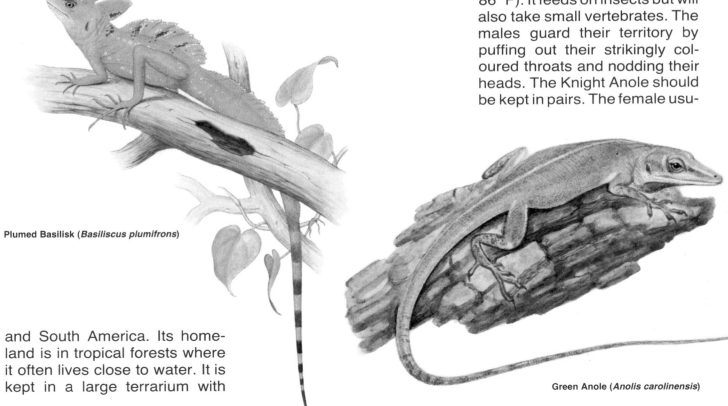

Green Anole (*Anolis carolinensis*)

Cayman Islands Ground Iguana (*Cyclura nubila*)

eggs underground. The young emerge from the eggs after two to three months. Diet is based on small insects to which calcium, minerals and vitamins must be added regularly.

The **Plumed Basilisk** (*Basiliscus plumifrons*) is distributed in tropical forests from Nicaragua to Panama, where it lives near water. As these creatures may be up to 85 cm (33 in) long, they

ally lays two eggs several times a year. The incubation time of the eggs is 60–70 days.

The **Curly-tailed Lizard** (*Leiocephalus carniatus*) is an inhabitant of dry, rocky places in Cuba and the Bahamas. In captivity it does well at a temperature of 24–30 °C (75–86 °F) in a semi-arid terrarium with large rocks. The Curly-tailed Lizard feeds on large insects, fruit, vegetables, curd cheese and similar food. It grows up to 30 cm (12 in) long and often lives in colonies where the lizards communicate by nodding their heads and curling their tails into a spi-

Agama (*Stellio stellio*)

Curly-tailed Lizard (*Leiocephalus carniatus*)

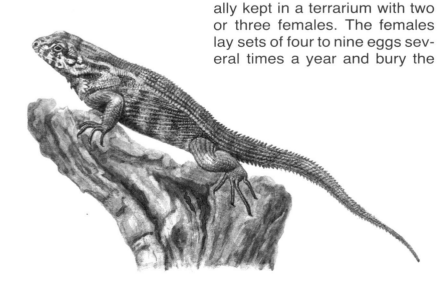

ral. In captivity one male is usually kept in a terrarium with two or three females. The females lay sets of four to nine eggs several times a year and bury the

need a large tropical terrarium with tree branches and plants and a shallow pool if possible. Pairs of basilisks should be kept at a temperature of 24–30 °C (75–86 °F) and fed with large insects, small vertebrates and fruit. Daily spraying is essential. The female lays 5–12 eggs several times a year and buries each set of eggs. About 60–80 days later the young emerge from the eggs.

The **Agama** (*Stellio stellio*), a lizard up to 35 cm (14 in) long, lives in stony places overgrown with shrubs in southwest Asia,

Agama sanguinolenta

northeast Africa and on some islands in the Aegean Sea. It requires a large semi-arid terrarium with large rocks and a temperature of 22–33 °C (71–91 °F). Its diet includes insects, flowers (e.g. dandelion) and soft fruit. Although the Agamas live in large communities in their natural habitats, it is recommended that you keep them either in pairs or that you stock the aquarium with one male and two or three females. Mating takes place in spring and the females lay 6–12 eggs on sand under a rock. The young hatch from August to October.

Agama sanguinolenta, growing to a length of about 30 cm (12 in), inhabits the stony semi-deserts and deserts of central Asia, Mongolia, Iran and Afghanistan. It is kept at a temperature of 24–33 °C (75–91 °F) in a large semi-arid terrarium decorated with large rocks. Its diet consists of insects and the juicy parts of plants. In April the female buries 5–14 eggs in sand and does the same again late in May. The young hatch after 50–60 days.

The **Toad-headed Agama** (*Phrynocephalus mystaceus*), from the sandy deserts of central Asia, Iran and Afghanistan, is at most 25 cm (10 in) long. It thrives in a small terrarium with a thick layer of dry sand where it is kept at a temperature of 25–35 °C (77–95 °F). The Toad-headed Agama feeds on insects and sometimes also on flowers. The female usually lays two to six eggs twice a year and the incubation period of the eggs is 60–80 days.

The **Oriental Water Dragon** (*Physignathus coccinus*) is up to 80 cm (31 in) long and lives on banks and around trees near water in southeast Asia. In captivity it needs a large aquaterrarium with branches and a large pool with the temperature between 24 and 30 °C (75–86 °F). It feeds on insects, small vertebrates, fruit and flowers. Water Dragons are kept either in pairs or in groups of one male and two or three females. The females lay eggs several times a year and the young hatch after two to three months.

The **African Spiny-tailed Lizard** (*Uromastyx acanthinurus*)

African Spiny-tailed Lizard (*Uromastyx acanthinurus*)

is a robust lizard up to 60 cm (24 in) long, living in the stony deserts and semideserts of north Africa. Its terrarium should be dry and should have numerous hiding places under stones. The temperature in the terrarium should be maintained at between 25 and 53 °C (77–127 °F). For the two coldest months of the year, however, it

Toad-headed Agama (*Phrynocephalus mystaceus*)

Schneider's Skink (*Eumeces schneideri*)

is recommended that you reduce the temperature to about 20 °C (68 °F). The Spiny-tailed Lizard is fed on insects, fruit and flowers. Although it lives a solitary life under natural conditions, several specimens can be kept in a group in captivity, because the Spiny-tailed Lizard is a peaceable species. The fe-

Common Chameleon (*Chamaeleo chamaeleon*)

Oriental Water Dragon (*Physignathus coccinus*)

male lays 4–20 eggs with a leathery skin and buries them in sand. Unfortunately, this lizard seldom reproduces in captivity. The **Garden Lizard** (*Calotes versicolor*), a lizard up to 45 cm (18 in) long, lives on rocks and in shrubs and trees, often very close to human dwellings, and is distributed over vast areas of southeast Asia. It is kept in a large terrarium with branches and plants, at a temperature between 24 and 30 °C (75–86 °F). In captivity it takes insects, fruit, sweetened curd cheese mixed with eggs, crisp leaves and flowers. About a month after mating the female lays 10–20 eggs and the young will hatch 60–70 days later. The **Common Chameleon** (*Chamaeleo chamaeleon*), the only chameleon found in Europe, lives on shrubs and in tree tops in the southernmost areas of the continent: in Spain, Portugal, Crete and Cyprus. Outside Europe it is distributed in the Canary Islands, north Africa, the Arabian Peninsula, India and Sri Lanka. It does well in a larger terrarium with good ventilation and with plants and tree branches. In summer the chameleon can also be housed in an outdoor terrarium. The temperature in the terrarium should be kept between 24 and 30 °C (75–86 °F). The chameleons are fed with insects collected by dragging: crickets, larvae of meal beetles and other small live food. Light spraying is recommended once or twice daily. Chameleons are best kept in isolation; if a pair or a group is kept, the terrarium must be furnished with as many heat sources as there are animals. It is even better to provide them with a few extra shelters. The females lay and bury 20–25 eggs, each with a leathery skin, and

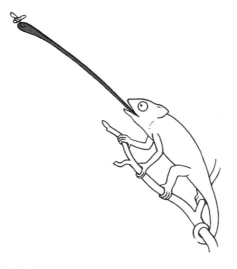

A Chameleon catching its prey

the young hatch after 70–80 days. The Common Chameleon grows to a length of about 30 cm (12 in).

Jackson's Chameleon (*Chamaeleo jacksoni*) is up to 30 cm (12 in) long, and is an inhabitant of the tropical forests of east Africa. It is kept in larger terrariums with plenty of branches and plants at a temperature of 25–30 °C (77–86 °F). Its diet is based on insects and small vertebrates (small mice and the like). The terrarium should be sprayed several times every day. Jackson's Chameleon is

an ovoviviparous species: the female bears 8–24 young.

The **Dwarf Chameleon** (*Chamaeleo pumilus*) is small, its length being only 8–11 cm (3–4.5 in). It is usually found in shrubs and tree tops in south Africa. Like other chameleons it needs a terrarium with plants and twigs heated to a temperature of 25–30 °C (77–86 °F). This little chameleon feeds on small insects. The female is ovoviviparous, bearing up to 14 offspring.

The **Ocellated Skink** (*Chalcides ocellatus*) grows up to 30 cm (12 in) long, living in dry, stony places with sparse trees and shrubs in north Africa, western Asia, Sardinia, Sicily, southern Italy and Greece and the adjacent islands. The terrarium in which the skink is to be kept should be dry and should have a thick layer of fine, washed sand on the bottom, plus some stones and logs or pieces of bark under which the creature could hide. A dish of drinking water must also be provided. The temperature in the terrarium should be maintained

at between 22 and 28 °C (71–82 °F). The Ocellated Skink can be kept in a group of one male and two to three females. They feed on insects, pieces of beef, soft fruit, curd cheese and the like. The female bears 4–15 offspring. The young often suffer from loss of calcium in their bones (rachitis), so their food must be enriched with calcium and other minerals, as well as vitamins.

Schneider's Skink (*Eumeces schneideri*) lives in forests, forest-steppes, stony semideserts and deserts in Central Asia, North Africa, Cyprus, Asia Minor and the northwestern regions of India. It grows to a length of 30 cm (12 in). In captivity it requires a dry terrarium with a thick layer of sand and stones, where the temperature is maintained at between 24 and 30 °C (75–86 °F). Its diet consists of insects and other invertebrates, and sometimes also pieces of sweet fruit. In summer the female lays 4–20 eggs and buries them in the sand. The young hatch within 60–70 days.

The **Blue-tongued Skink** (*Ti-*

Blue-tongued Skink (*Tiliqua scincoides*)

liqua scincoides), a member of the group of Australian skinks, grows to as long as 50 cm (20 in). Its homeland is in the sandy shrubby regions of Aus-

Dwarf Chameleon (*Chamaeleo pumilus*)

Ocellated Skink (*Chalcides ocellatus*)

tralia. To keep the Blue-tongued Skink successfully, the keeper must have a large dry terrarium containing a layer of sand and stones. The lizard will take both vegetable and animal food: insects, pieces of meat, boiled eggs, sponge biscuits, fruit and vegetables. It must be remembered that the lizards from Australia expect summer at a time when most of the other reptiles normally experience winter, and vice versa, so the temperature should be maintained between 25 and 35°C (77–95°F) from January to March and then, from April to June when it is cold in their homeland, the temperature should be reduced to 15–

Common Tegu (*Tupinambis tequixin*)

20°C (41–59°F). During their cold season the Australian lizards will take only a limited amount of food. Mating takes place late in October and the female bears two to four young in the latter half of February and in March.

Sungazer (*Cordylus giganteus*)

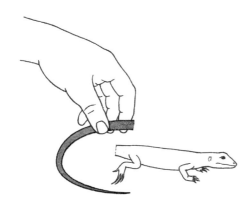

Some lizards, such as the genus *Lacerta*, have a plate of low-density bone tissue in the tail vertebrae whereby the tail easily breaks off. This is an important feature of passive defence: the predator will 'catch' the tail but the lizard is saved.

The **Sungazer** (*Cordylus giganteus*) is a robust lizard up to 40 cm (16 in) long, from south Africa where it inhabits dry savannas and sandy, rocky sites with sporadic shrubs and trees. It does well in a large terrarium with sand, stones and tree branches. Although it comes from arid regions, it drinks fairly frequently, so a dish of water is essential in the terrarium. The temperature in the terrarium should range between 25 and 35 °C (77−95 °F). The Sungazer feeds on large insects and small vertebrates. Plenty of minerals and vitamins should be added to the food in captivity. The female Sungazer bears two young, about 11 cm (4.5 in) long.

The **Common Tegu** (*Tupinambis tequixin*) is a large representative of the Tegu family and is distributed in the forest zone of the central area of South America. In its homeland it lives near water. In captivity it needs a temperature of 24−30 °C (75−86 °F) and is kept in a large terrarium with a shallow pool and thick logs. Its diet includes small vertebrates (mice) and insects, as well as fruit and vegetables. The Common Tegu is active during the day and loves basking in the sun. The female

buries 20−35 eggs in sand but keepers seldom rear the young successfully.

The **Glass Lizard** (*Ophisaurus apodus*) is a legless lizard, up to 140 cm (55 in) long, distributed from the Balkan Peninsula to Central Asia. It lives on dry hillsides, in forest-steppes and

Glass Lizard (*Ophisaurus apodus*)

steppes. The terrarium for the Glass Lizard should be large and dry and should afford suitable hiding places. The temperature in the terrarium should be between 22 and 30 °C (71−86 °F). The Glass Lizard feeds on insects, worms, molluscs and small vertebrates and will also take pieces of meat, boiled eggs and the like. In captivity it is a rewarding pet. The female lays 6−12 eggs in July and the

Dalmatian Algyroides (*Algyroides nigropunctatus*)

Sand Lizard (*Lacerta agilis*)

tributed from the southern regions of England and France throughout Europe as far as Asia and Lake Baikal; southwards it reaches the Pyrenees and the southwestern districts of Bulgaria. The Sand Lizard inhabits sunny places adjacent to forests and grassy, shrubby hillsides. Pairs of these lizards are kept in terrariums with various shelters and with a bowl of water from which the lizards can drink. In summer the temperature should be maintained between 22 and 28 °C (71–82 °F) but in winter the lizards should be kept in a cold place. From May to June the female lays one to two

young, light blue-grey with black cross stripes, hatch from the eggs six to seven weeks later.
The **Dalmatian Algyroides** (*Algyroides nigropunctatus*), up to 20 cm (8 in) long, lives on stone walls, in rocks and in the steppes and forest-steppes near the Adriatic coast of Dalmatia, Albania and Greece. It is kept in a dry terrarium with shelters of bark and stones where the temperature is maintained between 24 and 30 °C (75–86 °F). The food given to Algyroides should include insects, spiders and worms. The terrariums should be stocked with pairs of this lizard. It is recommended that you expose the terrarium to direct sunshine on sunny summer

Green Lizard (*Lacerta viridis*)

Eyed Lizard (*Lacerta lepida*)

days because the Dalmatian Algyroides loves basking in the sun. Mating takes place in April and the first two to three eggs are laid in the latter half of May. The first young will emerge from the eggs after mid-July.
The **Sand Lizard** (*Lacerta agilis*), up to 20 cm (8 in) long, is a common European lizard, dis-

155

sets of eggs which she buries underground or hides under stones. The young hatch after 45–70 days.

The **Green Lizard** (*Lacerta viridis*), only exceptionally growing longer than 40 cm (16 in), lives on stony hillsides overgrown with shrubs, in thin forests and in the vineyards and orchards of central and southern Europe and Asia Minor. In captivity it needs a large terrarium with hiding places and a bowl of water to drink from. The temperature in the terrarium should be 22–30 °C (71–86 °F) in summer. In the winter season it should be kept in a cool place at a temperature of 4–8 °C (39–46 °F). The Green Lizard feeds on insects and other invertebrates but will also greedily consume a piece of sweet fruit. Mating takes place in April and May and the female lays 5–20 eggs under stones or in hollows which she has dug. The young hatch after 50–90 days and are brown in colour, as distinct from the green adults.

The **Eyed Lizard** (*Lacerta lepida*), the largest lizard of the Lacertidae family, is up to 70 cm (28 in) long. It lives in the Iberian Peninsula, southern France, northwestern Italy and in Africa where it inhabits grassy and shrubby hillsides, forest margins, vineyards, large orchards and other such places. In captivity it requires a large semi-arid terrarium with logs, stones and numerous hiding places. The optimum summer temperature of 24–30 °C (75–86 °F) should be reduced for the winter. The lizards are fed on large insects, sweet fruit and small vertebrates. They are kept in pairs. The keeper must handle them with care to avoid painful bites. In spring the female lays 10–22 eggs in hollows in the ground or under stones and then buries

Desert Monitor (*Varanus griseus*)

them. The young hatch after about three months.

The **Common Wall Lizard** (*Podarcis muralis*), a slim lizard up to 22 cm (8.5 in) long, lives in the southernmost areas of Europe, from the Pyrenees along the Mediterranean coast to the Balkan peninsula; the northern boundary of its distribution runs through the Netherlands, Germany and the warmer parts of the Czech Republic and Slovakia. Its native environment includes dry and stony places with sporadic vegetation. The Common Wall Lizard does well in a dry terrarium with large stones, where the temperature is between 22 and 28 °C (71–82 °F) in summer. Its diet consists of insects and other invertebrates.

Varanus timorensis

Two to three times during the summer season the female lays 2–12 eggs and the young hatch after two to three months.

The **Mongolian Racerunner** (*Eremias argus*), a creature up to 20 cm (8 in) long, inhabits semideserts, forest-steppes and rocky areas along the Black Sea coast through the Caucasus and northern Iran up to northeast China and Mongolia. It is kept at temperatures from 24 to 30 °C (75–86 °F) in a dry terrarium with numerous hiding places. It feeds on spiders, insects and ants and its diet must be enriched with plenty of minerals and vitamins. The males are aggressive and may attack smaller reptiles, sometimes even their own offspring, so it is recommended that you keep them in pairs or in a small group of one male and two to three females. The female lays three to ten eggs and often does so twice a year. The young hatch after 60–75 days. If the Mongolian Racerunners are not allowed to hibernate they will fail to reproduce in captivity.

The **Desert Monitor** (*Varanus griseus*) is a bulky lizard up to 1.5 m (5 ft) long, that is native to the steppes and semideserts of North Africa and southwest Asia. To thrive in captivity, it requires a large terrarium or a commodious walkway inside a greenhouse with numerous hiding places. The temperature in the terrarium should be between 25 and 30 °C (77–86 °F) and in the place where the monitor warms itself the temperature may be as high as 40 °C (104 °F). Adult Desert Monitors are fed on small vertebrates; the young will take insects. They

ayan Monitor's diet is based on small vertebrates. The females lay 4–24 eggs and the young hatch after ten months. The young are easy to rear: they will take insects, larvae, young

up to 2 m (6.5 ft) long. There should be thick logs and suitable hiding places in the large terrarium in which this monitor is kept. The ideal temperature ranges from 24 to 30 °C (75–86 °F).

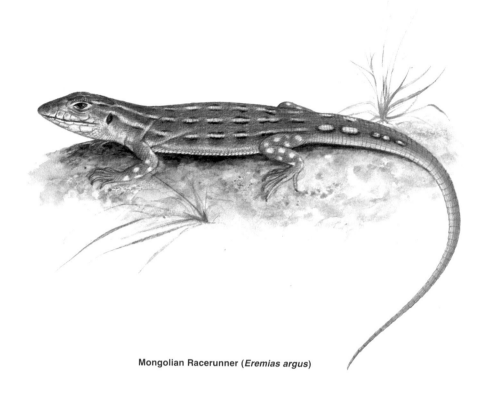

Mongolian Racerunner (*Eremias argus*)

can live for as long as ten years or more in captivity. In June and July the female buries 4–20 eggs deep in wet sand. The young that hatch from the eggs have black crosswise stripes and their striking colouring contrasts with the dull sandy mantle of the adults.

The **Malayan Monitor Lizard** (*Varanus salvator*), growing to more than 2 m (6.5 ft) long, is distributed in southeast Asia. It must live near water, so the terrarium in which it is to be kept must be large and have a shallow pool. Thick tree branches should also be provided for the creature to climb on. The temperature should be between 24 and 30 °C (75–86 °F). The Mal-

mice, small fish, lean meat and eggs.

The **Bengal Monitor** (*Varanus bengalensis*) lives in the steppe regions of southeast Asia, in places overgrown with shrubs and evergreen forests. It grows

Up to 30 eggs are laid in spring and these have an incubation time of five to six months. The young are excellent climbers in the shrubs and trees. Unfortunately, the Bengal Monitor seldom breeds in captivity.

Snakes (sub-order Serpentes)

The most outstanding trait of the Serpentes, of which about 2,600 species are known today, is their complete absence of limbs. Some groups of snakes, however, do still have a relic of

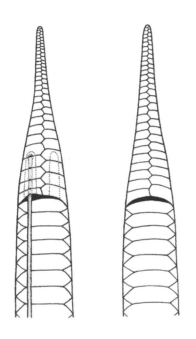

Diagram showing the method for identifying the sex of snakes. The probe can be pushed a much shorter distance into the body of a female compared with that of the male.

a pelvis, while the boas still have the bases of pelvic extremities. The eyelids of snakes long ago developed into a single transparent membrane. The jaws are connected by elastic and extensible ligaments that allow the

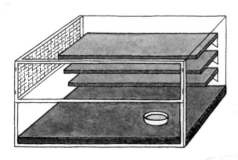

Terrarium with small shelves

snakes to swallow comparatively large chunks of food. Snakes' bodies are covered with horny scales and plates. They shed their skin from time to time: first the old skin sloughs off, beginning at the jaws and continuing until the whole skin is shed. To move, snakes push their large transverse ventral plates against uneven ground.

Snakes may be encountered in various surroundings: deserts, steppes, forests, under the soil's surface, in water. They feed exclusively on food of animal origin, from insects and birds' eggs to small and medium-size vertebrates. They kill their prey in different ways: some snakes wind themselves around the victim's body and suffocate it, others snatch the prey and swallow during which they bite the victim and then let it go. The poison may not act immediately and the animal may run a short distance before it dies. The snake's tongue, which combines the senses of touch, smell and taste, then enables the snake to find and swallow its prey. Snakes that have their poison fangs set back in their mouths hold the victim in their

Diagram of the venom gland

mouth until the venom begins to act.

The poison fangs are situated on the outlet of the paired poison gland. The fangs may be hollow or have a canal-like groove on the front. When the snake bites, it squeezes its facial muscles to eject venom which then flows into the wound to paralyse or kill the victim. The reserve of venom is regularly replenished and the poison

Dwarf Boa (*Tropidophis melanurus*)

fangs are replaced by new ones from time to time. The only remedy against snakebite is to inject a serum. By law venomous snakes may only be kept by

Boa Constrictor (*Constrictor constrictor*)

melanurus) from Cuba lives in wet places. It grows up to 1 m (3 ft). Wet conditions must also be provided in the terrarium. The best material to spread on the bottom is a mixture of peat and sand. Some peat moss or a moss cushion may be put in a corner of the terrarium which will help to hold moisture. Pieces of bark make good hiding places. In its habitat the snake feeds on small lizards and amphibians. In captivity it will also take small mammals and other vertebrates. The temperature in the terrarium should be 25–30 °C (77–86 °F) in summer, but for the period from November to January it should be reduced to 16–22 °C (61–71 °F). The mating season is from February to early May. The males often fight before mating, so pairs of this species should be kept in isolation. The pregnancy of the females is long, 8–11 months. Five to 12 young are born in each litter.

The **Boa Constrictor** (*Constrictor constrictor*) inhabits a vast area from southern Mexico

through Central America to northern Argentina, where it lives in forests and shrubby areas. In captivity this constrictor requires a large terrarium with thick logs and a shallow pool. The temperature should be between 24 and 32 °C (75–89 °F). The animals are fed on small vertebrates (mice, rats, rabbits and the like). They usually mate in autumn, but sometimes in spring. The female bears 10–60 young after seven months.

The **Green Anaconda** or **Water Boa** (*Eunectes murinus*) is one of the biggest snakes in the world and also one of the worst tempered: some specimens are as long as 9 m (30 ft). It lives

Boa's rest of the hind leg

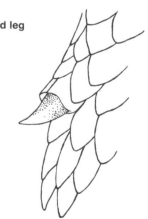

very experienced keepers or research institutes who hold an appropriate licence to do so.

Snakes reproduce either by laying eggs or by bearing live young that have developed in eggs inside the female's body. The **Sand Boa** (*Eryx jaculus turcicus*), growing to a length of up to 80 cm (31 in), lives in semi-deserts, steppes and forest-steppes of the Balkan Peninsula, Asia Minor and north Africa and is active at twilight and at night. During the daytime it hides under stones, in crevices in rocks or underground. It is kept in a terrarium with a layer of washed sand, large stones and a bowl with water. The optimum temperature is 24–33 °C (75–91 °F). The Sand Boa feeds on small vertebrates. Mating takes place in May and the female bears 4–20 young in September. This snake usually fails to reproduce in terrariums unless it is allowed to hibernate.

The **Dwarf Boa** (*Tropidophis*

Sand Boa (*Eryx jaculus turcicus*)

159

near water in the tropical forests in the basins of the Amazon and Orinoco Rivers. The anaconda is kept in a large terrarium with

land the Emerald Tree Boa eats predominately birds, but in captivity it will also take small rodents and amphibians. The

Female Indian Python (*Python molurus*) 'warming' her eggs

Green Anaconda or Water Boa (*Eunectes murinus*)

a pool where the snake spends most of its time. Both the water and the air should be kept at 25–30 °C (77–86 °F). The anaconda's diet consists of small and medium-sized vertebrates: mice, rats, rabbits, fish, chickens and so on. The pregnancy lasts seven to eight months and the female bears 10–70 young, 75–80 cm (29.5–31 in) long.

The **Emerald Tree Boa** (*Corallus caninus*) is a 2–2.5 m (6.5–8 ft) long tree snake from the rain forests of Guyana, Brazil, Peru and Bolivia. It lives in tree branches for almost all its life and only rarely does it come down to the ground. Anyone wishing to keep this snake must have a large and well-aerated terrarium with tree branches and a water bowl for the snake to drink from. The temperature in the terrarium should be 25–30 °C (77–86 °F). In its home-

Emerald Tree Boa is a biting snake that does not lose its aggressiveness in captivity. It is active at twilight and at night. The females bear 5–20 young after about seven months of pregnancy.

The **Rainbow Boa** (*Epicrates cenchria*), native to the tropical forests of Central and South America, from Panama and Costa Rica to southern Peru, Brazil and northern Argentina, is a snake about 2 m (6.5 ft) long,

that lives mainly on the ground. It needs a wet terrarium of medium size, heated to 24–30 °C (75–86 °F) and furnished with pieces of bark to provide hiding places. It takes small rodents as food. Outside the mating sea-

son each specimen should be kept in isolation, to be released in a mixed tank late in summer. Mating takes place from September to November. After five months of pregnancy, the female bears 8–35 young, 50 cm (20 in) long, which reach maturity at the age of two to three years.

The **Indian Python** (*Python molurus*) is distributed from Pakistan through India to southeast Asia, Java, Kalimantan, Sumatra and the Sumbawa Islands. This large snake, up to 6 m (20 ft) long, inhabits rocky

Emerald Tree Boa (*Corallus caninus*)

places with caves and overgrown by both deciduous and evergreen trees. It often lives near water. The terrarium

160

Green Tree Python (*Chondropython viridis*)

should be large, furnished with thick branches and a shallow pool, and heated to a temperature of 24–30 °C (75–86 °F). The pythons feed on small or medium-sized mammals. The

Rainbow Boa (*Epicrates cenchris*)

female lays eggs in leathery skin which she protects and warms among the coils of her body. The young will hatch from the eggs after 60–80 days.

The **Royal Python** (*Python regius*) is a small python up to 1.5 m (5 ft) long that lives near the margins of tropical forests in western and equatorial Africa. It should be kept at a temperature of 24–32 °C (75–90 °F) in a terrarium with suitable hiding places and a drinking bowl. Small rodents serve as food.

When the snake is frightened it huddles up and hides its head among the coils of its body. The female lays 5–20 eggs from which the young emerge after 65–70 days.

The **Green Tree Python** (*Chondropython viridis*) is a snake of less than 2 m (6.5 ft) long, lives in the forest regions of Papua New Guinea, the Solomon Islands and northern Australia. It is a tree snake, so the terrarium, large and thoroughly ventilated, must be furnished with tree branches; there must also be a small tank containing water. The temperature should be maintained at 24–30 °C (75–86 °F). The Green Tree Python

feeds on small rodents and birds. Both in its habitat and in captivity this python is a biting snake. In the terrarium the mating season is in spring or autumn and the female lays 10–30 eggs. The young will emerge after about 50 days. Unfortunately, this seldom happens in captivity. Any young that do hatch usually refuse food, and must be force-fed.

The **Grass Snake** (*Natrix natrix*), up to 1.5 m (5 ft) long, is still abundant near the grassy

Grass Snake (*Natrix natrix*)

edges of stagnant or slow-flowing waters in Europe, northwest Africa and western Asia. It is a good swimmer, requiring an aquaterrarium maintained at 22–26 °C (72–79 °F) in summer; in winter the temperature should be much less. It feeds on small fish and amphibians. In natural conditions it hibernates in shelters underground where a large number of these snakes may often gather. The mating season is in March and April. In June the females lay up to 70 eggs in various shelters and the young hatch after two months. Hibernation (the temperature successively reduced to 3–6 °C [31–43 °F] and maintained for three to five months) is essential for the successful reproduction of the Grass Snake.

The **Northern Water Snake** (*Nerodia sipedon*) is a 130 cm (51 in) long snake, living in the vicinity of stagnant and slow-flowing water in the eastern regions of the USA. It is kept in an aquaterrarium at a temperature of 22–28 °C (71–82 °F) and fed on fish, amphibians and small rodents. Like the majority of snakes of the genera *Natrix* and *Nerodia,* the Northern Water Snake sometimes emits a stinking secretion from its anus. Late in summer the female

Northern Water Snake (*Nerodia sipedon*)

bears 10–30 young, but successful reproduction requires hibernation for a period of three to four months.

The **Dark Green Racer** (*Coluber viridiflavus*), distributed from the northern Adriatic coast through Italy, France and Spain, and also in some Mediterranean islands, grows up to 2 m (6.5 ft) long. It inhabits shrubby steppes or thin forests, stony hillsides, vineyards and similar places. It is kept in a large terrarium with hiding places and a water bowl. The temperature should be maintained at 22–30 °C (72–86 °F). In natural conditions the Dark Green Racer feeds on small rodents, birds, lizards and large insects. In captivity it is fed on mice. Hibernation lasts from November to March. The female lays 8–15 eggs in spring and the young emerge from the eggs early in September.

The **Four-lined Snake** (*Elaphe quatuorlineata*) grows to a length of 2 m (6.5 ft). It lives in steppes, forest-steppes and shrubby stony places from southern Italy to western Asia. It feeds on small rodents and on birds and their eggs. It is a good climber in shrubs. The Four-lined Snake should be kept in a large, semi-arid terrarium, with branches to climb and shelters under stones and pieces of tree bark, at a temperature of 23–30 °C (73–86 °F). It is fed mainly on mice. Mating time is in spring following hibernation. The female lays 5–15 eggs. The young hatch after 50–60 days.

The **Great Black Coluber** (*Elaphe schrencki*), from northeastern China, Korea and the eastern regions of the former USSR, grows up to 1.8 m (6 ft) long. Its habitat is in forests and on shrubby hillsides. It does well in a semi-arid terrarium with branches and various hiding places, at a temperature of 22–26 °C (72–79 °F). Its diet should consist of small rodents, birds and eggs. From July to August, the female lays eggs in moss, leaves and other decaying organic waste where sufficient moisture is retained. The same conditions must be maintained in captivity if it is to reproduce. The young hatch after 60–70 days.

The **Corn Snake** (*Elaphe guttata*) is distributed in the southeastern and central areas of the USA and in northwestern Mexico where it lives on stony and shrubby hillsides, in coniferous forests and near water courses.

Four-lined Snake (*Elaphe quatuorlineata*)

Great Black Coluber (*Elaphe schrencki*)

It grows to a length of 180 cm (71 in). In captivity it needs a semi-arid terrarium with tree branches, stones and bark creating secure hiding places for the snake. The temperature should be maintained between 22 and 30 °C (71–86 °F) in summer. For the period of hibernation, which lasts three to six months, the temperature should be reduced to 5–13 °C (41–55 °F) for two to three months, although hibernation is not essential for successful breeding. The female lays up to three sets of 8–28 eggs a year and the young hatch after 60–75 days. The Corn Snake is popular among keepers, as it is easy to care for and breed from.

The **Milk Snake** (*Lampropeltis triangulum*) is an inhabitant of the forest regions of the south-eastern part of the USA and the north and centre of Mexico. It grows up to 1.5 m (5 ft) long and lives in hollow tree stumps, among the roots of trees, in shrubs and among stones. The semi-arid terrarium should be heated to 22–30 °C (71–86 °F) and should be furnished with large pieces of bark under which the snake will hide. The Milk Snake feeds on small rodents, birds, snakes and lizards. It is recommended to stock the terrarium with snakes of equal size, otherwise the large specimens may well swallow the smaller ones. Milk Snakes mate in spring. The female lays 2–25 eggs and the young hatch after 50–70 days.

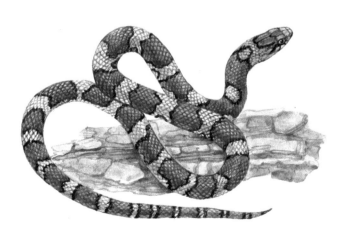

Milk Snake (*Lampropeltis triangulum*)

The **Common King Snake** (*Lampropeltis getulus*), which occurs in the same area as the Milk Snake, grows up to 2 m (6.5 ft) long. It is kept in a large semi-arid terrarium, with stones and bark, at a temperature of 24–30 °C (75–86 °F). It feeds on small mammals, snakes and lizards. The female lays 4–24 eggs from which the young emerge after about two months.

Common King Snake (*Lampropeltis getulus*)

In captivity the Common King Snake will take mice, young rats and chicks.

The **Common Garter Snake** (*Thamnophis sirtalis*), a small snake, seldom growing to a length of 1 m (3 ft), is native to a vast territory from Canada to Texas, where it lives in wet places near water courses. It will thrive in a terrarium with a large water pool and hiding places under stones and bark. The temperature in the terrarium should range between 22 and 30 °C (71–86 °F). The Common Garter Snake's food includes small fish, amphibians, earthworms, pieces of beef and small mammals. Mating takes place in spring. From ten to forty young are born from July to September. The Common Garter Snake is undemanding and easy to keep.

The **Egg-eating Snake** (*Dasypeltis scabra*), one of five related snake species that specialise in eating birds' eggs, is very popular among keepers. It lives in Africa, south of the Sahara, and in the western part of the Arabian Peninsula. It grows up to 90 cm (35 in) and it is very common near termite colonies close to the nesting places of birds, such as the Ploceidae. The Egg-eating Snake is kept at a temperature of 24–30 °C (75–86 °F) in a terrarium of medium size, furnished with tree branches and large stones. Because of its special requirements, in the wild this snake depends on the nesting season of birds, and the seasonal pattern of its feeding must be maintained in captivity. The Egg-eating Snake is active at dusk and at night. In the terrarium it will take the fresh eggs of pigeons, guinea-fowl, Japanese partridge and other birds, but hens' eggs are too large. If smaller eggs are not available, the snake may be fed by using a blunt-ended hose and a large syringe to introduce the mixed content of a broken hen's egg into the snake's digestive tract. The female lays 12–15 eggs in December and January and the young hatch from the eggs after three to four months.

Venomous Snakes

The **Long-nosed Vine Snake** (*Ahaetulla nasuta*), living on shrubs and trees in southeast Asia, is a slim snake, up to 1.5 m (5 ft) long, and an excellent climber. Its terrarium must be furnished with plenty of branches and creeping plants. The temperature in the terrarium must be maintained at 22–30 °C (71–86 °F). The Long-nosed Vine Snake is not easy to keep because in natural conditions it feeds on small lizards and amphibians and usually refuses to take any substitute food in captivity. Although it belongs to the group of venomous snakes of the subfamily Boiginae, its bite is not dangerous to people. The female bears eight to twenty young.

The **Mangrove Snake** (*Boiga dendrophila*) is venomous. It grows to a length of 2 m (6.5 ft) and lives in the tropical forests

Common Garter Snake (*Thamnophis sirtalis*)

may also be given small rodents. The female lays seven to ten eggs and the young emerge from them after 100 days.

The **Common Cobra** (*Naja naja*) is a very venomous snake, up to 2m (6.5ft) long, that inhabits the dry, stony hillsides, steppes and shore-side vegetation along the rivers of central

Long-nosed Vine Snake (*Ahaetulla nasuta*)

of southern Asia, Indonesia and the Philippines. It has grooved poison fangs set far back in its upper jaw and its venom is dangerous to man, so it is not suitable for inexperienced keepers. The Mangrove Snake needs a large terrarium with branches and a drinking bowl. The temperature in the terrarium should be maintained between 24 and 30°C (75–86°F). In its homeland it feeds on birds, snakes and lizards, but in captivity it

Common Cobra (*Naja naja*)

Mangrove Snake (*Boiga dendrophila*)

Asia, India and Indonesia. It likes to hide in rodents' burrows, in the structures built by termites, under stones and under fallen trees. In captivity it needs a large terrarium with a drinking bowl and hiding places. The Common Cobra feeds on small mammals, frogs, lizards, birds and birds' eggs. If it is frightened it erects the forepart of its body and extends its cervical vertebrae in a hood. Its venom is very strong and a serum must be used to treat any bite. It is dangerous to keep this cobra and it cannot be recommended to anyone but a very experienced and careful keeper. The Com-

165

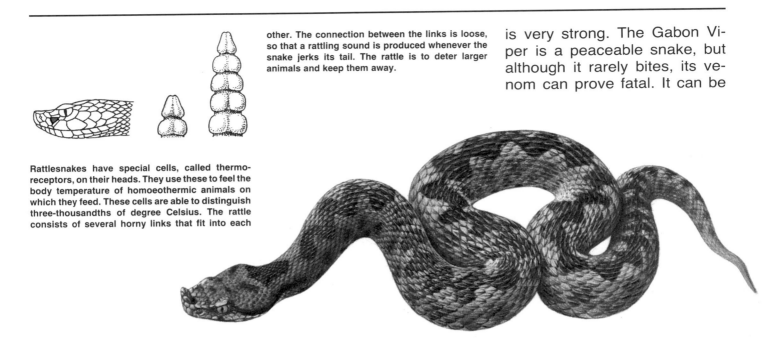

Rattlesnakes have special cells, called thermo-receptors, on their heads. They use these to feel the body temperature of homoeothermic animals on which they feed. These cells are able to distinguish three-thousandths of degree Celsius. The rattle consists of several horny links that fit into each other. The connection between the links is loose, so that a rattling sound is produced whenever the snake jerks its tail. The rattle is to deter larger animals and keep them away.

Sand Viper (*Vipera ammodytes*)

mon Cobra mates in late January and February and the female lays eggs in nests that she makes in sand. Both parents take turns in protecting the eggs. The young emerge from the eggs after 70–90 days.

The **Horned Viper** (*Cerastes cerastes*) is a small snake, up to 60 cm (24 in) long, from the deserts and semideserts of north Africa. It needs a dry terrarium with a layer of fine, clean sand and a temperature of 24–33 °C (75–91 °F). About 20 eggs are laid and the young hatch from them after 50–60 days.

The **Sand Viper** (*Vipera ammodytes*) is a fat snake up to 1 m (3 ft) long, distributed in the thin forests and stony hillsides of southeast Europe and western Asia. Its venom is dangerous, so this snake cannot be recommended for inexperienced keepers. Otherwise, the Sand Viper is easy to keep. It needs a temperature of 22–30 °C (71–86 °F) and a half-dry terrarium with stones and a drinking bowl. It feeds on small rodents. Mating takes place in spring and four to twenty live young are born in August and September.

In order to breed successfully, the parents must be allowed to hibernate at a low temperature. The **Gabon Viper** (*Bitis gabonica*) is a large, very strong snake up to 1.8 m (6 ft) long. It lives in the savannas and forest margins of the equatorial zone of Africa. Its poison fangs are up to 5 cm (2 in) long and its venom is very strong. The Gabon Viper is a peaceable snake, but although it rarely bites, its venom can prove fatal. It can be kept in a large terrarium, with hiding places, at temperatures between 24 and 33 °C (75–91 °F). Small mammals are given as food. The female bears 30–40 young.

The **Halys Viper** (*Agkistrodon halys*) is a 50–60 cm (20–24 in) long snake of the family Crotalidae (pit vipers or rattlesnakes),

Horned Viper (*Cerastes cerastes*)

found in the steppes, shrubby areas and near water east of the River Volga through central Asia and Siberia to the Far East. It is one of the venomous snakes and therefore dangerous. It is kept in a medium-sized terrarium with shelters and a small pool, at a temperature of 22–28 °C (71–82 °F). Its diet includes small mammals, birds and amphibians. Its mating season is early spring, soon after hibernation. Late in August the female bears 2–18 young.

The **Western Diamondback Rattlesnake** (*Crotalus adamanteus*) grows up to 2.5 m (8 ft) long. It is venomous and strong and therefore dangerous. This snake inhabits the dry, shrubby areas of the southeastern USA. It requires a large terrarium with hiding places and a bowl of water. The temperature should be maintained between 22 and 30 °C (71–86 °F). The snake feeds on small rodents and birds. All rattlesnakes have a special heat-sensitive pit behind their nostrils. On the floor of this pit there is a membrane densely interwoven with nerve endings that allow the snakes to sense the body temperature of

Halys Viper (*Agkistrodon halys*)

the warm-blooded animals on which they feed. With this organ, they are able, even at night, to trace any prey whose body temperature is higher than the temperature of its surroundings. The Western Diamondback Rattlesnake mates in spring and the female bears 2–20 young from August to September. During the breeding season the males defend their territories by fighting with each other.

Gabon Viper (*Bitis gabonica*)

Keeping Birds

The keeping of birds has a long tradition going back thousands of years in countries of the Far East (China, Japan, and Korea) and the ancient civilizations of Egypt, Greece and Rome. Today, birds are kept by aviculturists all over the world. Exotic species are especially popular because of the splendour of their colouring. Multicoloured large and small tropical birds are kept in cages or aviaries. A number of gallinaceous birds, or waterfowl, particularly ducks, are kept in large aviaries or allowed to roam freely, although with clipped wings, in gardens and parks.

If you wish to keep birds of any species the first thing to be considered is where they are to live. With a cage or aviary, or an enclosed place in the garden, it should always be borne in mind that the larger the space given to the birds, the better will be the

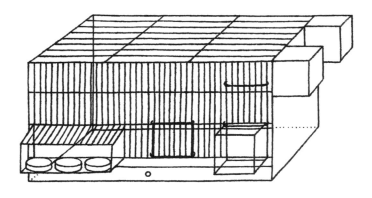

A cage for small songbirds.

conditions of their life in captivity. The minimum acceptable size of a cage for a pair of small birds is $100 \times 40 \times 70$ cm ($39 \times 16 \times 28$ in).

The best cages are the all-metal type. They leave no hiding places for parasites and can be washed with hot water and suitable disinfectants. As well as a front door, the cage should

substrate (sand, paper and the like) without having to catch and move the birds. Cages located in an indoors room have a strip of glass on the lower part of each side to prevent food debris from falling outside the cage.

There are also box-type cages with wires only in the front wall, the remaining walls being solid. Such cages should be

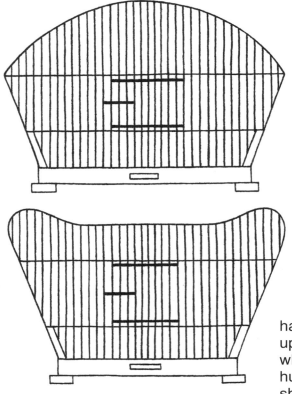

Decorative cages do not always provide the best homes for pet birds.

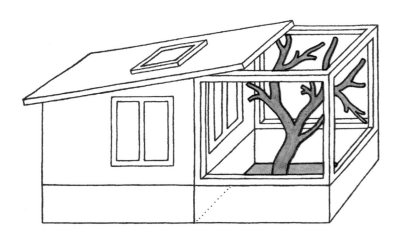

A garden aviary with a protective compartment.

have other openings in the upperparts of the side walls, where the nesting boxes are hung from the outside. The cage should have a removable bottom for easy replacement of the

painted white inside for reasons of hygiene and light. In such cages the birds feel safe. Sets of these cages may be arranged in vertical or horizontal rows. If the keeper has a box-type cage inside a room, it should face a window to provide enough light for the birds.

Glass cages are now increasingly used by keepers of small birds. They have a solid back wall, a ceiling of wire netting, a metal sheet on the bottom, and glass walls on the three remaining sides. A natural scene may be created inside such a cage, using sand, peat, moss, pieces of logs and tree branches and plants. The glass case should be at least 1 m (3 ft) long and 60 cm (2 ft) high. Nest boxes, holders for pots with plants, tree branches and similar objects are hung on the solid back wall. The cages are lit by fluorescent lamps. They may also have an air-conditioning system, heating and a source of ultraviolet radiation. To allow the keepers to clean the glass and rearrange the interior, the birds are driven into a separate area in which they can be enclosed, or a glass partition can be used to keep them clear ot the part of the cage being cleaned. Birds will soon destroy the interior of their cage, so the enthusiast must be ready to repair any damage as soon as possible.

Twigs of different thicknesses should be used as perches and frequently replaced. They should be distributed so as to force the birds to fly and not just hop from one perch to another; neither should perches be placed one above another or above the water or food dishes. River sand should be spread on the bottom of the cage to prevent the droppings from sticking to it. The birds will also like to peck at the sand because it helps them to digest the food. If grains of several plant species are used to feed to birds, there should be a separate dish for each kind of grain; if the grains are mixed the birds will scatter them all around, seeking out

A large aviary.

and eating only those they like best. Separate feeders for each kind of grain also allow the keeper to note what the birds' favourite food is. When the birds wash, they splash water around not only inside the cage but also into the room, so it is better to hang glass bath boxes on the side doors rather than using simple bowls.

Birds can be kept and bred with success in a large cage, located in a quiet spot, and containing a single breeding pair. To rear the finches (Fringillidae), the cage should be furnished with open, bowl-shaped wooden nests or wire nests with a lining. Songsters of the Estrildidae family require nesting boxes of different shapes with various sizes and positions of entrance. Some birds of this family like to nest in closed baskets or in coconut shells. If large enough, the cage may hold several boxes for the birds to choose from. The inner dimensions of the boxes should

be about 12×12×12 cm (4.8×4.8×4.8 in) to accommodate the nest itself, which the birds build from all kinds of material. The upperpart of the box should be removable to allow the breeder to check on the little inmates and to clean the box.

A walk-in, indoor aviary should be constructed in a suitable location — in a glazed part of a veranda, in a conservatory or another similar spot. In the lower part of the aviary there should be a small door through which the birds are fed. A large door, through which the breeder can easily pass, should be set in the aviary. The aviary floor should be covered with river sand, peat, garden soil and moss, or planted with grass. If a potted shrub is placed in one corner, some of the birds may build their nests there. Branches, among which the birds will fly, should be arranged on the opposite walls. There should be no live plants nor any water or food bowls under these bran-

171

ches. Nestings boxes, baskets and the like should be hung on the upper parts of the walls.

Gregarious birds have no problems in forming an integrated group in the aviary. Most of the decorative birds are quite peaceable outside the nesting season, but if they are released into an aviary with nesting boxes, each pair will defend its box and chase away any intruders. If, for example, a large aviary is stocked with several pairs of small Estrildids, there must be at least twice as many nesting boxes and baskets as there are pairs of birds, and these boxes should be set as far apart from each other as possible. There should also be dense shrubs in which any pursued birds may hide. Another good approach is to stock the aviary with bird species that are quite different from each other in the zoological sense, for example a pair of Estrildids may well share their aviary quite happily with a pair of pigeons or quails. In such cases the males usually see no competitive threat in each other's presence.

The indoor aviary may be equipped with an automatic, dry-grain feeder in which the grain is replenished only once a week. It is poured into each compartment and the amount left can easily be seen through a glass. A large shallow bowl, for example the kind of tray used in photographic dark rooms, will suffice for bathing.

To prevent parasitic mites from propagating in the aviary, once or twice a year it is necessary to remove all birds and wash out the whole aviary, feeders and boxes with a disinfectant solution.

Many keepers prefer to have a garden aviary with a separate compartment that is heated in winter to maintain the temperature above freezing point. The

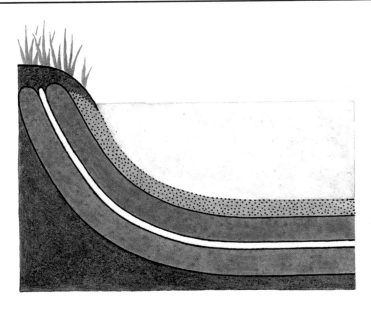

Cross-section through the structure of a small water basin.

roofed, inner part should be furnished with tree branches, nests or nesting boxes, feeders, bowls of water and the like. A layer of sand should be spread on the ground. There must be plenty of light inside the shelter because sometimes the weather may be too bad to let the birds out. A window may be located in a side wall or between the inner and outer wall of the aviary, and an exit opening may be set above the window. In size (about 30 × 40 cm/12−16 in diameter) it should be comparable with the sizes of the birds. It is opened and shut by a shutter to which a rope is attached from the outside. If you keep gallinaceous birds the entry and exit hole should be on the ground. The window must always have wire netting on both sides to prevent the birds from flying into the glass. There should be grass outside the roofed area, which should be mown frequently to promote thick growth. Parrots, except for some species such as those of the genus *Neophema,* would soon destroy the grass and shrubs, so they should have only branches,

which will have to be replaced frequently. On the other hand, there are birds, such as the Estrildidae and Amadinae families and the insect-eating species, for which live shrubs need to be planted in the aviary because they nest among the branches. A branch or perch for night roosting should be provided for gallinaceous fowl, and, as they like to nest on the ground under a thicket, dwarf conifers or non-poisonous evergreen shrubs should be planted in their aviary.

For those who keep waterfowl, it is ideal to have a small brook in the garden, for then there is no problem about building a pond. However, most enthusiasts must construct a concrete-based pool with the bottom sloping towards an outlet hole. If PVC lining is to be used, the ground under the lining must be firm. It must be filled in with stones, covered by a layer of gravel and finished with a sandy surface; the PVC lining is then spread over the sand.

Many of the exotic birds kept in Europe feed on grain and, except for most of the parrots, the major ingredient of their diet is millet, which replaces the grass seeds normally eaten by these birds under natural conditions. The millet grain should not be dehusked. Sometimes it is advisable to use grain soaked in water or sprouted, containing vitamin E. Canary grass is also important in their diet. The birds also like hemp seed, which, unfortunately, contains too much oil, so birds eating a large amount will become too fat. Consequently, only a small amount of hemp seed should be added to the diets of birds which spend the winter in garden aviaries. Dehusked oats are excellent feed for most parrots and many grain eaters. Sunflower seeds and fruit are the main ingredients of the diet of most medium-sized to large parrots. Green forage is an essential supplement to the feed of all grain-eating birds; they may be given spinach, lettuce, radish leaves, dandelion leaves, chickweed and other green plants. Vegetables bought from a greengrocer must be washed thoroughly to remove any traces of fertilisers and pesticides. In winter it is advisable to leave soaked millet, wheat, barley or oat grains to sprout to several centimetres long, and to put the

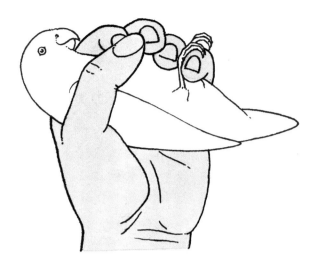

The correct way of holding a bird in the hand.

dish of sprouted grain into the aviary or cage. The birds will also take all kinds of fruit. An egg supplement (a mixture of hardboiled egg with grated carrot and bread crumbs) is an excellent source of nutrients during the period when the parents feed their young.

Most of the insectivorous birds will grow accustomed to an egg supplement. Meat meal may be used as a partial replacement for dried ant pupae and other insects. Cooked, minced beef, curd cheese and fresh or dried elderberries or rowanberries may be added to the feed

given to larger insectivorous birds. Live insects or fresh ant pupae should be given to the nestlings of insectivorous birds. It is recommended that keepers living in cities should maintain a reserve stock of insects, such as mealworms, crickets, greater wax moths and the like.

It is essential that food given to young and adult birds should contain minerals. Calcium is supplied in the form of cuttlefish bone or crushed eggshells. Limestone and bone meal contain calcium and phosphorus. Sodium and chlorine are provided in cooking salt, which is

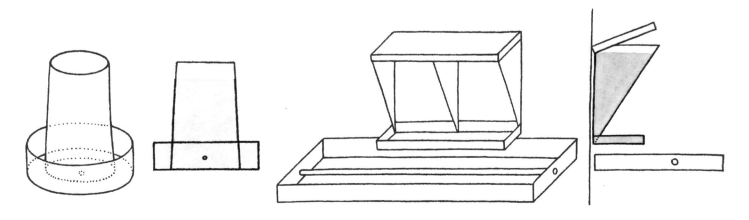

An automatic drinker and feeder.

sometimes added to the feed. If there is plenty of green forage and fruit, the birds will seldom suffer from a lack of minerals.

Vitamin deficiencies are mostly the result of a monotonous diet or insufficient exposure to sunshine. Carrot is the best source of vitamin A. B group vitamins are provided by adding dried yeast to the birds' food. Vitamin D is contained in green plants and also manufactured in the skin of birds exposed to the sun's rays. Sprouted grains are a source of vitamin E. Water-soluble vitamins may also be purchased and administered to the birds following the instructions given on the packet. Vitamins soluble in fat (A, D, E) must be emulsified in oil before they are added to soft food or grain.

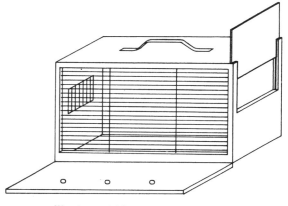

Wooden portable cage.

Parrots (order Psittaciformes)

Parrots have always enjoyed a special position as companions of people. This is due to their interesting habits and character and colourful plumage. Although the entire bird kingdom contains a remarkable range of colours, the colouring of parrots is the most striking of all. Some parrots are as small as a sparrow, others are much larger than a crow.

Parrots probably originated in New Guinea and northern Australia. Today there are about 350 parrot species distributed throughout southeast Asia, Australia, Africa and the American continent. All parrots are very good climbers; for this they use their hooked beaks and their short, strong legs whose shank is shorter than the fore digit. When a parrot walks on the ground its movements are uncertain and awkward.

Male and female parrots usually have the same colouring. Parrots live in pairs but outside the nesting season they gather to form flocks, sometimes small, sometimes extremely large. Spring is the nesting season for the majority of these birds. Nesting is preceded by courtship, which is interesting although not very unusual: the male follows the female everywhere and

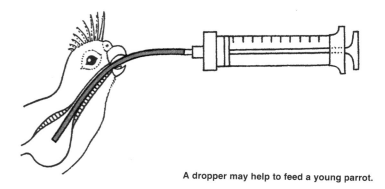

A dropper may help to feed a young parrot.

feeds her from his crop. Most parrots nest in hollow trees and other hollows which, in captivity, can be replaced easily by nesting boxes of different sizes.

Vegetable food predominates in the diets of parrots. Small species prefer grass seeds, cereal grains and small berries; the larger parrots will also take large fruits and nuts. In captivity parrots are not very choosy about food; they can be given apples, pears, carrots, unripe maize, nuts, sunflower seed and oats. Honey may be added to the food given to lories. Their need for water varies with the species. Some of these birds stay close to water sources, while others only appear at a watering place early in the morning and late in the evening.

Parrots may be kept either in large outdoor aviaries with branches on which they can climb, or indoors in large cages. It is more likely that young will be reared when the birds are kept in an outdoor aviary where they have more flying room, sunshine, wind and atmospheric humidity. The correct size of the garden aviary depends on what each species requires. Part of it must be roofed to give the birds shelter in bad weather. Dishes or feeding tables must be placed in the aviary, as well as bowls of water or a small pool. Nesting boxes are hung on the wall under the roof. Early in winter the parrots should be transferred either to a heated extension or to cages indoors. The majority of Australian parrots, however, have no special requirements as to temperature and they can be left in an outdoor aviary with an enclosed shelter that is draught-free and where the temperature can be maintained at about freezing point and daylight prolonged by artificial light-ing in the mornings and eve-nings. There are some parrot species that can withstand tem-peratures as low as −10°C (14°F).

Small parrots are mostly kept in cages on to which nesting bo-xes are hung from the outside. It is advisable to let the bird out to fly free about the room at least once every day. The relation-ship between the male and fe-

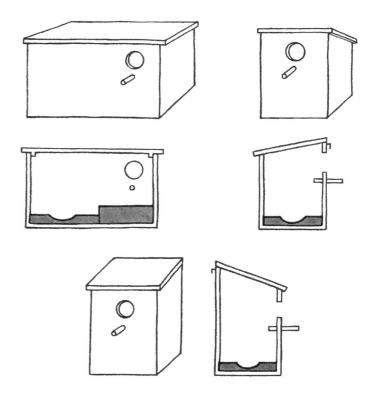

Various boxes for parrots.

male of each pair is very impor-tant for a successful breeding. Some pairs are quarrelsome and often fail to mate; some-times the female lays infertile eggs. If a male and female are not able to stay together despite all the keeper's care, it is neces-sary to replace one of them. About a fortnight after courtship

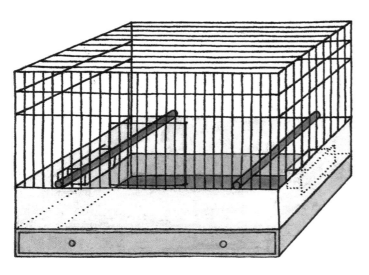

Cages for parrots kept indoors.

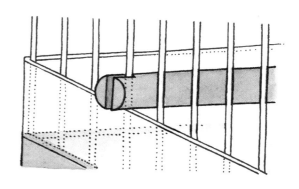

How to fix a perch.

have the same colouring. *Cacatua alba* inhabits the northern and central islands of the Moluccas. It feeds on seeds and grains, nuts, fruits and small insects. It is an undemanding bird and can endure cold weather. Its cage must be large. It enjoys nibbling at wood, fresh branches and bark.

The **Lesser Sulphur-crested Cockatoo** (*Cacatua sulphurea*) is about 33 cm (13 in) long and lives in the Indonesian islands of Celebes, Butung, Lesser Sunda and Flores, where it mostly sits in the tops of tall trees. It feeds on forest fruits, bananas and nuts. In the vicinity of human dwellings, it pecks at unripe ears in maize fields. The female lays two to three eggs. *Cacatua*

a) White-crested Cockatoo (*Cacatua alba*)
b) Pink-crested Cockatoo (*Cacatua molucensis*)
c) Lesser Sulphur-crested Cockatoo (*Cacatua sulphurea*)

begins, the female lays her first eggs in the nesting box. The eggs are white. Some parrots lay three to four eggs; others lay six to ten eggs altogether.

The **Umbrella** or **White-crested Cockatoo** (*Cacatua alba*) is a typical representative of the cockatoos, an attractive group among the larger parrots. Their typical feature is a handsome crest of long feathers on the head: if the bird is at rest its crest is folded flat, but whenever it is disturbed, its crest stands upright. The cockatoo has a very strong beak and its lower jaw is wider than the upper. Cockatoos use their beaks as general-purpose tools with which some are even able to open a complicated lock on the cage. An adult cockatoo is 46 cm (18 in) long and the male and the female

Rainbow Lorikeet (*Trichoglossus haematodus*) and some colour variants

sulphurea is easy to tame, it likes to snuggle and seldom pecks to hurt.

The **Moluccan Cockatoo** (*Cacatua molucensis*) grows up to 52 cm (20 in) long, and is among the most beautiful of cockatoos. There is hardly any difference in the colouring of males and females, although the female is a little whiter. This parrot species is distributed in the southern parts of the Moluccas, Ceram and Amboina. It lives in the tops of trees and flies silently. The female lays two to three eggs. If frightened, this cockatoo erects not only its crest but also the feathers on its neck, nape and breast. The young soon learn to mimic words or to whistle.

The **Green-naped Lorikeet** (*Trichoglossus haematodus*) is about as large as a starling. It is a good and fast flier, a trait typical of all lories. It lives in Bali, Papua New Guinea, the Solomon Islands, the New Hebrides, New Caledonia and eastern Australia. Lorikeets should be given runny food, such as boiled rice with honey or raspberry juice, sweetened milk and fruit juices. They seldom learn to talk. They need a large aviary or, if kept in a cage, must often be allowed to fly about the room. Unlike other parrots, lories do not peck much at wood, so they cause almost no damage inside the home.

The **Chattering Lory** (*Lorius garrulus*) exists in three races and is found in the Moluccas. Like the other lories, it has a brush-like tongue and is fastidious about food: it should be given honey, milk, baby foods, syrup, fruit juice, cold custard and soaked sponge biscuits. In its native habitat it drinks nectar from the flowers, sucks the juice from tropical fruits, eats soft fruits and catches small insects. Individual pairs must be kept in

isolation because lories are quarrelsome birds. They must be kept in a heated room during winter. The adult *Lorius garrulus* is about 30 cm (12 in) long.

The **Black-capped Lory** (*Lorius lory*) is one of the most popular lories. It is native to the northwestern part of Papua New Guinea and the adjacent islands. It grows to 30 cm (12 in)

Black-capped Lory (*Lorius lory*) and Chattering Lory (*Lorius garrulus*)

long, and exists in seven different regional forms. It is a fastidious bird, which must spend the winter in a sheltered room at a temperature of at least 10 °C (50 °F). Like other lories, it feeds on liquid and mashed food. In a large aviary it can be kept in the company of other lories, except if any of them are nesting. The Black-capped Lory easily learns to repeat words or whistle short tunes.

The **Budgerigar** (*Melopsittacus undulatus*) is a very small member of the group of flat-tailed parrots. Its homeland is Australia where small flocks live a strictly nomadic life by river banks, in savannas and in sparse forests. The male differs from the female by having a deep blue or bluish cere around its beak, whereas the fe-

male's cere is brown. However, this rule applies only to adult birds; in the young the colour of the cere varies, so it is not easy to identify their sex. The Budgerigar is very easy to tame and feed. It takes various seed mixtures (mainly millet), scrambled eggs, green fodder and different kinds of bread and pastry. Most of these birds refuse fruit. The Budgerigar comes from arid regions so it does not drink much.

Getting the bird used to sitting on your hand.

find and will often fly to a table to peck at the food on the plates. There is a wide range of colour mutations in the Budgerigar, which have been developed by cross breeding. In their native land these birds all have a uniform green mantle, but in captiv-

ful, it flies to farmyards where it likes to feed with poultry. *Psephotus haematonotus* is hardy and does well in a European climate, so it can be kept in roofed outdoor aviaries during the winter. It is an ideal bird for the beginner because it is easy to pair.

It has no problems in overwintering because it is frost-hardy, although if there is a severe frost and the birds are exposed to a draught, their legs may get frost-bitten. The Budgerigar may be kept in pairs or groups but if a bird is to be taught to talk it must be kept in isolation. The Budgerigar nests without problems in boxes in either an aviary or a cage. The female lays five to six eggs. If you wish to teach the young to talk, they must be taken from the nest early and fed with a dropper. Only males are suitable for this purpose because females seldom become tame. A tame Budgerigar will feed on almost anything it can

Zebra Parakeet (*Melopsittacus undulatus*)

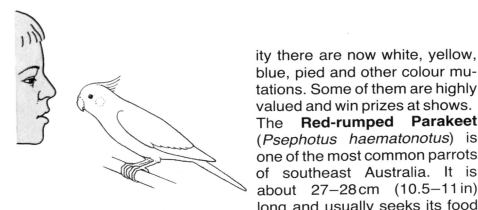

Teaching a parrot to repeat words.

ity there are now white, yellow, blue, pied and other colour mutations. Some of them are highly valued and win prizes at shows. The **Red-rumped Parakeet** (*Psephotus haematonotus*) is one of the most common parrots of southeast Australia. It is about 27–28 cm (10.5–11 in) long and usually seeks its food on the ground. Being very trust-

It will also rear the young of other parrot species, such as the rosellas, if their eggs are placed in its nest.
The **Turquoisine Grass Parakeet** (*Neophema pulchella*) is native to southeast Australia, but today it is very rarely found in the wild and is on the list of protected fauna. It finds its food of grass seeds on the ground. It

grows up to 21 cm (8.3 in) long making it one of the smallest of all parrots. In captivity it is fed on a mixture of seeds, including millet, small sunflower seeds and canary grass. This parakeet does not destroy green shrubs in the aviary, and it may be kept safely with smaller birds. Nesting lasts a long time – from August to December, the Australian spring and early summer – and the female lays four to six eggs.

Bourke's Parakeet (*Neophema bourkii*) is native to Western Australia and New South Wales but is now much more abundant in captivity than in its natural habitat. It is the least shy of all the Australian parrots and does not hesitate to visit farms in

Turquoisine Grass Parakeet (*Neophema pulchella*)

Bourke's Parakeet (*Neophema bourkii*)

search of water. It is undemanding, tame and easy to keep. Its diet consists of a mixture of seeds to which plenty of green fodder is added. Bourke's Parakeet will not bathe in a bowl but it enjoys flying in the rain. It has no problems with nesting in an outdoor aviary, although it will seldom nest in a cage inside a room. The female lays three to six eggs.

The **Rosella Parakeet** (*Platycercus eximius*) grows to a length of about 30 cm (12 in). It lives in the southeastern regions of Australia. It used to inhabit the open savannas but when Europeans arrived and felled large expanses of forests, the Rosella Parakeet also became an inhabitant of parks in large cities. Pairs of this species must be kept in isolation because during the nesting season they defend their territories and chase other birds away so ruthlessly that they may kill the intruder. They are, however, indifferent to smaller birds. The

Rosella Parakeet feeds on grass seeds, fruit, insects and larvae. In captivity it will take the same food as other flattailed lives in Tasmania and the *Platycercus eximinus ceciliae* lives in southeastern Queensland and the northeastern areas of liest of all parrots and any keeper's pride. It exists in three geographical forms in eastern and southeastern Australia. Its characteristics and requirements are roughly the same as those of the Rosella and the method of keeping and caring for it is also the same. It is one of the

Red-rumped Parakeet (*Psephotus haematonotus*)

parakeets, such as the Budgerigar. It nests twice in one season, which lasts from September to January, and each clutch comprises four to nine eggs. The Rosella Parakeet is hardy and can safely overwinter in a garden aviary with a walled extension. The birds like to nibble bark off branches and enjoy bathing. They have no particular talent for mimicry. The birds' sex is not easily distinguished: the colouring of the female is usually somewhat duller than that of the male.

There are three subspecies of the Rosella Parakeet. One, as we have seen, is native to southeastern Australia, another

Pennant's Parakeet (*Platycercus elegans*)

New South Wales. Today there are no pure subspecies in captivity.

Pennant's Parakeet (*Platycercus elegans*) is one ot the love-

180

cause great damage to fruit orchards.

The **Blue-cheeked Rosella** (*Platycercus adscitus*) is distributed throughout the western parts of Queensland and the northern regions of New South Wales. The mainstay of its diet is grass seeds and all kinds of fruit, but it will also take insects. Keepers give it the same food as they give to other rosellas.

Rosella Parakeet *Platycercus eximius cecilliae* and Pennant's Parakeet (*Platycercus elegans*) with young

Stanley Parakeet (*Platycercus icterotis*)

larger species, so it needs an indoor or outdoor aviary (cages are too small). In winter it can withstand very low temperatures. At nesting time the pair is very intolerant of the presence of any other birds.

The **Stanley Parakeet** (*Platycercus icterotis*) is an inhabitant of southwestern Australia. It is the smallest of the rosellas that can be kept in large cages or greenhouses. One of the commonly kept rosellas, it breeds easily in captivity and does not mind sharing its aviary with smaller bird species. It is peaceable, quiet and resistant to cold. Plenty of twigs should be made available to this bird because it

enjoys nibbling at wood. Both *Platycercus icterotis* and *P. elegans* are very popular, so Australian farmers seldom shoot them, although they sometimes

Platycercus adscitus is increasingly popular among parrot fanciers. There are no problems about nesting and rearing its young; the female rarely aban-

181

dons her clutch. As a rule it nests twice in one season. It can be kept in an aviary with budgerigars and other small birds. It is

Blue-cheeked Rosella (*Platycercus adscitus*)

rigars and other rosellas, although unlike them it is easily startled.

The **Australian Cockatiel** (*Nymphicus hollandicus*) is the second most popular parrot after the budgerigar. Its homeland is practically the whole of Australia where it lives in bush and thin forest. It lives a nomadic life. In long periods of drought the birds leave their densely inhabited territory and migrate far away in search of food. They feed on various seeds and herbs. In captivity they are given grass seeds, oats, wheat, millet, sunflower seeds, apples, pears, oranges, bananas and green plants. They do not use their feet to hold their food nor do they carry it in their beaks. The Australian Cockatiel is easy to keep in

one of the swiftest fliers of all parrots. In captivity it can nest several times in a season but it is advisable not to allow the birds to lose too much strength by nesting more than twice. There are four to five eggs to one clutch. The male and female alternate in sitting on them, which, among parrots, is a rare exception.

Various mutations of cockatiel colouring have been achieved by intensive breeding, including pure white birds. The white pied colour mutation of the cockatiel often appears at shows, although it is not so easy to keep and breed. Australian cockatiels of all mutations are very popular among fanciers because they can easily be tamed and are able to learn several words and whistle melo-

dies, although their talent here is not as great as that of the Budgerigar. Cockatiels are very hardy and can be kept by the beginner. They can be left in an aviary outdoors but it should be remembered that a draught is harmful to them.

The **Ringneck Parakeet** (*Psittacula krameri)* comes from India, Sri Lanka, Burma, southeastern China, central and northeastern Africa and adjacent areas. It is one of the most popular parrots. It lives in forests but will also visit orchards and gardens where it can play havoc with the fruit. Large flocks of the Ringneck Parakeet also destroy cornfields. This parrot cannot be kept with other, smaller birds, because it would attack them and bite their legs. It is fed on sunflower seed, fruit, maize and wheat; the fruit it likes best includes apples, cherries, currants, pears and strawberries, but it will also take carrot, kohlrabi and various green fodder. The Ringneck Parakeet is a hardy bird that is easy to tame and to teach a few words.

The **Derbyan Parakeet** (*Psittacula derbiana*) comes from northeastern Assam, Tibet and western China where it inhabits dense tree tops on the edge of the jungle. If alone, it is a placid, quiet and undemanding parrot, but in the presence of other birds it is aggressive. In addition, its cry is very loud and unpleasant. It will destroy any wooden object within its reach, so it must be kept in a metal aviary. The beak of the male of the Derbyan Parakeet is coral-red, and that of the female is black. It is fed on cereal grains, fruit, vegetables and green forage, such as spinach or dandelion leaves. The branches in the aviary must be replaced frequently. This bird has no problems about nesting in captivity and the female lays a clutch of

Colour varieties of the Australian Cockatiel (*Nymphicus hollandicus*)

tive of southwestern Africa, especially the south of Angola, where it nests in cavities in the trunks of trees and sometimes also in the nests of weaverbirds. It grows to about 15 cm (6 in) long and like all related species it has a short, blunt-tipped tail. The sexes are difficult to distinguish, the only difference being the shape of the head. In its natural habitat this small bird causes great damage to cultivated crops. In captivity it is fed sunflower seeds, millet and other cereals with supplements of green forage, beaten eggs, grated carrots and soaked sponge biscuits. It will readily nest in a wooden box. Pairs of Rosy-faced Lovebirds must be

two to five eggs. It can remain outdoors throughout the winter. The **Plum-headed Parakeet** (*Psittacula cyanocephala*) has its habitat in the trees on the edge of the tropical forests and forest glades in India, Pakistan, Nepal, Bhutan and Sri Lanka. It nests regularly and reliably in captivity but problems often arise when pairing because some of the grown-up young, although looking like females, turn out to be males. Healthy birds start nesting as soon as they find a nesting box where the female lays four to six eggs. Seeds of sunflower, millet and oats are the main ingredients of the Plum-headed Parakeet's diet and should be combined with half-ripe maize and green fodder.
The **Rosy-faced Lovebird** (*Agapornis roseicollis*) is a na-

a) Plum-headed Parakeet (*Psittacula cyanocephala*)
b) Ringneck Parakeet (*Psittacula krameri*)

kept in isolation because they are aggressive towards other birds. The female lays an egg every other day, the clutch being three to five eggs. The Rosy-faced Lovebird must be well supplied with tiny twigs because it uses them as bedding on the bottom of its nesting box.

The **Masked Lovebird** (*Agapornis personata*) is one of the most frequently kept lovebirds. It is native to Kenya and north-eastern Tanzania. The male and female have similar colouring and can be distinguished only by a slight difference in the shape of the head. This lovebird is less hardy than the others but it usually nests without problems. Its young can be easily tamed but they will never learn to mimic a word or to whistle. The female lays four to six eggs, mostly within 14 days of finding a nesting box.

Fisher's Lovebird (*Agapornis fischeri*) is native to the northern part of Tanzania and the region south of Lake Victoria, where it flies in flocks. It is very popular with keepers because of the splendid colouring of its plumage. Nesting, feeding and keeping rules are the same as for the other species of the genus *Agapornis*. All species of that genus can be crossed with one another. Many species have been developed into a number of colour mutations.

The **Nyanza Lovebird** (*Agapornis lilianea*) comes from Tanzania, northwestern Mozambique, eastern Zambia, Zimbabwe and Malawi. It is one of the smallest species of the *Agapornis* genus, only 13.5 cm (5.3 in) long. It is less abundant than the other species. As it is quiet and not aggressive, several pairs of the bird can be kept together. In winter they must be kept in a heated room because they would die of exposure in an environment with a low tempera-

Derbyan Parakeet (*Psittacula derbiana*)

ture and damp atmosphere, although their general health is good. For nesting they need quite a large box. Their diet is the same as that given to other species of the genus.

The **Black-cheeked Lovebird** (*Agapornis nigrigenis*), which lives in northwestern Zimbabwe and southwestern Zambia, is seldom kept as a pet, although it is peaceful and tolerant and its stock in an aviary of adequate size may number several pairs. These parrots are well acclimatised, resilient and hardy, nesting and rearing their young without problems. Unfortunately, like *Agapornis fischeri*, they have frequent trouble with their plumage and many lose all the feathers on their breasts and bellies. They need a higher temperature than the other species of *Agapornis*. Otherwise, they are kept under the same conditions. The female is somewhat duller in colouring than the male.

The **Madagascar Lovebird** (*Agapornis cana*) is an inhabit-

ant of the islands of Mauritius, Madagascar, Rodrigues, Comoros, Seychelles, Zanzibar and Mafia. It grows to a length of 14 cm (5.5 in). It is more difficult to keep than the other species of the genus; the female attacks other birds in the nesting season, so the pairs must be kept in isolation, and nesting itself is not always successful. *Agapornis cana* is not very fastidious about food, although some birds may refuse certain seeds. The diet consists mainly of sprouted millet, but the monotonous menu may be enriched with soaked sponge biscuits. If the young are removed from the nest and reared in isolation, they become tame and affectionate. The female lays four to five eggs in the nesting box.

The **African Grey Parrot** (*Psittacus erithacus*), which is about 36 cm (14 in) long when fully grown, is native to the forests of tropical Africa. Small flocks of this parrot inhabit tree tops: they are very clumsy when they try to move around on the ground. Although it seldom nests in captivity, it is very popular with fanciers because it is easy to tame and to teach to talk. It has always been considered the most intelligent of all parrots – in fact of all birds. Not only birds in captivity but also those in the wild enjoy mimicking the sounds they hear around them, including other birds' songs or noises made by animals. The African Grey Parrot can be kept in cages or in aviaries, and tame birds may even be left to live freely in an apartment if a perch is provided for them in a corner using a branch, where the bird will remain sitting for hours at a stretch. In captivity it is very quiet despite its great activity in its natural habitat. It is very sensitive to cold, so it must be kept at room temperature until May when drops in temperature no longer put it at risk in an outdoor aviary. The diet of this parrot consists of sunflower seeds, wheat, hulled oats, different kinds of nuts, peanuts, maize, unripe wheat grains and regular supplements of grated carrot and green forage (spinach, chickweed, and the like). Fruit or boiled eggs may also be given from time to time. The African Grey Parrot enjoys nibbling at tree branches and also loves to bathe. The perches and cages should be located in a shady place because direct exposure to sunshine is harmful to this bird.

With due care the African

a) **Nyanza Lovebird (*Agapornis lilianea*)**
b) **Rosy-faced Lovebird (*Agapornis roseicollis*)**
c) **Black-cheeked Lovebird (*Agapornis nigrigenis*)**
d) **Back: Colour varieties of the Rosy-faced Lovebird**

Masked Lovebird (*Agapornis personata*)

Grey Parrot may live for 50–80 years or even longer. The keeper has practically no way of distinguishing a male from a female as the size and colouring of both are the same. For this reason it is not easy to pair the birds for breeding. In captivity they easily learn to imitate different sounds; they can whistle tunes and say whole sentences, mimic a cat's miaouw or the barking of a dog and so on. A Grey Parrot living in captivity from a young age will tame easily, learn to hold various objects and do a few simple tricks; this is why they are so often seen in circus or cabaret shows.

The **Blue-fronted Amazon** (*Amazona aestiva*) is an inhabitant of tropical forests in Brazil, Paraguay and northern Argentina. Although the female has the same colouring as the male, she is a smaller bird and thus distinguishable. This parrot is common in captivity. It can be kept in a cage or aviary but also freely in a room. They make affectionate pets and are almost as talented as the African Grey Parrot, easily learning words and melodies. The tame Amazon should be taken on the hand frequently and taught to pronounce short words. It will also learn a few tricks. Its diet consists of seeds, the kernels of forest fruits, maize, nuts, berries and other fruits, especially oranges and bananas. Only rarely does the *Amazona aestiva* nest in captivity.

The **Yellow-shouldered Amazon** (*Amazona barbadensis*), a native of the woody and rocky regions of Venezuela and the island of Aruba, is a rare bird outside its homeland. Both male and female grow to a length of about 33 cm (13 in); the female is more soberly coloured than the male. They seldom nest in captivity but are easy to tame and to teach to mimic words and other sounds and to whistle. They feed on the same seeds and fruit as the preceding species.

The **Cuban Amazon Parrot** (*Amazona leucocephala*) is small, being no longer than about 32 cm (12.5 in). Five races of this species live in Cuba, on the island of Pinos and in the Ba-

Fischer's Lovebird (*Agapornis fischeri*) — back;
Madagascar Lovebird (*Agapornis cana*)

hamas. These populations have declined drastically in recent years, so that this parrot is now included on the list of strictly protected species. Its diet is the

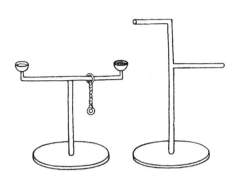

Perches for the African Grey Parrot

The **Blue-winged Parrotlet** (*Forpus passerinus*) is only 12 cm (4.8 in) long, and is distributed throughout northwestern Mexico, in shore-side thickets alongside rivers. Gathering in small flocks, parrots of this species chatter like sparrows. During winter they should be kept in a heated room, although they adapt well to weather in Europe and can spend a mild winter outdoors. They can be kept together with Budgerigars but may be dangerous to the Astrilds. Naturally, during the nesting season the breeding pairs will chase away any intruder. Their diet includes millet, oats and other seeds, similar to these given to the Budgerigar. The sexes are difficult to distin-

guish, except that the females are somewhat smaller than the males. They have no problems in nesting, but most of the young are males, so breeding pairs are difficult to form.

The **Mexican Parrot** (*Forpus cyanopygius*) is about 13 cm (5 in) long and lives in northwestern Mexico, the Caribbean islands and in the northern part of South America. It is not a common cage bird. Compared to the Blue-winged Parrotlet, it is livelier, less shy and more tolerant of the presence of other birds. The method of keeping both species is the same.

The **Celestial Parrot** (*Forpus coelestis*) has its range in the western part of South America alongside the Pacific coast from

same as that of the other Amazons. The Cuban Amazon seldom nests in captivity. Its power of speech is poorer than in its relatives, but it is easy to tame when young and will soon exhibit touching affection towards its keeper.

The **Senegal Parrot** (*Poicephalus senegalus*) has its homeland in the heart of western Africa where it causes great damage to maize and groundnut fields. In captivity it soon becomes tame and is able to learn many words. If it is not kept in a pair, it often makes friends with parrots of other species. This is a hardy little bird, able to withstand low temperatures. Its bill is strong, so its cage or aviary must be of strong wire – wooden cages are not recommended. Its diet consists of sunflower seeds, oats and fruit. *Poicephalus senegalus* is a small species (about 20 cm/8 in as an adult). It seldom nests in captivity.

a) Yellow-shouldered Amazon (*Amazona barbadensis*)
b) Blue-fronted Amazon (*Amazona aestiva*)

Ecuador to the northern regions of Peru. Unlike most birds of the genus *Forpus,* it is placid in a mixed aviary and several pairs can be kept together. The keeper's success largely depends on the weather; the adults, and

psitta monachus), an inhabitant of forest trees in hilly regions up to 1,000 m (3,280 ft) above sea level in eastern Bolivia, Argentina, Paraguay and Uruguay, is one of the hardiest South American parrots. It is a restless and agile bird, about 29 cm (11.5 in) long, with a constant piercing cry. In regions where it is abundant, large flocks raid the fields and cause considerable damage. The sexes can be distinguished only by the smaller size of the female's head or by observing the birds' behaviour before nesting. The Quaker Parakeet is the only parrot that does not nest in cavities inside tree trunks, but builds large nests among tree branches.

a) Mexican Parrot (*Forpus cyanopygius*)
b) Celestial Parrot (*Forpus coelestis*)
c) Blue-winged Parrotlet (*Forpus passerinus*)

especially the young, may die when the weather is cold, so it is recommended that they are kept in a garden aviary combined with a warm shelter. The female lays six to seven eggs but may sometimes fail to sit on them. As with all species of this genus, this parrot feeds on a mixture of various seeds.
The **Quaker Parakeet** (*Myio-*

African Grey Parrot (*Psittacus erithacus*)

188

Senegal Parrot (*Poicephalus senegalus*)

Individual birds or pairs are kept either in cages indoors or in an outdoor aviary where they nest more readily. In the aviary they must be given plenty of tiny twigs as building material for the nests. The female lays four to six eggs. The Quaker Parakeet is fed sunflower seeds, oats, hemp seeds, fruit, green fodder and the fresh twigs of nonpoisonous shrubs and trees. Its piercing screams are unpleasant, so it is not recommended that you keep a larger number of these birds at home. A Quaker Parakeet kept in isolation from an early age becomes tame but will seldom learn to mimic words. In many zoos these parrots fly freely. They are resistant to frost. The **Nanday Conure** (*Nandayus nanday*), from Bolivia, Argentina, Paraguay and the Mato Grosso in Brazil, lives in large flocks and often joins flocks of Quaker Parakeets. These parrots cause enormous damage to field crops. They are very popular among keepers, although it is not easy to pair them; both the

male and female are of the same size and colouring. The Nanday Conures are not such keen destroyers of wood as cer-

tain other species. They greet the daybreak with a loud cry. Nesting in captivity is not frequent, but cases are known of several females laying their eggs in the same box and then all sitting on them. It is advisable to keep the Nanday Conure in a heated room in winter, although the bird is not oversensitive to fluctuations in temperature. In a mixed aviary it does not mind the company of other birds. Fresh twigs must be supplied regularly to the aviary, otherwise the birds will bite and damage the wooden frames.

The **Jendaya Conure** (*Aratinga auricapilla jendaya*) comes from the eastern regions of Brazil and is commonly kept in aviaries. Although it has often been reared in captivity, success in rearing is far less frequent than with the Australian parrots. The bird is small, about 30 cm (12 in) long, but needs a large aviary. All parts of the aviary should be made of metal; wooden parts

Cuban Amazon Parrot (*Amazona leucocephala*)

and tender sprouting seeds. The size and colouring of both sexes are the same. The Blue and Yellow Macaw is too large to be kept as a pet indoors, so it is more frequently seen in zoos. It is placid and easy to tame and can be taught simple words. In captivity it is very agile. It nests in hollow trees in the wild; in captivity it will content itself with a large box in the aviary, but often fails to rear the young. Its diet consists of sunflower and maize seeds, nuts, rice, fruit and green fodder.

Quaker Parakeet (*Myiopsitta monachus*)

a) Blue and Yellow Macaw (*Ara ararauna*)
b) Scarlet Macaw (*Ara macao*)
c) Green-winged Macaw (*Ara chloroptera*)

would soon be destroyed. This parrot can be kept together with pheasants or large gallinaceous birds, but not with small species. Their diet is the same as the diet of other parrots. A bird of this species, kept in isolation from a young age, will often cuddle up affectionately to the keeper or to a parrot of another species.

The **Blue and Yellow Macaw** (*Ara ararauna*) is a large parrot, 86 cm (34 in) without the long tail, that is native to Panama, Colombia, Peru, Venezuela, Brazil, Bolivia and Ecuador. It is an inhabitant of forests and the mainstay of its diet is fruit, nuts

The **Scarlet Macaw** (*Ara macao*) is distributed from Mexico in the north to Bolivia and northern Brazil in the south. It is truly exotic in appearance. Its home damage to fig orchards. They easily adapt to the European climate, so they can be left in a garden aviary with a shelter during the winter season. Like gressive towards other people and because its beak is very strong, it may sometimes be dangerous.

The **Green-winged Macaw**

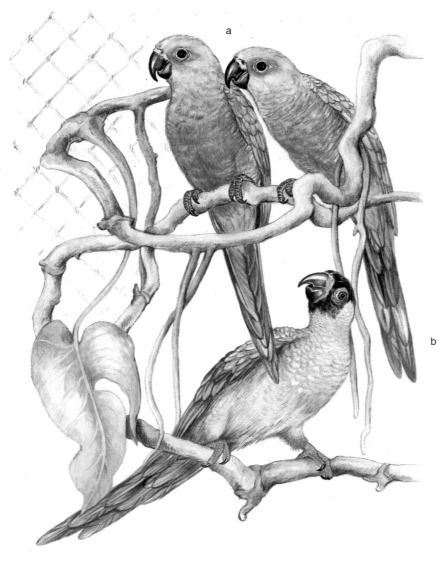

a) Jendaya Conure (*Aratinga auricapilla jendaya*)
b) Nanday Conure (*Nandayus nanday*)

(*Ara chloroptera*) inhabits the same areas as the Scarlet Macaw and usually lives in pairs, like most of the macaws; only exceptionally does it form small flocks. Its diet is the same as the diet of the preceding two species. In addition, the Green-winged Macaw requires a steady supply of fresh twigs and branches whose bark stimulates the bird's digestion. Attempts to rear this macaw in captivity are seldom successful.

is in the tops of tall trees in the tropical forests, although some birds will fly as far as the sea coast, where they cause great the majority of macaws, they require constant care and will cling to the keeper. However, the Scarlet Macaw may be ag-

The Small Songbirds (order Passeriformes)

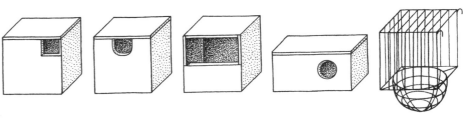

Boxes and a nesting basket for small songbirds

The majority of the finches (Fringillidae) and weaverbirds (Ploceidae), as well as many waxbills (Estrildidae), will live a long time in captivity if kept with due care. They mostly do best at room temperature of about 20 °C (68 °F) in winter, but from May to October should be kept in an aviary outdoors.

Millet is the mainstay of these birds' diet, supplemented with canary grass, niger seed, hulled oats, lettuce seed, linseed, poppy and rape seed; egg mix may be added from time to time, and fruit and green fodder should be given to the birds as often as possible. Mineral and vitamin supplements are also important ingredients of their diet.

Opened canary nests or abandoned nests of small European songbirds are put into finches' aviaries. The weaverbirds and waxbills usually build their nests in tall grass or dense shrubs, but some of them will put up with a nesting box. Fine hay, coconut and sisal fibre, feathers and the like are put into the roofed part of the aviary to provide the birds with building material for their nests. Varied food of animal origin should be given to them when the young hatch. Egg mix will also do, although not all of the birds will accept it. Small larvae of the meal beetle, aphids, insects collected by dragging, small crickets and other similar foods will make good sources of animal protein for the birds; the parents might evict their young from the nests if they do not have enough animal food. Dandelion and the

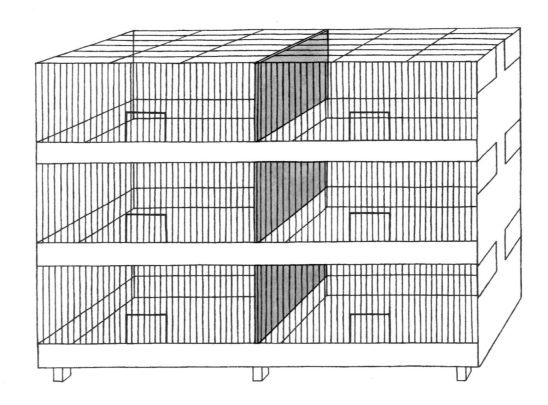

A set of cages

unripe spikes of millet, grasses and plantain will be greedily taken by most of the birds.

Some of the finches are not

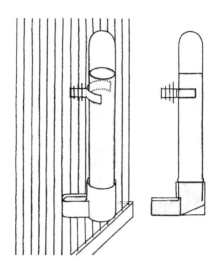

An automatic drinker

Painted Bunting (*Passerina ciris*) (a) and Indigo Bunting (*Passerina Cyanea*) (b)

too placid so it is better not to keep too many birds in a mixed aviary. The behaviour of all of them should be watched closely and any specimen seen to chase others must be removed.

Some attempts have been made to leave these small tropical and subtropical birds in a garden aviary during the winter; however, their adaptability has its limits and most of them must be overwintered in warmed compartments.

The **Common Cardinal** (*Cardinalis cardinalis*) is native to the southeastern and southern regions of the USA and to Mexico and has also been introduced into Hawaii. It is kept in large cages or in an indoor aviary and can withstand great drops in temperature. Its diet consists of cracked, hulled oats, canary grass, rapeseed, fruit and vegetables (spinach, chickweed and the like). Sprouted seeds and tree or shrub buds are fed in winter. Egg mixture and insects are added during the nesting season. The Cardinal will nest readily in a large cage. The female lays two to five eggs in a nest of dry grass or a similar material and both parents alternate in incubating them. The young hatch after twelve to four-

Common Cardinal (*Cardinalis cardinalis*)

teen days and leave the nest after another sixteen. The parents continue feeding them for two to three weeks afterwards.

The **Painted Bunting** (*Passeri-*

plenty of green fodder and fruit. The Indigo Bunting will sometimes nest in a cage, although it usually nests more readily in an aviary.

ing periods of drought. It is fed on millet, canary grass and foxtail. Like all waxbills, it needs plenty of animal food, including ant pupae, small insects or mealworms, especially in the nesting season. It also likes to peck egg mix, green fodder and unripe seeds of grasses. If the food does not contain enough vitamin D and calcium the females fail to lay eggs. The Star Finch has no problems in nesting and builds its ball- or bottle-shaped nest in dense shrubs or among the stems of grass. The female lays three to six eggs from which the young hatch after 12–14 days. They leave the nest after about 20 days.

The **Orange-cheeked Waxbill** (*Estrilda melpoda*) is found in western and central Africa. It is given various small seeds and animal food. The bottle-shaped nest, with another attached nest used as a 'bedroom', is built on the ground in grass or just above the ground in shrubs. Al-

a) Orange-cheeked Waxbill (*Estrilda melpoda*)
b) Golden-breasted Waxbill (*Amandava subflava*)
c) Lavender Waxbill (*Estrilda caerulescens*)
d) Star Finch (*Bathilda ruficauda*)

na ciris) is a relative of the Cardinal. It is about 13 cm (5 in) long and is distributed in the southern parts of the USA and in all the countries of Central America, except Panama. These birds also live in Cuba. They are known for their soft, rather monotonous song. They sing when in flight and late at night. Their diet includes millet, canary grass and niger seed. Fruit and green forage are their favourite foods.

The **Indigo Bunting** (*Passerina cyanea*) lives in the eastern parts of the USA and in Central America. It needs a large cage or an aviary. Besides millet and canary grass seeds, its diet should include rapeseed, niger seed, linseed, poppy seed, and

The **Star Finch** (*Bathilda ruficauda*) is native to northwestern and northern Australia and southern Queensland where it lives in pairs or small groups that gather as large flocks dur-

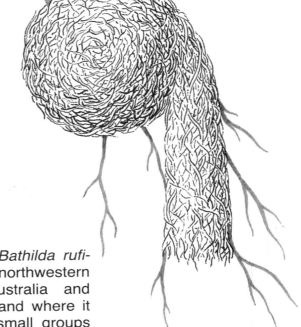

The Red Bishop's nest

194

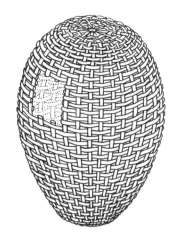

A basket for nesting

though nesting in captivity is common in this species, it is seldom successful. The female lays three to seven eggs and sits on them for 11—12 days.

courtship dress. It is interesting to observe Red Bishops building their nests. If they are given sisal or coconut fibres, bast, hay and similar materials,

do build their nests in cages, they seldom rear the hatchlings. Their diet consists of various seeds, millet and green fodder. Egg mix and insects should be

Red-billed Fire-finch (*Lagonosticta senegala*)

Red Bishop (*Euplectes fransciana*)

The young leave the nest after another 22 days.

The **Red Bishop** (*Euplectes fransciana*) is a representative of the weaverbird group, which is found throughout Africa. During the mating and nesting period it wears a striking

they will weave a suspended flask- or ball-shaped nest with a tube-like entrance. They hang the nest on branches or from the ceiling of the cage or aviary. The nest is built by the male and the female lines it with fine bedding material. Although weaverbirds

added when rearing young Red Bishops. The **Red-billed Fire-finch** (*Lagonosticta senegala*) is an inhabitant of dry steppes, savannas and the margins of deserts in central and eastern Africa, where it is often found in the vicinity of human dwellings. It is very tame and trustful. In captivity it is not choosy with food, and takes various species of millet and canary grass. The millet seeds may be left to sprout before feeding. As to feeds of animal origin, the birds are given egg mix, ant pupae and mealworms. Their nests of rootlets, hay and grass are ball-shaped with a side entrance and a feather lining inside. The nests are located either in the open or inside the box. The female lays four to five eggs and both parents alternate in incubating them. The young emerge from the eggs after 11 days and leave the nest after another 18.

The **Lavender Waxbill** (*Estrilda caerulescens*), native to the northwestern region of Africa, is a small bird, about 10 cm (4 in) long, inhabiting the steppes and forest margins and frequently found close to villages. Keepers feed it on millet and small half-ripe grass seeds; feeds of animal origin also form an important part of diet. The female lays two to four eggs in a nest built either in the open or in a box and the young hatch after about 15 days. They leave the nest 16–18 days later but return there at night.

The **Golden-breasted Waxbill** (*Amandava subflava*) is distributed in Africa from Senegal to Ethiopia and as far south as Transvaal, Natal and northern

a) Crimson-eared Waxbill (*Uraeginthus bengalus*)
b) Blue-faced Parrot Finch (*Erythrura trichroa*)

Cape Province. It is very popular among fanciers because of its splendid colouring, peaceful nature and hardiness in bad weather. It feeds on small seeds of grass and foxtail with supplements of animal food. Its size is 9–10 cm (3.5–4 in). The female lays four to six eggs in nests built in boxes or baskets. The young hatch after 11–12 days and leave the nest 20–21 days later.

The **Red Amandavat** (*Amandava amandava*) comes from both lowland and mountain areas up to an altitude of 2,000 m (6,600 ft) in India, in the Himalayas, southern China, Burma, Thailand, Cambodia, Vietnam, Java and Bali. It has been introduced and acclimatized in Egypt, the Comoro Islands, Sumatra, the Philippines, the Malay Peninsula and Hawaii. In Europe the first specimens appeared as early as the eighteenth century. Various species of millet form the mainstay of its diet, which has to be supplemented by green fodder and animal feed. This is particularly important during the rearing of the young. The Red Amandavat is the only species in the waxbill family Estrildidae that, like the weaverbirds or the why-

Red Amandavat (*Amandava amandava*)

dahs, changes its striking courting dress for a dull plumage when the nesting season is over. The amandavat nests and rears its young regularly in captivity. Its nest is usually located

fibre and the like. The female lays three to seven eggs. The young hatch after 11 days and leave the nest after 20 days.

The **Blue-faced Parrot Finch** (*Erythrura trichroa*), from Papua New Guinea and eastern Australia, is a gaily coloured bird, 12–13 cm (4.8 in) long. It makes its home chiefly in mountain and hilly areas. It is popular among keepers because of its easy and reliable nesting ability. Its diet consists of canary grass, millet, hulled oats mealworms, ant pupae, sponge biscuits, fruit and green fodder. For nesting, it prefers half-open boxes but may also nest in a basket or in a nesting box intended for budgerigars. Only rarely does it build a nest in a shrub thicket. The female lays four to five eggs and sits on them for 12–16 days. The young leave their nest 22–25 days after hatching.

The **Red-headed Finch** (*Amadina erythrocephala*) lives in pairs or small flocks in the open landscapes of south Africa, often staying in the vicinity of human dwellings. In captivity it prefers a large cage or an aviary. Its food includes millet, ca-

Red-headed Finch (*Amadina erythrocephala*)

close to the ground or in the lower part of the cage or aviary. The female lays four to six eggs and both parents alternate in sitting on them. The period of incubation is about 12 days and the young leave the nest 20–22 days after hatching.

The **Crimson-eared Waxbill** (*Uraeginthus bengalus*), native to the tropical regions of Africa, is one of the most commonly kept waxbills. It feeds on a mixture of small seeds of millet, sorghum, canary grass and foxtail, supplemented with animal food such as fresh ant pupae, mealworms, insects collected by dragging and egg mix. It makes its nest either in dense shrubs or in boxes in which one-third of the front wall is left open. The building material includes grass, hay, coconut and sisal

Zebra Finch (*Taeniopygia guttata*)

197

nary grass, poppies and spikes of Senegal millet. Egg mix, ant pupae and green fodder are given to the birds when they feed their young. The female lines the prepared nest with fine bedding and lays four to six eggs. The incubation, shared by both parents, lasts 14 days and the hatchlings leave the nest 22–24 days later.

The **Zebra Finch** (*Taeniopygia*

The **Long-tailed Grass Finch** (*Poephila acuticauda*) is a bird about 17 cm (6.7 in) long from Australia where it lives in sunlit savannas sparsely overgrown with eucalypts, in the tops of which it nests. In the wild it feeds chiefly on seeds of different grasses. In captivity it is given the seeds of any kind of millet and of canary grass (from time to time, both may be left to

which are incubated by both parents for 14 days. The young Long-tailed Grass Finches leave their nest after three weeks.

A nesting basket, suitable for a canary

Long-tailed Grass Finch (*Poephila acuticauda*)

The **Tri-coloured Munia** (*Lonchura malacca*) has its habitat in the paddies, cane fields and grasslands of India, Indo-China, southern China, Indonesia, the Philippines and Sri Lanka. It nests in the rainy season. In captivity it will thrive in an aviary where it is fed various kinds of millet, half-ripe grass seeds, green fodder, insects and ant pupae. During the nesting period the birds live in pairs but when nesting is over they gather to form large flocks. They build their nests in boxes and the female lays three to six eggs; the young will hatch after 14 days. However, nesting is seldom successful in captivity.

The **Java Sparrow** (*Padda oryzivora*), originally found only in the grassy, shrub-covered country of Sumatra, Java and the Molucca Islands, became a cage bird in Europe long ago. In the wild huge flocks of Java Sparrow cause considerable losses in paddies during the rice harvest. It can be kept either in a cage or in an aviary and given egg mix and millet with the addition of canary grass, mealworms and ant pupae. In a larger aviary it does not mind the company of other birds but in crowded or small aviaries it may prove dangerous to smaller

guttata), which originates from Australia, is a very rewarding cage bird. It feeds on various strains of millet, fresh or dry ant pupae, mealworms and bread soaked in water. It needs plenty of green fodder and calcium in its food. There are no problems with nesting. The female lays four to five eggs in the nesting box (it rarely builds a nest anywhere else) and the young hatch 11 days later. The young leave the nest after 18–20 days.

sprout before feeding). The diet should be enriched occasionally with mealworms, insects collected by dragging and the pupae of ants. The Grass Finch roosts in the nest overnight and builds another nest during the laying of eggs and rearing of its young. It can withstand great drops in temperature. It is seldom disturbed by the company of other birds. The nest, built in the box, is ball-shaped and in it the female lays four to six eggs,

birds. It likes frequent bathing. The female lays six to eight eggs in the nesting box and the young hatch after 14 days. Four weeks later the young leave the nest but the parents continue feeding them for another fourteen days. A white form and other colour mutations of the Java Sparrow are very popular among keepers.

The **Wild Canary** (*Serinus canaria*), originally living in the Canary Islands, is one of the most widespread and popular cage bird. It feeds on hulled oats, sweet summer rapeseed and canary grass, sometimes supplemented with poppy, linseed or niger seed. Fruit and vegetables, such as carrots, must be added to their diet as frequently as possible. When the birds

a) *Serinus leucopygius*
b) Wild Canary (*Serinus canaria*)
c) *Serinus mosambicus*

a) Pekin Robin (*Leiothrix lutea*)
b) Java Sparrow (*Padda oryzivora*)
c) Tri-coloured Munia (*Lonchura malacca*)

moult, their food should be enriched with egg mix, given twice a week. The water, not very cold, should be replaced frequently because canaries love bathing. Threads up to 8 cm (3 in) long, torn from a cloth, will be taken as building material for the nest, in which the first eggs will appear within a fortnight. The young hatch after 13 days and leave the nest when about 20 days old.

The **Pekin Robin** (*Leiothrix lutea*) is an inhabitant of northern India, upper Burma, southern China and the northern regions of Indo-China. It feeds chiefly on insects; if insects are not available, egg mix will do, enriched with dried mayflies or ant pupae, curd cheese, minced beef heart or meat. Several mealworms and some fruit may be added to their food every day. At nesting time a supply of live insects is essential, so plenty of insects should be collected by dragging every day or an auxiliary insect farm should be maintained to produce mealworms, crickets and the like. The bird builds its nest in shrubs and lays three to five eggs which both parents incubate. The young hatch in 12 days an the parents feed them for another 12 days.

Pigeons (order Columbiformes)

Some of the wild pigeon species (about 290 are known today) are particularly suited for aviary life. They can be kept together with quails and some species of pheasant. Most pigeons do no harm to other birds but they are often very quarrelsome when kept with other pigeons of the same or related species. For this reason they are kept in pairs as a rule.

All pigeons should be kept in aviaries. The warmth-loving species, which spend the winter in a heated shelter, should remain in the aviary from April to October. Small cages are not suitable for any of them.

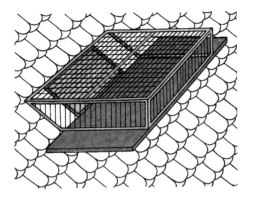

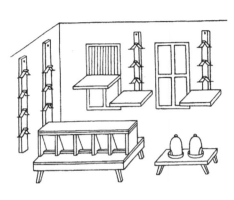

A settling cage.
Equipment inside the dovecote: a feeder and automatic drinkers; perches are fixed to the walls.

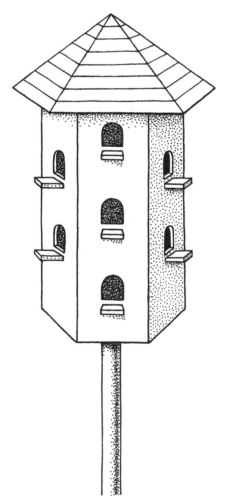

Wooden pigeonhouse

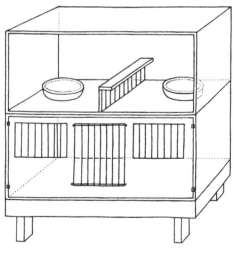

Diagram of a nesting box for pigeons

Pigeons are fed millet, wheat, barley, rice, vetch and some hemp seed in water. Smaller species are given canary grass seeds, poppy seed, spikes of Senegal millet, finely chopped green fodder and egg mix. Cal-

cium must be supplied daily in the form of eggshell, cuttlefish bone or lime. Grit must also always be available. These birds spend most of their time on the ground searching for berries and insects in the wild, and such food must also be provided for them in captivity, especially when they are rearing their young. For this reason, the cereal seeds in their diet must be combined with rowanberries and elderberries, currants, fruit chopped into small pieces, mealworms, small pupae and minced, boiled beef.

Females of most of the pigeon species lay two eggs. Their nests are very messy. Shallow baskets are hung in the aviaries and the pigeons build their nests in them. The young are fed in an interesting way: the parents pro-

a) Crested Bronzewing (*Ocyphaps lophotes*)
b) Bleeding Heart Dove (*Gallicolumba luzonica*)
c) Diamond Dove (*Geopelia cuneata*)

duce a high-protein substance inside their crops and regurgitate it to feed the hatchlings during the first five days or so. Later this mixture will contain increasing proportions of grain that has been soaked and softened in the parents' crops. The young are separated from the parents as soon as they can feed themselves, one month after hatching at the latest.

The **Crested Bronzewing** (*Ocyphaps lophotes*), found in the wild almost throughout Australia, is sometimes kept in aviaries. The main ingredients of its food are millet, hulled oats, maize, rice and finely chopped green fodder. The Crested Bronzewing grows to a length of about 33 cm (13 in) and can be kept together with pheasants because its young are able to fly as soon as they leave the nest. The female of this species incubates the eggs for 17—19 days. The young fly out of the nest when they are three weeks old and become entirely independent within another fortnight. This is when the young should be separated from the parents, otherwise the male will chase them away.

The **Bleeding Heart Dove** (*Gallicolumba luzonica*) is a pigeon about 26 cm (10 in) long. It comes from the Philippines where it lives in woods. It stays chiefly on the ground where it collects all kinds of berries and insects. The mainstay of its diet in captivity is millet, wheat and vetch which should be combined, especially at nesting time, with egg mix, boiled rice (with egg), white bread soaked in milk, minced lean meat, mealworms, small earthworms, small slugs and insects. Lettuce, dandelion, chickweed and fruit, all finely chopped, are the green fodder ingredients. In the autumn Bleeding Heart Doves should be transferred to a heated shelter because even mild frosts could harm their feet. In the aviary they spend most of their time on the ground but never nest there. Nesting baskets and boxes should be suspended in quiet places about 1 m (3 ft) high. These pigeons often abandon their eggs or stop feeding the hatched young after several days. If the hatchlings are to be saved and reared, reliable foster parents must be available.

The **Diamond Dove** (*Geopelia cuneata*), a native of inland Australia, is a suitable bird to keep in an aviary. It feeds on millet, canary grass and poppy seeds, spikes of Senegal millet and finely chopped lettuce, chickweed or dandelion. It can be kept in the company of other small birds except those of the same or related species. Before winter it must be taken from the aviary and placed in a heated room where the temperature remains above freezing point. A nesting basket containing some hay should be suspended about 1.5 m (5 ft) above the

Domestic pigeons

a trapdoor, worked by means of a pulled wire, on the front wall. When the new pigeon has settled down inside the dovecot, the keeper allows it to enter the settling cage from where it can observe the surroundings of the dovecot. A couple of days later the trapdoor is opened to allow the pigeon fly out. If nothing disturbs them in their flight, they will return to the dovecot later on. If nothing frightening happens during the first few days of freedom and the pigeons return home regularly, they can be considered as having become accustomed to their new home.

The basic equipment of the dovecot includes the nesting boxes. They are usually wooden, 80−100 cm (31−39 in) long, 40 cm (16 in) deep and 40 cm (16 in) high. There is a partition in the middle that is used to separate the young from the par-

ground. A reliable nester, the female, which has several breeds each year, lays two eggs. The young hatch after 13 days and leave the nest when ten days old.

Most pigeons kept loose in dovecots are undemanding and gregarious birds that like to live in larger communities, so it is advisable to keep a flock of at least five pairs.

Dovecots can be divided into two major groups: outside dovecots with separate doorways and chamber-type dovecots

An automatic feeder

with boxes inside a room. Pigeon fanciers mostly prefer the latter type, which allows the birds to be kept in closed rooms with one entrance for all. Several storeys of nesting boxes can line one wall or two opposite walls of the pigeon house. The entrance has a trapdoor, so the pigeons can be closed in.

The dovecot should be large enough (6−7 sq m/7−8 sq yd of floor area and 12−15 cu m/15.5 −19.5 cu yd of space is suitable for ten pairs) and it should be dry and easy to ventilate. Plenty of light should be provided throughout the year, including the winter season, by proper location of the windows. The equipment inside the dovecot must be simple and practical.

To accommodate new pigeons in the dovecot it is essential to have a settling cage. This cage, the size of a large nesting box (100×40×50 cm/39× 16×20 in), is attached on the outside of the entrance and has

Nesting dishes

ents when they produce another brood. The boxes are arranged in several rows, placed on top of each other, in the dovecot.

Artificial nesting bowls are also part of the basic equipment of the dovecot. These are round dishes, usually made of wood but they may also be made of plaster or fired clay. There should be several rows of perches in the dovecot: the birds will rest and sleep here outside of the nesting season.

Automatic feeders with vertical partitions for different kinds of grain are the best way to administer bulk feeds. A sufficient supply of clean water must be provided in drinkers, which are designed so as to prevent any dirt from getting into the water and allow easy cleaning and disinfection.

Pigeons love bathing, so the dovecots should be furnished with wide plastic or galvanised metal containers about 10 cm (4 in) high. The water must be removed after the birds have had their bath, to prevent them from drinking it. Various scrapers, shovels, rakes and other tools are used to clean the boxes, nests and perches.

Before the nesting season begins, the keeper must have inspected and prepared the nests and nesting boxes. Some pine sawdust should be poured onto the bottom of the nesting dishes. The birds will, of course, build their messy nests themselves but the keeper must supply them with enough building material, including leaves with stems, leafless stems of clover, alfalfa and the like, all chopped into pieces 13–15 cm (5–6 in) long.

The first eggs are laid six to eight days after mating and the parents take turns in incubating them. The young hatch from the eggs after 17–18 days. They are blind and almost naked, only sparsely covered with very fine down. During the first days of life the parents feed the hatchlings pigeon's milk, which is produced by glands inside their crops. Later, this early feed is replaced by half-digested grain. The young depend on their parent's care for about four weeks; then they leave the nest and live independently.

An appropriate diet is the main prerequisite for the good health of the birds and for successful breeding. Pigeons should be given cereals, including wheat, maize, oats and millet, and pulses, including garden peas, vetch and soya beans. Some oily seeds (linseed, hemp, rape and sunflower) may be used in small amounts to enrich the diet. Boiled flaked potatoes with an addition of some dry clover and alfalfa leaves, chopped nettles, spinach, grated carrot, and perhaps also dried yeast, are used as a supplementary feed. Pigeon food should be as varied as possible and contain plenty of minerals and vitamins in both summer and winter.

The best possible living conditions and strict hygiene should be maintained in the dovecot and its surroundings. Emphasis should be laid on protection from harm and prevention of disease rather than on the treatment of sick birds. The pigeons should be provided with adequate food, clean water and access to plenty of sunshine. Dirt must be removed regularly. Once in every two months a vitamin supplement should be added to drinking water. This can be purchased from a good pet shop or your vet. Follow closely the instructions on the packet.

The health and behaviour of the birds must be observed regularly and sick birds must be separated from the healthy ones immediately. In addition to regular cleaning, the whole dovecot must be thoroughly disinfected once every fortnight. The nests must also be thoroughly cleaned and disinfected when the young leave them. The whole dovecot and all its equipment should be cleaned thoroughly twice a year – in autumn when nesting is over and in spring.

The pigeon has the highest number of breeds of all domesticated animal species. About 200 breeds of pigeon, some subdivided into several dozen varieties, are listed in the handbooks. Popular types include tumblers, rollers, fantails, racers and homing pigeons.

Golden Pigeon

Quails and Pheasants (order Galliformes)

The methods used for keeping quails and pheasants differ substantially from those of keeping parrots, pigeons or small song-birds. Quails and pheasants are gallinaceans, which do not feed their young, so the keeper must take their eggs, leave them to incubate in a hatchery, and then take over the duties of rearing

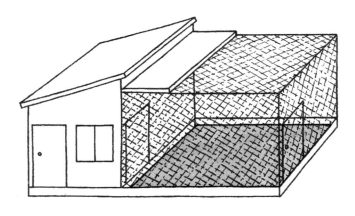

A type of garden aviary for pheasants

the young. The hatchlings of these species would die when their parents abandoned them if they are not replaced by suitable foster parents.

Quails and pheasants are aggressive towards birds of the same or related species, so pairs of each species must be kept in isolation. If there are two or more aviaries next to each other, the walls between them must be lined with wooden boards to a height of about 60 cm (2 ft), to prevent the cocks from seeing one another.

Animal food predominates in the diet of gallinaceans while they are young, while vegetable food predominates when they are adult. Vegetable food should include wheat, barley, oats, millet, hemp seeds, sunflower seeds, buckwheat and small-grained maize. In winter these birds should be given sprouted grains. Various berries (rowanberries, elderberries, currants etc.) are also important ingredients in the diet of quails and pheasants. The animal part of the diet can be replaced by high protein feeds, containing cereal meals, cooked flaked potatoes and meat or fish meal. Finely chopped green fodder, grated carrot or sugarbeet can be put into the mixture to increase its moisture content. A pinch of mineral supplement, and in winter a suitable vitamin supplement, should also be added.

In February the aviary should be prepared for nesting. If there are suitable shrubs and conifers, the female will find enough shelter for her nest. Reeds, straw and conifer branches leant against the walls of the aviary will also serve this purpose. The keeper should make hollows in these shelters and line them with moss and leaves to make a nesting place. The first food to be given to the newly hatched chicks includes egg mix, cottage cheese, fish or meat meal, and sometimes also boiled mayflies, all blended to produce a fairly wet mixture. The next day's mixture should be the same plus some protein meal, finely chopped green fodder and a pinch of lime. Later the proportion of egg is successively reduced until it is entirely eliminated from the mixture at the end of the second week. Simultaneously, the proportion of hulled millet and oat flakes must be increased. Older chicks can be given mealworms, grated carrot and cottage cheese. As they approach maturity, their diet should contain increasing proportions of larger grains until they are receiving the diet of adult birds.

The **Chinese Painted Quail** (*Coturnix chinensis*) has its range from India and Sri Lanka to southeastern China and Thaiwan, through Indonesia to Australia and as far east as New Caledonia and the Bismarck Archipelago. It makes its home in fields, meadows and grassy steppes. In captivity it requires an aviary overgrown with grass and in winter it should be kept in a heated shelter. In the aviary the quails usually incubate their eggs themselves, but in cages, although they do lay eggs, they will sit on them only for a few days or not at all; in such cases the keeper must try to incubate the eggs in a hatchery. The quails make their nests in grass on the ground. Tiny chicks emerge from the eggs after 17 days. They grow fast and need

Chinese Quail (*Coturnix chinensis*)

plenty of animal protein. The main ingredients of their diet include egg mix, a commercially produced high-protein mixture for chickens, ant pupae, mealworms, and later semolina, wheatgerm, soya bean and oat flour, poppy seed and small-grained millet. A supplement of finely chopped green fodder and calcium is essential. The quails do no harm to small birds but always fight with smaller gallinaceans. The adult quail is 12 cm (4.8 in) long.

The **California Quail** (*Lophortyx californica*), native to the Pacific coast of North America from southwestern Oregon to lower California, has also been introduced in Washington state, Utah, Arizona, New Mexico, Hawaii, New Zealand and Chile. It grows up to 24 cm (9.5 in) long. In captivity it can spend the winter in an aviary with a shelter. During the warm season the female will lay many

eggs but almost always fails to incubate them. A suitable foster mother must then be found or the eggs may be put in a hatchery. If fresh ant pupae and mealworms are not available, the newly hatched young should be given egg feed with poppy seed, a commercially produced high-protein mixture for chickens, finely chopped green fodder, grated carrot and insects. Small-grain millet is later added to the ration.

The **Golden Pheasant** (*Chrysolophus pictus*), distributed in the mountains of western China, is one of the most beautiful pheasants. It requires no special care, so even the beginner may keep it without problems. It is recommended to stock the aviary with three to four hens per cock. The Golden Pheasant is hardy and can endure European winters easily, but it is advisable to build it a dry shelter of straw matting inside the roofed part of the aviary. It crosses easily with other pheasant species, so many of the birds kept by fanciers are crossbreds, especially with the Lady Amherst Pheasant. The female lays

California Quail (*Lophortyx californica*)

12–16 eggs. The young hatch after 23–24 days and are able to live independently at an age of three months. The hen of the Golden Pheasant is a good sitter and its care of its young is exemplary.

The **Lady Amherst Pheasant** (*Chrysolophus amherstiae*) native to the mountains of south-western China, southeastern Tibet and northern Burma, is another pheasant that is seldom found in its purebred form in captivity. It does well in a large aviary that is densely overgrown

Lady Amherst Pheasant (*Chrysolophus amherstiae*) – a cock and a hen

Impeyan Pheasant (*Lophophorus impeyanus*)

Golden Pheasant (*Chrysolophus pictus*)

with shrubs, and has no problems overwintering in Europe. The ideal sex ratio is one cock to three or four females. In April and May the female lays 15–20 eggs which she incubates for 23–24 days. The chicks of this species are somewhat less hardy than the chicks of the Golden Pheasant.

The **Silver Pheasant** (*Lophura nycthemera*) lives in the hilly regions of Burma, Thailand and Indo-China, southern China and Hainan Island. It is one of the pheasants that even an absolute beginner can keep. The best stock in the aviary consists of two or three hens per cock. Late in April the female lays 15–20 eggs and sits on them steadily. The young hatch after 25–26 days and if the aviary is large enough the hen will look after them very carefully. They need plenty of green fodder and animal protein.

The **Impeyan Pheasant** (*Lophophorus impeyanus*) is an inhabitant of high mountains from eastern Afghanistan to Bhutan and southern Tibet. Hardy enough in its homeland, it can withstand severe frosts in captivity. In high summer it must avoid direct exposure to sunshine. This pheasant can be left

Silver Pheasant (*Lophura nycthemera*)

The **Blue-eared Pheasant** (*Crossoptilon auritum*) from eastern Tibet and western China, is an undemanding and tame species, ideal for keeping loose in the garden provided it is safe from foxes and cats. It takes all the food mentioned on page 204. At the end of May the female lays eggs in a small hollow scraped in the ground. The young are very agile after hatching and less sensitive to low temperatures than the chicks of other pheasants.

The **Brown-eared Pheasant** (*Crossoptilon mantchuricum*), a native of western China, is kept either loose in a safe garden or in a large aviary. If the aviary or garden is not large enough, however, and does not afford adequate shelter in shrubs, the female will fail to incubate the eggs. The clutch of 10—12 eggs is laid in a hollow on the ground and the young hatch after 26—27 days. They take much the same type of food as other pheasants.

to range freely over the garden providing no cats or foxes can get in. If it is kept in an aviary there must be an area of at least 40—50 sq m (48—60 sq yds) per pair and plenty of shelters among the shrubs. In April the female lays four to six eggs from which the young hatch after 27—28 days. They are fed egg mix, live insects, plenty of green fodder and finely chopped fruit. The young are sensitive to damp, so it is recommended to keep them in a shelter with an infrared heater in rainy weather.

a) **Blue-eared Pheasant (*Crossoptilon auritum*)**
b) **Brown-eared Pheasant (*Crossoptilon mantchuricum*)**

207

Ducks (order Anseriformes)

A description of a suitable pool or lake built for waterfowl kept in the garden is given on page 172. A larger lake may have a small island where the sitting adult, and later the young, will be safe from predators.

Many ducks can stay outdoors in the garden in the European climate if a suitable shelter is built for them. Even the less hardy ducks can overwinter at a temperature of 3–5 °C (37–41 °F). Part of the water surface must be kept free of ice and the ducks' diet must be high in energy-giving food in winter.

To prepare nesting places, the keeper must know the ducks' nesting habit in the wild. Shallow pits are dug in places hidden among plants and then lined with dry grass; small boxes or barrels containing bedding and with an open front wall may also be used. For ducks that nest on the ground, the boxes are buried underground and only the roofed passage to the

entrance is left open. For the tree ducks, the boxes are placed on trees or posts about 1.5 m (5 ft) above the ground. The box for small and medium-sized ducks should be 30 × 30 × × 40 cm (12 × 12 × 16 in) in size and the diameter of the entrance should be 15–17 cm (6–6.7 in). For successful nesting there should not be too many birds in the lake, while on the other hand, there should be many hiding places. Nevertheless, in the majority of cases the eggs will have to be entrusted to a dwarf domestic hen or duck.

The main ingredients of the ducklings' starter diet include duckweed and a soft food prepared from bread soaked in water or milk, oatmeal or wheat bran, cottage cheese or hard-boiled egg, protein meal, chopped lettuce, dandelion or nettles, dry ant pupae or mayflies and meat or fish meal. Mineral supplements should be added.

At the age of two to three weeks ducklings begin to take small grains, preferably millet soaked in water. The adult diet is successively introduced from their fourth week. It is based on

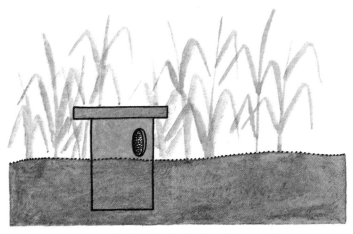

Nesting box for ducks on the ground

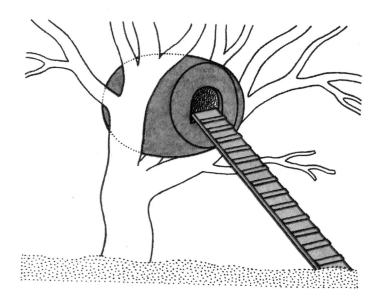

Nesting box for ducks in a tree

cereal grains and soft food of the following composition: one part boiled potatoes, three parts soaked bread, two parts crushed barley, one part crushed maize, one part wheatgerm, one part fish meal and a pinch of mineral supplement. In summer this mixture is enriched with green fodder and in winter with boiled carrots.

The **Mandarin Duck** (*Aix galericulata*) is distributed from southeastern Siberia to China, Korea and Japan where it nests chiefly in tree tops. To provide suitable conditions for the duck in captivity, boxes are fixed on a tree or a post about 1.5 m (5 ft) above the ground. As soon as the young hatch, their mother guides them to water. The mainstay of their diet is duckweed with ant pupae. Duckweed can be replaced by finely chopped lettuce, spinach or dandelion. As the ducklings grow, their soft food should contain increasing amounts of minced fresh or boiled meat, oat flakes, millet and wheat, and later also boiled potatoes; in this way the diet of adult ducks is gradually introduced. In winter the ducks are left on the pool but there must be a shelter littered with straw somewhere near, where they can hide whenever they like.

The **Wood Duck** (*Aix sponsa*) has its range in North America, especially in the eastern parts of the USA and in southern Canada. The box for this typical tree duck should be suspended from a tree or set on a tall post. The young hatch from the clutch of 8—12 eggs after 32 days and six weeks later they are able to live independently. If the female does not sit on the eggs herself she has to be replaced by a domesticated duck or hen. The first food of the young is ant pupae and duckweed. Egg feed and small grains are added later.

The **Baikal Teal** (*Anas formosa*) lives in northeastern Siberia during the summer season and migrates to China and Japan for the winter. It needs plenty of animal food (small slugs, worms and insects).

a) **Mandarin Duck** (*Aix galericulata*)
b) **Wood Duck** (*Aix sponsa*)
c) **Baikal Teal** (*Anas formosa*)

Keeping Small Mammals

Mammals are most popular among the public and many fanciers keep them. First of all it must be noted that small mammals are intelligent, dexterous and adventurous creatures, so they cannot be left to run freely

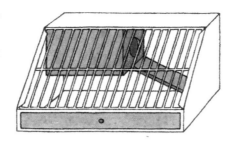

This all-metallic cage is safe. Even the Golden Hamster, an escape artist, cannot get out and cause damage in the flat.

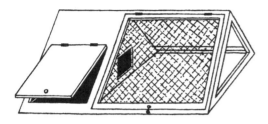

A portable cage suitable for guinea-pigs and rabbits. When the animal is to be left to graze, the bottom is removed.

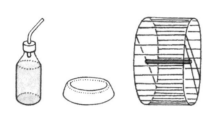

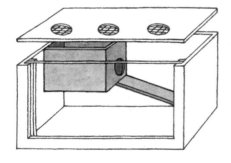

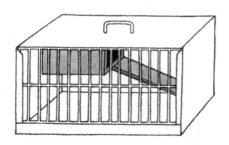

Different types of cages for mice. A cage with a glazed front wall is suitable for observation. The closed bedroom is cleaned from above. The equipment includes a drinker, a feeder and aids to allow sufficient exercise for the animals, such as a tread-wheel.

over an apartment. They cannot be trained as easily as cats or dogs, so freedom of movement could be dangerous for them, to the furnishings and even to the keeper's family. Hence, the first thing the keeper must provide is suitable housing for the newcomer. Its accommodation must meet the animal's requirements and, of course, must leave no chance of escape. For example, the material used to make a cage or terrarium must be resistent to rodents' sharp teeth and eliminate any attempt made by the pet to escape. Terrariums, either of the all-glass type or combined with a dense, hard metal mesh or a metal grating, are the best quarters for small mammals such as mice, hamsters and the like. There must be no wooden parts in the housing facilities for mice, hamsters and gerbils. Only guinea pigs do not gnaw and seldom seek ways to escape, so they could be kept in a small wooden pen.

A small terrarium is suitable only for animals that do not move about much and will therefore be content with limited exercise such as in a wheel. The more agile animals, such as squirrels, dormice, and chipmunks, or even small harvest mice, must be given more space, preferably in a cage made of sheet metal and dense netting with a mesh up to 8 mm (0.3 in). The small species, such

as the harvest mouse, will be content with a cage about 80 × 80 × 40 cm (31 × 31 × 16 in) in size, with a cylindrical extension to hold reeds or other stems on which the little creature can climb. A squirrel will need a larger cage, of at least 100 × 100 × 150 cm (39 × 39 × × 59 in). Small beasts of prey and monkeys or small primates need large aviaries, preferably

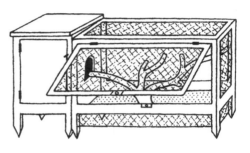

Smaller and simpler equipment for rearing ground squirrels and other small mammals. If the sides are buried in the ground they must extend at least 20 cm (8 in) below the surface to prevent the animals from undermining the wire netting and escaping.

out of doors, because most of them produce an odour that is often very offensive. It is not difficult to keep such animals in a typical European climate: all they need is a large, strong aviary and a garden house where they can shelter during the winter. However, a high temperature and often also high

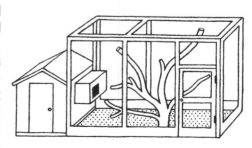

Tree animals, such as squirrels, need a lot of space and a box accessible from the rear.

humidity must be steadily maintained if exotic species are kept. For this reason accommodation for primates and monkeys is costly and these costs will be recouped only by very experienced keepers who specialize in rare creatures.

Of course, various species of farm animals also make good pets. Rabbits, especially the small breeds, are very popular; they are kept in an ordinary rabbit hutch.

Small hoofed animals, especially miniature horses and donkeys, have become very popular in recent years, particularly in the USA, where the best specimens are highly prized and sold for large sums of money. These small animals, as well as dwarf goats and miniature pigs, require stables, byres and sties just like their larger relatives. They also need a free range where they can run about. Their requirements in terms of space are considerable as they need a lot of exercise, so they are really not suitable pets for most people. Of course, the keeper can always walk his or her pet on a lead in the country, but this takes up much time and such a walk is not exactly what the animal would prefer.

Money and material should not be spared when facilities for breeding small mammals are

The Racoon is a playful but not very reliable animal. It requires a lot of care and is not a suitable pet for children.

Breeding thoroughbred rabbits can be recommended to everyone. This Castorex with lovely velvety fur is a good example.

built. Except for the smallest pets, all mammals need a solid, safe building that is easy to clean (including the range): this is doubly necessary because mammals can sometimes be affected by diseases and parasites that are transferable to people. The building must also be sturdy because – as distinct from pets such as invertebrates, the majority of fish or most birds – the larger mammals live to a good age (ten years or more) and hate changing their surroundings and routines.

Rodents

Rodents are the cheapest and most easily available small mammals, so they are commonly kept by beginners. Nearly all of them exist in the wild; the Guinea Pig, a domestic animal

Small rodents are vulnerable to diseases and external effects. The state of health of a mouse is reflected by its appearance and posture. Top: a healthy animal. Bottom: a sick animal.

kept by Peruvian Indians, is the only one to have undergone a long history of coexistence with people.

The **Guinea Pig** (*Cavia aperea* var. *porcellus*) bears all the common traits of a domestic

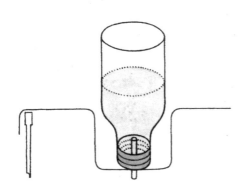

Water contaminated with the excrement of animals may be a source of infection. Hence, a hygienic drinker is a prerequisite for successful breeding.

animal, including variations of colouring and coat type: Guinea Pigs may be single-coloured or pied, short- or long-haired (Angora), and there are also some with hairs that are fanned out to form irregular rosettes. Guinea Pigs are undemanding, peaceable and quiet. They are kept in threes or fours in wooden boxes about 100×50 cm (39×20 in) in size. The side walls of the box are about 30 cm (12 in) high. Oat straw, wood shavings and paper can be used as bedding. There should be no colour print on the paper if newspapers are used; guinea pigs love to eat paper and might become poisoned by the toxic ink (they are very sensitive to chemicals). They do well at room temperature but can also withstand greater cold. They are, however, sensitive to wet and draughts. They should not be left out in the rain and only in exceptional cases should they be bathed. As they need a hiding place, the keeper should provide a small wooden or cardboard box for this purpose. Their summer diet includes green fodder with an addition of grain (oats) or oat flakes. In winter they will take hay, grain and vegetables, such as carrot. Besides this, Guinea Pigs love bread (both white and brown), lettuce, cabbage, fruit, dandelion leaves and the like, and should be given water to drink. In summer they may be left in a small enclosure in the garden but must be protected from excessive exposure to sunshine, from rain, and against cats and other animals that could harm them. A tame Guinea Pig may be left to run freely in flat or house. It will not damage the furniture and is easy to catch. It is easy to tame a Guinea Pig and it will soon recognise the people who look after it. Guinea Pigs breed twice or thrice a year. The female is

The Golden Hamster is a playful and nimble companion. There are many colour varieties and types of coat.

pregnant for up to 65 days and the young (two to six) are born with their coats on and their eyes open. The day after birth they will eat vegetable food and they will be weaned after two weeks of taking milk from their mother. A box $30 \times 20 \times 20$ cm ($12 \times 8 \times 8$ in) in size with a handle and air holes can be used to carry your pet from one place to another. If properly cared for, a Guinea Pig may live for up to eight years.

The **Golden Hamster** (*Mesocricetus auratus*) is another popular rodent. Many colour mutations have been developed (white, gold, black and white and others). Unlike the Guinea Pig, the Golden Hamster never stops gnawing and trying to escape, so it must be kept in a terrarium or in a box $40 \times 30 \times 30$ cm ($16 \times 12 \times 12$ in) in size, lined with sheet metal and covered with perforated metal or strong metal netting. Hamsters are active at night. They need plenty of bedding (hay, wood wool, sawdust); when building a nest they will also use cotton wool or another fine fibre. The terrarium should be furnished with toys, such as ladders, wheels and tree branches. The floor covering should be replaced once a week; the nest is replaced less frequently. The Golden Hamster feeds on green fodder, hay, grains, vegetables and fruit. Boiled eggs, meat or insects (mealworms, crickets) may be added from time to time. Nothing sweet should be given. Clean water should always be available for drinking. The Golden Hamster is a prolific breeder. The female remains pregnant for only 15–17 days. The 4–16 young are blind and naked when they are born, but reach maturity at the age of five months. Hamsters are aggressive, so the young

must be separated from their parents and each other as they approach maturity. They usually live to the age of three to four years.

The various species of Dwarf Hamsters, including those of the genera *Phodopus* (**Striped Hairy-footed Hamster** – *P. sungorus* – and **Roborovsky's**

Gerbils (genus *Gerbillus*) and Jirds (genus *Meriones*) have also become very popular in recent years. There are about 15 species in these genera, all from the deserts of Asia and Africa. They are kept in large terrariums at a temperature of about 25 °C (77 °F). The terrarium must be well sealed with a per-

The Gerbil needs plenty of exercise, so its cage should be as large as possible.

The Striped Hairy-footed Hamster is smaller and somewhat less agile. It is a good companion for children.

Dwarf Hamster – *P. roborovskii*), or *Cricetulus* (**Migratory Hamster** – *C. migratorius*, **Striped Hamster** – *C. barabensis* or **Chinese Hamster** – *C. griseus*), are much more peaceable. The care they require does not differ from the requirements of the Golden Hamster. The Dwarf Hamsters are smaller and are easy to tame and breed in captivity. They have about ten young several times a year. The gestation period lasts about 20 days and the young reach maturity within half a year, so they can start breeding in the same year they were born. They live to be about three years old.

forated cover because Gerbils and Jirds are very agile and are able to jump high on their long legs. In the wild they live in shallow holes in the sand and in captivity they require a hiding place, such as a small box, or should be allowed to dig a burrow. They take both animal and vegetable food: fodder crops, grains, nuts, vegetables, insects. Two to four times a year the female bears about four young after a three-week pregnancy. In captivity Gerbils and Jirds live up to five years. Both genera are typical nocturnal animals.

Perhaps the most modest animals that can be kept as pets

are the various species of the mouse, the **White Mouse** (*Mus musculus* var. *alba*) being the most popular of them all. They can be kept in glass containers (simple aquariums) or terrariums measuring 40 × 20 × 15 cm (16 × 8 × 6 in), on a litter of sawdust or wood shavings, 2–2.5 cm (0.7–1 in) deep. Some material (hay, cottonwool) should be available for nest building. The temperature should be maintained above 20 °C (68 °F). The mice feed on oats, oily seeds, vegetables and dog biscuits. Water should be provided preferably from drinkers. The period of gestation is 18–20 days. The young are blind and naked when they are born and the mother cares for them for six weeks. After eight weeks they are able to reproduce. They live for two years at most, but the females are suitable for breeding for only eight months.

The **White Rat** (*Rattus norvegicus* var. *alba*) is more entertaining and intelligent than a mouse. It requires the same conditions as the White Mouse but, of course, the feed rations and terrarium must be proportionally larger. The gestation period of the White Rat is 21–23 weeks. The young are weaned after 25 days and reach maturity after about 60 days. Like mice, they can be kept in groups of four females and one male. As a rule, the White Rat will be able to reproduce for only one year, although it will live for as long as three to four years if well cared for. Crossing the White Rat with the original grey form produces various colour mutations, ranging from beige to black with white patches, or to coffee-coloured specimens. A well-cared-for White Rat is easy to tame and is very playful.

Many people are repelled by rat-like rodents, which are associated with sewers and disease. On the other hand, the tree rodents are all very popular, though they require much more care in captivity.

The **Red Squirrel** (*Sciurus vulgaris*) is a lovely creature, and popular among keepers in Europe. This squirrel is now almost extinct in Britain. The **Grey**

The Fat Dormouse is a perfect animal for breeders who need something special: a beautiful nocturnal creature which is protected by law in many countries.

Squirrel (*Sciurus carolinensis*) is common throughout Britain. Squirrels need a large cage or aviary and cannot be left to run freely in your home because they will always gnaw at something and there will be problems with hygiene. The minimum size of cage for a squirrel is 100 × 100 × 150 cm (39 × 39 × 59 in). Squirrels are quarrelsome, so you cannot keep more than one squirrel in a cage. They seldom breed in captivity. Inside the cage there must be a hiding box, branches on which the squirrel will clamber and a place where it will find shelter from wind and rain. Sawdust is a good bedding material to spread on the bottom of the cage. The bedding should be replaced once a week. Squirrels feed on various seeds, fruits and vegetables, and drink water. The gestation period of the squirrel is about 40 days. The three to six young are naked and blind when they are born and open their eyes after about 30 days. After eight weeks they are able to live independently and reach maturity at 10–12 months. The lifespan of the Red

The American Grey Squirrel is more flexible than the Red Squirrel and is easier to keep.

Squirrel is eight years or more. Taming is successful only when the young are taken early from the nest.

Other exotic squirrels have the same requirements as the Grey and Red squirrels.

Dormice, another large group of rodents, can also be kept in large cages and aviaries. It must be remembered that dormice are protected by law in many countries. Four species live in Europe and the **Fat Dormouse** (*Glis glis*) is the commonest of these. Although the Fat Dormouse does well in captivity, it is difficult to tame and will bite the keeper without hesitation. The **Common Dormouse** (*Muscardinus avellanarius*) is much easier to keep as a pet. Not much larger than a house mouse, it is a fascinating little creature and also peaceable. The **Forest Dormouse** (*Dryomys nitedula*) lives in the wild only in the eastern part of central Europe and is very shy. The **Garden Dormouse** (*Eliomys quercinus*) is rare and on the verge of extinction in many countries, so it should not be taken from the wild.

All dormice should be kept in a secure cage because they will try every method to escape. Unlike squirrels, which are active during the daytime, dormice are exclusively nocturnal creatures, staying in their hiding place or nest throughout the day. They

The African Spiny Mouse is undemanding and placid but requires a higher temperature and numerous hiding places.

feed on fruit and nuts in shells and their diet should be enriched from time to time with insects, eggs and pieces of meat. It is recommended that you feed them in the evening. They will drink water from drinkers suspended on branches or hung on the walls of the cage. Dormice are shy, so their cage should stand in a quiet place. The temperature need not be high but must not rise or fall too much, which would be harmful to the animals. In the wild dormice hibernate in winter, so healthy and well-fed specimens should be left in an unheated place for at least part ot the winter season in order to have their winter rest. Dormice do not reproduce frequently in captivity. The female is pregnant for about three weeks and the young (four to eight) are naked and blind when they are born. They leave the nest after 20 days, and the following day they reach maturity. Dormice can sometimes be kept in pairs but never in groups; only the Common Dormice are tolerant of their own kind.

The group of creatures called ground squirrels enjoy special popularity among keepers. This group includes the **Burunduk**, **Chipmunk** and **Chickaree**. In the wild, in places where they are not disturbed by people,

The Degu, from South America, is very hardy and is able to reproduce in very basic conditions.

these prettily coloured, agile animals are quite tame. They can be kept in a large terrarium, well sealed to prevent escapes, and furnished with a tree stump, thick branches or a stone, under which they normally build their nests in the wild; in captivity in a terrarium they should be given a box for this purpose. The ground squirrels feed on various seeds, especially those rich in oil, fruit, mushrooms, insects and other invertebrates. Each animal has its own territory which it defends against intruders, so they must be kept in isolation or at the most in pairs. They reproduce only in spring when the female bears a litter of four to six young that are blind and naked. Reproduction in captivity is a rarity. They seldom hibernate. In captivity they do not live longer than four years.

The **Harvest Mouse** (*Micromys minutus*), an inhabitant of corn fields or large reed stands, is a delightful pet. It is adept in climbing up and down the stalks, where it builds its small, round nest. It is mostly kept in a tower terrarium which offers good opportunities for climbing. The terrarium should contain a pot with a sturdy plant to climb up, eg. dry reed stems. The diet of the Harvest Mouse includes grains and oat flakes, pieces of nut, seeds and green fodder. Overfeeding of the tiny mice must be avoided. Harvest Mice are kept in pairs or small groups of one male to two females. The gestation period is 21 days. There are five to nine young in the litter and the young will take vegetable food after 26 days. They do well in captivity and are easy to tame. They do not live longer than two years.

Other rodents kept as pets are the **Chinchilla** (*Chinchilla laniger*) and the **Short-tailed Chinchilla** (*Chinchilla chinchilla*). Chinchillas were first farmed

as fur skin animals in the 1920s. In 1934 they were introduced into Europe and have been kept there ever since. They do not need much space, so a large cage will be sufficient. The temperature should be maintained at about 18 °C (64 °F) and the air humidity must be low. The cage should contain shelves or branches where the animal can climb. To keep their coat in good condition, chinchillas like to 'bathe' in fine sand. They are fed green fodder, groats, sprouted grains or oily seeds; water

Chinchilla

should be supplied for drinking. The gestation period of these animals is very long – about 50

days. The one to four young are born with their coats on, their eyes open, and with developed teeth. They begin to take food on the third day but are not weaned until after about 50 days. Sexual maturity is reached after about three months. Chinchillas are kept in pairs or groups with one male. They can be tamed easily and make lovely pets. They live for a very long time, many up to 20 years.

Rabbits and Hares

These animals used to be classified with the rodents. Their teeth include continuously

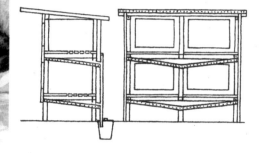

There may be different types of rabbit cages, but all must have a double floor: the lower floor should be inclined to allow urine to run down. Good hygiene prevents infection.

Fanciers keep uncommon species and breeds. The Japanese Rabbit is noted for its special colouring.

The hare, which is bigger, and the rabbit are relatives living wild in Europe. The picture shows the diference between them.

taken from the wild. The gestation period of the hare is 45–50 days and the two to three young are born with their coats on and their eyes open. The mother suckles them five times daily at first and later three times daily, but otherwise takes little care of them. If a young hare is found that really has been abandoned (it will be emaciated, bristling and restless), it should be given condensed milk, thinned one

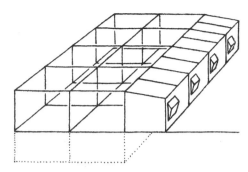

Keeping rabbits in a cage in the garden.

growing incisors and, like rodents, they constantly need to sharpen them by gnawing on twigs and the like, which must be provided in their hutches. However, in all other respects rabbits and hares differ significantly from rodents.

The **Brown Hare** (*Lepus capensis*) is shy and seldom reproduces in captivity: hence it is encountered in captivity mostly as a rescued orphan or injured adult. A healthy adult or well-fed youngster should *never* be

The Siamese Sable is popular both in its normal and dwarf sizes.

It is useful to have a removable plate under the slatted floor.

part to one part with carrot juice. To obtain the juice, carrots should be grated on a plastic grater and the juice pressed from this while held in a cloth. This basic food should be enriched with vitamins and minerals. For drink, the young hare should be given water or cool camomile tea if it has diarrhoea. Its belly should be gently massaged. Older hares can be given the same food as the domestic rabbit. The hare will become tame but it will never overcome problems of hygiene. Inside a house it will damage furniture with its incisors, so it

must be kept outdoors in a strong hutch from where it cannot escape by digging or biting through the walls. Such a tame animal cannot be released later to live wild, for it would soon fall prey to dogs or people, of whom it will not be afraid. A captive hare may live for eight to ten years.

The **Rabbit** (*Oryctolagus cuniculus*) is in many ways a domestic animal. There is a wide range of rabbit breeds, ranging from those weighing 9 kg (20 lb) to dwarf breeds not reaching 1 kg (2 lb). Rabbits are kept for meat and fur and also just as pets. They are easy to tame, and can be kept in pens, hutches and outdoor enclosures or runs enclosed by wire netting. The size of the facility where they are kept depends on the size of the breed. Adult rabbits, especially the females, must be kept in isolation because they are quarrelsome. At breeding time the male is allowed to stay with the female only for the time needed for mating. The gestation period lasts about 30 days and the female often bears as many as ten young. Most keepers reduce the number of the young to between four and six, depending on the mother's condition. The young are left to stay with their mother at least six weeks; they are kept together until they are four months old and then the males and females are separated. The age at which maturity is reached depends on the breed and ranges between five and six months. However, it is advisable not to allow young rabbits to begin to breed until two months later. Rabbits feed on green fodder, hay, oats, groats, vegetables, bread and the like, and food should be given twice daily. Water is best for drinking; it is recommended that you use tough, earthenware dishes that cannot be overturned.

The choice of breed depends

Chinchillas are among the most undemanding rabbit breeds. They may be either large or small.

Dwarf rabbits make good pets. They are kept in many colour varieties and coat types, from the wild type to the Albino Ermine.

on the purpose for which the rabbit is to be kept. Breeds of the medium sized and large types are the hardiest: these include the Chinchilla Giganta, the Flemish Giant and White British Giant Rabbit. Small and dwarf breeds predominate among the rabbits kept as pets. The weight of the small breeds is about 2.5–2.75 kg (5.5–6 lb) and that of the dwarf rabbits about 1 kg (2 lb).

The Small Chinchilla is one of the popular small breeds. Also popular is the Siamese Sable Rabbit, which has dark patches on its nose and paws and a dark stripe along its back, the Black and Tan Rabbit, with red patches (black was originally the basic colour but now there are also blue and brown rabbits of this breed), and the Dutch and Himalayan rabbits. The English Butterfly Rabbit is a popular breed at shows, in which the excellence of the pattern on the coat is evidence of the keeper's breeding skill. The Silver Fox rabbits, whose fur is white at the tips, are also impressive.

The most common dwarf breeds are the Red- and Blue-eyed Polish rabbits. It is a handsome general-purpose breed whose skin is used in the furrier industry. Rabbits of this breed are cuddly and easy to tame, content with a small living space and not fastidious about food. They have a pleasing appearance with short ears, a large round head and short legs on a plump body: the adult rabbits look as if they have never grown up. Besides the Polish Rabbit, there are dwarf varieties of all the small breeds, including the Siamese Sable, Black and Tan, Chinchilla, Himalayan and Dutch rabbits, as well as the various types of single-colour rabbits.

The Rex rabbits are another interesting group. They were bred for their fur but are kept as showing breeds because of their handsome appearance and velvety coats. They are not easy to keep, however, because they are sensitive to draughts and damp and have special requirements as to food and care. The weight of the Rex rabbit ranges from 3.50 to 3.70 kg (7.5–8 lb) and their coats must not have hair longer than 2 cm (0.75 in).

The Japanese Brindled Rabbit, with its striking black and yellow stripes or blotches, is a typical show breed, that can also be kept as a pet. It is large and plump, weighs about 4 kg (9 lb), has a somewhat coarse coat and develops slowly.

All rabbits are prone to contagious diseases, so good principles of hygiene must be strictly observed. Some diseases can be prevented by vaccination. During periods of infection, it is illegal to transport any rabbits, including pets, from affected areas to those that are disease-free, and vice versa. Quarantine regulations apply to imported rabbits just as to any other domestic animal.

Small Predators

Many predators are noted for their elegance of motion, attractive appearance and intelligence and many keepers long to test their skill at breeding them.

However, most small beasts of prey are difficult to keep. The facilities they require are rather complex, with great emphasis placed on safety. This is the main reason why it is inadvisable for children or adolescents to keep them. The smaller animals are extremely nimble and clever and seize the slightest opportunity of escaping. It is

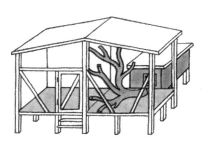

A large cage in the garden is necessary to keep the small predators, especially Martens.

then that trouble with your neighbours can begin! Such animals can play havoc with livestock, and may even escape into the wild to become a much feared pest.

There is a long tradition of keeping the **Ferret**, the partially domesticated **Polecat** (either *Putorius eversmanni* or *P. putorius*). Ferrets, both natural and albino varieties, were kept instead of cats in the households of the ancient Romans. The **Ferret** (*Mustela putorius furo*) is a rather sturdy creature, weighing almost 1 kg (2 lb); it is strong and pugnacious and for this reason it has been used to chase rabbits out of their burrows. The ferret bites quite viciously, so if it is to become accustomed to human company, it must be given a great deal of attention from a very young age. Ferrets and dogs hate each other, and small animals, such as guinea pigs, are in great danger when a ferret is nearby.

Originating in the Mediterranean region, the ferret must be kept in dry, warm, draught-free conditions. Its pen, similar to those in which rabbits are kept, must be located in a quiet place.

To rear the young, the ferret needs a small box with a removable roof, and must not be disturbed. Sawdust is used for the bedding and the nest is made of hay. The bedding must be replaced every week. Ferrets feed on meat, fat, and a mixture of oat flakes or groats and milk. If raw meat is given to them it must be of high quality, fresh and fit for animal consumption. Food leftovers must be immediately removed and the dishes washed every day.

The ferret's gestation period is 42 days, after which the female bears a litter of five to eight, all naked and blind. The young will open their eyes after a month, become independent

The Ferret is a domesticated form of the Polecat; it may have either a wild or white colouring. It emits a powerful smell, so it is best in the garden.

by three months, but will not reach maturity until six to nine months old. Those used for reproduction must be at least one year old. They live for about eight years. When frightened, they emit a strong smell similar to that of the polecat.

The **Stoat** or **Ermine** (*Mustela erminea*) and **Weasel** (*Mustela nivalis*) are smaller and more demanding than the Ferret. They are hardly 25 cm (10 in) long but are very lively, active and untamable. (Of the two, there is a greater chance of taming a young Ermine than a Weasel.) They are kept in a large terrarium of at least 100×70×70 cm (39×28×28 in) in size, which must be securely closed. On the bottom there should be a layer of sand, peat or other material, plus tree branches, roots, stones, a heavy dish containing water, and a box. The Ermine and Weasel

The Marten has always lived close to people, so it is easy to tame and keep.

feed on small vertebrates, chiefly mice, but not on pure meat. They will consume one dead mouse or chick every day but can be left to fast once or twice a week. They should be allowed to leave their terrarium only in an empty room, free of any places where the animals could hide. They cannot be let loose outdoors because they would soon escape. In captivity they do not reproduce, and live no longer than two to three years. **Martens** (*Martes martes* and *M. foina*) are much nicer pets, intelligent and easy to tame. If they are handled correctly at a very young age they will follow the keeper like small dogs. They need a large cage or aviary 1.8–2m (6–6.5ft) high, 8m (26ft) long and at least 2m (6.5ft) wide, with a wooden box in which to hide and many branches for climbing. The wire nett-

ing should be strong and dense (2.5cm/1in mesh maximum). They cannot be left to run about in the house because they can easily be injured if they come into contact with heating elements, sharp edges and the like. Martens can be left outdoors all year round, especially if they are given a double-walled box. Their home should be located out of the prevailing wind, in a partly shaded place with a layer of coarse sand or peat on the ground. Martens feed on meat, fat and eggs and in addition 10–20 per cent of their diet should consist of fruit, vegetables, oat mash and the like. Whole dead mice, chicks or large insects are strongly recommended to vary the diet. These animals seldom reproduce in captivity. Their gestation period is nine months and the young, naked and blind, are born in spring. Five weeks later they open their eyes, at two months they leave the nest and reach maturity the following year. They live for up to 15 years.

Various types of **Mink** (*Lutreola vison*) are kept as fur-skin animals on farms but they can be kept equally well as pets. Unfortunately, they are difficult to tame and do bite. They need a cage made of wire netting and a run. They feed on meat and have no difficulty reproducing in captivity.

Exotic carnivores are much rarer pets, requiring great skill and experience on the part of the keeper. Of the Viverridae, some fanciers keep the **Genet** (*Genetta genetta*), which also lives wild in southern Europe, various species of **Egyptian Mongoose** (genus *Herpestes*) and others. They are managed in the same way as Martens, but must be kept in heated accommodation and cannot live outdoors during winter. **Racoons** (Procyonidae) are another inter-

esting group of exotic predators; they are lovely to look at and very playful. The **North American Racoon** (*Procyon lotor*), kept in many zoos or as a fur skin animal, is the most common of this family. It needs a large, very strong cage with a 15 litre (3 gallon) pool (larger if possible), a tree to climb and a large box measuring 85×75×65cm (33×30×26in). It is given a mixed diet containing meat and fish, and also vegetables and fruit. The Racoon can spend the winter outdoors and sometimes hibernates.

The **Kinkajou** (*Potos flavus*), also called the honey bear, is perhaps the loveliest pet of this group. It is very gracious and playful, and has a monkey-like tail. As it comes from the tropics,

The Pastel Mink is not only splendid looking but also very valuable. A perfect individual is very hard to obtain.

it is sensitive to cold and fastidious about food.

Foxes and **Arctic Foxes** are the most commonly kept Canidae (apart from dogs, of course). Unfortunately, they can be rather dangerous and also produce an offensive smell. The most attractive pet of this family is perhaps the **Fennec**, which can be kept indoors like a dog. It is easy to tame but must be kept in warm conditions and away from the general bustle of the household. It feeds on

The Mink is bred for its fur but may make a nice pet. However, it is difficult to tame. The black-cross type of colouring is among the most interesting.

The Common Fox is a fine and interesting animal but needs special conditions in captivity.

Miniature Hoofed Animals

Hoofed animals are among the oldest domesticated animals, having lived with people for more than 10,000 years. They are still considered indispensable in many regions of the world. Some miniature breeds have been developed. These do not have the working abilities of their larger relatives but can be kept as pets purely for pleasure, so people who do not have the conditions required for keeping a full-sized horse or donkey

boiled meat, mice, artificially cultivated insects and fruit. It can walk on a lead like a little dog, even if the temperature is below zero. However, it must not get soaked and then allowed to get cold. In captivity it will survive for several years.

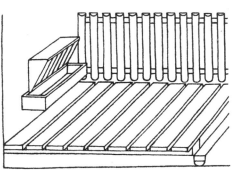

The necessary equipment of a stable: a manger, crib and slatted floor. If several animals are kept, there must be partitions between the stalls.

need not be deprived of caring for smaller members of these species. Miniature ungulates are not easy to care for and this is why they are so very expensive to keep.

Miniature Horses are the most widespread of all. The smallest of them are only 70 cm (28 in) high at the wither (the size of a large dog); most are about 80 cm (31 in). These small horses do not need special housing because they are so small, and they feed on the same fodder as normal-sized horses. Overfeeding must be avoided. Such horses can never be used for riding; their backs are too weak to carry even small children. They need a lot of exercise, so

The Saharan Fennec Fox is an affectionate pet but requires a very warm environment and is fastidious about food.

223

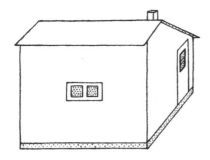

Miniature ungulate animals can be kept in brick or wooden sheds.

the keeper must play games with them, take them for walks and encourage them to trot. The breeding of such small horses is only practical for landowners and farmers; a household without the space of a farm can only keep one as a rule, to whom the keeper must give a great deal of attention to make up for the lack of companionship of its own kind.

Miniature Donkeys should be kept in wooden stables of an appropriate size, with all the usual equipment, including a manger, drinker and adjacent run. They are given the same fodder as large donkeys.

Special care should be taken of horses' and donkeys' coats and hooves: they require daily grooming, picking out of the feet, trimming of the hooves by a farrier and wiping of the eyes, muzzle and dock.

An inexperienced person should think twice before buying a mini-horse or a mini-donkey, because both animals can live for several decades.

The **Dwarf Goat** is a delightful pet, although it is a bit overinquisitive and somewhat smelly. The East African Dwarf, no higher than 40 cm (16 in) at the withers, is very common among goats kept as pets. It is very agile and is able to clamber up sloping tree trunks, so its enclosure must have a really strong

fence. It is bred in black, brown or red and white colour varieties. The hairs on its chin form a long beard and all dwarf goats, including the young, are horned. Old billy goats have huge horns and can use them with great force. Otherwise these animals are undemanding, feeding on green fodder in summer and hay in winter, occasionally supplemented by grain or vegetables and fruit. They do well in a European climate and can stay outdoors all year round if they have a sufficiently warm shelter. Goats can live to be ten years old or more.

A recent fashion is to keep **Miniature Pigs**, the dwarf form of the Domestic Pig (*Sus domesticus*). Originally these were bred as laboratory animals, either from the Vietnamese and Chinese forms (black or pied) or from American pigs, noted for their thick, red, hairy coat. Today there are also miniature white pigs. Some keepers like to walk their pig on a lead, wearing

A foal of the Miniature Horse: its birth weight is as low as 6 kg (13 1/4 lb).

Currently there are several dozen breeds of the Ponies and Miniature Horses. The spotted-colour varieties are very popular.

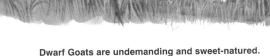

Miniature Pigs are winning increasing popularity. They are intelligent and quick learners. They can be taught to walk to heel almost like dogs. The harness should be tailored to fit the animal's dimensions.

a harness like that used for small dogs. Small pigs are not difficult to keep (breeding, of course, takes place only on farms because a sow with a dozen piglets would hardly be an ideal pet to keep in a house). The Miniature Pig is usually kept in a small sty with washable floor, well insulated or even heated. The mainstay of this pig's diet is pig swill – a mush of milk, groats, boiled potatoes and the like; the pig is an omnivorous animal, so it will also take meat or any other scraps. Miniature pigs are quick to learn and are playful and will soon get used to human company. They can learn simple commands as readily as a dog does. Of course, perfect hygiene is essential; fortunately, despite their reputation, pigs are very clean animals.

Dwarf Goats are undemanding and sweet-natured. Some breeds may be very useful.

Large Tree Shrews and Primates

Today the amateur primate keeper, especially the beginner, has no chance of acquiring these very sensitive, exotic animals, the majority of which are on the list of endangered species. The International Primate Protection League, supported by the International Union for the Conservation of Nature and Natural Resources (IUCN) and the World Wildlife Fund (WWF), is fighting against the illegal trade in poached and smuggled animals. In countries that are signatories to a special agreement that bans the trade of endangered animal species and their related products (called the CITES – Conference on International Trade in Endangered Species – or Washington Agreement) it is illegal to import such animals. Exceptions are allowed only for zoological gardens where the best conditions exist for such animals to reproduce, and for some other institutions that meet the same requirements. High-quality facilities, excellent care and experienced personnel are needed for the breeding of primates. Breeding in captivity may save an endangered species that is condemned to extinction in the wild. This applies, for example, to the South American **Silky Marmoset** (*Leontopithecus rosalia*) which is found only in a very small area in its native country where, in 1985, its number was estimated at only 200 individuals, far below the number needed for survival in the wild. This primate was so seriously endangered that emergency action had to be taken. The zoological institute of a renowned university in Germany began the controlled breeding of the animal. Now the number reared in this way is

The South American Silky Marmoset is a very rare and expensive animal. In the wild it is very strictly protected; it is only possible to buy young specimens born in captivity.

greater than that of the animals living in the wild. Of course, this is scientifically approved breeding in the best conditions, undertaken because of an ex-treme emergency. The ordinary amateur keeper can hardly hope that any primate will repro-duce with success or that the young could be reared under the conditions he or she is able to provide. Such animals are, in fact, lost for the future of their species. For this reason, we do not recommend primates as pets and mention them here only as a point of interest.

Large Tree Shrews are strange animals that used to be classified with the primates but now represent an order of their own. They are tropical animals, native to southeast Asia. They look like squirrels but are a spe-cial and very old group, ranked between the insectivores and the primates.

The **Common Tree Shrew** (*Tupaia glis*) is the commonest of the large tree shrews; it is a very agile diurnal animal, similar to the squirrel in its nimbleness and activity. The difference is in the diet; large tree shrews feed on insects and also love eggs, meat, sweet fruits, lettuce and milk.

The **nocturnal arboreal primates** are unusually beautiful and interesting animals, but un-fortunately most of them are seriously endangered. The Bushbabies, Lorises and Pottos are the nocturnal arboreal primates most frequently en-countered in captivity. The Galagos (six species in two genera) live in Africa and are heat-loving. These lovely, agile creatures are adept at climbing trees and move by leaping when on the ground. They feed on tropical fruits and leaf vege-tables, raw eggs and insects; they also like to drink milk. Visitors to zoological gardens are astonished at how delightful and tame galagos are, but it would be no pleasure to own one, for they have a nasty habit, as do all primates, of perfuming

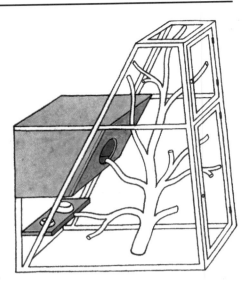

A large and solid shed is necessary if a monkey is to be kept. No monkey can be allowed to move freely around a flat or house.

their paws with their extremely offensive-smelling urine, which then leaves an odour trace on anything they touch. The habit is connected with territorial claims. The **Lorises** (genera *Loris* and *Nycticebus*), which come from tropical Asia, are far less agile than the galagos. They are noc-turnal animals, as suggested by

Galagos are beautiful and interesting, but besides a nocturnal way of life, they have some bad habits, so the 'bushbaby' as the Galago is also called, is an animal to be kept by an experienced fancier.

Marmosets are delightful inhabitants of zoos but, unfortunately, they belong among the endangered species. The Silver Marmoset, still abundant in its natural habitat, is available to fanciers.

their large eyes. They are very timid and when frightened will defend themselves by biting. Lorises feed on the same diet as galagos – fruit, leaf vegetables, insects and eggs. They can live a long time in captivity: some specimens are known to have lived for up to ten years.

The **Pottos** (genera *Arctocebus* and *Perodicticus*) are native to Africa. They have much in com-

A young Marmoset is so small that it can be held in one hand. Even in adulthood it will remain tiny.

mon with the lorises: they are active at night and very shy, and when frightened they hide their head between their forepaws. Their diet is the same as that of the galagos and their life span is eight years or more.

The **Marmosets**, from South America, are perhaps the love-liest of all the primates. There are dozens of species of these tiny monkeys, but most of them are critically endangered. Only a few seem able to rear their young in captivity, such as the **Common Marmoset** (*Callithrix jacchus*), the **Pinché Marmoset** (*Sanguinus oidipus*), the **Silky Marmoset** (*Leontopithecus rosalia*), the **Silver Marmoset** (*Callitrix argentata*), and some tamarins. All are agile and playful, always on the move, and need a temperature above 25 °C (77 °F). Their food is varied. They will take different kinds of fruit and vegetables, nuts, eggs, oily seeds and insects; keepers also enrich their diet with sprouted grains, rice or oat gruel and vitamins. Marmosets are very graceful inhabitants of zoological gardens and if well cared for they can live for as long as ten years. *Leontopithecus rosalia* may live up to 20 years. Unfortunately, all are very susceptible to contagious diseases, even to those that affect humans, and the common cold may kill them. They are also very shy and timid and so have to be kept in quiet conditions.

Monkeys

All children and many adults would love to have a monkey as a pet, but what has been said of primates generally applies to the monkeys, too. Besides this, they are really difficult animals to keep, having very specific requirements for housing, feeding and care. They take up much more of the keeper's time than other animals, and may often be dangerous. All are gregarious, living in groups in the wild: if they are deprived of the company of others of their kind they suffer from stress, become nervous and are inclined to bite. They cannot be kept in a normal household because no monkey

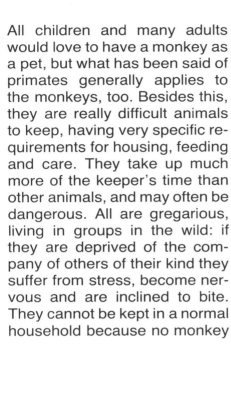

The rare Macaque called Vanderu is a beautiful animal to look at but it is not a good companion because the male may be aggressive.

Macaques, especially Rhesus Monkeys, are the most frequently kept primates.

can learn about cleanliness and order: being tree animals, they will leave litter everywhere. Due to their inexhaustible energy and inquisitive minds, they can destroy the most solid and well-secured furniture and equipment, and can even pick tiles off a wall. The monkey's deftness in opening locks and undoing knots is amazing and their teeth are also able to overcome many obstacles. Monkeys prove that they are related to people by their ability to find and use tools – mostly to break fragile objects. Therefore, even if there was no danger of monkeys becoming extinct, even if there were no bans and other protective measures to prevent it, there would still be many other good reasons why they are not recommended as pets. A monkey just will not be happy in the house because it can never be-

come accustomed to the various restrictions of a house; while people, no matter how much they love animals, cannot adapt their homes to a monkey's requirements. Problems even arise in zoological gardens where monkeys are kept, shown by the frequent injuries suffered by attendants and by the damage caused by monkeys both inside and outside their cages and pens if they succeed in escaping. What is more, monkeys are susceptible to human diseases and often fall victim to an infection that is common among people.

Monkeys are tropical animals which need a high and stable temperature (above 20 °C/68 °F) and degree of humidity; they cannot stand draughts or noise. Their diet is remarkably varied. In the wild they feed on leaves and all kinds of fruit, insects, eggs, small vertebrates and oily seeds. In captivity their diet should be enriched with vegetables, boiled meat, sprouted seeds and an essential vitamin and mineral supplement. There are many species of monkeys and each of them shows food preferences that are different from the others. As to rearing of the young, even specialists encounter all sorts of problems, owing to the monkey's susceptibility to so many diseases and because they harbour so many internal and external parasites.

It will be interesting to look at some of the small and less-demanding species that used to be kept by circuses as well as by keepers. Some of them showed extraordinary hardiness under the adverse conditions of circus life. Nevertheless, it should not be imagined that even the commonest monkeys can be kept by amateurs. The wild populations of even the hardiest monkeys are now diminishing because

their habitat is shrinking, and they, too, must be protected.

The **Squirrel Monkey** or **Saimiri** (*Saimiri sciureus*) is a lovely monkey, about 30 cm (12 in) long, agile and attractively coloured. It is kept in most zoological gardens, where it regularly reproduces. It can only be kept in groups (one male and several females) in large aviaries. Meat and insects are essential everyday ingredients in its diet.

The hardy South American **Capuchin** monkeys are also lovely and playful. There are four species of the capuchin and a whole range of subspecies. They are perhaps the best example to demonstrate what a problem their inventiveness, dexterity and agility pose for the attendants: capuchins love to break things using different tools and can escape from almost anywhere. At Prague Zoo

The South American Saimiri is attractively coloured but it requires a lot of care.

Barbary Ape (*Macaca sylvana*)

they were even able to cut step-like shapes into a high wall — a sophisticated feat. Capuchins live for more than twenty years. Sometimes they are pugnacious and may bite.

The **Macaques**, typical monkeys of the Old World, are one of the hardiest groups. These were the monkeys that used to accompany organ-grinders and also appeared in circuses. The Barbary Ape (*Macaca sylvana*) lived in southern Europe (Gibraltar), the **Rhesus Macaque** (*Macaca mulatta*) is found at altitudes of up to 4,000 m (13,000 ft) and the **Japanese Macaque** (*Macaca fuscata*) has no problems wading in snow.

Macaques are not fastidious about food: their diet includes fruit, vegetables, boiled maize and other such inexpensive feeds. However, the majority of macaques living in captivity are not pets but are kept as laboratory animals for use in medical research. Research using the Rhesus and other macaques has saved human lives, and the significant rhesus factor of human blood groups derives its name from the Rhesus Monkey.

The **Guenon** monkeys, especially the smaller ones, are among the most popular of all monkeys, including **Moustached Guenon** (*Cercopithecus cephus*) and the **Dwarf Guenon** (*Miopithecus talapoir*). Although the large Guenon monkeys are very beautiful creatures, they are aggressive and cannot be kept outside specially built facilities. As they come from tropical Africa, they need a high and stable temperature and atmospheric humidity. In the wild Guenon monkeys live in large groups, so they are unhappy when kept in isolation; they will start biting and become shy. They are also difficult to feed, because they waste more than they eat.

Primates are not the only group of animals to enjoy international protection and a ban on trade in live specimens. Exclusive pets, such as the Puma, Cheetah and Ocelot, are now also on the list of endangered species and are subject to strict protective regulations. People should never attempt to keep an animal for which they are unable to provide fully satisfactory conditions and appropriate care. The good keeper will only enjoy keeping pets that are healthy and happy.

Familiar Pets

Cats

The human tradition of keeping cats is long. Nevertheless, over the years some bad habits have become deep-rooted among keepers because for thousands of years cats were half-wild and without control. Today many cats can be seen roaming at will, coming home only when hungry and often giving birth in hidden places. In such conditions it is easy for many of them, especially unneutered males, to live wild. Cats that wander come in contact with injurious substances and may thus get hurt or contract contagious diseases. They often kill and eat small game and songbirds. These are all good reasons why purebred cats should not be left to roam at will. If the cat has plenty of room to exercise and play in, if it is well fed and has opportunities for sun-bathing, it will not need to go outdoors as much as a dog and should never need to leave the garden at all.

Cats prefer lying in raised places. The post underneath, covered with a coarse matting or carpet serves for sharpening the claws.

Equipment suitable for a flat that meets the requirements of a cat and will protect the furniture from damage. For a larger number of cats, a 'scratching post' with several resting places is ideal. There should be planks or blocks for the cats to sharpen their claws on.

The home or apartment that you wish to share with a cat needs some adjustment. The first thing to be done is to remove from reach all poisonous plants, all unstable objects that could be toppled by the cat and, for safety's sake, all other pets that could trigger its hunting instincts: although the cages and terrariums of pet birds and small mammals are strong, frequent attacks by a cat will cause great stress to those little creatures. A suitable spot should be found for the cat to sleep and a place established for its feeding bowl and litter tray. The cat is a natural climber and it loves to watch the world go by, therefore its bed – a wicker basket or a wooden box containing a warm blanket – preferably sheltered from draughts, should not be on the ground. It should be placed in a quiet, secluded position. The scratching post fitted for the cat should be a simple well-fixed structure made of wood or covered with coarse coconut matting or other material suitable for the cat to sharpen its claws on. There should be a separate bed for each cat if you intend to have more than one. To prevent the furniture from getting scratched, do not place the cat's bed on valuable pieces.

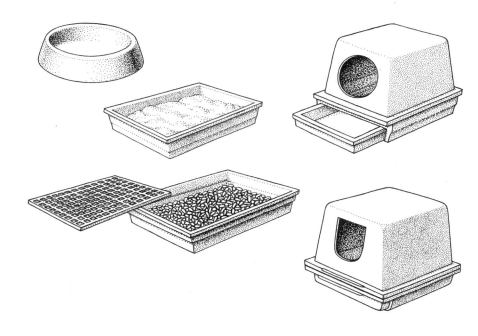

Food should be offered in a place that is easy to clean and where nothing will disturb the cat. It is essential that the floor should be covered by tiles, vinyl or another washable floor surface. A bowl of water (always fresh) and another containing food should be placed on the ground. The most suitable bowls are those made of heavy earthenware, porcelain or glass – light plastic bowls are not recommended. Raw or boiled meat or fish is the mainstay of the cat's diet supplemented, if necessary, by a good-quality tinned cat food. Eight-week-old kittens should be offered food four to five times a day and the frequency of feeding should be reduced with age: adult cats will eat twice a day. A dessert spoonful of food is enough to feed a kitten, but the ration should be increased as it grows older, of course, depending on the type and size of the adult cat. Food that is not eaten should not be left in the bowl for more than a few hours. Not all cats like milk; if milk is given, what is left over must be disposed of imme-

diately because soured milk may cause digestive troubles.

The cat's litter tray is a sturdy plastic container containing a layer of sand, earth or special grit that absorbs odours. The best place for the litter tray is in the bathroom or a downstairs cloak room; naturally the cat should always have free access to it. The tray should be placed in a box or on paper because cats like to dig up the filling after using the tray and will scatter it all around. The litter tray, as well as the cat's bed and feeding bowls, should always be kept clean: the filling in the litter tray must be replaced regularly and the tray itself throughly washed and disinfected with a solution that does not leave behind a strong smell.

A balcony or window is the place where the cat will like to bask in the sun. It will be happy to doze there on a blanket, but as lively cats will sometimes leap at a flying bird, it is advisable to construct a low obstruction at the window to prevent the cat from leaping out. Some keepers, especially those who own several cats, build a large cattery for them in the garden.

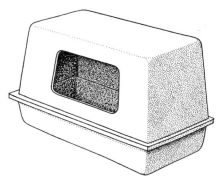

Besides bowls for water and food, a cat also needs a litter tray. A simple tray filled with a material that absorbs odours may suffice, but it is better to put the litter tray in a box, so the cat cannot scatter the contents around.

When the cat's home is ready, the next thing to do is to acquire a kitten. If you wish to have a pedigree cat, it is advisable to visit a show of purebred cats first or to consult an experienced breeder who specializes in a certain breed. The kitten is taken from its mother when it is about eight weeks old. A healthy kitten is nimble, has clean eyes, a smooth, tidy coat, clean ears, and must not be nervous. Great emphasis must be laid on checking that the kitten has no parasites or diarrhoea. The breeder will tell you what food the kitten is used to.

It should never be lifted by catching it under its forepaws and leaving its rear legs hanging loose; this could cause an umbilical hernia. To lift a kitten, always put a hand under its belly and hold its neck gently. Carry an adult cat in your arms, with one hand supporting its hind legs and letting it hold on by itself. When travelling with a cat, you will need a portable cage, wicker basket or wooden box, large enough for the cat to lie or sit in comfortably. Such a box must have good ventilation and preferably a door with a grating, a firm and reliable catch and a strong handle by which to carry it. Put a blanket on the floor of the cage or basket. The cat should not be fed before a journey. Even in a car a cat should not travel freely, but al-

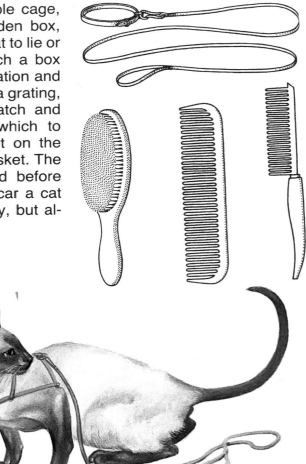

Some cats can be taught to walk on the lead like a dog. Combs and brushes for different types of fur are essential.

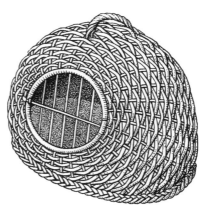

Cats cannot safely be transported in your arms. A tied cloth bag put into a shopping bag may suffice, but it is better to use a purpose-built carrier with good ventilation and a solid base.

ways in a basket or box, or if nothing more suitable is at hand, in a bag from which its head can peep out. The basket, box or bag must be placed safely inside the car to ensure it cannot fall off a seat or bump against anything hard. *Never* put a cat in the boot of the car.

Some cats can be taught to walk on a lead. However, collars are not suitable so it is better to fix the lead to a harness similar to that used for small dogs. The lead must be adequate in length: a line that is too long, or the self-winding type of lead intended for dogs, is not recommended.

The cat is noted for its cleanliness, but this is not to say that the keeper can leave his or her pet entirely to its own devices. Even smooth-haired cats have to be groomed every day and the longhairs must be combed. Every morning the cat's eyes must be wiped clean of mucus.

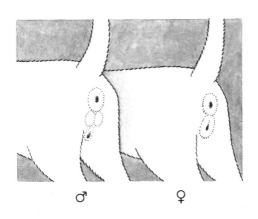

It is not easy to distinguish the sex of kittens. The distance of the sexual pore from the anus is one indication.

234

The ears can be cleaned with a small cotton swab and their condition should be thoroughly examined. Ear parasites are among the commonest pests of cats, especially those that have the run of the garden or associate with cats that live wild.

Cats do not usually require baths. A bath will be needed only if the animal's coat becomes soiled with an adhesive or dangerous substance. Bathe it in warm water (38–40°C/100–104°F), using a special shampoo acquired from your pet shop or a solution of potash soap well shaken in water. Cats are much more sensitive to chemicals than people, so ordinary shampoos or soap should not be used. After bathing, the cat's coat must be thoroughly towelled and allowed to dry in a warm, draught-free room. A hair-drier should not be used for two reasons: cats hate noise, and the drier might overdry its coat. A cat should never be bathed just before a show because for a few days after a bath its coat loses its gloss. As far as possible, longhairs should not be bathed at all. Excess grease is removed from their fur by using a special powder, which is then brushed out thoroughly.

Although the cat is a carnivorous creature, it must be given a little vegetable (boiled carrot or spinach, but never cauliflower, pulses or cabbage, which cause flatulence) and also grass. Grass seed can be sown in a pot and the grass left to grow to a height of at least 10 cm (4 in) and then made accessible to the cat. The consumption of grass helps the cat to eject hairballs that form in its stomach from the hairs swallowed during its own daily grooming of its coat.

A cat needs plenty of exercise, so things on which it can climb, such as a ladder, fixed logs or sets of poles, as well as toys, must be placed in the room where it is kept. The toys may be of hard rubber, leather or other natural materials. Painted rubber or wood, foam rubber and plastics are not recommended. The cat may well take a fancy to such items as a rubber ring or a buffalo bone suspended on a cord, which it will swing and chase.

Cats are adult at about a year old. The females come into heat (oestrus) two to three times a year. The oestrus lasts for 8–14 days and is usually accompanied by particular sounds and movements. Pregnancy lasts 56–65 days. Owners who do not want to rear young are advised to have their pets, both male and female, neutered.

Special powder is useful in grooming cats.

235

Longhaired Cats

Persians are undoubtedly the most popular of all the longhaired cats. This group consists of the highest number of recognised breeds – that is, colour varieties officially recognized by FIFé (Fédération Internationale Féline) as separate breeds. Persians have a massive body conformation, short and stocky legs, a tail just reaching the ground, a large head with a fairly flat face, large round eyes and, their most distinctive trait, a high-quality coat of long silky hair. The coat forms a conspicuous ruff around the neck, the ears must be very hairy with tufs inside, the tail should have a full brush, and long tufts must appear on the toes. Persians are robust and quite undemanding. Slenderness is not as essential as it is in the Siamese and Oriental cats. The hunting instinct of Persians is not as strong as in other breeds, and they are not very agile so they can be kept indoors without problems. It is not recommended to let them loose outside without control because their splendid coat could easily be damaged by squeezing through shrubs where dirt, seeds and fruit could catch in their fur. Persian cats should be combed and groomed every day. They should be bathed only in exceptional

Different colour varieties of Persians: Tortoise-shell, Tabby and Bicoloured.

cases. Dry powder is used as a grease and dirt remover, but there must be no sign of it in the cat's coat when competing at a show.

Persians were originally kept only in their white and black colour varieties; the blue colour did not appear until just before the end of the last century, soon to be followed by other varieties. Self-coloured Persians are the most popular. Most of them have orange or copper eyes (Black, Orange-eyed White, Blue, Red Self, Cream, Lilac, Chocolate and others). Only the

Whites may have blue or odd eyes (for example one eye blue, the other yellow).

Orange eyes can also be encountered in the rare **Smoke Longhairs** which have a silvery undercoat, light-coloured ear tufts, whiskers and ruff but are otherwise black, blue, chocolate, cream or lilac.

Tabby Longhairs are more common. They have several stripes on the forehead forming the shape of the letter 'M', a pattern resembling a butterfly wing on the back, and a whorl on the flanks. The Silver Tabby Longhairs with a black pattern have green eyes; the Black Tabbies with a ground colour of sand have copper eyes. Tabbies are kept in all possible colours and combinations and the colour of the eyes should correspond to the ground colour.

Tortoiseshell Longhairs are very popular and widely bred, owing to their variation of colouring. Different colours, for example red and black, alternate on their bodies in irregular

The Blue Persian displays a striking contrast between its blue coat and orange eyes.

The Persian Smoke cat has an interesting coat colouring.

patches. The Tortoiseshell Longhairs are always females; the toms are usually red. The eyes of the Tortoiseshell Longhairs are of different shades of copper. A red blaze in the middle of the forehead is especially favoured. The Tortoiseshell-and-white Longhair is also appreciated for its interesting colouring. Many cat fanciers prefer bicoloured cats, especially the bicoloured Black-and-white and bicoloured Red-and-white varieties, although other combinations are also recognised. The

eyes of these cats are always copper. In showing emphasis is placed on the purity of the coat colours, their clearly defined patches, and the distribution of the patches over the body.

The **Chinchilla** is one of the loveliest of the longhaired varieties and has grown in popularity in recent years. It is somewhat slimmer than most, with a finer conformation, its undercoat is pure white and its guard hairs are black-tipped. Its expressive bluish-green eyes and pink muzzle are rimmed with black and its lips are black. Chinchilla kittens are sometimes born with a hint of tabby which disappears by the time they are adult. This popular breed has become a basis for the breeding of other interesting colour varieties of longhairs. The tips of the hairs of the original Chinchilla were black but now there are also blue, chocolate and lilac Chinchillas. The undercoat of all these colour varieties is pure white. On the other hand, the undercoat of the **Voile** and **Shaded** cats should be light-coloured but never white; the Voiles are lighter, the Shaded cats are darker. Their green eyes betray their kinship to the Chinchilla. Similar cats, called **Cameos**, were bred in the USA. They have a white un-

dercoat and the hairs of the mask and on the back, flanks and tail have black tips. Besides the ordinary Cameo, which comes in different colours, there is also a Shaded Cameo with a more marked tipping. The Red Cameo and Cream Cameo are especially popular.

The latest type of Persians are the **Colourpoints**. They were genetically engineered in the USA by crossing Persians with Siamese cats. These cats should have the colour of the Siamese cat and the conformation of the Persians. A Siamese head type is a serious fault. All these cats should have deep blue eyes. They are semi-albi-

Cameo is 'modern' colour type in cats. The undercoat is pure white and gains colour gradually.

nos whose young are born white, and acquire the points after several months. They may be dark brown (Seal Colourpoint), chocolate (Chocolate Colourpoint), red (Red Colourpoint), blue (Blue Colourpoint), lilac (Lilac Colourpoint), and also cream, tortie and tabby-pointed in various colours.

Many new types keep arising among the Persians, all with a quiet temperament which suits them for homes in the city.

Persians with 'Siamese' colours are called Colourpoints. Their kittens are white and gain colour gradually.

Semi-longhaired Cats

These breeds are much less widespread than the longhairs (Persians). The origin of some of them, for example the Turkish breeds – Angora and Turkish Van – is really ancient. Others, however, have been bred more recently, such as the Somali cats, which received recognition by FIFé in 1982. Their common trait is that they are more difficult to keep than the Persians and they are not as even-tempered. For this reason they remain curiosities and are much more frequently seen at shows than in family homes. The ancient **Angora** cat has been known since the Middle Ages when the first specimens were imported into Europe; yet it is still often confused with the White Longhair, from which it differs by having a slimmer body, larger ears, a smaller head of a different shape, and blue or green eyes,

Somali cats are longhaired relatives of Abyssinians. The ancient Angora shows considerable differences in body conformation from the Persians, though people often confuse these two groups of cats.

a long nose and light amber eyes. It has red spots on its head and its tail is also red. This cat is an excellent swimmer and, like the Angora, it is much more agile and fiercer than the Persians.

The **Birman**, or the **Sacred Cat of Burma**, is actually a semi-longhaired cat. It was first put on display at a show in France in 1931, but it comes from Asia and has only been further bred in the West. It has the same colouring as the Siamese, the only difference being that the Birman's ground colour is goldish. Its eyes are a beautiful blue. The white 'gloves' on all paws are a typical trait of cats of this group. Their heads are small with full cheeks that should not resemble those of either the Siamese or the Persian. The tail is also longer than that of the Siamese cat, and is bushy. The fur of the Birman is long, silky and slightly wavy. Colour vari-

The Birman differs from the Colourpoints by having white gloves on all four paws. The Turkish Van is an ancient breed.

which may sometimes be of different colours. In Europe this is not yet a recognised breed, unlike, for example, the **Turkish Van**, which comes from the same part of the world. The latter is also white, its head is wedge-shaped with large ears,

eties of this group include Seal-, Chocolate- and Blue-point.

The **Norwegian Forest Cat** is a very special type of cat. Its

238

The Maine Coon has small bristly tufts on its ears.

basic features are similar to the European Shorthair to which it is undoubtedly closely related. In summer it has a very similar shorthair coat which may show all the colours of the European cat. Not even the eye colour is important: the only trait of importance is the quality of the fur, which is very long and thick in winter, with a warm undercoat. The tail, in particular, is often very bushy and is as long as the body. This cat is well adapted to the harsh climatic conditions of its homeland where it is kept half-wild, as many cats used to be in country homes. The temper of this cat corresponds to its tough outlook, so it is not as easy to keep as the Persians, for example.

Somali cats look rather strange. They were bred in the USA in the 1960s. It was not until 1979 that they received recognition in the USA and not until 1982 that they became accepted in Europe. The Somali is, in fact, a longhaired Abyssinian, but the longhair gene is recessive (that is, not dominant), so it is very difficult to breed this variety. Its typical trait

is the ticking, which means that every guard hair bears several colours and is distinctly ringed, the tip always being dark. The eyes of this interesting cat are green or amber. Originally, like its Abyssinian ancestor, this cat was bred in ruddy and sorrel colour varieties but now Blue Somalis and a beige fawn colour variety may also occasionally be seen, the latter being a more flaxen colour rather than fawnish-red.

One of the largest cat breeds in the world is the **Maine Coon**. The weight of the tom is 8–10 kg (17.5–22 lb) and the females weigh about 5 kg (11 lb). The breed was developed in North America in the nineteenth century and has been seen at shows since 1860. It has a rather rectangular body shape, set on tall legs; its typical features

are large ears and a bushy tail with flattering hairs. This breed likes swimming. It has a very greasy coat, so powder, commonly used to clean the coats of other cats, should never be used on the Maine Coon. Otherwise, the care of its fur is easy; occasional combing (once a week) will suffice because the coat is not inclined to become matted. The Maine Coon may be either ticked (the agouti factor) — that is, with rings of different colours on each hair, a trait typically occurring in a South American rodent called the agouti and also in the European hare — or non-ticked, self-coloured, without the agouti factor (this is the preferred purebred form). Cats of this breed are very independent and have a well-developed hunting instinct.

The Norwegian Forest Cat is bred in different colour varieties. The large difference in the length of its summer and winter coats is its typical feature.

British Shorthaired Cats

The popularity of cats in Britain and British cat breeding traditions led to the development of British Shorthair cats, which differ considerably from other types, especially the Orientals. There are 65 officially recognised breeds (colour varieties in fact) of the British Shorthair show specimens. As the muscular body of the British Shorthair is required to be heavily built, the cats should be given quality food and opportunity for enough exercise, especially when young. Kittens kept in the home need attention and should be allowed to scamper and play only the White Shorthairs may have blue eyes. The strict standards insist that the coat of the self-coloured Shorthairs should be absolutely free of any white hair and any trace of marking or tabby pattern. In the Bicoloured British Shorthair the colours should be well balanced and the

British Red: Striped, Tabby and Spotted forms.

which are easily distinguished from the European Shorthair. The British Shorthairs are of medium size and stocky, with comparatively short, strong legs and a short tail. The wide, round head set on a strong neck has small ears. Its cheeks are full and the short nose is broad and straight. A typical characteristic is its fur – short and thick, but not too close-lying. For centuries the British Shorthair has been kept in the harsh, rainy climate of the British Isles, so it is sturdy, undemanding and needs no special care. The coat is easy to keep in good condition but daily grooming is recommended for as much as they like. Frail conformation, a long or pointed head, large ears, an open coat, a long tail and other features reminiscent of the Oriental cats are considered shortcomings.

The different colour types of these cats have been bred to perfection and great emphasis is laid on them and on the eye colour. Defects in colouring are a reason for eliminating such specimens from breeding. The self-coloured British Shorthairs (black, blue, red, beige and other colours) have, as a rule, orange or copper eyes like the Persians: green eye colour is not allowed for self-colours and patches of colour should be clearly defined with no intermingling or overlapping. The eye colour (usually orange) should match the colour of the coat.

The **Tabby British Shorthairs** of various colours enjoy great popularity. Both breeders and show judges pay particular attention to the distinctness and accuracy of the pattern, which is similar to that of Persians but must be much more pronounced and precise. There must be a distinct 'M' on the forehead, wide longitudinal stripes on the back, a symmetrical pattern resembling butterfly wings on the shoulders and closed circular

Bicoloured British Shorthaired cats

whorls on the flanks. The harmony of the colours is most desirable: various modifications of ground colour and the colour of the pattern are allowed but they must always match each other and the colour of the eyes. The Silver Tabby British Shorthair has a different eye colour: green and yellow.

Some fanciers are fond of Spotted British Shorthairs. The back and sides of the spotted cat should be covered with small round spots: the more spots the cat has, the higher the show rating. Of course, the distinctness of pattern and colour harmony are also important.

Some novel colour modifications have recently appeared to enrich the spectrum of this old and well-established group of original British Shorthair cats. These include the Smoke British Shorthair in various colour shades, Chinchillas, Shaded cats and the still unrecognised Voile Shorthairs. All these types are known among the Persians, but in the Shorthairs the colour effects are different. For example, the tipping (dark tips of hairs on a light ground colour) is much more distinct in the Short-haired than in the Longhaired breeds. These types are difficult to breed because the breeding specimens must be selected with the utmost care. The Chinchilla has tipping of various colours on a white ground colour and its eyes are sea-green. The eyes of the Smoke and Shaded Shorthairs are usually orange.

Another two representatives of the British Shorthairs enjoy great popularity among keepers: the Tortoiseshell British Shorthair and the Tortoiseshell-and-white British Shorthair. The harmony of colours is especially striking in the latter, which are always females: if males do occur they are infertile, so the queens can be mated only to self (red) toms. The colours should be clear, distributed in large, well-defined patches, well separated from the white. The colour of the eyes is orange.

Three types of blue cats: the British Blue, Korat and (at left) Russian Blue

European Shorthaired Cats

The **European Shorthair Cat** is of medium body size, robust and long-necked. Its head is slightly elongated and its tail is round-tipped and of medium length. The general impression is that the European Shorthair is slimmer and loftier than its British counterpart but it should not be too slender or frail. It must be a well-muscled creature, light in its movements and with a well-balanced conformation. Its coat is dense, hard and glossy.

This cat has been kept half-wild or in households in Europe for centuries without any breeding efforts. The majority of the cats still kept this way in Europe have no certificate of origin but

Different types of self-coloured European Shorthaired cats

A Tortoiseshell European Shorthaired kitten

specimens with perfect conformation may be bred from them after a thorough examination.

The European Shorthairs may be self-coloured, tabby, striped, spotted, tortoiseshell, bicoloured, and of various new colour shades.

The self-coloured European Shorthairs may be white (blue-, orange- or odd-eyed), black, blue, lilac, cream or red, which are all required to have orange eyes; green eyes are a common fault of the black cats, for which reason they may be eliminated from breeding.

Bicoloured European Shorthairs must have pure colours, forming clearly defined patches. Their eyes should be orange. Green or yellow-green eyes are allowed in the tabby, striped or spotted cats, but are always required to match the ground colour and the colour of the pattern. The pattern should be distinct and clear, as in the case of similar colour varieties of the British Shorthair cat.

The European Shorthair may also appear in a tortoiseshell colour variety, a trait associated with male sterility, implying that tortoiseshells can only be females. The same applies to the blue cream variety, which is unusual and, in fact, not particularly attractive, with intermingled tiny patches of blue and cream. A good-quality colouring is very difficult to achieve because toms of other colours have to be used in the breeding. The best results are obtained when a self-cream cat is mated to a blue tom: such a mating will usually produce self-coloured males and blue cream females. The blue cream females are then crossed with cream toms. It is also possible to use a reverse procedure, that is to cross a blue cat with a cream tom to get blue cream females and blue toms. The lightest-coloured kittens, free of spots or tabby pattern, are selected for breeding. Besides this unusual colour variety, which also exists in the Persian group, there is also the smoke variety of the European Shorthair in which the ground colour is silver and the tips of the hairs are black or of another colour.

The European Shorthair cat is sturdy and hardy, requiring no special care. The females are usually very good mothers and can be used to rear the kittens of other breeds or even other species. On the other hand, it is much livelier than the Longhairs or British cats, tends to wander and is often violent when in heat. This is why keepers who do not like noise often have their European Shorthair pets, both female and male, castrated. Toms usually mark their territory with a strong odour: castration will eliminate this.

Of course, the international standards that strictly define the traits of every breed also apply to European Shorthairs. Nevertheless, unusual types, still waiting for international recognition, can often be encountered at cat shows in many European countries. For example, a combination of white with tabby patches occurs fairly frequently. The required eye colour is the greatest problem in breeding the pedigree European Shorthair cats. As cats of this breed are very

A European Striped cat playing

prolific and sturdy, much effort is required to abolish the many congenital defects that occur in their breeding. I kept under normal conditions, the European cat will seldom become obese.

The very temperamental Red Tabby cat has to be held really firmly if its body temperature is to be measured accurately.

243

Shorthaired Cats of Western Origin

As well as the European and British Shorthairs, special shorthaired breeds of cats were developed in Europe and America. The **Russian Blue** is one such breed whose origin is uncertain. It is said to have been brought to the United Kingdom on trade ships from the Russian port of Archangel. This is why the breed used to be known as the Archangel cat. It was subjected to further breeding refinement in Britain, from where it was taken back to Russia where it was allegedly kept by the family of the Tsar. Today the best specimens of this breed are kept in the UK and Scandinavia. This cat differs markedly from other types of European blue cats by having almond-shaped green eyes, long legs and tail, a flat wedge-shaped head and large pointed ears that are thin and almost naked inside. The coat is very short, thick and silky; it should have a silvery sheen. Although the Russian Blue cat looks frail, it is hardy and very intelligent. Its coat requires regular care. Overfeeding must be avoided.

The **Chartreux**, said to have been bred in a monastery by the Carthusian monks who produced the renowned liqueur Chartreuse, is almost the opposite of the Russian Blue. It is a cat of medium size and powerful, robust and muscular build. The head is broad and has strong jaws, full cheeks and round eyes that should be as deep and orange as possible. The coat of the Chartreux cat should be light grey-blue, free of any tabby markings, brown shading or white hair; it has a special type of coat, not close-set but standing out from the body like an otter's fur.

Another interesting breed is

The Manx Rumpy and Manx Stumpy

the **Abyssinian** cat. In 1869 a cat was brought by its owner from Abyssinia (Ethiopia) to Britain, where it was subjected to long and careful breeding to produce offspring resembling the cats seen in the ancient Egyptian frescos. It is of medium size, long and sleek, with a long, pointed tail. Its head is wedge-shaped with a slightly pointed nose. The ears are largish and pointed and set wide apart. The almond-shaped eyes may be either green or amber. The typical features of the breed are a dark line around the eyes and a silky, fine, close-set coat. Neither the body build nor the ear shape of the Abyssinian cat should bear any resemblance to the Siamese, and no white spots should appear anywhere on the body (it sometimes happens that the cat has a white chin and white lips). The agouti ticking of the Abyssinian's coat is a distinctive feature of the

breed. Each hair has two to three dark bands. The original wild colouring is deep orange with black or dark brown ticking and a dark eel-like band running down the cat's back. Simple ticking is preferred at shows. There are several colour varieties of the Abyssinian cat, in-

The Brown Burmese cat (brown is its original colouring)

cluding the Sorrel, Blue and Beige Fawn (dull beige with dark cream ticking).

The **Manx** is one of the strangest cat breeds of Europe, coming from the Isle of Man in the Irish Sea. Animal populations that have developed on islands without contact with other populations of their species sometimes bear very special traits, and the Manx demonstrates this clearly. The Manx is tailless (some tailless cats are also known in Japan). A truncated or absent tail is not the only characteristic feature of the Manx: it also has conspicuously long hind legs so that its gait is somewhat rabbit-like. Mating between two Manx cats may produce true Manx kittens with a dimple at the base of the spine where other cats have their tails, kittens with a short truncated tail, or kittens with a tail of almost normal length. Problems arise when the cat is bred for full taillessness: a lethal factor then becomes involved and the kittens are often born dead. The tailless Manx is called 'rumpy' and a cat with a stump of tail is called 'stumpy'. The large round head of this medium-sized cat has a longer nose than the British shorthaired cat; its ears are wide and pointed and its eyes are round. All colour varieties are acceptable. Emphasis is laid on the quality of the coat, which should be soft and double, showing a dense undercoat and an open top coat.

Another special type of cat is the **Burmese**. In 1930 a brown cat was taken from Rangoon to the USA. As the cat was originally thought to be a Siamese of a different but interesting colour, it was mated to a Siamese tom. The crossing resulted in a new breed. The first attempt to bring the cat to Europe (in 1947) failed. In 1957 it began to be bred in England and since 1957 it has also been kept in other continental European countries. The Burmese cat is more robust and better muscled than Siamese cats; its head is wider and wedge-shaped, with a strong chin. The tail is of medium length and slightly tapering, and the ears are small with rounded tips. The eyes are set wide apart and should be golden-yellow. The fine satin coat should have a typical lustre. The original Burmese cat is the Brown Burmese, having a seal brown coat, just slightly lighter on the chest and belly. The overall tone of the kittens is much lighter, but they become darker as they grow. The brown colour variety remains the most popular, although many others are also officially recognised (Blue, Chocolate, Lilac, Red and Cream Burmese, and the Brown, Chocolate, Lilac and Blue Tories). White patches, blue eyes and other traits typical of the Siamese cats are regarded as faults.

The **Rexes**, breeds with a special type of coat, were developed separately in Britain, Germany and the USA. The curly coat first appeared in 1940 in the Blue Longhair cat. Purposeful breeding of these cats began in the 1950s. Breeding gave rise to the **Cornish Rex** with a wedge-shaped head, almond eyes and plushy coat, recognised in all colour mutations; and to the **Devon Rex** with a short wedge-shaped head, large round-tipped ears and large almond-shaped eyes whose colour, either yellow or green, should match the coat. Its coat, showing slightly modified guard hairs, is short and soft, and curled all over the body. All colours are recognised. The crossing of the British Rexes with the Siamese cats produced the blue-eyed **Si-rex.**

Cats with curly coats: Cornish Rex, Devon Rex and German Rex.

The **German Rex** was developed in Germany and was internationally recognised in 1982. It is a robust cat with a wide head, large ears with rounded tips and a velvety coat, showing no guard hairs. All colours are allowed.

Siamese Shorthaired Cats

The **Siamese** cats originated in the Far East, probably in Siam (now Thailand), from where they were brought to France in 1870. The first Siamese cats to appear in Britain were brought from Bangkok in 1884, which was, in fact, the beginning of wider breeding of these animals. The original variety is referred to as the Seal-point Siamese.

A number of breeds with markings of other colours have been developed since the first imports and today 18 colours are recognized. Siamese cats are among the most popular breeds, although some keepers might have objections to their temperament and harsh, almost sobbing voice. They are prized above all for their elegant and sleek body, a long marten-like head set on a long neck, blue eyes and short, fine coat of unusual colour. Siamese cats are semialbinos – their kittens are born white with blue eyes. (True albinos do not occur among cats.) The colour markings

The Siamese cat is a semialbino: its kittens are born white and the markings colour gradually.

occur on the extremities of the body, those parts most exposed to cold: the ears, nose, tail and legs (this feature is called acromelanism). Most of these cats hate milk, which can cause them to develop serious digestive disorders. Some of them do not like children's company, and when the young are being reared the female may even be aggressive towards her owner. In the earlier periods of breeding some Siamese cats showed degenerative changes in the tail, which used to be stumpy, twisted or kinked (a little hook or kink in the tail was once even regarded as a distinctive trait of the breed). This fault has been eliminated by thorough breeding selection, and today's Siamese cats should have a slender, tapering and perfectly straight tail. Any change in the tail is undesirable, as are white toes. Heavier conformation, small ears and a round head are also regarded as faults.

The points may be of a single colour, tabby or tortoiseshell. The ground colour is always light – cream, peach, milk-chocolate or even magnolia-white.

The body colour of the Seal-point Siamese is cream, shading into a darker colour on the back. The mask, ears, legs and tail are dark brown. The dark

Lilac-point and Chocolate-point Siamese

colour of the ears and the mask should not merge. The Blue-point Siamese should have a glacial-white body colour and blue points, but the ears must not be darker than the other points. The Chocolate-point Siamese should have an ivory-white body colour and light chocolate points. The Lilac-point

Tortie-point Siamese

red. The Cream-point is rather dull compared with other Siamese cats; its coat is cream-white, the points are a pastel-cream shade. The Tortie- and Tabby-point cats have a darker body colour than the cats described above. Basically they are cream-coloured and darker (up to milk chocolate) on the back. The Tabby-point used to be called the Lynx. The points colour of the tabbies is most pronounced on the head, tail and legs. The ears should be dark, not tabby, with a typical spot. Various colours of the tabby points are recognised; it is essential that the tabbying should be restricted to the points, without penetrating into the ground body colour.

The Tortie-point Siamese is undoubtedly the strangest of all Siamese cats. Like all torties, they are invariably females. Their body colour is cream and much darker on the back, the

mask, ears, legs and tail have dark brown and red, chocolate and red or some other marbling. The colours must be distinct and the spots well balanced, not merging. Tabbying is a fault as are any white spots or individual

A white Siamese cat

hairs. The breeding of these cats is very difficult and the desirable colour is hard to achieve; dilute patches of various colours may appear even in the ground colour, especially at the end of the back. Toms of another type must of course be used for the breeding. The kittens are lighter than adults in colour but not white.

New colour varieties of Siamese cats have appeared in recent years, including those with blue and cream, chocolate and cream, and lilac and cream points.

Siamese is off-white with pink-grey points. The body colour of the Red-point Siamese is also off-white, shading into peach on the back; its points are goldish-

Tabby-point Siamese

Oriental Shorthaired Cats

These cats are, in essence, colour forms of the Siamese cats. They have an elegant, slender body with fine bones, a long flat head resembling the head of a marten, a thin tail tapering to a point and large, erect ears, set wide apart. The Oriental-shaped eyes of these cats are not blue, but green; yellow eye colour is a fault. Forty-one col-

Oriental Chestnut – Havana

free of points. Most popular among them is the Havana (Oriental Chestnut), known for its strange brown colour, matching the colour of the world-renowned Cuban cigars. Its colour and conformation differ from those of the Burmese cat. The other colour varieties include black (ebony), blue, lilac and red. The Oriental Tortoise-shell Tabby often attracts the attention of show visitors; it occurs only in the female sex and is crossed with self-coloured toms of various types, depending on what colour shade the breeder wants to produce.

Patterned (Tabby) Orientals come in three tabby-pattern types – mackerel, blotched and spotted. They differ from other shorthaired cats of these colours by having green eyes and a different conformation, corresponding to the Siamese type. The green colour of the eyes should be particularly deep in the dark cats; the deeper the eye colour, the better. A sturdy

body build, a squint, yellow eyes, white patches or white hairs are regarded as faults. The tail should be free of any kink or hook. Show judges also place emphasis on the colour of the muzzle, eyelids and foot pads. The hind legs are somewhat longer than the fore. The self-coloured Orientals should be free of any hint of tabbying or other marking. A round head and a short, thick tail are undesirable features. Kittens have hints of tabbying that disappear as they reach maturity.

Though Oriental cats were developed from the Siamese, today most of them come from Europe or the USA.

The **Korat**, on the other hand, is a truly natural Oriental breed. In 1959 it was brought from Thailand to the USA, where it was recognised in 1965, and from there to Europe. The FIFé did not recognise it officially until 1982, although it had been recognised in Britain seven years earlier. The Korat is of medium size, strong and well muscled, with a thick tail, rounded at the end. Its face is distinctly heart-shaped, its eyes are conspicuously large and its nose has a distinct stop. The ears are large, round and wide, different in shape from the ears of the Siamese cat. The eyes of the

Oriental Black – Ebony

our varieties have been developed so far and only one of them, the Oriental White (Foreign White), bred in the USA, is allowed to have bright blue eyes. The Oriental cats are kept only in self-coloured varieties,

Oriental Striped

mature Korat are brilliant green or amber and its coat close-lying, thick and blue with silver tipping.

There is a number of breeds that are not recognised by the FIFé, for example the **Balinese**, which are longhaired Siamese cats, differing at first sight from the Colourpoint Longhairs by having no ruff.

The **Ragdolls**, developed in the USA, bear no kinship to the Siamese, though they are of similar colour, except for the white gloves and white tip of the tail. They may have seal, blue and chocolate points and are noted for their unusual passivity; they will hang over the owner's hand like a living ragdoll.

In the 1960s, a longhaired form of the Manx was bred in the United States. The breed is known as the **Cymric** but is not recognised in the United Kingdom. Of the other nonrecognised longhaired breeds, the Pekinese attracts attention at cat shows. The nose of this Siamese-type cat is as short as the nose of the Pekinese dog.

Shorthaired Persians are popular in the USA where they are kept in the most diverse colour shades and types, including the exotic Golden Chinchillas and Silver Shaded Shorthairs. On the whole, 85 colour varieties of these shorthair Persians are recognised in the USA.

The **Japanese Bobtail** is an interesting cat with a truncated tail only 10–12 cm (4–4.75 in) long. Part of the tail is hidden in the coat so it appears to be shorter still. The **Scottish Fold** is an unusual mutation that appeared in Scotland as recently as 1961. It is, in fact, a British shorthair with folded ear flaps, and can be kept in any colour. The folded ear is a recessive trait that would soon disappear if the animals were not carefully selected for breeding. Cats with folded ears have also been reported from China and other countries, but are now extinct there.

The **hairless cats** are an even stranger mutation. According to well-researched reports they used to be kept in China and some older sources

Oriental White (Foreign White)

also refer to hairless cats in Bohemia. They were also kept by the Indians in Mexico and perhaps by other nations too. These cats are, however, exceptionally delicate and have died out almost everywhere. The only hairless cat now in existence is the **Sphynx**, developed in 1966 in Canada. Like any hairless animal, the Sphynx has a higher body temperature than haired members of its species and is very sensitive to fluctuations in temperature, damp and other unfavourable factors. Breeding is difficult because Sphynx kittens often die.

In the late 1950s, American breeders attempted to re-establish the original Egyptian type of cat and developed a breed called the **Egyptian Mau**, using cats taken directly from Cairo. The Egyptian Mau is a slender spotted cat with green or yellow eyes, hardly differing from the other shorthaired cats.

Oriental Red Tabby

Dogs

It is much more difficult to keep dogs than cats, as the keeper must be prepared to commit more time to the care of a dog. It is always advisable for the owner of a large dog to have a well-made kennel set in a large well-fenced yard. Even dogs that can be left to run freely in the garden will be happy to have an enclosed yard as their own territory, and this is also an advantage for the keeper as the yard can be closed to keep the dog in, while the rest of the garden may have to be open at times. Even when the owner is absent the dog may be left in the yard. There should be a wire netting fence around the yard. The lower part of it should be buried underground or should be set into a concrete base so that the dog cannot dig its way out underneath it.

It is recommended that you pave the area around the kennel

The diversity of dog breeds has no parallel in the animal world.

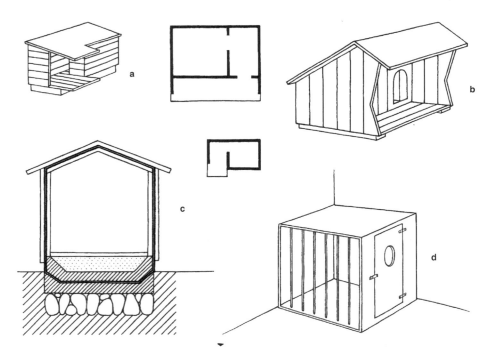

Different types of kennels: a) a simple kennel; b) a kennel for use throughout the year under harsh climatic conditions; c) the floor must always be thoroughly insulated from the ground; there must be double walls and one of the walls or the roof should be detachable to allow cleaning; d) a short-stay facility like this will be useful if a temperamental dog is kept in a flat.

with bricks (concrete is too cold). The kennel should always be wooden, with double walls and a removable roof for easy cleaning. A kennel in which the dog is to be left all year round must be thoroughly insulated against frost and protected against damp. A shelter out of the wind is the best solution for breeds that are unhappy in an enclosed space. The yard and kennel should be located in a place protected from wind and partially shaded during the heat of the day.

The breed of dog you intend to keep, and its purpose, must be taken into account when the yard and kennel are built. If the dog is to stay in the kennel all year round, and especially at night, the yard should be large and the kennel solid. The kennel may be simpler if it is intended say as a temporary shelter and

The fenced yard should be sited in a quiet, sunny place protected from wind.

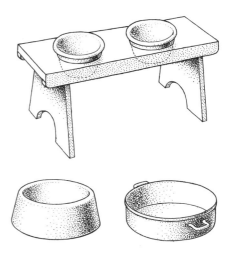

A dog should always have plenty of fresh water, preferably in a heavy stoneware bowl which cannot be knocked over easily. Discarded kitchen utensils are not suitable. Bowls fixed to a stand are best for taller dogs.

the area can be smaller. Hardy breeds with a thick coat, for example the Newfoundland or sledge dogs, must be protected from direct exposure to hot sun, whereas the more delicate breeds require a sunny place. All dogs dislike damp and permanently shady places. Dogs must also be protected against noise and should not be constantly disturbed especially when eating or sleeping. The dog needs, on an average, twice as much sleep as a person. It sleeps most of the day, so the kennel and the yard should not be sited in a busy place. Even a guard dog needs rest when it is off duty. The dog should never be tethered, not even to a long wire stretched over the garden.

Dogs kept indoors also need a permanent sleeping place. For a large or agile dog, a closable kennel in a quiet place is recommended. This will avoid problems with visitors, whom the dog might bother or even threaten. A well-trained and even-tempered dog should not need to be closed in, but it should have its own bed, raised several centimetres above the ground. Draught is harmful to dogs, as is lying on the bare floor, especially on cold tiles. An easily washable blanket should be placed in the animal's bed, which must be long enough for the dog to stretch out its body. The bed should be regularly cleaned and washed, and, if necessary, disinfected, both in the kennel and indoors, because your dog may easily bring home parasites such as fleas from its meeting with other dogs in the street. Dogs prefer lying on a firm bed; very soft cushions and mattresses are far from comfortable for them and are difficult to look after, so it is better not to allow the dog to become accustomed to them. Even the most delicate dog will be happy lying on a blanket folded several times or a bean bag.

The dog. must also have its own eating place, where fresh drinking water is always available. In the yard it is advisable to stand a heavy earthenware bowl on a raised platform, easily accessible to the dog. This will ensure the water remains clean and prevent it from spilling. The bowls with the water and food should be protected from rain and from falling leaves and dust. The food should always be fresh; cooked food should be given lukewarm. Puppies younger than eight weeks are fed six times a day, those up to three months eat five times, up to six months four times, later three times, and adult dogs, that is those older than nine months to a year, depending on the breed, should be given food twice a day if they work. Dogs that do not have regular exercise should be fed once daily. Regular feeding hours must be maintained every day. Unconsumed food must be removed because it would decay and attract flies and rodents in the yard, and the dog might get used to taking too long over its food.

The food should contain plenty of animal protein (meat) (16 per cent), vegetables and fibre (for example oat flakes, groats, rice and the like). The dog should not be given too much starch (up to 50 per cent) and fat (5 per cent at most). Vitamins and minerals are, of course, essential. The diet can be supple-

Both the box and the bed must correspond to the dog's size. The box should allow the dog to sit and stand inside. The bed should allow the dog to lie full length.

251

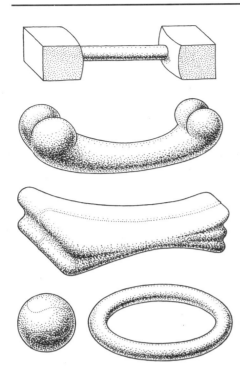

Dogs need toys which encourage them to play and to strengthen their jaws by biting. Toys of leather or hard rubber are best; wood and plastic are less suitable materials.

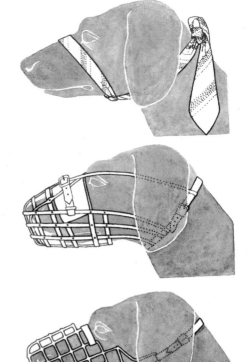

its mother. The new owner has to be very understanding: he must, in fact, replace the puppy's mother and siblings at this stage. This is when the puppy's close emotional attachment to its new owner usually develops. A young puppy should never be left alone in an outdoor kennel.

Puppies must be trained from the very first day in their new home. The first thing a puppy is to learn is its name, which it must hear as frequently as possible. The owner uses the puppy's name to call it to come, and praises it when it obeys. The meaning of 'No' is another im-

mented with good-quality tinned dog food.

When buying a dog, the first thing to decide is which breed to buy and from whom. It is always better to buy a puppy with a pedigree: this guarantees that the puppy really will grow into the breed originally chosen and that it can take part in shows or field trials. Pedigree parents and a reliable and reputable breeder will guarantee that the puppy is healthy and has all the traits required of its breed.

Puppies should never be taken away from their mother before they are seven weeks old, and preferably even later. Kennel clubs advise that puppies should be taken away at the age of 8–12 weeks. Instructions concerning their diet and care should be provided by the breeder. It is a big change in the life of a puppy when it leaves the kennel and

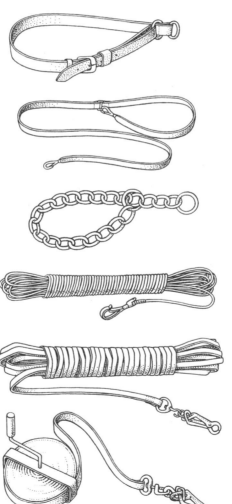

A collar and lead are essential. A choke chain can be used for disobedient dogs or those that are hard to manage. A long lead affords the dog more freedom.

It is not just a matter of the rules: it may well be that the dog's mouth will have to be secured to prevent it from biting someone. Any wide and firm piece of cloth or belt will suffice in an emergency. Muzzles may be made of leather, light plastic or metal; all must be wide enough and must not chafe the dog's mouth or nose.

portant thing to teach the puppy. Punishment should be rare. The puppy should learn to wear a collar and to walk on a lead,

A dog's corner in the flat, with an elevated bed and a washable wall lining. The floor should also be washable.

which should never be used to punish it.

The collar must be wide and lined with felt. Later a choke chain (a chain loop) may have to be used if the dog pulls or is hard to control. Dogs of some breeds hate collars and should wear a harness instead, for example the toys (Chihuahua, Miniature Pinscher, Pekinese), dogs with a special type of coat (Chow Chow), or dogs with a sensitive neck. A harness is also essential for some working dogs — a tracing type of harness for police dogs, a draught type for sledge dogs, and a special harness for guide dogs for the blind.

Dogs are often seen wearing different kinds of jackets. One type covers the dog's kidneys. When the weather is bad, such a blanket is suitable for dogs of the oversensitive breeds (the smooth-haired Miniature Pinscher, Chihuahua and others) or dogs that are sick. A healthy and agile dog needs no such protection, even in winter. Jackets protect the coats of some toy dogs (mainly poodles) from rain and dirt. Such attire is perhaps necessary in city streets in winter, but not in clean surroundings. Where chemicals have been used to thaw the ice on the roads in winter, the dog's paws may need to be protected with a special cream or small boots. Dogs hate wearing these, so it is better to carry small dogs or to avoid chemically treated areas.

Some working dogs wear blankets for identification. Bright-coloured blankets with a red cross are worn by avalanche and rescue dogs; blankets with a number are part of the equipment of racing dogs.

It is essential to have some basic equipment for the daily care of the dog. All dogs, including the smooth-haired breeds, need a brush, comb, a towel for their muddy paws and a bath towel. Regular grooming and combing is necessary for the dog's appearance and health. External parasites transmit various diseases, including those caused by intestinal parasites (tapeworms) as well as mite- and flea-borne conditions. The care of the coat depends on the standard of each breed. The dog's eyes should be wiped every day and the ears regularly inspected at least once a week,

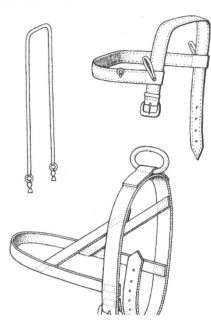

Different harnesses for working breeds.

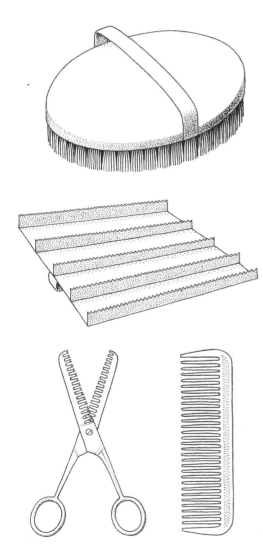

The essential equipment for keeping a dog includes a brush, a curry comb and a comb for cleaning and combing the dog's coat, a trimming knife or scissors for rough-coated dogs, and other aids, depending on the type of coat.

especially in breeds with folded ear flaps. The odour glands around the anus should also be regularly checked: if these do not empty spontaneously, they have to be cleaned, otherwise they may become infected. Most dogs do not need frequent bathing and the wire-coated breeds should not be bathed at all. Special dog shampoos or finely diluted potash soap should be used to bath a dog. After the bath it should be rubbed down with a towel and left to dry in a warm room.

The breeds are classed according to the purpose for which the dogs are kept, such as working dog, gundog, and toy groups, but many no longer fulfil their original purpose; a number of dogs originally intended as gundogs or working dogs are now kept in city homes as much-prized companions. The great popularity of Dachshunds, Cocker spaniels, or Collies provides good evidence of this. It is essential with these breeds to

The Australian Cattle Dog, called Kelpie in its native country, is clearly a relative of the collie.

insist that only those that have passed the required trials and possess proven, desirable working qualities may be used for breeding, otherwise the general quality of the breed may deteriorate.

Working dogs are often subdivided into police and military dogs, cattle dogs, guard dogs and others. There is no unity in this classification and the groups are not clearly defined: for example the German Shepherd, originally included among the herding dogs, is now the most popular breed used as a guard, with police and military, and dogs for the blind. The original purpose of the Rottweiler was also to drive and guard livestock. The mountain dogs are sometimes regarded as herding dogs and sometimes as guard dogs. Some authors classify

sheepdogs as a separate group and include other farm dogs, as well as the sled dogs, police dogs, some gundogs (Bloodhounds), the small Schnauzer and Miniature Pinscher among

the so-called utility breeds. It is more logical to divide dogs according to their kinship: there are distinct groups of terriers, hounds, retrievers and others. The official FCI classification is perhaps the best, because it is easy to follow.

It is essential that the owner should take into account the inherited and acquired characteristics of each breed before choosing a particular dog. He or she must know that spaniels or the Hamilton Stovare have a hunting instinct, that terriers have an active and busy nature and that the Chow Chow is aloof and dignified. Dogs of each breed should be treated and trained according to their nature and the owner must give up his or her free time to the care of this new pet.

Obedience is the main thing

a dog has to learn. This is essential for the large and working dogs, although small luxury 'toys' should also be taught to obey. The dog is a gregarious animal, always trying to win the highest possible status in the pack. If its pack is a human family whose members dote on it and are lacking in firmness, the pet will soon become spoilt and be a nuisance to everybody. The owner should supply all the dog's needs and be kind and understanding; nevertheless, he or she must also always be firm and remain the undisputed leader of the pack.

Gundogs or utility dogs should be used for their original purpose. If the owner does not feel able to train the dog himself, he can join a club or send the dog to a good dog trainer. Most dogs, including the toy breeds, dislike their talents being left unused.

Training a dog is a long process during which numerous difficulties will arise. The main thing is that the owner should be patient and should understand the needs of the dog. There is no general pattern to follow in training a dog because all of them, even puppies from the same litter, have their own individual temperament. The dog must have confidence in its owner and must not be afraid of him or her. A good owner or trainer avoids punishing dogs: verbal reproof will usually suffice, except in cases of real misdemeanour (attacking the trainer, other dogs or other people). Dogs should never be punished, despite the mischief they may have done, if they come to their owner when called without being forced to do so. The punishment must always follow immediately after the deed, otherwise the dog cannot understand why it is being punished. The dog should never see its owner losing his or her temper and should never be forced to do things it is unhappy about doing – climbing difficult obstacles, carrying heavy or nasty-smelling objects and the like. Negative feelings such as fear, nervousness and aggression must be overcome gradually, with endless patience. A trainer who wants to be successful and control a dog well, must control himself first. Even a well prepared dog often fails in trials simply because its master is nervous.

It is necessary to note that good training is very important because some dogs, if poorly trained, can be extremely dangerous.

In the UK, many breeds are now required by law to be muzzled.

The owner should constantly check the dog's state of health, have it vaccinated against contagious diseases such as rabies (in many countries this vaccination is compulsory), and prevent it being a source of infection to other dogs; this, of course, also applies to all parasites, including fleas and tapeworms. If puppies are to be reared or a dog is to be used as a stud, the breeding regulations must be thoroughly observed. Such a dog must attend shows and the owner must strictly follow the instructions of the breed society. The bitch comes into season twice a year. The dog is able to mate all the year round. Gestation lasts 63 days on average, usually ranging from 58 to 70 days. The litter size is usually large (10–15 puppies), especially in the big dog breeds.

a

b

c

d

e

f

What is wrong and what is right in dog training: a) It is useless to try to catch a dog; the best way to attract a dog is to adopt a friendly posture and call it in friendly tones. b) Violence will not help a dog to overcome an obstacle. Assistance of a whipper-in is very useful during such training. c) Pushing the dog forcibly back with the knee will help to teach the dog not to jump on its master. d) It is essential that the dog should walk by its master's heel. e) On hearing 'Down!' the dog should neither loll nor sit unconcernedly. f) Feeding by hand spoils the dog. Food belongs in the dog's bowl and should always be given in the same place and at regular times. Of course, a reward for a special performance can be given by hand.

The Herding Breeds

Most of the herding dogs are large or of medium size, small ones being an exception (Shetland Sheepdogs, Welsh Corgi). Their great agility, hardiness and thick 'waterproof' coat, as well as their aloofness, are associated with their original purpose. Their inborn alertness means that they will make good watchdogs after due training. Many of these breeds make fine companions for children: they are good-natured and will also be protective of the children. They are not, however, suitable for life in a city flat where they would suffer from lack of exercise. In the countryside they guard premises and stock, which they do not chase. Their hunting instinct is not very strong.

The herding breeds constitute a vast group, subdivided according to the environments where they first developed. The mountain dogs, once kept on mountain farms, serve people in many ways: they are used as

The best-looking of the Swiss shepherd dogs: the Bernese Mountain Dog.

The popular Scottish sheepdog: the Rough Collie.

guard dogs, herding dogs for livestock (mainly cattle), and even as draught animals. The Swiss mountain dogs are perhaps the most famous of this group; they are handsome in appearance and good natured. Sometimes they are used as police dogs. The longhaired **Bernese Mountain Dog**, the most commonly kept Swiss mountain dog, standing 66–68 cm (26–27 in) high at the shoulder, is of strong and harmonious build and has sparkling dark eyes, small drop ears and a straight bushy tail. Its coat is glossy, mostly jet black with clear russet points on legs, cheeks and above the eyes, and clear white symmetrical spots on the head and chest; white paws and a white tip to the tail are appreciated. The coat should be slightly wavy, but never curly. Light-coloured eyes and defects of jaw and of body build are considered faults.

The remaining Swiss mountain dogs are shorthaired. The **Great Swiss Mountain Dog** is the largest of them (up to 70 cm/28 in high) and heavy, weighing up to 58 kg (128 lb). The **Appenzell Mountain Dog** is smaller, up to 58 cm (23 in) at the shoulder, with a curled tail, and the smallest, the **Entlebuch Mountain Dog**, is up to 50 cm (20 in) high, with only a stump of tail or no tail at all, which is an inborn trait. All these mountain dogs have the same colouring and all are loyal and affectionate. They have speed and stamina and are alert and eager to defend their owner.

Another herding dog of great ability is the **Collie**, a lively and agile long-legged dog, 61 cm (24 in) at the shoulder, and weighing up to 30 kg (66 lb). It has a handsomely shaped head with almond eyes, small, half-erect ears and a very thick coat. The longhaired Rough Collie has a wealth of ruff, mane and trousering and a bushy down-swept tail. The shorthaired Smooth Collie is less popular than the rough variety. The most popular coat colours of the Collies are golden-yellow or sable, always with a white ruff and white markings on the legs and tail. There are also self-coloured varieties, gold or blue merle, in which the wall, or blue-flecked, eye is permissible, and a tricolour variety. The Collie is an intelligent dog, able to undergo all kinds of training: it has been used as a police dog. It needs plenty of exercise and fair treatment, and its coat needs constant care.

The **Shetland Sheepdog**, 'Sheltie', is a miniature Collie. It is longhaired, 34 cm (13 in) high, with a maximum admissible weight of 18 kg (40 lb). It is suitable for city life and can live happily in a flat.

The **Briard**, often known as Berger de Brie, is a French representative of the rough-coated shepherd dogs, with a height of up to 68 cm (27 in) and a weight of 30 kg (66 lb). It is an agile dog with a thick coat. The coat should not cover the eyes, which are dark and intelligent. French breeders crop the Briard's drop ears. This is illegal in the UK. The bushy tail reaches down to the heels. All colours are allowed with the exception of white. Dark colours are preferred. Pied body colouring or white markings on the paws dis-

The rough-coated French Briard really is a giant among sheepdogs.

qualify the dog at shows. A light-coloured or spotted nose, light eyes, a curly soft coat and small size are considered faults. The long coat of the Briard, which is wavy and stiff, requires constant care with occasional bathing and no clipping at all. The Briard is a well-mannered, intelligent dog and easy to train. It needs a lot of exercise, sensitive handling, and good housing in cool conditions. It is an affectionate animal and happy with children it knows. It makes a good family dog.

One very specific group contains the steppe cattle dogs that have a coat similar to that of sheep, although it tends to become matted. These breeds come from Asia but are most widespread in Hungary. The **Hungarian Komondor**, a massive and strong dog, up to 80 cm (31 in) high and weighing up to 60 kg (132 lb), is a well-known representative of this group. It is kept exclusively in the white colour variety. Its fine wavy coat forms ropes or dreadlocks. Unlike other breeds, combing of this dog's coat is undesirable.

The longer and more felt-like it is the better. However, it is not easy to maintain a coat like this for such a dog will be happy only in a clean, natural environment. It is cautious with strangers but affectionate to its owner. Originally kept to guard and protect flocks of sheep, it is not very suitable for any work except shepherding.

The smaller **Puli** (44 cm/17 in; 15 kg/33 lb), which is black, white or grey; the silver, grey or black **Pumi** (44 cm/17 in; 13 kg/ 29 lb); the black, white, or black and white **Mudi** (47 cm/18.5 in; 13 kg/29 lb); the **Polish Lowland Sheepdogs** (52 cm/20 in; 20 kg/44 lb); or the white, yellowish or steel-coloured **South Russian Ovczarka** (70 cm/ 27.5 in; 35 kg/77 lb) have qualities similar to those of the Komondor. All of these dogs have a very lively temperament and are sometimes suspicious of strangers. A flat is not a proper setting for them.

Sheep breeding is a traditional occupation in the mountain regions and that is why moun-

Hungarian sheepdog breeds typically have a coat similar to that of sheep. The Hungarian Komondor is the largest.

tain breeds predominate among the sheepdogs. They all share many of the same characteristics and even experts may easily confuse them, although they come from regions that are far apart. All of them are strong, with tall, straight legs, a large head and a very thick, long and often slightly wavy coat. White, or at least light shades of other colours, predominate in their coat colouring. The conformation and temperament of these dogs are in keeping with their work in the mountain terrain and the coat is likewise suited to the harsh climates. The dogs are white to distinguish them from wolves attacking the flocks in times of poor visibility or at night. The mountain conditions also shaped the nature of these dogs: they are alert, fearless or even aggressive, willing to at-

A representative of the white mountain sheepdogs: the Slovakian White Sheepdog.

Three breeds of very similar appearance: this one is the Hungarian Kuvasz.

tack and fight animals, and not easily controlled. They are not suitable for activities other than shepherding, the males being particularly stubborn and difficult to train.

In Europe the mountain sheepdogs are represented by three breeds, very similar to each other: the **Slovakian White Sheepdog, Hungarian Kuvasz,** and the **Polish Mountain Sheepdog**. The Kuvasz is the largest of them, 75 cm (29.5 in) at the shoulders, and weighing up to 60 kg (131 lb). The Polish Mountain Sheepdog is not as tall, but it is massive in build, weighing up to 55 kg (121 lb). The Slovakian White Sheepdog is the lightest in conformation; although it is 70 cm (27.5 in) high, it weighs only 44 kg (97 lb). The skull of the Kuvasz is rather flat, with a slightly arched nose and an indistinct stop. The Slovakian White Sheepdog has a shorter, straight nose, a distinct stop and a much rougher coat than the Kuvasz. The Polish Mountain Sheepdog has a short and slightly tapering nose and brown eyelids (the eyelids of the Kuvasz are covered with thick white hair; those of the Sheepdog are black). The differences are really slight. All three are happy in a country setting where they can have a large yard and can be kept outdoors all year

The imposing Polish Mountain Sheepdog.

round. Their coats require minimum care. They are excellent guard dogs, careful with strangers and sometimes aggressive. They are not suitable for keeping as pets in city flats.

The **Pyrenean Mountain Dog** bears a close resemblance to the preceding three breeds but is still larger, up to 80 cm (31 in) high and weighing about 55 kg (121 lb), with an abundant white coat. The Italian **Maremma Sheepdog** and the **Sheepdog of Abruzzi** are very similar to each other (their standards were unified in 1941). Their height is up to 73 cm (28.5 in) and weight up to 40 kg (88 lb). Their small triangular ears taper to a narrow point. The **Asian Mountain Sheepdogs** are of a similar type with the exception of the coat colour which may be yellow, grey (like a wolf's coat), dark brown or piebald. In regions where the dogs may still encounter wild predators, their ears, and sometimes also the tail, are docked.

The **Welsh Corgi** is a specific type of cattle dog, occurring in two forms: the Cardigan, which is smaller (up to 30 cm/12 in and 12.5 kg/27.5 lb) with a medium-long tail, carried horizontally; and the Pembroke (up to 31 cm/ 12 in and 11.5 kg/25 lb) with a very short tail. Both have a long body, erect ears and keen sight. They are very agile and sturdy. They are said to have been used in Wales for pony and sheep herding. Today they are very popular pets, intelligent and good natured, and suited for life in a city flat. Some people object to their tendency to bark, announcing every stranger. The coat of the Welsh Corgi is strong and short or medium-long. The Cardigan may be of any colour except white, the most popular colour varieties are red or blue merle with white markings. The most fre-

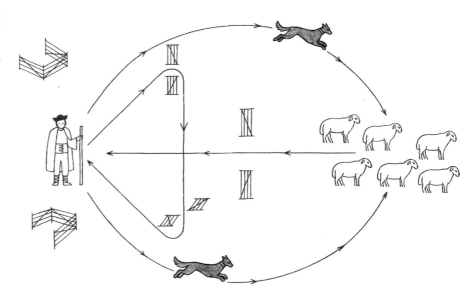

Sheepdog competitions have strict rules. Dogs may compete either individually or in well-matched pairs. The route along which the sheep are to be driven is precisely marked out.

quent coat colours of the Pembroke are rust, brown or black with white markings allowed on legs, chest and underparts. The Corgis are hardy and require no special care.

The training of sheepdogs and cattle dogs is lengthy and difficult and is usually started when the dog is young. The dogs' guarding and herding abilities are largely inborn, inherited from the hunting tactics of the wolf pack – the ancient ancestors of the dog. The first things to teach the herding dog are obedience and tolerance of the tended animals, without losing aggression towards strangers and wild animals, particularly predators. The dog is first taught to keep the herd together, to gather in strays and then to drive the herd or flock in the required direction. The training procedure varies according to the environment and the species of livestock. Field trials are frequently organised for sheep-

dogs in Britain and Germany. The herding dogs are also noted for their excellent sense of direction and common sense even in busy streets: they are even able to drive a flock across a busy road. They are assertive, and will try to show their herding abilities during family walks, which may be a nuisance if one of the company wants to go off alone before the whole group returns home. Strangely enough, with the exception of the German Shepherd Dog, these dogs are not suitable for training as guide dogs for the blind.

Police and military dogs form a special category among the working breeds. They have the widest range of abilities – capable of exacting work in training, they are also sturdy enough for police and military use. Various breeds – the Collie, Airedale Terrier, Newfoundland, German Mastiff and others, have been used in the past in many countries as police dogs. At present, police and military dogs are mainly recruited from the following five breeds: the German Shepherd Dog, Boxer, Rottweiler, Dobermann and Giant Schnauzer. Standard and Miniature Schnauzers may also be used for special purposes, for example at European customs offices.

The **German Shepherd Dog** is one of the most popular and widespread breeds in the world. It has a rectangular outline and its body is massive and strong. The height of the males is 60—65 cm (24—26 in). The weight is not specified but the dog should not look heavy or cumbersome. German Shepherd Dogs may be shorthaired, longhaired and, rarely, wire-haired. The permit-

The most versatile and widespread utility dog: the German Shepherd Dog.

The Boxer is somewhat less assiduous but very reliable. Docking the ears used to be compulsory in Europe but, today, Boxers' ears can be left in their natural shape.

ted colours include black, wolf-grey, sandy and tan, usually with a black saddle on the back. Brown or light grey markings are allowed; white spots are a fault. The German Shepherd Dog is an energetic, tireless, alert and lively creature. Eagerness to work is its inborn quality, so it needs good training and plenty of exercise. It is able to serve people in any way needed: Ger-

man Shepherd dogs are good trackers, guard dogs, leaders of the blind, rescuers, avalanche dogs and watch dogs, as well as fine companions. They can be housed outdoors. For details on training see pages 300—301.

The **Boxer** is a dog of medium size, square in outline, 57—63 cm (22—23 in) high, well mus-

The Rottweiler, originally a cattle dog, is now used as a military and police dog.

cled, with a typical shortened upper jaw. Docking of the ears and tail of the Boxer was usual in Europe until recently; in Britain this practice was given up some time ago. Boxers with ears and tail left in their natural form perhaps lose their keen appearance, but on the other hand the puppies avoid a painful operation and the adult dogs avoid the risk of being disqualified at shows for a nonstandard ear. The coat of the Boxer should be smooth and should lie close to the body. Its colour is fawn, red or brindle; the muzzle is black. White markings should not cover more than one-third of the dog's body surface. The Boxer is good natured and playful and quick to learn. It does not have the endurance of the German Shepherd Dog and is less resistant to cold. It makes a fine family pet, after careful training and if given plenty of exercise.

The **Rottweiler**, up to 68 cm (27 in) high, weighing about 40 kg (88 lb), is used as a police dog in much of Europe. It is robust and well muscled. Its coat

The most commonly kept colour variety of the Giant Schnauzer is black.

is short and black in colour, with tan markings; white hair is undesirable although a small white spot on the chest is tolerated.

The ears are small and drooping, the eyes dark with close-lying lids, and the tail is docked. Some puppies are born bobtailed but even then the stump is docked. The Rottweiler is intelligent and a quick learner, suitable for heavy police service. It is a natural watchdog. These dogs require firm handling and thorough training. They can be quick tempered and dangerously aggressive towards strangers.

The **Dobermann** has somewhat similar requirements for training and handling. It bears a distant resemblance to the Rottweiler but is far less robust. Its head is wedge-shaped and the body square and slender. Its high-set ears are cropped in Europe but not in Britain and the

tail is docked to about 6 cm (2.3 in). The height of this dog is up to 68 cm (27 in) and its weight up to 36 kg (79 lb). The Dobermann is intelligent, swift, fearless, but very cautious with strangers and often unwilling to accept a new owner. It requires a very sensitive approach combined with firm discipline, and needs plenty of exercise. If it is improperly handled it may become aggressive and may even

bite. Its coat is short and is black, brown, or blue and tan.

The **Giant Schnauzer** is a robust, well-muscled dog, even-

The temperamental Dobermann requires great patience and perseverance on the part of the trainer.

tempered, hardy and hardworking. The maximum admissible height is 70 cm (28 in); the weight is up to 50 kg (110 lb). Its black or grey (pepper and salt) coat is coarse, tight and thick. It has prominent eyebrows and a beard on its muzzle. The tail is set high and docked. The Giant Schnauzer is the only European police dog to require clipping and trimming. The jutting eyebrows and a well-maintained bristly beard are important features of the dog's appearance. Character-wise the Giant Schnauzer is a little slow to learn and to begin with needs a firm hand. It is, however, good natured and affectionate. It is suspicious of strangers but does not bark much, unlike the Standard and Miniature Schnauzers. Housing out of doors is recommended as this will help to maintain a good-quality coat.

The Mastiff Breeds

These dogs are mostly ancient breeds; only a few have been refined by breeders in more recent times. They derive from the famous ancient Molossus hounds. They are massive to heavy in body build, and are not very agile. They are usually shorthaired, with a heavy skull and excessive skin which forms large wrinkles on their face. Their ears are pendant, but are docked in Europe in many of these breeds. Since ancient times they have served chiefly as watch and guard dogs because they do not have the stamina and agility for other kinds of work. They are usually

The Mastiff is among the most powerful of dogs.

The Bordeaux Mastiff demands respect.

docile and some of them make affectionate pets, especially when young. The disadvantages of these dogs are their large food consumption, their need of space for exercise, and breeding difficulties.

The **Mastiff**, 80 cm (31 in) at the shoulder and 90 kg (198 lb) in weight, is one of the largest dog breeds. It has a broad, massive head with a short nose and a powerful body, set on strong,

straight legs. Its coat is thick with a dense undercoat in fawnish-brown, silver, apricot or brindle. Rearing is not easy, because if the puppy is to develop well it needs good-quality food and sensitive training. The war years 1939–45 took a great toll of the Mastiff population, so the existing stock is not always of top quality, making it difficult for breeders to produce specimens with perfect conformation, well-

developed muscles and desirable bearing. In spite of its size, the Mastiff is obedient, responsive and good with the family. As a watchdog it is intimidating and alert.

The **Dogue de Bordeaux** is robust and well-balanced in appearance in spite of its rather short legs. Its height is up to 66 cm (26 in) and its weight at

The Neapolitan Mastiff, like every good fighter, has short-docked ears.

least 45 kg (99 lb). Its heavy head is imposing, with a prominent lower jaw at least 1 cm (0.3 in) longer than the upper jaw. The coat is dense and silky, bright bay, apricot, brownish-red or sable; there should be a distinct mask on the face. The Bordeaux used to serve as a military dog, so it has a rather suspicious, sometimes dour temperament, and is not easy to train: it needs firm handling. This is an excellent guard dog, very loyal and good with children. It will not take readily to a new owner. Like the Mastiff, it is drop-eared and its ears and

The white Argentine Mastiff is lighter and more agile than other mastiff breeds.

long tail are left undocked. It is intimidating as a fighter.

The **Neapolitan Mastiff**, a dog of Italian origin, bears a very close resemblance to the Dogue de Bordeaux. It is enormous in size, and very strong. Its height is 75 cm (29.5 in) and weight 75 kg (165 lb); its head is heavy and short, with numerous wrinkles. Unlike the Dogue de Bordeaux, the lower jaw may be only slightly longer than the upper jaw. In Europe its ears are docked. The eyes are quite large and chestnut in colour.

The coat should be close-lying and its colour may by glossy black, grey or brindle. There may be a white spot on the chest. The Neapolitan Mastiff is a somewhat cumbersome dog with plenty of character and if badly handled it could be dangerous. However, it will be very affectionate towards its family and if really well trained is obedient and faithful, watchful and calm. This mastiff's behaviour towards other dogs is sometimes unpredictable.

The **Argentine Mastiff** is a smaller, square-set dog up to 65 cm (35.5 in) high and weighing up to 45 kg (99 lb). It is a well-muscled and agile dog that, in its native land, was used for hunting wild boar and other wild beasts. It is rarely encountered in Europe. The Argentine Mastiff is bred exclusively in white; it is short-haired. In countries other than Britain its ears are docked short. This mastiff breed can be trained successfully as a guide dog for the blind.

The **Great Dane** is the most remarkable of all mastiffs. It is large and strong, up to 90 cm (35 in) high and weighing up to 60 kg (132 lb). Unlike the other mastiffs, it is svelte and elegant and its head is quite long, with no excess skin. In much of Eu-

rope its ears are docked, but British keepers, and since 1987 also those in Germany, leave their Great Danes' ears undocked. The tail is long, reaching down to the heels. The coat is short, smooth and glossy and must not stand away from the body or be coarse. The breed's colours are golden, blue, black or harlequin, which must be pure white with black or blue patches. The light-coloured dogs may have a black mask. Great Danes of all colour varieties have dark eyes, claws and nose, only the harlequin may have lighter eyes and claws, although the dark colouring is preferred. The blue Dane may have lighter eyes. It is not easy to rear a Great Dane. The puppy must have plenty of good-quality food and a lot of exercise to let it develop a harmonious form and strong musculature. The Great Dane is an intelligent dog, although not a quick learner. It needs thorough training. While young it is playful and good-natured but it may become aggressive with age. It can even take police training and makes a good guard dog.

The most elegant of the Mastiffs – the Great Dane or German Mastiff.

Large Working Breeds

As distinct from the mastiffs, whose appearance elicits the respect of strangers, the dogs of this group are generally regarded as trustworthy and, despite their size, they are usually reliable and even-tempered. For this reason, many of them have been used as rescue dogs and all are ideal companions for children.

The **Newfoundland** is a very popular dog, up to 75cm (29.5in) at the shoulder and weighing 62kg (136lb). It is a giant of a dog, rectangular in outline, with a large, well-arched head, pendant ears and a long, shaggy tail. Its thick coat is long and silky, and oily enough to repel water. It is bred exclusively in black which should be free of any tinge of brown. This dog is a powerful swimmer and certainly strong enough to drag a man from the sea. It is very intelligent and is suitable for police training. In summer heat it often feels uncomfortable. Newfoundland puppies are not easy

The Newfoundland is a powerful swimmer with a zeal for rescuing people from drowning.

to rear. They are big eaters and need plenty of exercise. They should not, however, be allowed to jump over obstacles before they are one year old, to avoid exposing their growing joints to excess stress. They also need clean water in which to swim. Stagnant water is not suitable because it may be a source of leptospirosis or other diseases. The Newfoundland is a splendid family dog and able to adapt to any environment. However, it will be happiest in the country where it can live outdoors, take plenty of exercise and may be allowed to swim. It is reliable with children. Unfortunately, like all heavy dogs, the Newfoundland does not have a long life span.

The **Landseer** is the white-and-black variety of the Newfoundland. Its legs are longer, and its height at the shoulder may be as much as 80cm (31in); it weighs up to 55kg (121lb). The coat of this dog is white with black patches but there must not be too much black. The Landseer's coat is not as dense as that of the Newfoundland. Landseers were popular in the last century but today they are rare. It is a good swimmer, as good as the Newfoundland.

The Landseer is the white-and-black – and very rare – variety of the Newfoundland.

The **Saint Bernard** is one of the most popular dogs. It was said to have been able to predict storms and avalanches and was used to sniff out lost travellers. The original type of this dog was lighter than today's Saint Bernard: now they are 75 cm (29.5 in) in shoulder height and weigh 85 kg (187 lb). The Saint Bernard has a massive head with a short, broad nose and a good-natured expression. Its ears hang flat and its tail is straight. This dog is bred in white with red patches and in two coat types, the longhaired type being far more popular than the shorthaired. The face often bears a dark mask. Drooping eyelids are a problem in this breed. The Saint Bernard is a very intelligent creature, being even-tempered and friendly. If given appropriate training, it will

large but harmoniously built animal. It is 80 cm (31 in) high and weighs 80 kg (176 lb). Bred in Leonberg, Germany, this is a longhaired, rugged dog and is bred in a 'lion' colour, varying from yellow to reddish-brown, with a black mask. The Leonberger is resistant to disease and, unlike the preceding breeds, has great agility and stamina. It makes a first-class watchdog and companion; in the past it frequently accompanied its master on horseback. The Leonberger is very clever, careful and fearless but needs firm training in order not to become dangerous when on guard. It is exceptionally loyal, and as a children's companion it is very reliable.

The **Hovawart** is a very old German breed, used as a house guard. It is much smaller and lighter than the other dogs of this group: its height is up to 70 cm (28 in) and its weight up to 40 kg (88 lb). This is a shapely, handsome animal with an abundant long coat, a neat head, and an alert and intelligent expression. Kept for centuries in southern Germany, this breed was refined and given its present appearance before the Second World War. It has retained its

Many of the original dogs kept in the St. Bernard Monastery were short-haired.

good qualities, including hardiness, docility and alertness. Originally a farm dog, the Hovawart has proved itself to have other remarkable abilities and it has been trained for police work. It is bred in three colour varieties: mid-blond (which may have a white star on the chest and tail end), black, or black and tan (these may also have small white spots, 6 cm/2.3 in across at the most, on the chest). The Hovawart is a fine dog, but without due training it might become suspicious and even aggressive towards strangers. Today few dogs of this breed are kept as pets.

The famous saviour of those who lost their way: the Saint Bernard.

make a good watch dog, and is good with children. Puppies and adult dogs both need large amounts of food and require a great deal of exercise.

The **Leonberger** is an outstanding guard dog. It is a very

The Leonberger, a versatile working dog.

The Sledge Dogs

People who live in the snowy areas of the North have always used dogs to pull sleds or the simple drags on which loads were carried when there was no snow. Dogs also served as beasts of burden, carrying loads on their backs. Sledge dogs are still invaluable in northern countries, where the successful breeding of good sledge dogs used to be virtually a matter of life and death. Today these dogs are used not only for practical purposes but also for sport: races between individual dogs or teams are now gaining popularity even in countries where the use of dogs for pulling sleds has never been a tradition.

Most of the breeds of sledge

The Alaskan Malamute bears a close resemblance to the Husky, but is much more robust and stronger.

dogs are very old, and have only been slightly refined by breeders. The fastest of them all is the **Siberian Husky**, up to 59 cm (23 in) high and weighing 22 kg (48 lb). This is a slender dog of compact body build and smooth gait, with a narrow skull, pointed erect ears and rather slanted eyes, blue or brown in colour. It is well-furred, with a bushy tail and densely coated paws. The tail is carried above the back. All colours are permitted, including white, although wolf-grey or silver-grey are preferred, with a typical white mask on the face. The Siberian Husky is docile, eager to learn and very adaptable. Of course, it requires plenty of exercise to work off its energy and the owner must spend plenty of time with it. The Husky should be kept out of doors and should be protected against heat.

The **Alaskan Malamute** bears a close resemblance to the Husky but is much more robust. Although about the same height as the Husky, it weighs 38 kg (83 lb). It really deserves its name 'the tractor of the north' because it is the most powerful sledge dog, holding many long-distance records. The prevailing colours are grey or black, with

a typical white facial mask. It is slant-eyed and its eyes are dark; it has small pointed ears and a tail curled up to form a ring. The Malamute is an all-purpose dog, and does well in the harsh conditions of the North. It has a quieter nature than other sledge dogs and is very intelligent. It needs exercise and adequate conditions, so is unsuitable for a town flat.

The **Eskimo Dog** (up to 64 cm/25 in high; weighing 42 kg/92 lb) and the **Greenland Dog** (up to 68 cm/27 in and 45 kg/99 lb), both bred in various colours, are also very an-

The picture of the Greenland Dog shows that it is a relative of the Spitzes.

cient breeds. Both are unsuitable for apartments because of their wild and untamable nature.

The **Samoyed** makes a much better pet. It is beautiful, agile and sturdy, with a handsome head and magnificent snow-white fur. It is up to 55 cm (21.5 in) high and weighs up to 30 kg (66 lb). This very ancient breed was originally kept by the Siberian peoples who used it as an all-purpose working dog.

The Siberian Husky with its conspicuous porcelain-blue eyes.

After the first Arctic expeditions, the Samoyed was introduced into northern Europe and Alaska and from there into the USA.

As this is one of the hardiest sledge dogs, it became very popular, especially in the early twentieth century; today it is even kept as a pet in town flats. This intelligent and very active dog needs strict training and plenty of exercise. Its coat is 'open', – that is, standing away from the body – so it is especially sensitive to rain.

The most recent breed of sledge dog to be developed is the **Czech Mountain Dog**, bred for practical purposes using stock of Canadian sledge dogs, the Slovakian White Sheepdog, and the Saint Bernard. It is robust and very agile, 70 cm (28 in) high and weighing 45 kg (99 lb). It is longhaired and is bred in two colour varieties: the

The snow-white Siberian 'tractor', the Samoyed, makes a very fine pet.

ground colour is always white and there are either black or deep yellow plates or patches on it. The Czech Mountain Dog is well muscled and moves smoothly. It has a massive head with drooping ears, a medium-long bushy tail and a fine, thick coat, with a rich undercoat. Under mountain conditions it has proved its worth as a good sledge dog, and is noted for its friendly, pleasant character. The main reason for the development of this breed was Czech conservationists' efforts to reduce the damage caused by motorised traffic in the mountains by replacing such traffic with dog teams. For one whole season a team of these dogs carried the mail in the Giant

A brand-new breed – the Czech Mountain Dog – has proved to be very strong in harness.

Different types of dog teams: the fan-wise Indian dog team, also used by the Labrador Eskimos; the two-dog team of the Yenisei Ostiaks; the alternate team, commonly used by Giliaks in eastern Siberia; the Canadian tandem in which the dogs pull the traces.

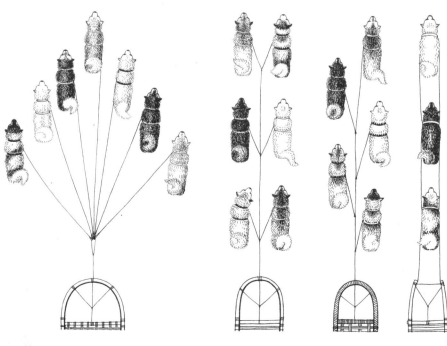

Mountains and also took part in many races. The dog is not easy to breed and keep, being a big eater and requiring good-quality food and plenty of exercise. The quality of the dog's coat suffers if it is kept in heated rooms, so it must be kept outdoors.

The Spitzes

The Spitzes are a remarkable group of dogs, which come from countries with a harsh climate. They have a magnificent thick coat, standing out from the body, and typically a head with a pointed muzzle and small, erect ears. The hindlegs stand square and the tail is carried over the back. All Spitzes are lively and courageous, and will make themselves heard with their penetrating bark. Such a noisy little creature is by no means an ideal pet for a city flat, although otherwise they make intelligent, docile and affectionate companions. Originally used for hunting and guarding, they can make excellent watchdogs and are reliable companions for children if they are kept in the country.

European Spitzes come from the Baltic and North Sea coast. The **German Spitz** is the most widespread of them, existing in three varieties – Large, Standard and Miniature. The **Wolfspitz,** wolf-grey in colour, also belongs to this family. The Large

The Spitzes are not all alike. The rust-coloured Finnish Spitz is an outstanding gundog, whereas the white Large Spitz is a general-purpose guard dog.

Spitz is up to 40 cm (16 in) high; the Standard is 28 cm (11 in), weighing 3.5 kg (7.5 lb); the Miniature Spitz weighs about 2.8 kg (6 lb). The Wolfspitz is the largest of them all, growing to a height of up to 45 cm (17.5 in). The colour varieties of the German Spitzes include white, black, dark brown, orange, silver and, most recent of all, champagne.

Spitz fanciers in the Netherlands keep the **Keeshond** instead of the Wolfspitz. Another breed kept in the Netherlands and also in Belgium is the smart **Schipperke**, used as a watchdog on barges. The Schipperke may be either miniature (height up to 26 cm/10 in; weight 4.5 kg/ 10 lb) or standard (up to 30 cm/ 12 in high; weight 9 kg/20 lb). This vivacious little dog has a fairly smooth black coat, but on its neck it has an abundant mane that often bristles. The bobbed tail is a distinctive feat-

The short-haired Schipperke, a reliable guard on barges. Its bark is very loud.

ure of the breed and puppies are born with this. The Schipperke is a very temperamental little dog, but has many good qualities. It has, however, a louder bark than the average Spitz, which, together with its constant restlessness, makes it unsuitable for life in a city flat.

Many Spitz breeds are native to Scandinavia. One of the most beautiful of these Scandinavian

The wolf-grey colour is typical of the German Wolfspitz (in the picture) as well as the Dutch Keeshond.

The Karelian Bear Dog is a game-hunter among the Spitzes.

dogs is the **Finnish Spitz**, with its splendid reddish-brown coat. Its height is up to 48 cm (19 in) and its weight about 20 kg (44 lb). This hardy and persistent breed is a very independent dog that hunts game, stops it and calls its master by barking. The Finnish Spitz can be trained as an all-round gundog, agile, strong and bold enough to hunt even wild boar. However, it is not suitable for central European hunting grounds, and as a pet it can be rather boisterous, although otherwise intelligent and docile.

The **Karelian Bear Dog** has similar qualities but is quieter than the Finnish Spitz. Dogs of this breed are not abundant in central Europe, though some specimens may be encountered. Their height at the shoulder is up to 60 cm (24 in) and their coat is black-and-white, short and dense, and lies close to the body. Their tail forms a bushy ring. The Karelian Bear Dog is a courageous and sturdy hunter, and has been used in its native country to hunt large game, including bear. Although a hunter at heart, it can make

a good watchdog on an estate or a farm. It is hardy, undemanding and resistant to disease, but does not like heat and rain.

The Spitzes are widespread all over Asia as far as Japan, where several native breeds are kept, each of a different size. One of the largest Japanese dogs is the **Japanese Akita**. This heavy-duty work-dog is large and powerful, up to 69 cm (27 in) high. It has a large head with a broad front, small, dark, triangular eyes and small, prick ears. Its coat is hard and has a thick, woolly undercoat. The coat colour can be red, white, wheaten, black, grey, silver, steel-blue, black-and-tan or brindle. The Japanese Akita is used for hunting and can also make a very good watchdog or police dog. It is very intelligent but needs to be trained by an experienced handler. It is not commonly kept as a pet in continental Europe or Britain.

Another dog native to Asia is the popular **Chow Chow**, a massive dog up to 53 cm (21 in) high and weighing 25 kg (55 lb). It has a robust body build, a heavy head and a magnificent, thick coat. There are also smooth-coated Chows but they are much less popular. The colours, solid throughout, can be black, red, blue, cream, white or cinnamon. The Chow Chow is one of only two breeds of dog with a blue tongue. (The other is the Shar-pei.) Dogs of this breed are not easy to train: the Chow is aloof and suspicious, and can be stubborn. However, if a member of the family wins its affections, the Chow makes a most devoted and delightful friend.

The mysterious looking blue-tongued Oriental dog, the Chow Chow. Its puppies are the loveliest clowns.

The Hounds

This group of dogs is so different from all others that some experts believe hounds must have had a different ancestor to other dogs. They are tall, slender and keen-sighted, and are the fastest of all four-footed animals. They are hard to control and not always easy to train. They need a large, enclosed area or regular running exercise. The track dogs require a special diet to replace the energy lost on the track without affecting the dog's body outline. These short-track runners cannot store and utilise body fat reserves, so they need plenty of good-quality meat (at least two-thirds of the daily ration), cooked vegetables and oat flakes. Vitamins and plenty of calcium and other minerals are essential.

Equipment for dog races: on an oval, grassy track the dogs chase a mechanical hare. Originally the dogs were released by hand, but today starting gates are commonly used. On the track the dogs wear a wire or plastic muzzle and a blanket with a number. A collar is inadmissible during races. Separate races are held for different breeds and for dogs and bitches. They youngest age at which a dog is allowed to race is 15 months. Whippets race on

The long- and short-haired runners. The Afghan Hound is more impressive but the smooth-coated Greyhound holds the speed record.

shorter tracks (350 m/382 yards) than the larger breeds.

The **Greyhound** is the best-known racing dog, up to 76 cm (30 in) high and weighing at most 25 kg (55 lb). Greyhounds are bred to race at the highest possible speed, so breeders pay little attention to the coat colour or other traits not associated with movement. The

short, smooth, firm coat may be of any colour or combination of colours. The head is long, with reclined rose-shaped ears. Neither the tail nor the ears are ever docked. The Greyhound is able to run at over 60 kmph (37 mph) and in short bursts its speed is even higher. It is unsuitable for any kind of training and has problems with obedience. It is usually unreliable in families with children or cats, so it is better kept outside the home, in a warm place with a raised bench to sleep on.

The **Whippet** looks like a miniature Greyhound, up to 50 cm (20 in) high, weighing 12 kg (26 lb) at the most. Like the Greyhound, it is also a powerful racing dog. There are both smooth-coated and longhaired Whippets; the latter, bearing a resemblance to the Borzoi, are very rare. Unlike the Greyhound, the Whippet makes a very good pet. It is essentially a family dog, although by no means eager for training.

The smaller star of the racing tracks, the speedy whippet.

The **Afghan Hound**, up to 73 cm (29 in) high and heavier than the Greyhound (up to 30 kg/66 lb), is a very popular breed. It is much slower than its typical racing counterparts but looks magnificent with its long coat. Its distinctive features are a graceful body build, a handsome head and, in particular, the quality of the coat, which must be silky, smooth and thick, and short only on the face and back. All colours are allowed. The Afghan's coat should be

Massive body and powerful jaws: this is what the Russian Borzoi needed when hunting wolves.

The Saluki or Gazelle Hound derives its nobility and grace from its ancient origin.

well brushed, and when in the countryside care should be taken that the dog avoids thorns and dense shrubs which could damage its coat. The Afghan Hound is an aristocrat and an animal of style and beauty but the potential owner must be aware that this dog will need plenty of exercise, has a complex and aloof character and may sometimes attack other dogs.

The **Borzoi** is sometimes called the king of hounds. It is a tall dog up to 82 cm (32 in) and heavy, weighing up to 40 kg (88 lb). It looks spectacular with its long, wavy, silky coat, with a ruff around the neck and feathering on the legs and tail.

The Borzoi's most frequent coat colour is pure white with golden or black patches, and also golden, red or black. Tan is acceptable but not desirable. The Borzoi was originally used as a coursing dog to hunt large game animals. Although not as fast as some other hounds, it is a dog of great stamina and endurance, and even able to cope with a wolf. It was used for hunting in a pack and was kept in kennels, not in the household. On the track it reaches a speed of about 50 kmph (31 mph). This is an independent and aloof dog, which is not easy to train, and needs plenty of exercise

and daily care of its coat.

The **Saluki** or **Gazelle Hound**, an oriental dog with drop cars, long silky hair and a long-feathered but not bushy tail, is the swiftest of all hounds. Its coat is smooth and soft, with slight feathers on the legs and ears, although some Salukis may be smooth-coated throughout. The coat colours may be cream, golden, red or grey with yellow or rusty markings, as well as tricoloured. Originally a coursing dog, the Saluki has retained its coursing abilities

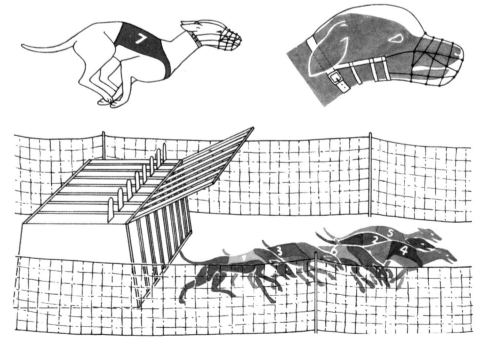

The short-track dog runners wear a light blanket with a number and a wire or plastic muzzle of minimum weight.

Today, starting gates are commonly used at all stadiums for dog races.

and is also a good guard dog. Its coat requires daily care.

The mighty **Irish Wolfhound** is one of the tallest and most powerful of all dogs, never less than 79 cm (31 in) at the shoulder and weighing 54 kg (119 lb). The breed faced extinction in the mid-nineteenth century and was laboriously revived by a breeder called Captain Graham. This tall, rough-haired dog of elegant carriage has grey, red, black, white and fawn colour varieties. Its head is long and narrow with longer hair over the eyes and under the jaw. Its eyes are deep set and the ears are rose-shaped. The Irish Wolfhound is a rare breed and requires great care especially during the first year of life. It is not easy to produce a dog of the desired carriage with good musculature, nor is it easy to maintain a good-quality coat, which is often too soft. The Irish Wolfhound is calm, aloof and reserved, but is neither aggressive nor noisy.

The **Scottish Deerhound** is just a little smaller in size (height 75 cm/29.5 in, weighing up to 42 kg/92 lb); it differs from the Irish Wolfhound in having a flatter skull without a stop. Its coat is softer on the head than on the

The tallest dog in the world, the Irish Wolfhound, once facing extinction, was laboriously revived.

body. On the back and legs the coat is long and wiry. The most popular colours are grey, with dark or light brindling, blonde, sandy-red, or reddish-fawn with black ears and muzzle. The Deerhound is a dog of greater speed and endurance than the Wolfhound; it has keen hunting abilities and requires gentle handling, otherwise it might become snappy. Bathing should be kept to a minimum to avoid softening of the coat. The prospective owner must be aware that the dog will need plenty of exercise. Both the Wolfhound and the Deerhound need suitable accommodation; not too warm, which would spoil the coat. Both dogs are tough and hardy.

The **Pharaoh Hound** is a dog of great antiquity, being depicted on the walls of ancient caves and tombs. It has been maintained in its purest form on the island of Malta. This dog is not large (height about 55 cm/23 in, weight about 20 kg/44 lb) and its short coat is usually tan or rich tan with white markings. In the past it was found throughout the Mediterranean region

The Pharaoh Hound, one of the most ancient breeds of the world.

The Ibizan Hound is a close relative of the Pharaoh Hound. It is native to the Balearic Isles.

but it is now extinct in the north of Africa. It cannot tolerate rainy weather.

The Pharaoh Hound is presumed to be one of the ancestors of a number of Mediterranean breeds, namely the **Ibizan Hound**, the **Portuguese** and **Spanish Podenco**, and the **Spanish Galgo**. All of these dogs are somewhat smaller than the large hounds, but resemble them in their body build. They are very friendly and can be used as gundogs when hunting small game. The Spanish Galgo (height 65 cm/25.5 in; weight up to 25 kg/55 lb) is most like the European hounds. Its

The Azawakh Hound, from the Sahara, has long been confused with the Sloughi.

coat colours are cinnamon, red, black and tawny-yellow with white markings, and its ears, like those of the hounds, are tilted backwards. The Ibizan Hound, up to 66 cm (26 in) high and weighing up to 22 kg (48 lb), is native to the Balearic Islands off the coast of Spain. Its ears are erect like the Pharaoh's. Most of the Ibizan Hounds are smooth-haired but there are also rough- and long-haired varieties. The European Podenco breeds, with smaller ears, seldom occur outside the Iberian Peninsula.

The African hounds, including the **Azawakh Hound**, the **Sloughi** and the smaller **Sinai Sloughi**, are perfect antelope hunters. The first two breeds had long been confused with each other until the Azawakh was recognised as a separate breed in 1981. The nomadic tribes kept them for centuries in the semideserts and steppes of northern Africa. It is interesting to note that the diet of these dogs is almost vegetarian: they are given milk and cereals and only during the hunting season do they eat meat. Nevertheless,

these dogs are robust, 70 cm (28 in) high and weighing up to 35 kg (77 lb), and they possess great stamina and endurance. They are fearless and when in a pack they will not hesitate to attack large beasts of prey. The Azawakh differs from the Sloughi in having longer legs and a shorter back.

The smaller size of the Sinai Sloughi distinguishes it from the other two breeds. All three have a close-lying silky coat, a long, thin tail reaching down to the hocks, and triangular drop ears. Azawaks are usually tawny-yellow to red, rarely tan, with white markings and sometimes with a black mask. Spots are undesirable. The Sloughi's coat colouring is tawny-yellow, sometimes with a black mask, and the Sinai Sloughi is white or grey with a black mask, or light brown. Dogs of these breeds are rarely encountered in Europe and are not, in fact, much suited to European conditions. They do not like rain and frost, nor do they like training and they have problems with obedience. These dogs are not used for racing and have failed when used for coursing on European hunting grounds.

The Arab Sloughi is widespread in Arabia and Africa.

Gundogs: Setters and Pointers

Gundogs are the shooter's indispensable companions. A number of setter breeds have been developed for various types of hunting and to be used with different groups of game. The breeds were developed in specific conditions in their native regions, so each of them has its distinct character. They are all-round gundogs, robust and comparatively tall, perfect in movement, with a very keen sense of smell, and with the much appreciated ability to point or set up game, in which respect they differ from other dogs. A dog of this group, on finding a bird or hare, neither barks nor hurls itself at its prey; it stops and assumes a posture that indicates where the game is and sometimes even what it is. These dogs are also able to retrieve shot game and work enthusiastically in field, forest and water. Most possess good temperaments and are obedient, docile and friendly towards other dogs and animals. Hardy and well behaved, they do not require much care and make really fine companions. Prob-

Two smooth-haired gundogs: the English Pointer and a representative of the continental Pointers, the German Smooth-haired Pointer.

lems seldom arise in keeping a pointer or setter, although they should be vaccinated against infectious diseases and should be protected against external parasites such as ticks. The owner should never allow the dog to eat any part of the shot game, especially the guts which are a frequent source of infection.

Possibly every region of every European country has its own setter breed. Several dozen of these all-round gundog breeds are internationally recognised. For a clearer understanding they are divided here into British/Irish and continental European dogs.

The smooth-haired **Pointer**, one of the world's best specialists at scenting, is perhaps the most distinct representative of the British Isles branch of this gundog group. It is about 70 cm (27.5 in) high, weighs up to 30 kg (66 lb), has a conspicuous stop (the boundary between the forehead and muzzle) and a somewhat concave muzzle outline. It is a well-muscled and strong-backed dog of great poise and elegant bearing. Its ears are covered with fine hair and its medium-long tail tapers to a point. The coat is smooth and close-lying, with a very definite sheen, usually white, with black, red or yellow patches; solid-coloured specimens of the above-mentioned shades are also seen. The Pointer learns quickly and has an outstanding gundog temperament, although

Three long-haired British Setters: Irish, English and Scottish Gordon.

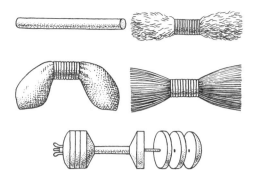

Retrieving is among the important jobs of Setters. Various training aids are indispensable.

it is not such a complete all-rounder as the continental European setters; for example, it is unwilling to retrieve some types of game. The Pointer requires plenty of exercise in the field, good training and good-quality food containing sufficient protein, vitamins and minerals for good development of the skeleton.

Great popularity is enjoyed by three setter breeds, particularly the mahogany-coloured **Irish Setter**, up to 67 cm (26 in) tall and weighing almost 30 kg

Basic commands to gundogs: Sit down. Lie down. Retrieve. Drop. Retrieving from water.

(66 lb), with a splendid long, smooth, glossy coat and a noble, dignified expression. This is a very intelligent animal with a rather gentle temperament, requiring sensitive handling. The Irish Setter, free-flowing in movement, is a vivacious hunter with an excellent nose, and may also become a good retriever. It makes a fine pet but it should be borne in mind that its original purpose is to be a gundog. Its coat requires thorough care.

The **English Setter** is somewhat shorter and less lofty in appearance. Its coat may be white with black, yellow, liver or bicolour flecking. It is calmer than the Irish Setter, likes to work in water and is good at retrieving game.

The **Gordon Setter** is the most powerful of all setters. It is well boned and has a larger, deeper head than the English Setter, with a distinct elevation on the back of the skull. The ears are heavy and profusely overgrown with long hair, as is the tail. The long coat is soft and close-lying, wavy or straight, but not curly. The coat colour is always black with mahogany markings. The Gordon Setter's height is 68 cm (27 in) and its

weight about 30 kg (66 lb). This is an intelligent dog, with a quiet, gentle character, and eager to learn. It makes an affectionate pet that loves children. Although rather careful with strangers, it is easy to control. It has a perfect nose.

All setters need sensitive training, plenty of exercise out of doors and daily care of their splendid coat, especially the

German Longhaired Pointer and Hungarian Viszla

long hair on the ears and the abundant hair on the tail.

Continental European setters and pointers offer a large choice indeed, comprising all types of coat: smooth, rough, long or wire. The **German Smoothhaired Pointer** is the most widespread of them all. This is a symmetrical dog of a strong body build, up to 70 cm (28 in) high and weighing 32 kg (70 lb). Although very lively, it is also quite manageable, intelligent and docile. Its coat is short and rather hard, brown in colour or white with brown patches, or pepper and salt; black specimens may also occur but they are rare. The German Smoothhaired Pointer is drop-eared, with its tail docked to about two-fifths of its natural length, which is, in fact, common practice among all smooth-haired continental European setters.

The **German Longhaired Pointer** is of about the same height, weight and coat colour. It has similar qualities to the Smooth-haired Pointer and is also an all-purpose hunting dog. However, unlike the Smooth-haired Pointer, it has an undocked tail with a profuse flag, long wavy hair on its ears and trousering on the legs. The coat on the back is 3–5 cm (1.5–2 in) long, thick and glossy, but not silky. There must also be thick hair between the toes on the paws, but it must not be longer than the toes themselves. This is a hardier dog than the Short-haired Pointer and is particularly suited to work in water.

The **Hungarian Vizsla** is another highly rated gundog. It is lighter and smaller (up to 30 kg/66 lb) and 64 cm (25 in) and is used for all gundog purposes. There are three types of Vizsla: Smooth-haired, Wirehaired and Longhaired, all of a deep wheat colour – the darker the better, but dark brown is undesirable, as are white markings. The Vizsla is manageable, quiet, very tough, hard-working and docile. Like other pointers and setters, it makes a good

The Weimaraner attracts attention by its striking colour.

pet, but it requires plenty of exercise. Otherwise, it requires no special care or attention.

The **Weimaraner** is a striking, noble dog of harmonious outline with a short, soft and very dense coat, silver-grey in colour. Its eyes are light: sky blue in the puppies and light amber in the adults. The Weimaraner's

height is up to 70 cm (28 in) and its weight up to 28 kg (62 lb). There is also a longhaired type whose coat is 3–5 cm (1.5–2 in) long. The Weimaraner is calm, usually silent, manageable and very affectionate with family. It can be suspicious of strangers and needs firm handling. However, like all dogs of this group, it needs a generous amount of exercise in order to work off its excess energy. Its coat does not need much care and if the dog is well fed (with plenty of protein, vitamins and some cod liver oil from time to time) the

The small Munsterlander and Czech Wirehaired Pointer

German Wire-haired Pointer

coat will remain sleek and glossy. It is beneficial to brush it frequently and to wipe it over lightly with a flannel cloth to remove dust.

The large and middle-sized varieties of the **Munsterlander** should also be mentioned among the longhaired pointers. The height of the large Munsterlander is about 62 cm (24 in), while the small variety is about 10 cm (4 in) smaller. The large Munsterlander is white with black patches, or spots, or else the black and white hairs are intermingled. The middle-sized Munsterlander is white with brown patches. In the former the brown colour is a fault; in the latter the end section (one-third) of the tail should be white. Both are close relatives of the Longhaired Pointer but are not so meek and docile. Their training is harder and requires experience. If they are not given thorough obedience training they may cause problems, especially when taken out in the country. Otherwise, they are affectionate and make good companions. The tail of the Large Munsterlander is sometimes shortened by about 2 cm (0.75 in).

The **Rough-haired Pointers** form a large group of popular gundog breeds. Chief among them are perhaps the **German Wire-haired** and **Spiny-haired Pointers** and the **Czech Wire-haired Pointer**. The **Pointing Wire-haired Griffon**, bred by E. K. Korthals late in the nineteenth century and still referred to as the Korthals Griffon in France, and the **Poodle Pointer** also rank among this group. All are about 65 cm (25.5 in) high, only the Griffon is about 5 cm (2 in) shorter, and their weight is about 30 kg (66 lb). All are docile and suitable for general purpose use in hunting. To an inexpert eye these Rough-haired Pointers may look the

Poodle Pointer

same. The tails of all of them are docked: the Czech Wire-haired Pointer's tail is shortened to about two-fifths, the Wire-haired, Spiny-haired and Poodle Pointers' by about one-third, and the Griffon's to a third or quarter of the natural length. All have a rough, thick coat with a fine undercoat. There is a bushy mass of hair over their eyes and under the jaw. The colours of all these breeds are also much the same: mostly various shades of brown. The Poodle Pointer is perhaps most easily recognised: the outline of its nose is somewhat concave like the Pointer's and its coat colour is brown. White, black and light brown colours are considered a fault, as is flecking. The remaining rough-haired pointers have somewhat arched (ram-like) noses. The Griffon has short hairs mixed with long on its ears; it is bred in the steel-grey variety with chestnut splashes, white with brown or yellow patches, or brown with pepper and salt. The undercoat is especially dense, the guard hairs are almost bristle-like but should not be curly.

The remaining three breeds differ mainly in their coats: the coat of the German Wire-haired Pointer is really very rough, hard and close-lying and can be of any colouring. The coat of the Spiny-haired Pointer is about 4 cm (1.5 in) long, straight, hard and bristle-like, brown or brown with white. The Czech Wire-

haired Pointer has three kinds of coat: a soft and dense undercoat, about 1 cm (0.3 in) long, a half-covering coat 3–4 cm (1.3–1.5 in) long, and wiry hair up to 7 cm (2.8 in) long on the chest, back and flanks. The Czech's colour is also brown or brown and white. The characters of all these dogs are also much the same. They are docile, reliable, even-tempered, sharp with vermin, and suitable for many purposes. When not working they are very good-natured and friendly towards other animals. With the family they make very good companions. However, if they are badly

Griffon

trained and not given enough exercise, they may play havoc among poultry and become much-feared fighters. They can live outdoors as they are hardy. They need good-quality food, and good care must be taken of the coat which must not become soft; they should be bathed only in very exceptional cases. The old hairs should be removed by pulling with a trimming knife rather than with a comb; the eyebrows and beard, being the dogs' most distinctive features, should be treated with particular care.

The Trackers

As distinct from the pointers and setters who are the all-round workers of the hunting field, the trackers are specialists, whose job is to flush small game from shelters in thickets, reeds and tall field crops. The trackers are smaller than the pointers and setters and all have a long, thick coat that protects them against injury in the thickets. Unlike the pointers, the trackers are easy to list; only one breed of this family comes from continental Europe, the others being spaniels bred in the British Isles. The single continental European Tracker is the **Wachtelhund**, or German Spaniel. This is a noble dog whose appearance and character resemble the Longhaired Pointer. It can easily be distinguished from this pointer by its much shorter legs; its maximum height is 52 cm (20 in). Its tail is shortened by about one-third. This dog has drop ears that should not be too long (they can be stretched to

the tip of the nose). They are overgrown with long wavy hair that is dense although not as profuse as the ears of the spaniels. The coat should not be silky and is either brown throughout out or brown and white. The Wachtelhund is docile and adaptable, excellent in hunting small game and a fine companion. It is powerful and hardy, does not bark enough to be a nuisance, and attracts everyone with its intelligent expression. It loves to show off the tricks it has learned, is good with children and avoids fight with other dogs.

However, the general popularity once enjoyed by the Wachtelhund has now been usurped by the **spaniels**, a large and varied group of dogs who can serve as gundogs. They range from tiny 'ladies' toys', who have maintained their hunting abilities despite their small size (up to 25 cm/10 in at the shoulder), to the water spaniels, the largest of whom are about the size of the Pointers. The **Cocker Spaniel** is undoubtedly the best known and the greatest favourite among the spaniels, and has become more of a luxury dog than a hunter. The Cocker Spaniel has a shoulder height of 41 cm (16 in) and should weigh about 12 kg (26 lb). Like all spaniels, it has moderately long ears set low on the head and well feathered. These ears cause many a prob-

Representatives of the large family of spaniels: an American Cocker Spaniel, a Cocker Spaniel puppy, a Golden Cocker Spaniel, a Welsh Springer Spaniel.

lem to the dog and its owner. They often become dirty during walks or when the dog dips them in water or food and, unfortunately, the dog also suffers from inflammation of the ear. It is essential that the ears of all spaniels, particularly the Cockers, should always be kept clean. The tail is docked to allow the dog to move it freely: it should be neither too short nor too long, depending on the standard. The coat is silky, abundant and glossy and its colours may be golden, red, black, white with single-colour

Irish Water Spaniel

splashes or spots, or brindle; black and tan Cockers and tricolour specimens are also seen.

Very similar, but heavier, is the **Clumber Spaniel**, up to 45 cm (17.5 in) high and weighing 25 kg (55 lb), and pure white with yellow markings; the golden-brown **Sussex Spaniel** (height 40 cm/16 in; weight 20 kg/44 lb); the black, liver or mahogany **Field Spaniel** (height up to 46 cm/18 in; weight 22 kg/48 lb); the white **Breton Spaniel** with orange patches, about 50 cm (20 in) height, and a number of others.

The **Springer Spaniel** and **Welsh Springer Spaniel** will frequently be seen out hunting. Both are taller than the Cocker and are temperamental, agile and sturdy. The height of the Welsh Springer Spaniel is up to 48 cm (19 in) and its weight about 22 kg (48 lb); the Springer Spaniel is somewhat taller. The former is white with deep red patches; the latter is usually white with black patches, although all colours are allowed except pure white, red and white, and white with lemon markings. Both of these dogs are deft in the field and tireless even in the hardest conditions. However, they have a somewhat peculiar character and are not easy to train; a strong hand and an understanding and sensitive approach are perhaps the best combination for successful training. All spaniels can make agreeable and playful pets of a pleasing, handsome appearance, but a badly trained spaniel may be pig-headed, disobedient, and even quarrelsome and snappy with other dogs. The beginner should start with a bitch, who will be meeker and more affectionate.

Of the spaniel family, the **Water Spaniels** (Irish and American) are the greatest specialists. They have a brown coat, similar in structure to that of the Poodle, and their tail is left undocked. They excel in water retrieving. The Irish Water Spaniel is 60 cm (24 in) high and weighs 30 kg (66 lb). The smaller American Water Spaniel is about 45 cm (17.5 in) high and weighs 20 kg (44 lb). Used for nothing else but hunting, they are not easy to manage.

The New World contributes another fine breed to the spaniel family: the **American Cocker Spaniel**, a splendid-looking dog up to 32 cm (12.5 in) tall and weighing up to 12 kg (26 lb). It is

Springer Spaniel's head

more robust than its British counterpart and has a very abundant coat and profuse wavy feathering on its ears, chest, abdomen and legs. Although a gundog by name, it is really a luxury dog, requiring extraordinary care. To keep its coat in good condition it must be combed every day and some parts of it must be lightly trimmed from time to time. Special attention should be paid to the ears. Its colour varieties include black and other colours with lighter flags, sometimes with a white spot on the chest, and also bicolour with whitish splashes, as well as black with brindle.

The Coursers

As hunting techniques and regulations developed, this very ancient type of hunting dog underwent significant changes during the last century. The coursers' original purpose was to chase game in rough terrain, working individually, in twos or in a pack, while barking in a high, far-reaching voice and thus enabling the hunter to identify the position of the dogs and the game. This type of hunting is practised on a very limited scale today and dogs of this group are now given different assignments; for example, they may be used instead of Bloodhounds. The official standards of some of them (such as Slovakian Kopov), have been modified to comply with this new wider range of their use: their height has been reduced and sometimes even their shape has changed. Many breeds have almost disappeared or are bred only as pets. Of course, only quiet and even-tempered dogs make good pets, such as the **Bassets** or the **Beagle**. Most of the coursers are too agile and noisy to be kept in a city flat and they are not easy to train.

Switzerland is the country of origin of many courser breeds,

Different types of Coursers: the tall Lucerne Laufhund and the Beagle with a puppy.

The Courser works in rough terrain.
Its job is to help the hunter identify the position of both dead and wounded game.

most of them existing in two varieties: tall and short-legged. Some examples of these are the **Jura Laufhund** or Hunting Dog of Jura (heights 46 and 38 cm/ 18 and 15 in; weight 30 kg/ 66 lb), which is yellow to reddish-brown with a black saddle; the large and small **Schweizerischer Laufhund**, or Swiss Beagle (heights 53 and 38 cm/ 21 and 15 in; weights 30 and 20 kg/66 and 44 lb), both white with red patches; the tricoloured **Berne Beagle** (46 cm/18 in; 30 kg/66 lb) and another version of the same breed that is smaller by 10 cm (4 in); or the **Lucerne** pair of Laufhunds, of the same size as the preceding breed with a special 'blue' coat (grey-white in colour), with black spots and tan. All these Laufhunds are short-haired and have very long, thin ears, set low on the head and covered by fine hair. Their long and comparatively thin tail is not docked.

Most of the European coursers are referred to as jowlers. There are so many different types that they cannot all be mentioned here. Every country and perhaps even every district has its own jowler breed. Dozens of them were bred in France (*braques*), and in Scandinavia, too, where they are called *stövare,* as well as in Russia, the Czech Republic, Slovakia and other countries of Europe.

The **Dachsbracke**, no smaller than 34 cm (13.3 in) and no taller than 42 cm (16.5 in), is an all-purpose gundog that is still in use. Unlike the Dachshund, its forelegs are straight. The Dachsbracke is a sturdy, agile dog, hardy and with stamina. Its close-set coat is dense and hard, with a thin undercoat. The colour varieties include deer red with a black mask, black and tan, and red with a black saddle. Yellow colouring and white markings are undesirable. The Dachsbracke is suitable for mountain terrains.

Most central European game dogs are used for hunting small game, but the **Slovakian Kopov**, a smallish Carpathian dog, can even cope with deer, boar or large beasts of prey. It was originally quite big, up to 60 cm (24 in) high, but new game-management regulations forced the breeders to develop a smaller type. Today the Kopov should be no higher than 50 cm (20 in) nor heavier than 35 kg (77 lb). Even so, this well-muscled, smooth-haired dog still gives a remarkable performance. A perfect tracker and steady runner, it is now used chiefly for chasing vermin and driving wild boar. Its coat is black with mahogany markings. This dog has also proved to be good at following a scent and is irreplaceable in mountain terrain. Although smooth-haired, it can withstand

One of the best mountain hunters – the Slovakian Kopov, together with the Dachsbracke.

The coursers used on small game also include the **Bassets**, short-legged but otherwise fairly powerful dogs developed in France. This group comprises a whole range of smooth- and rough-haired types. The most popular of them is perhaps the smooth-haired tricoloured Basset Hound, up to 38 cm (15 in) high and weighing 23 kg (50 lb). It has very long pendulous ears and its mild, somewhat melancholy temperament is reflected in its expression. This hound is an ideal companion, being quiet, tolerant, obedient and reliable.

The Basset is a pet rather than a gundog today.

frost well, and goes into deep snow without hesitation because its undercoat grows thick in winter. This is an independent animal that requires a firm hand in training, otherwise it could become headstrong or even aggressive, especially towards other dogs.

The Basset Hound from southern France.

Bloodhounds and Retrievers

Some gundogs can be used for many purposes, while others are very specialised. The bloodhounds are among such specialists: held on a long lead or

Hannoverscher Schweisshund and Bayerischer Gebirgsschweisshund

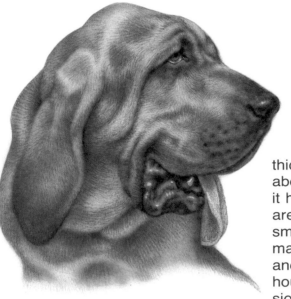

The English Bloodhound with its typical deep folds on the head.

left to work by themselves, they are expected to track down and find wounded game. They are the best of all tracker dogs. A keen sense of smell is their prime quality, provided they are thoroughly trained. Trainers use part of a game animal, dragged on a string, to mark the trail. The training is difficult and lengthy but well worth while: a well-trained bloodhound is able to follow a trail several hours old and will stay on it over many miles of difficult terrain until it tracks down its quarry.

The **English Bloodhound** is the largest of this group, up to 72 cm (28 in) high and up to 49 kg (108 lb) in weight. It is powerful in appearance and rectangular in shape. Its skin is thick and loose, particularly about the head and neck, where it hangs in deep folds; the ears are fine and long. Its coat is smooth and comes in black with masking, and tan, and also red and reddish-brown. This Bloodhound has a worried expression; it used to serve as a police dog but today it is bred mostly as a companion, being a loving, gentle pet, quiet and reliable, playful and warm-natured. However, its good nature makes it a poor watchdog. Its coat needs constant care, especially in summer when dirt in the skin folds may cause irritation and inflammation. Its lower eyelids may sometimes be too heavy and hang open, producing a haw, which could lead to conjunctivitis.

Two breeds still prevail among dogs of the Bloodhound type that are used in gamekeeping. These are the **Bayerischer Gebirgsschweisshund** (height 60 cm/24 in) and the **Hannoverscher Schweisshund** (50 cm/ 20 in). Both have short legs (so that they are rectangular in form), a smooth coat, drop ears and a long straight tail. A typical feature is their matt, non-glossy coat, although the Hannoverscher Schweisshund may have a dull silky lustre. The most common coat colour of both dogs is reddish-brown with a dark mask; yellow or red with grey are less common in these breeds. Both Schweisshunds are loyal and reliable, although the Bavarian is more lively. They make fine companions, are quick to learn and are entertaining and playful.

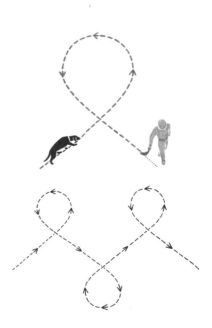

Training Bloodhounds: part of a game animal is dragged on a string to mark the track with the animal's blood.

There is no doubt that blood-hounds are useful game dogs. Wounded game, if not trailed and found by a bloodhound, would suffer for a long time, and the sportsman's venison and trophy would be lost. Keeping a retriever, on the other hand, is a sportsman's luxury. There are few retrievers in Europe because retrieving is usually done by the setters. In America and Britain, however, these dogs have a place among gundogs and are also very popular as pets.

All retrievers are robust, powerful dogs. The **Golden Re-**

The Golden Retriever, a beautiful dog both in its colour and its build.

The most popular colour variety of the Labrador Retriever is black.

triever, a sturdy dog of up to 63 cm (25 in) in height and 33 kg (73 lb) in weight, is the most popular of all. It is symmetrical in body build and has an abundant wavy, water-repellent lustrous golden coat. Puppies have a very pale coat colour when they are born and may even look pink as they develop. The Golden Retriever's need to retrieve is legendary – it is not

afraid to leap into icy water to do its job and is never as happy as when fetching and carrying. The Golden Retriever is a good-natured dog, friendly to children and other animals, but obedience is not among its major qualities.

The **Labrador Retriever**, up to 65 cm (25.5 in) high and weighing 30 kg (66 lb), is another popular breed of the retriever family. Unlike the Golden Retriever, it is smooth-haired, tawny-yellow or black in colour. It is a powerful swimmer, even better than its Golden rival, being a close relative of the Newfoundland. Its smooth coat is very dense and hard to the touch, and it is always self-coloured with no spots allowed. The Labrador is suitable for families and good with children.

Some other retriever breeds have been developed in America, such as the **Curly-coated Retriever** and the **Chesapeake Bay Retriever**. The coat of the latter is slightly wavy but never curly.

Curly-coated Retriever and Chesapeake Bay Retriever

Dachshunds and Terriers

These smallest specialists among the gundogs have some peculiar features and abilities that are associated with their work. First, they must be small enough to penetrate a fox's or badger's lair or a rabbit warren. Most of them are long-bodied and short-legged but in spite of their size they have great physical strength and very strong jaws. They are well muscled and robust, with a massive head. Working underground, these dogs must be able to take care of themselves, consequently they are difficult to control, stubborn and assertive. However, they are friendly little animals with people, so they are also favourites as pets.

One of the most widespread breeds in the world is the **Dachshund**. There are four weight varieties of this breed and three coat styles: long-haired, smooth-haired and wire-haired. The heavier type is 20–25 cm (8–10 in) high and weighs 7–9 kg (15–19 lb); the lighter

The Dachshund in all its three coat types – Long-haired, Smooth-haired and Wire-haired – is undoubtedly among the best earth dogs.

type weighs 4–7 kg (9–15 lb); the Miniature Dachshund weighs 3–4 kg (6.5–9 lb) and the smallest type of Dachshund up to 3.5 kg (7.5 lb). As with all breeds, the bitches are smaller and lighter (a weight difference of 500 g/1 lb). Dachshunds are

well known and need not be described here in detail. Correct body form, the required posture of the forelegs, a correct bite and the setting of the ears, which should neither have folds nor stand off, are the main criteria. Bulging or light-coloured eyes and defects of coat are serious faults. Dachshunds are bred in many different colours: self-coloured, with markings, and pied. The most popular colours of the longhaired Dachshunds are mahogany and black with mahogany markings. With the Wire-haired Dachshunds, emphasis is laid on coat quality, which should be short and hard, not standing off, and should form a beard on the chin and bushy eyebrows over the eyes.

The Dachshund is intelligent, unusually clever, sturdy and lively. If well trained, it is an ideal family pet, loyal, watchful and playful, but requiring plenty of attention. It is sensitive to cold and its long back should not be exposed to excess stress by frequently running up and down

Terriers of excellent hunting qualities: the Smooth-haired Fox Terrier, the Welsh Terrier, the short but strong Czech Terrier and the German Terrier.

stairs. Susceptibility to spinal diseases usually has a genetic background. The risk is reduced by good muscling, which requires regular and adequate exercise in the country.

A group of digging dogs that rivals the Dachshunds in popularity, the terriers originally came from the British Isles. Few terrier breeds were developed on the European continent, the **German Terrier** proving to be the best gundog of them all. Its height is up to 40 cm (16 in) and its weight up to 10 kg (22 lb). The colours of its rough coat include black, deep brown with lighter markings, reddish-brown, brown and sand. The German Terrier is courageous, sharp with vermin and a really passionate hunter, hence not a good dog to keep in a city flat. The **Czech Terrier** has a much calmer temperament. It is 27–35 cm (10.5–13.5 in) high and weighs up to 9 kg (20 lb). Its coat, greyish-blue or light coffee in colour, is dense and soft with a silky sheen, and requires laborious clipping. Although a gundog, it is quiet and non-aggressive, fitting well into a family. The FCI recognised this breed in 1963.

One of the varied range of British Isles terriers, the **Fox Terrier,** 39.5 cm (15.5 in) in height and weighing 8 kg (17.5 lb), takes first place with its excellent hunting abilities. There are two types, Smooth and Wire, with coats of white with black or black and tan markings. The Wire's coat has to be clipped and trimmed. Once a hunting dog, it has retained its hunting instincts. This is a sharp, lively little animal that needs a firm hand and thorough training.

Similar in body build is the **Welsh Terrier**. Its wiry coat is black and tan or black grizzle and tan. A hardy, lively and assiduous dog, perhaps even more courageous than the Fox Terrier, it would not hesitate to stand up to a large wild beast. The Welsh Terrier is, in fact, an all-round gundog. With its temperament and sharpness, it is more suited for a gamekeeper's lodge than a city apartment, although many Welsh Terriers are kept as pets today.

The two short-legged terriers, the black or wheaten **Scottish Terrier** (height up to 28 cm/ 11 in; weight up to 10 kg/22 lb) and the white **Sealyham Terrier** (up to 30 cm/12 in; weight 9 kg/20 lb) are much better suited to the urban lifestyle than the Welsh Terrier. Although both are very good diggers, they are rather quiet and easy to manage, and the bitches are

The white Sealyham Terrier is one of the ancestors of the Czech Terriers.

especially playful, loyal and affectionate. Both have coats that need expert clipping and trimming.

The terriers include many breeds which can be used for several different purposes, not only as hunting dogs.

The **Airedale Terrier** is the largest of the terriers, powerful, well muscled, square in body shape, up to 62 cm (24 in) high and up to 20 kg (44 lb) in weight.

The Scottish Terrier is now more popular as a pet than as a gundog.

Its coat is dense and hard and requires plucking or stripping; its colour is black and tan or tan and dark grizzle. The tail is shortened by one-third of its length and the small triangular ears are not cropped. The stripping is very complicated and is done for two purposes: to enhance the shape of the head and the body and to help maintain the required hardness of the coat. The Airedale is an intelligent all-rounder, once used as a police and military dog, although its original purpose was hunting larger game, including work in water. Today it is no longer used by the police or army, being considered less efficient than the German Shepherd Dog and other police breeds and because of the great amount of care its coat requires. Its present assignment is companionship and guarding. Obedience training is essential. Experienced owners may have problems coping with its strong will and assertive temperament.

Similar problems are faced by owners of other large terriers such as the Irish **Kerry Blue** (height to 50cm/20in; weight 15–17kg/33–37lb), the **Lakeland Terrier** (38cm/15in; 8kg/17.5lb) and the **Irish Terrier** (46cm/18in; 10kg/22lb). The soft, thick, silky coat of the Kerry Blue is most difficult to maintain: it should be partly clipped and partly trimmed. The whiskers, which are considered particularly important, require special care because this inquisitive dog will always be poking them into something. The Kerry Blue gives an impression of elegance, but is a hunter at heart (once used to hunt badgers and otters), and a great fighter. The Lakeland Terrier also requires complicated clipping and trimming because its double coat (soft undercoat and a hard, wiry outer coat) looks untidy if not given proper care. It was used to chase foxes and otters but its character is somewhat gentler than the Kerry's. It needs plenty of attention and plenty of exercise and can be trained to be a pleasant companion.

The Manchester Terrier is one of the most elegant dogs. The Airedale Terrier is noted both for its appearance and its reliability.

Two British natives: Lakeland Terrier and Irish Kerry Blue Terrier.

Owners of an Irish Terrier do not have so much trouble with their pet's coat. Although the trimming regime is about the same as with the Airedale and Lakeland Terriers, the Irish Terrier's short, hard coat, with a short undercoat, is much easier to maintain. However, this untameable hunter of vermin causes trouble of another kind. It attacks cats and also other dogs and may play havoc with domestic livestock. It is an arduous task indeed to teach this 'red devil' to be obedient. Otherwise the Irish Terrier is a very affectionate and loyal pet, and will be calm in a quiet household. During the First World War it was famous as a patrol- and courier-dog.

Like the Irish Terrier, the smooth-coated **Bull Terrier** is a dog with a tough nature: It has a distinctive body form and a powerful wedge-shaped head. Up to 54cm (21in) high, it may weigh as much as 34kg (75lb). Unlike its elegant relatives, who cannot do without trimming, the Bull Terrier requires little groom-

The Irish Terrier has a splendid soft 'wheat'-coloured coat.

ing. Its smooth coat is hard and flat; the ears and tail are not docked. The coat is either white or of any other colour with white markings, so long as the white does not predominate. Brindle is the preferred colour. The Bull Terrier is a hard and and fearless fighter and guard dog; it has excellent scenting powers. This is primarily a hunting dog, unafraid of any game. With its assertive temperament it will not tolerate harsh treatment but if trained carefully and patiently the Bull Terrier becomes a fine companion and an excellent watchdog. With their own people, Bull Terriers are playful and happy.

Another smooth-coated dog of the same group, the **Manchester Terrier**, is a breed with a long tradition. It has been bred in England since the sixteenth century and its original work was ratting. It is 40 cm (16 in) high and weighs 8 kg (17.5 lb). Although slender, this is a very sturdy animal and a great fighter. A miniature variety – the **Toy Manchester Terrier** – was bred from the original form. It is

at most 35 cm (14 in) high and its weight is from 3–5.5 kg (6.5–12 lb). Its short, hard coat, which is a glossy deep black with mahogany markings, needs no trimming. Originally the ears were cropped to a pointed shape but today cropping is forbidden in Britain. Although small, the Manchester Terrier is stout-hearted and an excellent watchdog and guard. It is somewhat noisy in a city flat, but can be lovable and affectionate. This dog has contributed to the development of many other breeds.

Many terrier breeds are now included among the pet group, irrespective of their original purpose. The **Bedlington Terrier** is a typical example. Today it is a luxury pet, 40 cm (16 in) tall and weighing about 10 kg (22 lb). Its history can be traced back to 1782. Originally this was an all-round gundog, which, being a remarkable runner, used to excel in chasing hares. It was also very good at ratting, at fighting in an arena, and, with its keen sense of smell, it was also used in mines to warn miners of dangerous gas. Although no longer used in hunting, the Bedlington has retained its remarkable abilities. It is either blue or sandy in colour, and its coat, crisp but not wiry, and standing out from the skin, requires daily grooming. This is a lively, playful little dog and good with children. Although high-spirited, it is not as hard-headed as other terriers: it is obedient and placid and will not fight unless provoked.

Far from being obedient and placid are the group of small terriers that are very similar to one another – the **West Highland White Terrier** (height 28 cm/11 in; weight 7.5–8 kg/16.5–18.5 lb), **Cairn Terrier** (25 cm/10 in; about 5 kg/11 lb), **Norwich Terrier** (25 cm/10 in; 5 kg/

11 lb) and others. All are small but robust, hardy and self-confident. They have small, pointed, erect ears and a short erect tail, scarcely 15 cm/6 in) long. All have an independent temperament. Their coat is hard; the Westie's is pure white (a yellow sheen is a fault), the Norwich's is rusty, wheaten, grey or black with markings, and the Cairn's coat may be of any colour except white. All these little creatures are very lively, alert and noisy and difficult to train. They will impress with their happy disposition. It is to their advantage that their coat needs no trimming: general grooming is quite enough. If obtained from a good breeder, these terriers will enjoy good health. Although they may do well in city flats they are not ideal pets for nervous owners.

The **Australian Terrier** 25 cm/10 in; 4–5 kg/9–11 lb) is a blend of the short-legged terriers, chiefly the Cairn. Its coat is longish, hard and straight, blue-black or silver-black with rich tan, sandy or red markings on the head and legs. This is

The Bull Terrier is a dog of dubious reputation but possesses outstanding qualities.

a good gundog, used in hunting small game, and is sharper than its European relatives. Its coat needs trimming from time to time.

The Australian Terrier was crossed with the Yorkshire Terrier to produce the only Australian toy dog, the lovely **Sydney Silky Terrier**, 20–25 cm (8–10 in) high and weighing 3.5–4.5 kg (7.5–10 lb). The Silky's coat is silky indeed, and up to 15 cm (6 in) long.

The **Yorkshire Terrier** is a miniature member of the terrier family. Its height is 20–24 cm (8–9.5 in) and its weight 1.5–3 kg (3–6.6 lb); the smaller the size the more prized the dog is at shows. Nevertheless, its body build should be strong. Correct occlusion of the teeth is also important. The coat should be glossy, fine, silky, straight and long, reaching to the floor. The coat colour should be golden-tan on the head, tan on the

The Bedlington Terrier has won its way up from working in the mines.

Different types of terriers: Smooth-haired Terrier from America, white West Highland Terrier from Scotland, Skye Terrier from the rough island of Skye, with a splendid coat. Rear: the rare Australian Terrier.

ears, cheeks and legs, steel-blue on the back and tail. The tail is shortened by one-third; the ears are carried erect or half-erect. The Yorkshire Terrier is playful and affectionate. Its coat requires much care and should be protected from unfavourable factors, especially from getting wet, and from the dirt and grease of city streets. The bitches are sensitive, sometimes even timid.

Another short-legged terrier with a splendid coat is the **Skye Terrier**. Although far from tall (25 cm/10 in high), it is strong and long, measuring more than 1 m (3 ft) from the tip of its nose to the end of its tail. Its weight is 5–7 kg (11–15 lb). A native of the Isle of Skye off the west coast of Scotland, this hardy and courageous little dog used

The owner of the longest coat: the miniature Yorkshire Terrier.

beautiful coat, at least 14 cm (5.5 in) long. The Skye is bred in different shades of blue and silver-grey or cream with black markings. The coat is quite hard and requires regular combing and grooming, but no trimming.

The **Boston Terrier** is entirely different in appearance. With its short head, robust, square-shaped body, large, erect ears and short tail, it looks more like a French Bulldog than a terrier. Its height is up to 45 cm (18 in) and its weight up to 12.5 kg (39 lb). Unlike the French Bulldog, the Boston Terrier should have no wrinkles on its head. The coat is short, fine and glossy, black or tan with white markings. It must not be pure black, liver or light grey, nor have a flesh-coloured nose or a docked tail. There are three weight varieties of the Boston Terrier. Boston Terriers make affectionate pets. They are intelligent and, although they need no special training, they will take to training with enthusiasm.

to hunt foxes and badgers. It is much admired for its equable, yet somewhat stand-offish nature, stylish appearance and

Family of Kerry Blue Terrier

289

The Toy and Utility Breeds

The **Poodle** has a special position among this group of dogs. This very ancient breed, still extremely popular today, exists in three sizes, two types of coat and a whole range of colours. The Standard Poodle's height is up to 60 cm (24 in) and its weight up to 30 kg (66 lb). The respective data for the Miniature Poodle are 35–45 cm (13.5–18 in) and 5–7 kg (11–15 lb); and for the Toy Poodle up to 35 cm (13.5 in) and 5 kg (11 lb). Nowadays most poodles are bred with curly coats; those with a coat hanging down in cords up to 20 cm (8 in) long are rarely

Poodles can be chosen by size, colour and type of coat; in addition, there are different styles of clip.

clip to the lamb-clip. They are ideal companions, intelligent, willing and able to learn, playful, affectionate and manageable. They are not noisy and do not shed their fur so they make very good flat dwellers. Of course, their coat needs regular clipping and styling and their eyes and drop ears should be thoroughly cleaned. Poodles with the cord-type coat require particular care and it is difficult to keep these dogs tidy. All poodles should be protected from dirt because frequent bathing is not advisable.

Tabbying is a popular colouring of the Bulldog.

seen. The coat colours should always be solid. They include black, white, brown, silver and orange (apricot). No white markings are allowed. Poodles can be clipped in many ways, ranging from the traditional 'lion'

The high rump is a typical characteristic of the English Bulldog.

The **English Bulldog**, bred to fight bulls in the past, is now kept as a companion and pet. Although barely 40 cm (16 in) high, it weighs 24–30 kg (53–66 lb). This dog does not need much care. It is rose-eared. The ears are not cropped but must be kept perfectly clean because their inside is exposed. The short tail is not docked and the short, fine coat requires no special care. All colours are allowed except black and black and white. The extremely short nose gives the Bulldog an intimidating appearance but it is not aggressive: they are perfect pets and companions. This dog finds it difficult to tolerate harsh treatment or a change of owner. Although an excellent watchdog and guard, it does not take well to training for other purposes. Owing to the quality of its coat the Bulldog should be warmly housed in winter. This dog is rare in continental Europe.

The neat little **French Bulldog**, up to 34 cm (13.3 in) high and weighing at most 14 kg (31 lb), is seen much more frequently in European cities. Its appearance is rather friendlier than that of the English Bulldog. It is an ideal companion in a city flat; its coat is short, dense, fine and easy to maintain. This is not a noisy animal and gets along well with other dogs and with people; it is also easy to train. The breed's standards emphasise the correct shape of the head with a shorter upper jaw, an arched back, the correct set of the short tail, and a black or brindle coat colouring without excessive white markings. The French Bulldog is sensitive to cold and susceptible to certain diseases, so the rearing of the puppies is often problematic, as is the birth. The owner must pay extra attention to his or her pet's health, for even hot weather can prove harmful to it.

The **Pug**, a small but robust dog up to 35 cm (13.5 in) high and weighing 3–4 kg (6.5–9 lb), has a bizarre grace similar to that of the French Bulldog. Its nose is shortened and the expression on its wrinkly face is enhanced by a black mask. The coat is velevety, the ears have overhanging tips and the tail is curled above the rump. The Pug is a very ancient breed, imported from Asia and regarded as a close relative of the Pekinese. Its coat colours are silver, apricot, grey and (rarely) black. A black line or trace of it along the back is essential. The lively, playful and intelligent Pug is a quick learner and very self-confident. It is not noisy and makes an ideal pet for a town flat. It is not oversensitive but it must be protected from rain.

The opposite of these solid little dogs is the **Italian Greyhound**, a fine frail-looking creature. It is the smallest of the hounds, 32–38 cm (12.5–15 in) tall and weighing up to 5 kg (11 lb). The breed has been known for centuries. It has a neat body build and is rose-eared, with an arched neck and back, slender feet and tail, and large, expressive, but not bulging eyes. The silky coat may be of any colour, but white spots on the chest and legs are a fault. The Italian Greyhound is lively and nimble and may even be a good racer. It is not noisy. Dogs of this breed are often nervous and possessive and are sensitive to cold and damp, so owners should cosset them a little. Their good-quality food must be accurately rationed.

Three perfect pets for the urban flat: the Pug, the Italian Greyhound and the French Bulldog.

The Toy Spaniels

The history of these smaller relatives of the Spaniel gundogs can be traced back a very long way, but it was not until the seventeenth century that they were refined by breeders in England. They enjoyed tremendous popularity in Britain during the early twentieth century. The **King Charles Spaniel** is divided into four varieties according to colour: King Charles Black and Tan, the Blenheim, the Ruby and the Prince Charles. The King Charles Black and Tan is a rich black and mahogany in colour. The Blenheim is chestnut and pearl-white, broken-coloured. The Ruby is whole-coloured rich chestnut-red, and the Prince Charles is tricoloured (white, tan and black).

Over the years the faces of these spaniels grew shorter and shorter. The **Cavalier King Charles Spaniel** is the result of efforts to breed back a long nose and restore the older type of the breed. The Cavalier's head is almost flat between the ears and the muzzle is long with a very shallow stop. The King

King Charles Spaniel of traditional type, Ruby, Cavalier King Charles Spaniel and the Little Lion (Tenerife) with the prescribed style of clip.

Charles's head is massive, the nose is short and the stop is deep. The Cavalier is taller and heavier (up to 32 cm/12.5 in and 6 kg/13 lb) than the King Charles (26 cm/10 in; over 3 kg/6.5 lb). All these Spaniels are agile, with large dark eyes and long ears. All are vivacious, lovable and affectionate creatures. If given plenty of exercise, they may prove remarkably hardy and resistant to adverse conditions, but they do require regular grooming. It is not difficult to rear a puppy, but pampering may easily spoil it.

The English spaniels' continental European counterparts are the **Papillon** (Butterfly Dog) and the **Phalène** (Moth), which is another variety of the same breed. The Papillon is a well-balanced dog, 20–25 cm (8–10 in) high and weighing up to 4 kg (9 lb). The Phalène is about the same height but may be one kilo (2 lb) heavier. Both have a finer head and a narrower nose than the English spaniels. Their eyes are large and almond-shaped, and their tail, left undocked, is set high, its tip laid over the back. The Papillon has well-fringed erect ears which give the dog its butterfly-like appearance and its unusual name. The Phalène has drop ears, covered less abundantly with hair that stands off, so that the shorter feathering looks different from that of the spaniels. The ground colour is white, on which there are brown or black spots which

The most conspicuous trait of the Papillon is its well-fringed erect ears.

must be symmetrical on the head. Care of the hair on the ears is essential, especially in the male dogs whose ears are feathered more abundantly. The Papillon and Phalène have been bred in southern Europe since the twelfth century. They are sturdy and not oversensitive. With their vivacious, affectionate and docile nature, they make lovable companions although they can sometimes be too active and noisy. However, good obedience training can improve this behaviour.

Another very old breed is the **Tenerife**, 27–30 cm (10.5–12 in) high and weighing up to 3 kg (6.6 lb). Ancestors of this dog can be seen in medieval paintings, but the modern form of the breed was developed in 1880. The Tenerife is a variety of the Bichons: it has a comparatively short nose, drop ears, a tail carried high over the rump and a dense, silky and slightly curly coat that is trimmed in the old-fashioned 'lion style'. On the head, neck and shoulder the coat is left long, whereas the legs and the back part of the body are clipped clean. Rings of

longer, though trimmed, hair are left on the legs, and the tail has a tassel that falls lightly onto the rump. The coat colour can be pure white, or with beige or grey spots. This breed is quite rare today because the coat style, requiring expert modelling, is a bit out of fashion. Tenerife's character is not steady, perhaps because it is seldom kept in a pure-bred form.

The **Maltese**, one of the most ancient pure-bred dogs, was a favourite of the nobility in ancient Greece and Rome. It should be called 'Mljetese' rather than Maltese, as it does not come from Malta but from the island now called Mljet in the Adriatic, off the Croatian coast. It has a pink skin and an extraordinarily abundant, long silky coat, pure white in colour. Its height is up to 30 cm (12 in) and its weight up to 4 kg (9 lb). The eyes are dark brown with black eye rims; black-pigmented eyelids are desirable. The nose is pure black and should not be small or pointed. The head is rather long. The silky coat is of the same length all over the body and has no undercoat.

The Moth (Phalène) differs from the Papillon by having drop ears.

This little dog requires a considerable amount of care, daily grooming and very careful bathing, otherwise it would look untidy. As the hair on its forehead tends to fall over the eyes it is tied up in various ways. If the eyes are irritated, chronic conjunctivitis may develop. The Maltese is lively, intelligent, manageable and full of self-confidence, but because the minimum weight of 1.5 kg (3.3 lb) is considered ideal, many specimens are nervous, timid and consequently noisy.

The Blenheim, the Maltese with a remarkably abundant specially trimmed coat, and the King Charles Spaniel.

Tibetan Spaniel

The Pinschers and Griffons

These are breeds belonging to the toy dogs, although they were once working dogs. Their small size allowed them to live in households, where they kept mice and rats under control in the Middle Ages. Because of their noisiness and alertness, these little dogs soon also acquired the role of watchdogs. The hunting abilities of the little pinschers are reflected in their names.

The **German Smooth-haired Pinscher** is a typical representative of the pinscher family. It is well balanced, sturdy, compact, well muscled and 43–48 cm (17–19 in) high. The coat colour of this dog is different shades of brown or black with sharply defined rust markings. The tail is docked short and is carried a little high. In some countries of continental Europe the ears are docked to give the dog a sharp expression. Today this breed is fairly abundant in central Europe although it was on the verge of extinction late in the nineteenth century and had to be revived by cross-breeding with black and tan English Terriers. The German Pinscher is a very lively and noisy dog but also manageable and willing to accept training appropriate to its size.

The miniature variety of this breed is the **Miniature Pinscher**, only 28 cm (11 in) high and weighing 3–4 kg (6.5–9 lb). The tail and ears of this dog are also shortened in Europe. Its coat is smooth and glossy, and comes in 'fawn' (red-brown), yellow, solid brown, grey-blue and black with rusty markings: markings are also allowed with other colours, especially the blue.

Chief among the rough-haired

The German Smooth-haired Pinscher with its popular colour variety of black with rust markings and the Miniature Pinscher. In contrast to them, the hard-haired Griffon Bruxellois (undocked).

pinschers is the **Affenpinscher**, 25–28 cm (10–11 in) high and weighing less than 4 kg (9 lb). It has a solid body with a round head, short nose, pendant V-shaped ears and slightly bulging eyes. The tail is docked to leave three vertebrae, as with the smooth-haired pinschers. The coat is hard and wiry, black in colour and may have brown or grey markings. The Affenpinscher is a very alert and independent dog.

The **Griffon Bruxellois**, a small but strong dog bearing some resemblance to a small Schnauzer, is the most widespread form of the rough-haired griffons developed in Belgium. Its height is 21–28 cm (8–11 in) and its weight 3–5 kg (6.5–11 lb). It has a round head with an arched forehead, a short nose and a slightly undershot jaw. There is a visible stop in

front of the large dark eyes. The ears are cut to a pointed shape in continental Europe; the tail is shortened to a third. The abundant coat is hard and forms profuse whiskers and eyebrows. It is bred mainly in red and rusty-

The Prague Ratter is easily distinguishable from the German Pinscher by having erect uncropped ears.

brown, with a black mask and whiskers. The **Belgian Griffon** is very similar to the Bruxellois except for the coat colour, which is black or black with tan.

An extinct breed revived: the Ratter of Karlsbad.

Belgian Griffon

now being revived, and the **Ratter of Karlsbad**. A typical feature of the Prague Ratter is its erect ears, which are left uncropped. The Ratter of Karlsbad was probably white with small black spots and cropped ears.

In recent years, the extinct pinschers and their relatives have been replaced by the little dogs of the smallest breed of all, the **Chihuahua**, imported from Mexico. They are 16–23 cm (6–9 in) at the shoulder and weigh 0.5–3.5 kg (1–7.5 lb), although weights between 1.3 and 1.8 kg (2.8–4 lb) are preferable. Its 'bat' ears are large and erect; the tail is not docked; the size of the eyes should correspond to that of the nose, so that the onlooker will see three dark spots of about the same size. There are two Chihuahuas: the Long-coated and the Smooth-coated. The long-coated variety has a soft coat, long feathering on the ears and legs, a ruff on the neck and a flag on the tail; the tail may be turned upwards. The coat of the smooth-coated variety is dense, close-lying and glossy. All colours are allowed.

The only smooth-coated griffon of the Belgian griffon family is the **Petit Brabançon**, also regarded as a smooth-coated variety of the Griffon Bruxellois. It is rather sturdy, 21–28 cm (8–11 in) high and weighing 3–5 kg (6.5–11 lb). Its head is round, with large eyes and a markedly undershot jaw, like all griffons. The tail is docked by one-third; the ears may be cropped (only in Europe) or overhanging and V-shaped. The short coat is usually red with a black mask, or black with tan.

Some of the breeds of this family are extinct today, for example the Czech ratters such as the **Prague Ratter**, which is

A set of miniature dogs: the Petit Brabançon, the long- and short-coated Chihuahua and the Affenpinscher.

The Oriental Breeds

Many exotic breeds have been brought from eastern Asia to Europe and North America where they became popular during the last century.

The most widespread of them

A maximum contrast: the abundant coat of the Tibetan Shi Tsu and the Pekinese, which are far from being as rare as the Chinese Crested dog, which has only several hairs on the head and tail.

all is the **Pekinese**, 15–25 cm (6–10 in) high at the shoulder; the weight of the dogs is 5.5 kg (12 lb) and bitches 5 kg (11 lb). The head is wide and flat between the ears and the upper jaw is shortened to a mere 2 cm (0.8 in). The large eyes are dark, clear and lustrous; the hanging ears are heart-shaped with abundant feathering; the feet are large and flat, the front feet turned slightly out. As the dog walks, it shows a slow rolling gait in front with a neat, close gait behind. The heavily feathered tail (the hair up to 30 cm/ 12 in long) is carried over the

rump. A profuse ruff is worn on the neck. The silky coat can be of any colour except liver; albinos are eliminated from the pedigree Pekineses. The first Pekinese dogs were brought to England in 1860, where they were developed to the present standard.

The **Japanese Chin**, or Japanese Spaniel, is a very decorative breed, dainty in appear-

The Mexican Hairless and the Japanese Chin – from different ends of the world but both are perfect companions.

ance, with a smart, compact carriage, 18–28 cm (7–11 in) high and weighing 2–4 kg (4.5–9 lb). Its face is flat but the nose is not as short as that of the Pekinese. The drop ears are V-shaped. The typical coat colour is black and white or red and white. Reds range from sable, brindle and lemon to orange. The white should be clear. Good distribution of the patches is required. This dog was sent to Germany as a gift from the Empress of Japan in 1880; otherwise the export of dogs of this breed was strictly forbidden. Both the Pekinese and the Japanese Chin are very companionable and intelligent. Their coats, however, require regular grooming.

The Tibetan breeds are not yet commonly known in continental Europe where they appeared very recently. They are better known in Britain and the USA. These are very ancient breeds and it is believed that they may be the ancestors of both the Pekinese and the Japanese Chin.

The **Tibetan Spaniel**, 24–28 cm (9.5–11 in) high and weighing 4–7 kg (9–15.5 lb), has nothing in common with Eu-

ropean spaniels. Its muzzle is short, its eyes are large, its densely feathered ears are set on high, and its heavily feathered tail is carried over the rump. The coat is long and silky, forming a ruff on the neck and shoulders. The most frequent coat colours are white, golden, cream, brown, grey-brown and black; tricolours may also occur. Its standard was recognised by the FCI in 1961.

The **Tibetan Terrier** is much taller, 35–40 cm (13.8–15.8 in) at the shoulder, and its weight is 13–15 kg (28.5–33 lb). Its nose is not shortened but the jaw may be slightly undershot. The eyes are large and dark, the medium-sized ears are V-shaped, and the tail is carried in a gay curl over the back. The Tibetan Terrier has a long coat with profuse whiskers and eyebrows falling deep over the eyes. The coat is double – the undercoat, of any colour, is fine wool and the outer coat is long and straight, not silky. A white stripe on the forehead and a white-tipped tail are desirable.

Another Tibetan breed is the **Lhasa Apso**. Some experts assert that this is not an original Tibetan breed and that it really came originally from China where – so it is believed – it was

seen by Marco Polo in the thirteenth century. It is small, in height 25–28 cm (10–11 in) and in weight 5–7 kg (11–15.5 lb). Its head is rather narrow and its nose should not be too short. The wide-set ears are covered with long hair; the tail is curled up. The coat should be heavy, straight, hard and dense, with an abundant undercoat. All colours are allowed but golden and 'lion' colours are considered best.

The Tibetan breeds are often confused with one another. Their quality coat does not need everyday care, but all require plenty of exercise and the rooms in which they are kept should not be overheated.

As well as the profusely coated Orientals, there is a group of hairless dogs. The **Chinese Crested Dog**, 28–33 cm (11–13 in) high and weighing 4.5 kg (10 lb) at most, exists in two types: the lighter (deer) type and the heavier type. They are not entirely hairless: there are silky tufts on the crowns of their heads, on the tips of their tails and on their feet. The Crested Dog is very delicate, with a body temperature slightly higher than is normal in other breeds. It is difficult to breed, and may

Tibetan Terrier

sometimes lack a full set of teeth. Hairlessness is controlled by a recessive gene, so thorough selection is needed to maintain the breed. The **Mexican Hairless** is perhaps the most easily bred of the hairless dogs. There are, in fact, two varieties of this breed. The **Xoloitzuintle** has a height of 30–50 cm (12–19.5 in) and weighs 6–8 kg (13–17.5 lb). It is very variable, the skin being usually brown, grey or black. A little hair remains on the head and tail. Like the Chinese Crested, the Xoloitzuintle also tends to have poor dentition: the premolars are normally absent. Light marks on the body are allowed. The smaller **Mexican Hairless** barely measures 28 cm (11 in) and should not weigh more than 5 kg (11 lb). It has no hair on its body and its dentition also develops irregularly. The skin must be smooth and free of folds. The ears are erect and set high. Its general appearance resembles the Chihuahua. All hairless dogs have to be protected not only from cold but also from direct exposure to sun. They are playful and affectionate and bark very little. They are fairly rare in Britain and Europe. Their price reflects the difficulty of their breeding.

Lhasa Apso

Exotic Breeds

People are always interested in anything new or exotic, and this is just as true of dogs.

The African hunting dog, the **Basenji**, is a good example of this. It is of medium size, has long ears, small almond-shaped eyes and wrinkles on its forehead which give it a worried expression. Its white-tipped tail is tightly curled. Otherwise its short coat is chestnut-red, pure black or black and tan – always with white feet, chest and tail tip. A white blaze on the head and a white collar are allowed. This dog was first bred outside Africa in 1937 but is still not widespread. It is rather lively and difficult to train. Instead of barking it utters a cry that is a mixture of a chortle and a yodel. The Basenji is very sensitive to cold.

Another exotic breed is the **Canaan Dog**, bred from the street dogs in Palestine by a Mr and Mrs Menzel in 1938. It is 50–60 cm (20–24 in) high and weighs 20–25 kg (44–55 lb). This is a slender dog with short, erect ears and a curled tail. There are two types of this breed: the Dingo and the Collie. The tail is slightly feathered, otherwise the coat is short. The

One of the few representatives of tropical Africa: the Basenji, which does not bark although it is a hunting dog. Also the Chinese curiosity, the Shar-pei with numerous folds on the skin, a feature particularly conspicuous in puppies.

A descendant of the pariahs – the Canaan Dog.

298

ears are often not held erect. Any colour is allowed, ranging from light sand to black, with a mask, and with or without white marking. The FCI recognised this breed in 1966. The Canaan can be kept in the household where it proves to be a reliable watchdog. Being sensitive and easily frightened (especially the bitches), it is not very suitable for training.

In Australia a special breed of cattle dog has been developed. Called a **Kelpie** in its native country, it is also known as the **Australian Cattle Dog**. A sturdy animal of powerful body build, 43–50 cm (17–19.5 in) high and weighing about 25 kg (55 lb), it is thought to have originated from imported Scottish (Rough) Collies and out-crossed with Dingoes and perhaps other breeds. The result is a hardy, agile and swift dog with a short, hard coat that protects the body perfectly. It has pointed ears and a medium-long tail with a brush. The coat may be black, black-brown, red, red-brown, chocolate or smoke. It is noted for its ability to run across the backs of sheep in a tightly packed flock. In Australia it has been bred for over a hundred years and took its name in 1870 in memory of a famous bitch called King's Kelpie. The Kelpie seldom occurs outside Australia: it is not suitable for life in the home and its temperament is really difficult to manage. It is an excellent sheepdog, but its working methods do not comply with the European rules of field trials.

A really interesting breed is the **Shar-pei**. This is a massive dog of medium size, kept for centuries in northern China and Tibet. It is 45–50 cm (17.5–19.5 in) high at the shoulder and its weight is 18–25 kg (39.5–55 lb). This dog has small ears with overhanging tips, a wide, blunt muzzle, a tail carried over the rump and a blue tongue, all of which indicate relationship with the Chow Chow. Its most marked feature is its skin with its numerous folds. The coat, in cream, beige or black, may be of two types: the so-called 'horse' type with short, hard, bristly hair, and the 'brush-like' type with hair about 2.5 cm (1 in) long, standing at a 90-degree angle from the skin. Irregularities frequently occur in this breed. For example, the pups may be born with either a long or a stunted tail. In 1978 the Shar-pei was considered to be the most expensive dog in the world. Today it is bred not only in America, where it was brought from China soon after the last specimens of the breed were discovered, but also in many countries in Europe. Once used for hunting, herding, fighting and food, it has now become a pet and companion dog. Its character is similar to that of the Chow Chow, so it is not suitable for everybody. Its skin often suffers from inflammation, caused by dirt which accumulates in the skin folds, so the Shar-Pei is not the best dog to keep in a city.

Two close relatives – the Welsh Corgi and the Pembroke, a dog with a stunted tail; both used to be favourite pets of kings.

Breeds not yet recognised by the FCI crop up almost every year, including rediscovered ancient breeds, revived extinct breeds, and newly developed ones. The pool of dog types available for breeding is almost inexhaustible. The FCI's 1982 list recognises almost 50 breeds of herding dogs, the same number of guarding and other working dogs, 25 terriers and one Dachshund, more than 20 coursers for hunting big game and 60 for small game, 35 continental and four English pointers and setters, about 20 trackers and retrievers, 12 hounds and about 40 toy breeds – altogether more than 300 breeds. However, there are also other breeds not yet recognised, or breeds covered by a single common name. Most of the recognised breeds come from Europe.

A prospective owner has great choice, limited only by expense and the place where he or she lives. It is sensible, of course, to learn something of the characteristics, abilities and requirements of your chosen breed before you commit yourself.

The Hovawart owes its name to the fact that it used to be a farm guard.

Dog Training

Unlike other pets, the dog requires at least fundamental training. Even the tiniest toy dog must learn the simplest rules of obedience: coming, working at heel, lying down and otherwise respecting orders. Owners who believe that training a dog involves being cruel to it will raise unmanageable and nervous creatures. Training is not a nuisance to the dog; on the contrary, it is fun and an opportunity to demonstrate its abilities, especially when done in the company of other dogs. Training is also necessary for the dog's safety; an untrained dog cannot be left to run free without the risk of it being injured on the road, fighting with another dog or chasing livestock, to say nothing of incidents with people.

Obedience training should begin as early as possible – the bitch herself administers discipline quite firmly and her admonitions may seem severe to the

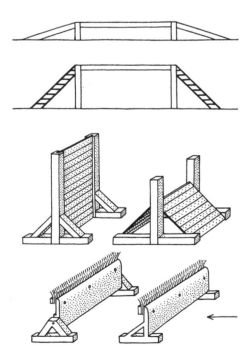

Equipment for dog-training: balancing beam; ladder with a beam; a barrier and folding obstacle for the dogs to climb; obstacles for practising high and long jumps.

human eye. People, of course, must not punish a puppy frequently or too hard: it is better to keep it occupied and teach it through play. The most important thing is to establish confidence and firm mutual affection. Then the training is easy. The first thing to teach the puppy is its name, which should be repeated persistently, especially in pleasant situations. Next is training the dog to come when called. If the trainer squats down and extends an arm, the puppy will run up with joy. It may be rewarded with a titbit, a pat or a romp. A good trainer never forgets to praise the puppy for every command obeyed. On the other hand sharp words or punishment should be used only in dire circumstances – otherwise, their effect is weakened. Any scolding must follow *immediately* after the misdemeanour: if there is a delay the puppy will fail to understand what it is being scolded for.

Patience is the most important virtue of a good dog trainer. The first simple obedience exercise should be taught in a place where it does not matter if the puppy fails to obey immediately or perhaps even runs away. The trainer must have enough time because the training must not be hurried. The amount of training should be increased successively and the formal training started at a suitable age, depending on the dog's development and the difficulty of the exercise. It should be borne in mind that the large breeds reach maturity later than the small breeds.

It is advisable that owners train their dog themselves, even at the cost of early mistakes. Sending the dog to a professional dog trainer will deprive the owner of an interesting experience and of understanding the whole complexity of the

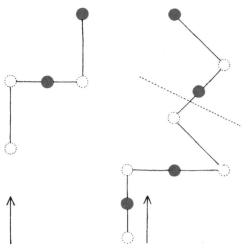

Training by tracking: the track must be pointed and in its course some objects are laid, which the dog is to find.
Types of tracks. Red circles denote the left objects, the dotting shows crossed trails.

dog's nature. The training should not follow a fixed pattern; every dog has its own personality and requires a specific approach to enhance its good qualities and suppress those that are less desirable. It is essential that the dog should always consider its trainer or owner as the only authority.

There are as many training techniques as there are dog breeds. The difficulty of training depends on the dog's duties: the training of dogs to be used by the police, army, rescue teams, mountain rescue service and other such groups is perhaps the most exacting. Training for each of these purposes follows a complex system; it re-

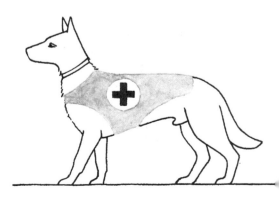

A perfectly manageable dog with a very good sense of smell can serve in locating people trapped under an avalanche or ruined buildings. The red cross is the symbol of its job.

quires plenty of time, special equipment and skilled trainers. Such special training is practised on special training grounds under expert supervision.

It is equally exacting to train guide dogs for the blind. The choice of dog is of prime importance. Such dogs must be highly intelligent, calm and manageable. Bitches are temperamentally more suitable than dogs. A special harness and other equipment are necessary.

The training of other working breeds, for example sheepdogs, is governed by special rules that are available from the respective kennel clubs of each country.

The training of gundogs is entirely different from the training of police or military dogs. The basic principle of gundog training is to make the best possible use of the inborn abilities of the dog. It was to this end that special breeds, with genetically fixed abilities and a suitable temperament, were developed for each kind of gundog work. Gundogs can only be trained in the open, in the hunting field, under the supervision of experienced sportsmen. Special equipment is needed for the training of some breeds, for example an artificial burrow for the training of Dachshunds or terriers.

It is comparatively easy to train the toy breeds, as here simple obedience training will suffice. Unfortunately, many luxury pets are far from even-tempered, so their obedience training is often lengthy and requires sound knowledge of the breed psychology. Toy breeds differ from one another in their demands, temperament and disposition, and each needs a specific approach. The playful and tireless Poodle always likes to perform a task to demonstrate its abilities, whereas the proud Chow Chow hates such demonstrations. Some toy breeds are oversensitive, for example, the toy spaniels or the Maltese, whereas others have the resistance and hardiness of the larger breeds, such as the Miniature Spitz, the Miniature Schnauzer and the Miniature Pinscher. Consequently, the selection of a toy breed is even more difficult than picking a working breed.

Dogs with the best abilities and suitable temperament can be trained to be guide dogs for the blind. Special 'trucks' teach the dog to avoid obstacles that could be dangerous to the guided person.

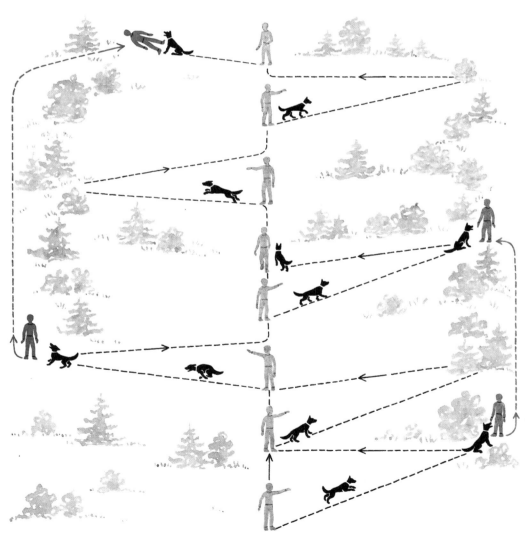

Ranging – the seeking of persons and objects in rough terrain – is among the most difficult of field exercises.

Field Trials

Trials are a logical and inevitable conclusion of the working dog's training and a verification of its success. In many countries working and gundog breeds must complete successful field trials as one of the required conditions for including them in the official pedigree stock. A dog that has not passed such a test is not recognised for breeding no matter how excellent its conformation or other qualities may be. This apparently strict requirement is based on disappointing past experience, especially with some gundog breeds. The good looks of some attractive breeds, such as the Cocker Spaniel, were overemphasised and their hunting abilities deteriorated so much that dogs of excellent conformation were no longer fit for hunting. The trend went so far as to separate working dogs from show dogs.

The trials of dogs of working, police and other breeds usually consist of several stages. The minimum knowledge trials are the first stage in a young dog's career. These first trials allow the trainer and the judge to check the dog's chances of further working use. Then follows intensive training and trials according to national and international rules. For the working breeds, including the German Shepherd, Boxer, Dobermann, Rottweiler, Giant Schnauzer, Hovawart, Belgian Shepherd Dog, Beauceron, Briard, Pyrenean Mountain Dog, Lapinkoira, Finnish Spitz and Bouvier des Flandres, the FCI (International Cynological Federation) organizes international championships at which the dogs can win the certificate of Candidate International Work Champion (CACIT) or International Work Champion (CAT). These trials

are governed by international rules (IPO) grade three. (The fitness trials of working dogs usually have three grades [I, II, III], the third being the most exacting.) The International Work Champion must win at least two CACIT certificates in two different countries, and at an international show where the CACIB is awarded, the dog must win at least the 'very good' mark.

Of course, champions are very rare. However, any well-trained dog can pass at least the first-grade trial of basic training. Besides these general trials there are others, in tracking, guarding and the like. Dogs with special assignments such as the rescue, avalanche and herding dogs, undergo special trials based on specific national or international rules.

With gundogs the situation is perhaps more complicated because there are special trials for each type of gundog. Pointer and setter trials, especially those in all-round work, enjoy the greatest popularity. There are national and international trials and also international championships. For the majority of dogs, the spring and autumn gundog trials are the goal; having passed these, the dog can be included among the approved pedigree animals and can be used in the field. These trials are held separately for setters and pointers and also for the small breeds. In addition, there are special national and international trials for terriers, scent dogs and trackers, either open or individual breeds or breed groups. For example, scent trials and competitions are held for Dachshunds or for terriers. The conditions vary in different countries and under different kennel club rules.

There are also popular speed and draught races, which hold the same importance as the

Trials of service dogs consist of three events. Obedience trials include overcoming a barrier; defence trials include checking an offender; in track tests the dog must scent the track perfectly. The specialist trackers should also 'bark the tracked person out' and identify the person in a line of people.

trials; they allow verification of how much of the original abilities of their breed each dog has retained.

The trial and race results are entered into the dog's pedigree because they give important information about the dog's performance and provide evidence of its quality and the dog trainer's good work. When judging the different breeds at shows, their field trial results are taken into account.

At many working dog and gundog shows, categories with and without field trial results are judged separately. Working dogs have a higher value when sold or evaluated, for example, for the purposes of insurance.

A dog in a car should not be allowed to travel with its head out of the window.

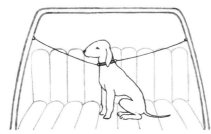

For safety purposes it is advisable to tie the dog at two points. However, the lead should not be too tight: it should not prevent the dog from lying down.

Shows and Judging

Good looks are among the most important traits of toy and pet animals. Both breeders and owners pay great attention to this. However, this is not just vanity. All details are prescribed for the toy dog breed and if a breed is to maintain its character all these prescribed traits must be closely observed and non-standard animals eliminated from breeding.

The major characteristics of each breed are specified in the breeder's standard. This is a detailed description of the breed with emphasis on all the desirable and undesirable traits: the latter, of course, affect the judges' decision or may even disqualify the animal. The standards may be international, approved by the FCI, or national, referring to breeds not yet recognized internationally. The international standards are binding in all FCI member countries, although they may be modified. The national standards of breeds not yet officially recognised by the FCI may vary in different countries. There are particularly large differences in judging the breeds of dogs and cats in Europe and in North America.

Showing a cat or dog is not an easy task. First of all, an entry form with all the relevant data

It is most convenient to transport a dog in the rear part of the car, separated by a flexible net.

Baskets for transporting dogs.

must be sent in. The animal must have a recent veterinary certificate to say that it is healthy and that there are no contagious diseases in the vicinity of its keeper's home. Owners are advised to take the vaccination certificate everywhere they travel with their pets, because at show events they will be asked to present certificates proving the animal has been properly vaccinated.

In addition, if a dog is to be shown, it must be in show condition, it must be absolutely healthy and free of parasites, it must not be in moult and its coat must be in perfect condition. Of course, the bitch must not be in season. The show condition of the coat is prescribed for each breed. Dogs of the rough-coated breeds, which have to be trimmed, must be prepared for the show several months in advance to ensure their coats have grown in correctly by show time. Bathing just before the show is not recommended because it will soften the coat and deprive it of its sheen.

The dog must be trained for the show. It must learn to walk to heel perfectly and show good general obedience; it must allow strangers to handle it and examine its teeth, ears and so on. It must not attack other dogs in the ring and, on command, should assume a posture in which all its merits are shown to best advantage. Undisciplined behaviour during the show will affect the judgement (because the dog's character is also assessed) and may even lead to the dog being ordered out of the ring and disqualified.

Shows differ in grade and importance. There is not much at stake at a small club or local show with local judges; nevertheless, even these require thorough preparation because their results are entered in the pedigree and are sometimes required if the dog is to be used for breeding. National shows are more important, especially those where the certificates of fitness for the International Beauty Championships (CA-CIB) are awarded. Such a certificate entitles the dog to appear at major international shows where it may win the CIB title (International Beauty Champion).

Big shows are organized for the owners to show off the beauty of their pets. Club reviews, with an assessment of

Deerhound

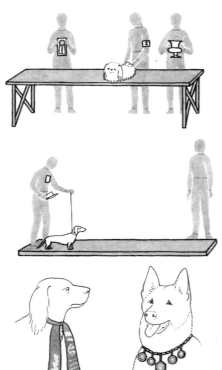

It is important to teach the dog the 'show posture'.
Small pet breeds are judged on benches.
Solid ground is needed for evaluation of the height and posture of the dog.
Various trophies may be won: from medals to cups.

the qualities of young dogs, are smaller in size but their importance is greater. Selected judges and breed advisers estimate the merits of young dogs and bitches and, from them, select those suitable for breeding. No titles, medals or even ribbons (blue: excellent, red: very good, green: good) are awarded at the club reviews, nor is the public's interest so great as at the big shows, but the young dogs must be prepared just as carefully because this is an event at which their future is decided. It is important for the breeder to be present at reviews of breed groups and litters. Although every litter has to be appraised by the breed adviser or society at any event, it is more appealing to the dog-owning community to show whole litters at club shows; these are indeed the best occasions to show off the parent stock's merits and the

breeder's abilities. The kennel name is the breeder's trademark, so he or she must seek every occasion to enhance its reputation.

The Health of Pets

Pets live in close contact with people, sharing their homes, and often having frequent contact with their children. These are good reasons for owners to take the utmost care of their pets from the very first day. A vet should be consulted whenever an adult dog or cat, pup or kitten is to be brought into the household. The vet's advice is important when a puppy is bought; a poor state of health or a congenital defect justifies the new owner returning the puppy to its breeder. Still more important is a health check of adult animals, especially those about whose past life little is known (animals found abandoned, those received as gifts or being re-homed). Such animals may have parasites or suffer from a hidden ailment.

Cats and dogs are plagued by many internal and external parasites. Some diseases are very dangerous, especially those caused by protozoans (coccidiosis, formerly known as toxoplasmosis, which is transmissible from cats to people and is dangerous, mainly to preg-

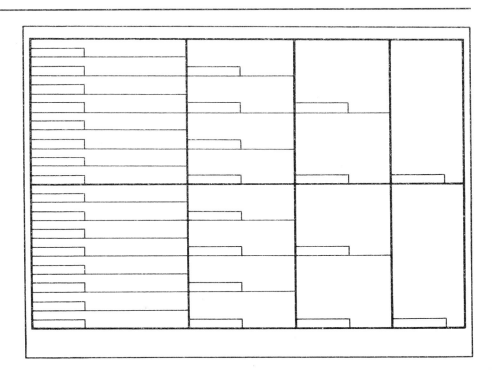

The pedigree contains a list of ancestors back to the great-great-grandparents.

The prescribed trimming of the coat is a prerequisite for a good score for the dog.
a) The Bedlington: parts denoted 1 should not be clipped but combed up – only on the breast is the coat combed down; part 2 (the coat) is clipped short six weeks prior to the show; part 7 three weeks to the show, and the rest a week before it. The parts must run smoothly into one another.
b) The Scottish Terrier: part 1 should be plucked six months before the show and should be combed downwards; part 2 should be trimmed ten weeks before the show, part 3 should be clipped with a clipping machine at the same time; the tail should be thoroughly plucked eight weeks before the

show and finished two weeks before the event to a conical shape; part 5 should be completely plucked 14 days before the event and the beard should only be combed.
c) The Kerry Blue Terrier: Clip 2 to 6 weeks before the show. Parts 1 and 3 should be clipped short, part 2 should be clipped over a comb, part 6 should be short, part 2 should be clipped over a comb, part 6 should just be clipped with scissors and parts 4 and 5 should not be clipped, only combed.
d) The Poodle: traditional trimming: Clip the coat on the feet (1) with scissors, clip parts 2, 4, 5 and 7. Trim part 3 and the end of tail with scissors. Trim part 8 with scissors.

nant women whose foetuses it may affect) and those caused by worms. Round worms and tapeworms commonly occur in cats and dogs. The *Echinococcus* tapeworm is dangerous to people. Others are less important, but the dog should still be regularly inspected and dewormed if necessary. The raw entrails of any animal, especially of shot game, should never be eaten by dogs or cats, because this is a common cause of infection. No dog should ever be allowed to eat food it finds for itself. Cats should not be allowed to roam, and if they catch mice they should not be allowed to eat them. Cats kept principally to control rodents should not be regarded as pets and neither children nor pregnant women should stroke them.

The external parasites of cats and dogs are numerous, ranging from hardly visible mites up to ticks as big as a human finger nail. Parasites must be thor-

305

oughly controlled as they are both annoying and dangerous: for example, fleas spread tapeworms and other diseases. Parasites are best controlled by keeping clean animals in clean surroundings, giving them good food and preventing them from having contact with cats and dogs that run wild.

Pet and toy animals suffer from various ailments and contagious diseases of which rabies is the most dangerous. The vaccination of dogs to control rabies is compulsory in some countries. Cats can also be in-

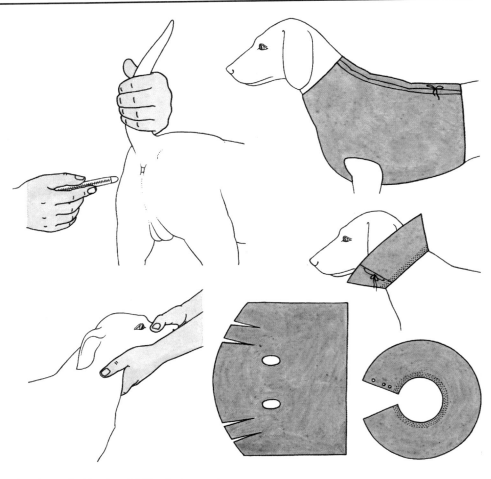

Routine medical treatment: taking the temperature; holding the mouth for examination.
The 'waistcoat' and collar prevent the dog from tearing the dressing.

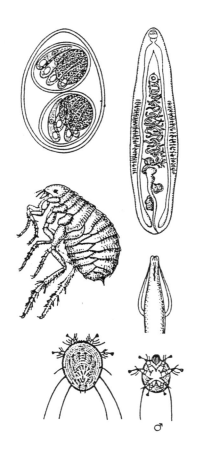

Parasites of cats. From the top: a cyst of coccidium from a cat's intestine, the cat fluke, the cat flea, the front part of the cat threadworm and a pair of cat mites.

oculated against rabies, especially those that are allowed to roam out of doors. Inoculation can also be used to control distemper, parvovirus and liver diseases in dogs. Cats can be inoculated against feline distemper, diseases of the digestive tract and liver and some other diseases.

Many ailments are caused by improper handling. Small breeds, castrated tom cats and neutered bitches are exposed to the danger of obesity with all the ensuing risks. A polluted environment may be responsible for skin diseases and for lung cancer, the incidence of which has been increasing rapidly in re-

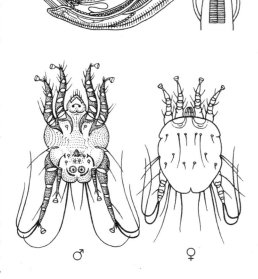

Above: dog threadworm, the rear part of the body of the male and the front part of the female. Below: the mite Otodectes cynosus from the external ear of the dog.

306

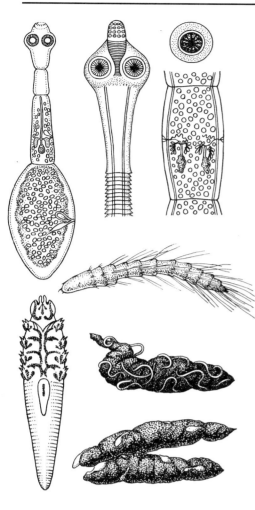

Dogs' parasites: tapeworm *Echinococcus* (left) and the dog tapeworm (*Dipylidium caninum*) – the head, the egg and a ripe segment. Centre: a larva of the flea.
Bottom: left – the mite *Demodex canis*; the excrements of a dog with threadworms and tapeworm segments.

and many other chemicals. The dangers associated with these substances are a real threat to pet animals.

Veterinary surgeons should be consulted whenever a symptom or disorder occurs. The first thing to do in such cases is to find out what the animal may have been in contact with. One case was reported of a dog having died through eating the seeds of poisonous ornamental plants in the garden.

It is necessary to observe the animal's state of health constantly. Animals, unlike people, can withstand pain or discomfort without making a sound for a long time, and by the time they begin to moan it is usually too late to seek a remedy. Hence, the pet should be examined every day. Its eyes should be wiped and their brightness and correct reactions should be checked. The ears should also be wiped, as well as the teeth (using a small brush and a special dog toothpaste, *not* the human kind). The mouth should be free of odour and the tongue should be free of coating. The faeces should also be inspected

from time to time and food intake monitored.

When a drug has to be administered to a dog, a wet tablet should be put on the root of its tongue and its mouth should be held closed for a while; if a liquid medicine is used, it should be poured into the side of the dog's mouth, using a small spoon. If a tablet were crushed and added to its food, the dog would scent it and refuse to eat. Cats do not have such a fine sense of smell, so they can easily be deceived and will normally eat a powder hidden in a piece of raw meat.

Like a human patient, a sick animal needs care and should be kept warm and quiet. The vet's recommendations should be fully respected. Although a four-legged patient may recover spontaneously, its system may remain irreversibly damaged. It is wrong to leave an animal that is too old or incurably sick to suffer needlessly: the owners should have them painlessly killed.

Surgical nail trimming is another job for the vet. Some dogs have a dewclaw, that is a fifth

cent years. The skeletons of some pets exhibit degenerative changes: many dog breeds are susceptible to hip dysplasia, so some breed clubs insist on seeing an X-ray before they allow dogs to be included in the breeding list.

Injuries are very frequent and are caused mainly by traffic accidents. Pet and toy animals are also often poisoned. Pollutants and other noxious substances are abundant in the environment today; cats and dogs may come into contact with poisonous pot and garden plants, with dyes, bleach, pesticides

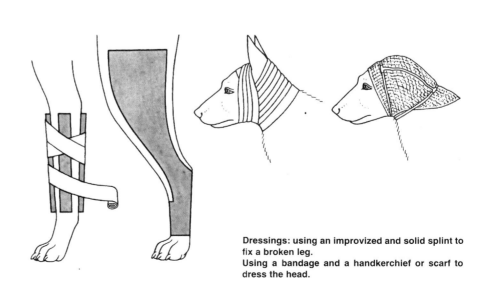

Dressings: using an improvized and solid splint to fix a broken leg.
Using a bandage and a handkerchief or scarf to dress the head.

claw, on the hindlegs. This abnormality should be removed by the veterinary surgeon as soon as possible. The tail is docked in many breeds during the first days of the puppy's life. Ears, on the other hand, can be cropped later, when the puppy is about three months old. In Britain cropping of the ears is forbidden and a similar ban was introduced in Germany in 1987.

Cats, Dogs and Human Society

There can be no doubt about the importance of pets. Cats and dogs first played a significant role in people's lives long ago, and still do today. The economic importance of many breeds (sheep dogs, guard dogs, etc) is diminishing now and they are increasingly becoming pure pets.

A companion animal is always an essential factor in its owner's life; it is a significant counterbalance to the stress of monotonous work, for lonely people they are friends, for sick and old people they provide stimulus for walks and exercise, and for everyone they are an opportunity to develop friendly contacts with the people around them: there is perhaps no easier way of making friends with other people than through a handsome and well-behaved animal.

Of course, keeping a companion animal implies many duties. First, maximum security must be provided for the animal in the flat or house where it will live and may have to stay alone for a few hours each day: it must feel safe and be able to move about and play without any risk of harm. Special temporary safety measures must be taken for young animals. The heating elements must be protected to

prevent pets from getting burnt, and cables and electric leads must be covered. There should be no unsteady objects onto which agile animals (cats) could jump, and no heavy objects that could fall on top of them. No poisonous plants or freely accessible drugs should be left in the room. Objects that the animals could destroy, bite or swallow should be removed.

Animals should *never* be sent by mail; the owners must always travel with them. In a bus or train dogs must wear a muzzle, collar and lead. Cats and small dogs must be carried in transport boxes with good ventilation and a waterproof bottom. The animal should eat nothing and drink only a little before a trip. Both cats and dogs can survive without problems for 24 hours or a little longer without food and water. During a long trip it is recommended that you take along a bowl and offer water to the pet from time to time; it will probably show little interest in food when travelling. Journeying with a pet in a car involves some risks. A pet should never sit next to the driver and should not be left to move freely inside the car. A small animal should be carried in a well-secured basket and a bigger animal should stay on a rear seat or in the rear part of a van or hatchback. Animals should *never* be carried in the boot! Looking out of an open window is dangerous for the animal's eyes and ears. The shelf beneath the rear window is not an ideal place for an animal in the car: it will obscure the driver's view and might be exposed to hot sun or to the dazzling lights of other cars at night; the animal might also be thrown off and injured in the event of a crash. For longer trips it is advisable to fit a large dog with a harness and fix it by two leads to two spots inside the

car: this will then act as a safety belt. Stress may occur during the ride and this can lead to a change in the animal's normal behaviour; for this reason it is safer to carry a cat in a box or basket. If there is a stranger in the car, the dog should wear a muzzle, however reliable it might otherwise be. In an aeroplane the animal must be placed in a transport box that complies with the airline's regulations; however, some companies do allow small animals to stay in the passenger cabin.

Even a well-trained animal may cause harm to a stranger. It is advisable to take out an insurance policy to cover such cases. Insurance is compulsory for dogs undergoing special training, for example police dogs, where such accidents cannot be excluded. Of course, the dog itself can also be insured, especially a valuable dog that can easily get injured, such as a gundog.

Pets in the Open

Pets accompany people everywhere, including on walks in parks and in the countryside. This causes a number of problems. For safety reasons all dogs should be kept on a lead inside towns and villages or by busy roads. In natural surroundings the situation is different, but it is still your responsibility to ensure that your pet does not chase game or sheep or otherwise annoy landowners or cause damage to fields, etc.

Hence, dogs should not be allowed to roam. Cats can also cause considerable damage, especially at the nesting time of songbirds, and to small feathered game, so a collar with a bell on it is a good idea. Dogs are also dangerous to wildlife.

Even though they are often unable to catch an animal and are only chasing it for fun, they disturb the peace of wild animals, which have anything but an easy life today.

However, there are times when a dog has to be allowed to run around in the open, without its lead during training or when performing a specific task. All loose dogs should wear a collar with an identity tag bearing the address and telephone number of the owner: if a sportsman with his dog wishes to visit another district, he must seek the permission of the local landowner or local gundog club.

How, then, can you move around with a dog in the countryside without harming the natural environment and without exposing your pet to unnecessary stress? A well-trained dog can follow at its owner's heels and run about in a close circle without a lead, but when the terrain is not easy to survey, even an obedient dog must be kept on a lead. A dog should never be allowed to get close to places where it could disturb sheep or game (reserves, pheasantries, places where game have their nests and rear their young during the breeding season) or in the proximity of game management facilities (aviaries, hatcheries, pheasant-mating aviaries and the like).

A dog lacking good training should never be allowed to chase game or to approach dead or wounded game animals. Nor should it be allowed to chase domestic animals, not even those that have entered its owner's premises. The dog's hunting instinct is easy to arouse but hard to suppress.

There are many other dangers that pets may encounter when walking in the countryside. They should never be allowed to drink from stagnant pools and other suspect sources, to run around in places where waste is dumped, or to go into polluted water or fields treated with pesticides. Dogs like running around freely in the open but they may contract an injury or a chronic foot infection on such occasions. In spring and autumn they should not be allowed to run through bushes or tall vegetation where ticks and mites abound. Having returned home the pet should be thoroughly inspected and all parasites, thorns and seeds attached to its coat removed; otherwise the animal will try to clean its coat itself by scratching and biting at itself and may damage its coat or skin.

The owner of a bitch should avoid walking her on a long lead when in season. She will certainly attract a large following of dogs. If it is really necessary to walk near other dogs with a bitch on heat, use one of the special animal deodorants may confuse the would-be suitors for a while.

Dogs need and enjoy exercise in the country, but good training is essential. A well-trained animal likes the company of its human friend. When its owner is around it feels safe and enjoys the walk much more than a solitary wander with all its risks.

The Breeder's Ethics

Livestock breeding has always been of great economic importance to people; the continued existence of whole groups of humans has often depended on the number and condition of the animals they kept. Economic reasons alone should convince a breeder of the advantages and necessity of careful handling and breeding of their animal stocks.

This is not true of animals kept purely as pets. It is sad to admit that toy, pet or companion animals, although often very rare and of great value, are frequently the victims of inexpert treatment or the ephemeral interest of the owner. Fashion, social prestige or irresponsible instantaneous decisions, may all be involved in choosing a pet. It is no wonder that the kennels for abandoned pets are overcrowded with unhappy creatures waiting for someone to adopt them or, in the worst case, to 'put them down'.

Therefore, at the conclusion of this book a few words on the ethical aspects of breeding are in order. Anyone buying an animal, no matter how insignificant and dull it may appear, should be aware of his or her respons-

Shi-Tsu

ibility for that little piece of living nature. He or she must understand that from then on the little creature with its own feelings, needs and perceptions, will be entirely dependent upon its new owner.

It is important to provide the pet with everything it needs for its well-being. This should have been provided before the new owner brings the animal home. Material provisions are not everything though; the owner has to learn all about the pet's needs and acquire desirable keeping habits. The pet should be bought from a reliable breeder or a good pet shop – never from a casual seller: the breeder will be glad to tell the new owner everything about the animal and the care it requires. As far as possible, the owner-to-be should collect the pet himself. Sending the animal long distances or by inappropriate means of transport should be avoided, especially when the young of birds and mammals are involved.

Keepers have duties not only to their pets but also to the people around them. They must control their pets (especially an ill-trained dog or venomous snakes) and are held liable for injury or damage done to peo-ple, other animals or property. The pets must be clean, tidy and healthy, so as not to become a source of infection to other animals. They should also be inoculated against contagious diseases in compliance with current veterinary regulations. It is the keeper's responsibility to prevent his or her pet from being a nuisance to people in the vicinity (through noise, smell or bad behaviour). Everything possible should be done to prevent any injury or damage the pet could cause.

Every devoted keeper wants to be a successful breeder and to rear his or her pet's progeny. However, this praiseworthy intention should not became detrimental to the progeny's health. In other words, prestige or profit should never be the chief motive of the breeder's effort. He or she should do their best to help the animals to thrive, not just to inflate their purse. Honesty should be the policy of any breeder, especially breeders of pedigree animals: breeder organizations often impose heavy penalties for any breeder misdemeanour. No breeder should produce animals with hidden defects or ailments or an unstable temperament.

Breeders and keepers often face situations when they must decide what to do with animals that are too old or sick to live long, or if a litter is too large. It is cruel to leave too many young with a mother who then cannot feed them all; nor should they be reared on substitute food which would only lead to producing weak progeny and to debilitation of the stock. Nor is it advisable to prolong the suffering of an incurably sick animal. Unwanted animals should never be given away without knowing what care the new owner can provide: it is better to have such an animal painlessly killed. Nothing at all can justify an animal being exposed to suffering or cruelty.

Pets are a source of joy. They enrich the keeper's life and help people to understand the wonder of nature. If the pets are to thrive, the owner must be a devoted fancier, willing to devote all the time, money and energy the animals require. Pets are living creatures and each has its own personality. They must be treated with interest, attention and patience. A successful breeder or keeper must have all these qualities. He or she should always attempt to understand the pet and win its confidence.